The Editor

GRACE IOPPOLO is the founder and director of the Henslowe-Alleyn Digitisation Project and is Reader in English and American Literature at the University of Reading. She is the author of *Dramatists and Their Manuscripts in the Age of Shakespeare, Jonson, Middleton and Heywood: Authorship, Authority and the Playhouse* (2006) and of *Revising Shakespeare* (1991). She has edited Shakespeare's *Measure for Measure* and Middleton's *Hengist, King of Kent*. She has published widely on literary and historical manuscripts, most recently as co-editor of *Elizabeth I and the Culture of Writing* (British Library, 2007), which contains studies of manuscripts by, to, or about Elizabeth I.

A NORTON CRITICAL EDITION

William Shakespeare
KING LEAR

AN AUTHORITATIVE TEXT
SOURCES
CRITICISM
ADAPTATIONS AND RESPONSES

Edited by

GRACE IOPPOLO

UNIVERSITY OF READING

W. W. NORTON & COMPANY

New York • London

W. W. Norton & Company has been independent since its founding in 1923, when William Warder Norton and Mary D. Herter Norton first published lectures delivered at the People's Institute, the adult education division of New York City's Cooper Union. The Nortons soon expanded their program beyond the Institute, publishing books by celebrated academics from America and abroad. By mid-century, the two major pillars of Norton's publishing program—trade books and college texts—were firmly established. In the 1950s, the Norton family transferred control of the company to its employees, and today—with a staff of four hundred and a comparable number of trade, college, and professional titles published each year—W. W. Norton & Company stands as the largest and oldest publishing house owned wholly by its employees.

Composition by PennSet, Inc.
Digital file management by Jay's Publisher's Services.
Manufacturing by the the Maple-Vail Book Group, Binghamton.
Book design by Antonina Krass.
Production manager: Benjamin Reynolds.

Library of Congress Cataloging-in-Publication Data
Shakespeare, William, 1564–1616.
    King Lear : an authoritative text, sources, criticism, adaptations, and
responses / William Shakespeare ; edited by Grace Ioppolo. — 1st ed.,
A Norton Critical ed.
        p.   cm.
    Includes bibliographical references.

    ISBN 978-0-393-92664-4 (pbk.)

    1. Lear, King (Legendary character)—Drama.   2. Shakespeare, William,
1564–1616. King Lear—Sources.   3. Inheritance and succession—Drama.
4. Fathers and daughters—Drama.   5. Kings and rulers—Drama.   6. Aging
parents—Drama.   7. Britons—Drama.   8. Tragedy.   I. Ioppolo, Grace,
1956–   II. Title.
    PR2819.A2I75 2007
    822.3'3—dc22

                                                              2007029213

W. W. Norton & Company, Inc., 500 Fifth Avenue, New York, NY 10110
www.wwnorton.com

W. W. Norton & Company Ltd.
15 Carlisle Street, London W1D 3BS

3   4   5   6   7   8   9   0

Contents

Adaptations and Responses

Introduction

In case it please God to provide you to all these three kingdomes, make your eldest sonne Issac [i.e., the son of Abraham], leaving him all your kingdomes; and provyde the rest with private posses-sions. Otherwaies by deviding your kingdomes, ye shall leave the seede of division & discorde among your posteritie.

—King James I to his eldest son, Prince Henry, in *Basilikon Doron*, 1603[1]

On December 26, St. Stephen's Night, 1606, Shakespeare's acting company, the King's Men, of which he was a sharer and the princi-pal dramatist, performed a play only recently composed, *King Lear*, in front of their monarch, and patron, King James I, and his court at Whitehall Palace as part of their Christmas celebrations. What James, the proud author of a number of political treatises, includ-ing *Basilikon Doron*, must have thought in hearing his very words about the dangers of dividing a kingdom, as well as the problems caused by allowing illegitimate sons (such as Ishmael) to share the inheritance of legitimate sons (such as Isaac) is not known, but can certainly be imagined. In fact the play has long tested the imagina-tion of literary and theatrical audiences, proving only too forcefully that

> The poet's eye, in a fine frenzy rolling,
> Doth glance from heaven to earth, from earth to heaven,
> And as imagination bodies forth
> The form of things unknown, the poet's pen
> Turns them to shapes, and gives to airy nothing
> A local habitation and a name.
> —*A Midsummer Night's Dream* (5.1.12–17)

Shakespeare's abstract and exquisite rendering here of the powers and "tricks" of "strong imagination" (5.1.7–18) in the mid-1590s was made only too real and brutal ten years later in *King Lear*, in which the most savage acts of cruelty are not imagined but staged for an audience who is made to feel complicit and culpable.

---

1. *Basilikon Doron* [*The King's Gift*]: *or His Maiesties Instructions to his dearest sonne, Henry the Prince* (Edinburgh: Robert Waldegrave, 1603), Books 2–3, signatures H1ᵛ-H2ʳ.

vii

King Lear is Shakespeare's most perfect embodiment both of his own artistic vision as a "poet" and of the tragic genre he and other early modern dramatists inherited from classical authors. The Greek philosopher Aristotle had claimed in *The Poetics* that tragedy must be "an imitation of an action that is serious, complete, and of a certain magnitude," complete with embellished language, and "in the form of action, not of narrative," with the result that through "pity and fear" would be effected "the proper purgation of these emotions." Aristotle did not make clear whether this purgation was to come through the pity and fear of the audience or of the characters or "the poet," as the dramatist Shakespeare referred to himself, or all of them; however Aristotle did decree that tragedy must involve the fall of a great man through a fatal flaw. The Roman dramatist Seneca offered an equally fatalistic model of tragedy, but one resulting from a family member's desire to extract vengeance for murder or an equally heinous crime. Less dramatically powerful was a more recent model, the "de casibus" tragedy, offered by Boccaccio in *De Casibus Virorum Illustrium* (1363) and adapted by Chaucer (most obviously in *The Monk's Tale*), showing, as Boccaccio's translated title suggests, the examples of famous men fallen from fortune. Yet this type of fall shows the usually awkward tension between the classical belief that the pagan goddess Fortune's spinning wheel controlled a person's fate and the medieval Christian tenet that God alone determined a person's fate, although that person could choose to reject God's fortune (or fortunate gifts) through the exercise of free will.

Early in his career, Shakespeare followed the formulaic model of Seneca, which had proved enduringly popular with Elizabethan audiences, in such revenge tragedies as *Titus Andronicus* and *Romeo and Juliet*. But by the early 1600s he began to experiment with tragedy, as in *Hamlet, Othello*, and *Macbeth*, which not only used both the Aristotelian and Senecan models but cross-referenced them, showing how the conflict between a character's need to exact vengeance and his own fatal flaw doomed him to a tragic conclusion from which he was powerless to extricate himself. In fact, the character's ultimate comprehension that he could not extricate himself provided him with redemption. By December 1606, the last possible date for the composition of *King Lear*, Shakespeare seems to have concluded that allowing his tragic characters the scope to challenge and reject their "promised end," as Kent will come to call it in the play's last scene, was worth exploring for five acts. In addition, Shakespeare appears to have decided that a character's redemption was no longer the poet's concern, nor was it his concern to encourage an audience to use their imaginations only to envision tragedy. He also seemed to mock the *de casibus* form of tragedy by allowing Lear to rant madly on the heath about his victimization by Fortune, all the while laying bare Lear's deliberate rejection of what the audience would have recognized as Christian fortune, which he comes to understand much too late.

Such a deviation in the Jacobean period from the standard norms of Elizabethan tragedy did not come without a cost. For Shakespeare, that cost was reinterpreting the graphic, but natural, brutality between two warring political families in *Titus Andronicus*, in which a powerful matriarch of one family destroys the patriarch of a rival family, as the graphic, but much more unnatural, brutality *within* one warring family in *King Lear*, in which two matriarchs destroy the patriarch of their own family, with another family easily appropriating such strategy. The revenge desired by Tamora for Titus's murder of her sons, Hamlet's for Claudius's murder of Old Hamlet, and Macduff's for Macbeth's murder of his own family and of Duncan in earlier plays gives way to Goneril and Regan's growing, and unexplained, resentment of Lear in the later play. By 1606 and the composition of *Lear*, motives are not required for the main tragic plot, and those required for the tragic subplot are petty and entirely personal. Shakespeare's domestication, and internalization, of motiveless, or at least ambiguous, tragedy in *King Lear* would forever change the tragic form and genre, paving the way for the great tragedies of the 1610s and 1620s, including *'Tis Pity She's a Whore* and *The Duchess of Malfi*, most basically in making female characters and their domestic world deserving of and, paradoxically, causing tragedy.

If Shakespeare did not feel constrained in *King Lear* to follow the models of contemporary tragedy, he was equally uninterested in strictly adhering to his main source, *The Chronicle History of King Leir*, which, although not printed until 1605, was almost certainly in performance on the London stage for some years earlier, possibly with Shakespeare in the cast. In this source play, the now-anonymous author followed his main sources, including chronicle histories by Holinshed and Camden and the popular poems *The Mirror for Magistrates* and *The Faerie Queene* (see Sources, pages 137–59), which presented all the basic elements of the Leir story: his long reign as king of Britain; his petulant love-test of his three daughters; the refusal of his youngest daughter to flatter him in her answer; his rejection of her, and her dowerless marriage to the kindly King of Gaul (or France); Leir's two older daughters' ultimate rejection of him, and his reconciliation with his youngest daughter, who with her husband helps him overthrow the armed rebellion of his older daughters; and, finally, Leir's triumphant return to power. Although the play *King Leir* ends at this point, the sources continue with the story of the youngest daughter's succession to her father's throne upon his death, and her peaceful rule for a few years until her usurpation by her evil nephews and her suicide in prison.

Although the Leir story was a seminal part of British history and folk-tale, Shakespeare tampered with it, altering the ending to tragedy, or at least moving up Cordelia's tragic end to a much earlier point; perhaps for this reason the original naming of *King Lear* as a "Chronicle History" on the title page of its first printing in 1608 in Quarto 1 was changed to a "Tragedy" in the First Folio in 1623. Shakespeare also adopted a subplot from another popular text, Sidney's prose romance *The Countess of Pembroke's Arcadia*, which recounted the blinding of the corrupt Paphlagonian king by his illegitimate son Plexirtus and his rescue by his legitimate son Leonatus (see pp. 153–56). Although Shakespeare may have borrowed the Leir story indirectly from Higgins and Spenser through the source play, he borrowed from Sidney directly, perhaps to salute him as one of the triumvirate of Elizabethan master-poets on whom Shakespeare drew for inspiration in using the "poet's pen." At any rate, what seems yet one more of the countless unhappy fables recounted in *The Arcadia* moved effortlessly and seamlessly into Shakespeare's imagining of the wider repercussions of Lear's increasingly cruel set of kingdoms.

Once it is understood that Shakespeare borrowed from his sources nearly all the physically and emotionally abusive behavior (including the misogynistic treatment of his daughters) and the graphically explicit violence in the play (including Gloucester's blinding, and the hanging of Cordelia, suggested by Sidney's presentation in *The Faerie Queene* of her eventual method of suicide), it is difficult to support uninformed critics from the eighteenth to the twenty-first century who have proclaimed their revulsion at Shakespeare's "invention" or "imagination" of such despicable and multiple forms of cruelty. Shakespeare did not imagine the blinding of Gloucester, Sidney did. Shakespeare did not imagine that a seemingly incestuous father would demand that his daughters publicly, and unnaturally, pledge their entire capacity of love to him above all others, Geoffrey of Monmouth and his succeeding historians did. Shakespeare did not first counsel a ruler, "Ye shall leave the seede of division & discorde among your posteritie," should he consider "dividing" the united British kingdom among his children into three separate kingdoms, King James did. Nor did Shakespeare first envision a monarch as possessing two bodies, the body politic and the body natural, the imbalance of which could lead to disease and corruption. For this proverbial myth and cultural truth he could look not only to James but James's immediate predecessors, Henry VIII, Edward VI, Mary Tudor, and Elizabeth I, all of whom waged their own battles, some more successfully than others, to prevent the body natural from destroying the body politic.

What Shakespeare did imagine were the repercussions if these warnings about familial and political struggles were not heeded. More basically, he may have witnessed in his own family, or heard about the accounts of witnesses in another family such as the Annesleys (see Sources, pp. 160–62), the jealousies and long-suppressed resentments that surface when a dying father divides family property. James, whose royal inheritance first in Scotland (as the heir of his imprisoned and executed mother Mary, Queen of Scots) and then in England (as Elizabeth's reluctant choice of successor) was fraught, to say the least, seems to be drawing on personal experience in his warning in *Basilikon Doron. King Lear* is certainly the product of a mature imagination in more ways than one; only the Shakespeare who has already spent more than a decade acting in and writing plays could have produced the incredibly subtle and exceptionally finely tuned characterizations and simultaneously spare and terse dialogue in this play. Nor are the visions of family strife part of a young writer's inexperience, but of an author in mid-life (just past the age of forty, as Shakespeare was), who had suffered the death of his elderly father in 1601, as well as of some of his siblings and one of his children (Shakespeare's mother would die in 1608, the same year in which *Lear* was first published). It is tempting to wonder if Shakespeare's *Lear* sprang from his own experience in seeing a once strong father (or grandfather?) become feeble and act so rashly, perhaps in a single moment, that he alienated his adult children, who finally feel justified in airing their long-simmering resentments against him and their siblings, particularly those thought to be "favorite" children. Such resentment often springs from the guilt of a child toward a parent and not a sibling, making the emotions all the more complex and intense. Any adult who has witnessed the family "division & discord" of which James speaks before or after a parent's funeral or the reading of a parent's will would surely understand that the Lear family is no different than any other. This is what Shakespeare understands, but Lear does not.

It may be this discomfort with facing up to repressed fear, anger, and guilt that has made the play so very uncomfortable and awkward for its audiences. Charles Lamb was not seriously challenged when he proclaimed in 1810 that "Lear is essentially impossible to be represented on a stage" (see pp. 172–73). Nor did critics disagree with William Hazlitt's brusque admission in 1817, "We wish that we could pass this play over, and say nothing about it. All that we can say must fall far short of the subject; or even what we ourselves conceive of it" (see pp. 173–74); according to Hazlitt, *King*

Lear is literally "nothing," but at the same time it is something that manages to enlarge our imagination on a conscious and unconscious level. The Polish critic Jan Kott, who had so shrewdly correlated the corruption caused by the Soviet occupation of his country to the events of *King Lear*, suggested that familial resentments could infect the wider culture and political structure. Kott recognized that "the attitude of modern criticism to *King Lear* is ambiguous and somehow embarrassed" (see pages 177–79), as if self-scrutiny of our most basic human relationships is so painful that we cannot acknowledge even the possibility of it.

Kott's trenchant commentary on *King Lear* as Shakespeare's most modern work finally succeeded in rehabilitating the play, both as a magnificent literary and cultural text and a powerful theatrical experience. Kott's was not an easy achievement. In 1681, the poet Nahum Tate announced that Shakespeare's *King Lear* so resembled "a Heap of Jewels, unstrung, and unpolisht; yet so dazling in their Disorder" (see pp. 169–70) that this "Heap" alienated Restoration audiences who were still being confronted by the bloody consequences of the Civil War (including the execution of King Charles I, the Interregnum and rule of Oliver Cromwell, and the return of the exiled British monarch in the person of Charles II). Tate was compelled to offer some solace in the form of his revision of the play, which "restored" the happy ending of the chronicles and the source play, while adding a love story between Edgar and Cordelia, who live happily ever after. Tate's revision was so comforting in its easy sentimentality, or Shakespeare's original was so intimidating in its intellectual force, that Tate's tragicomedy replaced Shakespeare's tragedy on the London stage for over one hundred and fifty years. Tate's version was "refined" by later writers, but it must be remembered that the great actors of the eighteenth and early nineteenth century who excelled in the role of Lear, including the much-praised David Garrick, John Philip Kemble, and Charles Kean, were performing in Tate's much inferior adaptation, in literary and theatrical terms, of Shakespeare's play.

All the while *King Lear* on stage remained Tate's for those one hundred and fifty years, it remained Shakespearean on the page. Due to the great vogue for editing Shakespeare's texts, multivolume editions of his plays began to appear every twenty years or so beginning in 1709, with each succeeding editor eager to point out the defects of preceding editors. The great editors such as Rowe, Capell, Steevens, and Malone were quick to dismiss the inferiority of Tate's version of *Lear* while struggling to offer some guidance to readers about Shakespeare's version. Typical of these editors was Samuel Johnson's somewhat stingy statement that the play "is deservedly celebrated among the dramas of *Shakespeare*." Dr. Johnson charitably noted that "so powerful is the current of the poet's imagination, that the mind, which once ventures within it, is hurried irresistibly along," but concluded by apologizing for Shakespeare: "Perhaps if we turn our thoughts upon the barbarity and ignorance of the age to which this story is referred, it will appear not so unlikely as while we estimate *Lear's* manners by our own" (see pp. 170–72). Yet Johnson failed to comprehend or acknowledge that this barbarity and ignorance sprang at least partly from Shakespeare's sources, not solely from his "imagination."

It was no surprise then that both Lamb and Hazlitt professed a lack of interest in engaging with Shakespeare's play of *King Lear*. Keats seemed to enjoy tasting the "bittersweet of this Shakespearian fruit" when sitting down to read Shakespeare's text (see p. 261), although he would not have been able to see it staged, for it was not until 1834 that William Macready courageously returned the original play to the stage (albeit with some "refinements"). Only the applause of his audience on opening night confirmed to the anxious Macready that he had done the right thing. Later nineteenth century productions, as Kott notes, struggled to make the play meaningful to audiences; if Shakespeare's *Lear* could be seen as "black theatre" to the Romantics, it was presented as such a purified embodiment of Victorian sentiment that its plot and its characters became "ridiculous" (see pp. 177–78). The great midtwentieth-century British productions of the play combined the formidable talents of directors like Harley Granville-Barker and Tyrone Guthrie and actors like John Gielgud and Laurence Olivier, and of critics like A. C. Bradley (who primarily saw the play through its characters and their movement toward Christian redemption; see pp. 175–76). Such productions succeeded only in reminding audiences that they should respect Shakespeare's achievements in *King Lear* if they could not bring themselves to admire them.

So, when Kott proposed in 1961 that the play should be read as a counterpart to the works of Bertold Brecht and Samuel Beckett, and that *Lear* could be recognized as a stylized and symbolic representation of the grotesque nature of modern cruelty, the British theatre director Peter Brook agreed. Brook's now legendary production of the play in 1962 for the Royal Shakespeare Company in Stratford-on-Avon, with Paul Scofield in the title role, was a result of his conversations with Kott, who emphasized, "There is in *King Lear*—and Mr Brook was the first to discover it—a combination of madness, passion, pride, folly, imperiousness, anarchy, humanity and awe, which all have their exact place and time in history" (see p. 178). Brook explained, "Experimentally, we can approach *Lear* not as a linear narrative, but as a cluster of relationships." Rejecting the modern convention of elaborate sets and costumes, Brook demanded a return to the play stripped bare in the type of vision offered by Kott, deciding that "the play is directly related to the most burning themes of our time, the old and the new in relation to our society, our arts, our notions of progress, our way of living our lives." As the theatre director Brook stressed, in direct contrast to the literary critic Charles Lamb, *King Lear* could be represented on the stage, for it is up to actors, not critics, to interpret this vision to their audiences: "If the actors are interested, this is what they will bring out. If we are interested, that is what we will find. . . . The meaning will be for the moment of the performance" (see pp. 179–81).

The visions of Kott and Brook, and later of the great film directors Grigori Kozintsev and Akiro Kurosawa, who were influenced by them, were rooted not only in theatre history but in a postwar world. As R. A. Foakes argues, the rise of the nuclear age displaced *Hamlet* and placed *King Lear* as Shakespeare's most modern, most accessible, and most representative play; no longer could *King Lear* be defined as a Bradleyian pilgrimage to redemption, but as Shakespeare's "bleakest and most despairing vision of suffering, all hints of consolation undermined or denied" (see pp. 240–43). With the application of postmodern theory, *King Lear* began to serve as Shakespeare's most extreme example of the cultural, political, and personal failures caused by strictures inherent in the modern age and inherited from the early modern age. For feminist critics especially, the Lear story embodied the ways in which women as mothers, daughters, sisters, wives, and lovers suffered primarily through their absence, and only secondarily through their presence, in a world that was dysfunctional because it was patriarchal, and patriarchal because it was dysfunctional. For both Lynda E. Boose and Janet Adelman, a father-daughter relationship which is not mediated by the mother, or is mediated by a "suffocating" absent mother, produces a contemptible female sexuality that gives birth not to healthy offspring but the incestuous pseudo parent-child relationship of monarch and subject (see pp. 194–226). But the play has not only been reinterpreted by theorists in recent years; for Stanley Cavell and Margot Heinemann, *King Lear* can teach us as much about our own time, in personal and political terms, as Shakespeare's (see pp. 227–40; 243–54). The physical blindness of Gloucester and the spiritual blindness of Lear are still relevant to a postmodern and post-theory world.

Without doubt, *King Lear* helped to change not only modern Shakespearean theatre production but all theatre production; the play changed not only modern Shakespearean literary criticism but all literary criticism. *King Lear* still has the power to provoke controversy and sweep away widely institutionalized beliefs about the very nature of "the poet's pen," for in the last thirty years the play has been at the forefront of renewed discussions of Shakespeare as author and reviser. Beginning with Michael Warren's influential reconsideration in 1978 of authorial revision in the play (see pp. 181–94), textual critics, literary critics, and theatre directors have increasingly come to accept that Shakespeare wrote two distinct versions of *King Lear*: one as represented by the text printed in the 1608 Quarto 1 (printed from Shakespeare's "foul papers" or original draft), and the other as represented in the 1623 First Folio of Shakespeare's works (printed from a later theatrical manuscript, checked against a copy of Quarto 2, which was largely reprinted from Quarto 1). Shakespeare revised the play sometime after its composition between late 1605 and late 1606 (judging from the play's use of sources and its topical allusions) or early or later performances (including at Whitehall in front of James I, and at the Globe for public audiences and Blackfriars for private audiences) and appears to have made hundreds of minor and numerous major revisions in his original text.

In fact, a collation of the two main texts (and the unauthorized Quarto 2) shows revisions in nearly every one or two lines of *King Lear* (see Textual Variants, pp. 117–33). Sometimes the revisions seem unimportant—a contraction to emphasize informal language—or functional—a contraction to ensure the meter is regular. Some revisions may have been done by other hands, including company bookkeepers (who kept track of the company's "book," now called a "promptbook"), such as the purgation of oaths on stage from 1606, or editors or compositors, who regularized exit directions or split lines. But the majority of small- and large-scale revisions between Quarto 1 and the Folio text show a number of sophisticated and consistent authorial patterns, including the enlargement of Lear's role and the reduction of the roles of those who surround him, including Kent and Cordelia, in order to further portray Lear's increasing isolation; the role of the Fool grows, perhaps because he symbolizes Lear's conscience. As if to forestall the kinds of critical attack launched on him by his later critics, including Tate, Lamb, and Hazlitt, Shakespeare appeared to soften the "barbarity" and "cruelty" of the play; the unbearably harsh "mock-trial" of Goneril and Regan by their father and his maddened companions in the Quartos does not appear in the Folio, and Lear apparently dies believing that Cordelia is still alive in the Folio, unlike in the Quartos, where he dies in total despair at the execution of his "poor fool". However the blinding of Gloucester in 3.7 is somewhat redeemed in the Quartos only, for Gloucester is not cast out alone after being blinded, as in the Folio text, but is followed by two sympathetic servants determined to help heal him by applying "flaxe and whites of egges" to "his bleeding face." Gloucester is denied this succor in the Folio text.

It may not be possible to decide definitively which version of the play is less "cruel" or more "redemptive" (or "better" or "worse"); perhaps Shakespeare is warning us that it is not important to decide. *King Lear*, in any given moment, can be a Jacobean tragedy, a primer on royal duty, a political treatise, a psychoanalytic investigation of dysfunctional families, an exploration of misogyny, a modern rendering of a post-nuclear culture, or a cathartic theatrical experience in which pity and fear are purged. Or it can simply be proof that none of these effects or concerns can be brought to this or any other play; that is, the play is a negation of anything we bring to it or imagine of it "in the moment," to use Brook's term. As Shakespeare shrewdly acknowledged in *A Midsummer Night's Dream*, it was the poet's pen that gave to "airy nothing" a "local habitation and a name," but it is the audience of Oberon, Hippolyta, and the others at court who judge the habitation and name given to *Pyramus and Thisbe* by its dramatists and actors in performance. In *King Lear*, so punctuated with the word "nothing," Shakespeare hands the poet's job to his audience, and it is for us, not Lear or Cordelia, or Lamb or Hazlitt, or Shakespeare, to make something or nothing come from airy nothing, and, as Brook reminds us, "If we are interested, that is what we will find."

The Text of
KING LEAR

M. William Shak-speare:

HIS

True Chronicle Historie of the life and death of King LEAR and his three Daughters.

With the vnfortunate life of Edgar, *sonne* and heire to the Earle of Gloster, and his sullen and assumed humor of
TOM of Bedlam:

As it was played before the Kings Maiestie at Whitehall vpon *S.* Stephans *night in Christmas Hollidayes.*

By his Maiesties seruants playing vsually at the Gloabe on the Bancke-side.

LONDON,
Printed for *Nathaniel Butter*, and are to be sold at his shop in *Pauls* Church-yard at the signe of the Pide Bull neere
S^t. *Austins* Gate. 1608.

Title page of the 1608 Quarto 1 edition of *King Lear.*

The Tragedy of King Lear

Dramatis Personae

LEAR, King of Britain
GONERIL, his eldest daughter
REGAN, his middle daughter
CORDELIA, his youngest daughter
DUKE OF ALBANY, husband of GONERIL
DUKE OF CORNWALL, husband of REGAN
EARL OF GLOUCESTER, courtier to LEAR
EDGAR, his elder son
EDMUND, his younger, illegitimate son
EARL OF KENT, courtier to LEAR
THE FOOL, attendant to LEAR
KING OF FRANCE
KING OF BURGUNDY
OSWALD, steward to GONERIL
CURRAN, servant of GLOUCESTER
OLD MAN, tenant of GLOUCESTER
CAPTAIN
HERALD
KNIGHTS
SOLDIERS
GENTLEMEN
SERVANTS
ATTENDANTS

Act 1, Scene 1

Enter KENT, GLOUCESTER, *and* EDMUND

KENT   I thought the King had more affected the Duke of Albany than Cornwall.
GLOUCESTER   It did always seem so to us, but now in the division of the kingdom, it appears not which of the dukes he

1.1. **Location:** King Lear's court.
1. **more affected:** preferred.

3

values most, for qualities are so weighed that curiosity in   5
neither can make choice of either's moiety.

KENT   Is not this your son, my lord?

GLOUCESTER   His breeding, sir, hath been at my charge. I
have so often blushed to acknowledge him, that now I am
brazed to it.   10

KENT   I cannot conceive you.

GLOUCESTER   Sir, this young fellow's mother could, where-
upon she grew round-wombed and had indeed, sir, a son for
her cradle ere she had a husband for her bed. Do you smell
a fault?   15

KENT   I cannot wish the fault undone, the issue of it being so
proper.

GLOUCESTER   But I have a son, sir, by order of law, some year
elder than this, who yet is no dearer in my account. Though
this knave came something saucily to the world before he   20
was sent for, yet was his mother fair, there was good sport at
his making, and the whoreson must be acknowledged. Do
you know this noble gentleman, Edmund?

EDMUND   No, my lord.

GLOUCESTER   My lord of Kent; remember him hereafter as   25
my honorable friend.

EDMUND   My services to your lordship.

KENT   I must love you, and sue to know you better.

EDMUND   Sir, I shall study deserving.

GLOUCESTER   He hath been out nine years, and away he shall   30
again. The king is coming.

> *Sennet. Enter one bearing a coronet, then* LEAR, CORN-
> WALL, ALBANY, GONERIL, REGAN, CORDELIA, *and* ATTEN-
> DANTS.

---

6. moiety: share (in the planned division of the kingdom).
8. breeding . . . charge: (1) upbringing was at my expense; (2) paternity was charged, or
legally named, as mine (about which Gloucester may remain unconvinced).
10. brazed: rendered shameless.
11. conceive: understand (but with a pun on "become pregnant" in Gloucester's response).
15. fault: (1) flaw; (2) moral transgression; (3) lost scent (in hunting), with pun on sexual
chase.
16. issue: (1) offspring; (2) result.
18. by order of law: i.e., legitimate.
20. knave: (1) rogue; (2) servant.   **saucily:** (1) lasciviously; (2) rudely or impertinently.
28. sue: proceed.
29. study deserving: i.e., learn to be worth your attention.
30. out: away.
STAGE DIRECTION sennet: a set of notes on the trumpet or cornet to signal character en-
trances or exits (OED).   **one bearing a coronet:** Lear's entrance is preceded by a servant carrying a coronet, a smaller and inferior crown to the one Lear is wearing; during the love-test
with his daughters Lear may proffer the coronet to each in turn.

LEAR   Attend the lords of France and Burgundy, Gloucester.
GLOUCESTER   I shall, my lord.   *Exit*
LEAR   Meantime we shall express our darker purpose.
    Give me the map there. Know that we have divided   35
    In three our kingdom, and 'tis our fast intent
    To shake all cares and business from our age,
    Conferring them on younger strengths, while we
    Unburthened crawl toward death. Our son of Cornwall,
    And you our no less loving son of Albany,   40
    We have this hour a constant will to publish
    Our daughters' several dowers, that future strife
    May be prevented now. The princes, France and Burgundy,
    Great rivals in our youngest daughter's love,
    Long in our court have made their amorous sojourn,   45
    And here are to be answered. Tell me, my daughters—
    Since now we will divest us both of rule,
    Interest of territory, cares of state—
    Which of you shall we say doth love us most,
    That we our largest bounty may extend   50
    Where nature doth with merit challenge? Goneril,
    Our eldest born, speak first.
GONERIL   Sir, I love you more than word can wield the matter,
    Dearer than eyesight, space, and liberty,
    Beyond what can be valued, rich or rare,   55
    No less than life, with grace, health, beauty, honour,

---

32. Attend: wait upon, look after.
STAGE DIRECTION *Exit*: Gloucester, having been sent out of the room by Lear, does not witness Lear's love-test of his daughters, as Edmund apparently does (there is no direction for his exit).
34. we: Here and throughout the play, Lear uses the royal "we," representing not only himself but his people; in effect, a king had two bodies, the body politic (representing his body of subjects) and the body natural (his own physical body). darker: sad or secret, with ironic meaning of "vile" or "evil."
35–36. divided / In three our kingdom: The Scottish king James VI, who had ruled England as James I for little over three years when this play was performed before him in 1606, was suspected by his English subjects of wanting to divide the multiple kingdoms of Britain.
36. fast: settled.
39, 40. son: i.e., son-in-law.
42. several dowers: individual dowries (i.e. payments made by a bride's family to her spouse).
45. sojourn: temporary stay.
49. doth love us most: This love-test appears in all the chronicle histories and literary sources that Shakespeare used for the play. However, in the source play, *King Leir*, in a preceding scene, Leir states to a courtier that he is about to choose husbands for his three unmarried daughters but worries that the stubborn Cordelia will not accept his choice for her. He plans to use the love-test to prove that Cordelia will not only pledge her true love to him but her willingness to accede lovingly to all his commands, including in choosing her future husband.
51. nature . . . challenge: i.e., filial love and worth prove the strongest challenger at the love-test.
53. wield: (1) express; (2) win.

As much as child e'er loved, or father found,
A love that makes breath poor, and speech unable,
Beyond all manner of so much I love you.
CORDELIA [*Aside*]   What shall Cordelia speak? Love, and be   60
  silent.
LEAR   Of all these bounds even from this line, to this,
  With shadowy forests and with champaigns riched,
  With plenteous rivers and wide-skirted meads,
  We make thee lady. To thine and Albany's issues
  Be this perpetual. What says our second daughter,   65
  Our dearest Regan, wife of Cornwall? Speak.
REGAN   Sir, I am made of that self-mettle as my sister,
  And prize me at her worth. In my true heart
  I find she names my very deed of love.
  Only she comes too short, that I profess   70
  Myself an enemy to all other joys
  Which the most precious square of sense possesses,
  And find I am alone felicitate
  In your dear highness' love.
CORDELIA   [*Aside*]   Then poor Cordelia,
  And yet not so, since I am sure my love's   75
  More ponderous than my tongue.
LEAR   To thee and thine hereditary ever
  Remain this ample third of our fair kingdom,
  No less in space, validity, and pleasure
  Than that conferred on Goneril. [*To* CORDELIA] Now, our   80
    joy,
  Although our last and least, to whose young love
  The vines of France and the milk of Burgundy
  Strive to be interest, what can you say to draw
  A third more opulent than your sisters? Speak.
CORDELIA   Nothing, my lord.   85
LEAR   Nothing?

---

61. bounds: boundaries (shown on the map mentioned at 1. 35).
62. champaigns: plains.
63. meads: meadows.
65. perpetual: i.e., perpetually endowed.
67. self-mettle: i.e., same strength of character; *Q* has the redundant "self same mettle."
69. deed: (1) act; (2) contract.
72. precious square of sense: dear measurement of feeling (?)
73. felicitate: made happy.
76. ponderous: weighty or profound.
77. thine hereditary: i.e., descendants.
81. least: youngest.
83. interest: entitled.
85–86. Nothing: These lines appear in *F* but not in *Q* and were probably added by Shakespeare to intensify this confrontation.

CORDELIA   Nothing.

LEAR   Nothing will come of nothing, speak again.

CORDELIA   Unhappy that I am, I cannot heave
My heart into my mouth. I love your majesty   90
According to my bond, no more, nor less.

LEAR   How, how, Cordelia? Mend your speech a little,
Lest you may mar your fortunes.

CORDELIA   Good my lord,
You have begot me, bred me, loved me. I
Return those duties back as are right fit,   95
Obey you, love you, and most honour you.
Why have my sisters husbands, if they say
They love you all? Happily, when I shall wed,
That lord whose hand must take my plight shall carry
Half my love with him, half my care and duty.   100
Sure, I shall never marry like my sisters,
To love my father all.

LEAR   But goes thy heart with this?

CORDELIA   Ay, my good lord.

LEAR   So young, and so untender?

CORDELIA   So young, my lord, and true.   105

LEAR   Let it be so, thy truth then be thy dower.
For by the sacred radiance of the sun,
The mysteries of Hecate and the night,
By all the operation of the orbs
From whom we do exist and cease to be,   110
Here I disclaim all my paternal care,
Propinquity and property of blood,
And as a stranger to my heart and me
Hold thee from this forever. The barbarous Scythian,
Or he that makes his generation messes   115

88. **Nothing . . . nothing:** Proverbial expression (*"Ex nihilo nihil fit"* in Latin), but suggest-ing the tension between the classical philosophical tenet that nothing comes from nothing and the Judeo-Christian tenet (Genesis 1.1) that God created the world from nothing; the latter tenet would have been familiar to Shakespeare's audience. *Q* uses "can" in place of the Folio's "will." "No thing" (i.e. "no penis") is also a pun on female genitalia (see *Hamlet* 3.2.108), from which something (a child) can come.
91. **no more, nor less:** Although she insists she cannot measure her love, Cordelia uses the same words of measurement as Lear and her sisters in this scene.
99. **plight:** pledge of marriage.
104. **untender:** (1) unkind; (2) unnatural, i.e., unfilial.
105. **true:** (1) truthful; (2) steadfast, loyal; (3) pure.
106. **dower:** dowry.
108. **mysteries:** secret rites.   **Hecate:** goddess of witchcraft.
109. **orbs:** planets.
112. **Propinquity:** close kinship.   **property:** possession or connection.
114. **Scythian:** i.e., an Asian warrior, characterized as brutal, as with the title character of Marlowe's *Tamburlaine*.
115. **makes his generation messes:** makes his offspring into his food; i.e., a cannibal.

To gorge his appetite, shall to my bosom
Be as well neighbored, pitied, and relieved
As thou my sometime daughter.

KENT   Good my liege—

LEAR   Peace, Kent!
Come not between the dragon and his wrath!   120
I loved her most, and thought to set my rest
On her kind nursery. [*To* CORDELIA] Hence and avoid my
    sight!
[*To all*] So be my grave my peace, as here I give
Her father's heart from her. Call France. Who stirs?
Call Burgundy. [*Exit* ATTENDANTS] Cornwall and Albany,   125
With my two daughters' dowers digest the third.
Let pride, which she calls plainness, marry her!
I do invest you jointly with my power,
Pre-eminence, and all the large effects
That troop with majesty. Ourself by monthly course,   130
With reservation of an hundred knights
By you to be sustained, shall our abode
Make with you by due turn; only we still retain
The name and all the addition to a king.
The sway, revenue, execution of the rest,   135
Beloved sons, be yours; which to confirm,
This coronet part between you.

KENT   Royal Lear,
Whom I have ever honored as my king,
Loved as my father, as my master followed,
As my great patron thought on in my prayers—   140

LEAR   The bow is bent and drawn, make from the shaft.

KENT   Let it fall rather, though the fork invade
The region of my heart. Be Kent unmannerly
When Lear is mad! What wouldst thou do, old man?
Think'st thou that duty shall have dread to speak   145
When power to flattery bows? To plainness honor's bound
When majesty falls to folly. Reserve thy state,
And in thy best consideration check
This hideous rashness. Answer my life, my judgment:

118. **sometime:** former.
121. **rest:** retirement in old age.
122. **nursery:** nursing or care.
126. **dowers:** dowries.
127. **plainness:** directness.
134. **addition:** trappings.
135. **sway:** authority.
142. **fork:** barbed head of an arrow (from archery imagery in l. 141).
145. **dread:** fear.
146. **plainness:** Kent adopts Lear's imagery from l. 134.

Thy youngest daughter does not love thee least,   150
  Nor are those empty-hearted whose low sounds
  Reverb no hollowness.
LEAR   Kent, on thy life, no more!
KENT   My life I never held but as a pawn
  To wage against thine enemies, ne'er fear to lose it,
  Thy safety being motive.
LEAR   Out of my sight!   155
KENT   See better, Lear, and let me still remain
  The true blank of thine eye.
LEAR   Now by Apollo—
KENT   Now by Apollo, King,
  Thou swear'st thy gods in vain!
LEAR   O, Vassal! Miscreant!
ALBANY   Dear sir, forbear.   160
KENT   Kill thy physician, and thy fee bestow
  Upon the foul disease. Revoke thy gift,
  Or whilst I can vent clamor from my throat,
  I'll tell thee thou dost evil.
LEAR   Hear me, recreant! On thine allegiance, hear me!   165
  That thou hast sought to make us break our vows,
  Which we durst never yet, and with strained pride
  To come betwixt our sentences and our power,
  Which nor our nature nor our place can bear,
  Our potency made good, take thy reward.   170
  Five days we do allot thee for provision
  To shield thee from disasters of the world,
  And on the sixth to turn thy hated back
  Upon our kingdom. If on the tenth day following
  Thy banished trunk be found in our dominions,   175
  The moment is thy death. Away! By Jupiter,
  This shall not be revoked.
KENT   Fare thee well, King, since thus thou wilt appear.
  Freedom lives hence, and banishment is here.
  [*To* CORDELIA] The gods to their dear shelter take thee,   180
    maid,

152. **Reverb:** reverberate.
155. **motive:** i.e., my motive.
157. **blank:** white spot at center of a target (from archery imagery at 1. 141ff).
158. **Apollo:** god of culture, poetry, and music, as well as archery.
160. **Vassal:** slave.   **Miscreant:** villain.
163. **vent clamor:** raise an outcry.
165. **recreant:** breaker of faith or allegiance.
168. **sentences:** judgments (i.e., punishments).
170. **potency:** royal power.
175. **trunk:** i.e., body.
176. **Jupiter:** god who controls the state and its laws.

That justly thinkst, and hast most rightly said.
[*To* GONERIL *and* REGAN] And your large speeches may your
   deeds approve,
That good effects may spring from words of love.
Thus Kent, O princes, bids you all adieu,
He'll shape his old course in a country new.   *Exit* 185

    Flourish. Enter GLOUCESTER *with* FRANCE *and* BUR-
    GUNDY [*and*] ATTENDANTS

GLOUCESTER   Here's France and Burgundy, my noble lord.
LEAR   My lord of Burgundy,
   We first address toward you, who with this King
   Hath rivaled for our daughter. What in the least
   Will you require in present dower with her, 190
   Or cease your quest of love?
BURGUNDY   Most royal majesty,
   I crave no more than what your highness offered,
   Nor will you tender less?
LEAR   Right noble Burgundy,
   When she was dear to us, we did hold her so,
   But now her price is fallen. Sir, there she stands. 195
   If aught within that little-seeming substance,
   Or all of it, with our displeasure pieced,
   And nothing else, may fitly like your grace,
   She's there, and she is yours.
BURGUNDY   I know no answer.
LEAR   Will you with those infirmities she owes, 200
   Unfriended, new-adopted to our hate,
   Dowered with our curse, and strangered with our oath,
   Take her, or leave her?
BURGUNDY   Pardon me, royal sir,
   Election makes not up in such conditions.
LEAR   Then leave her, sir, for by the power that made me, 205
   I tell you all her wealth. [*To* FRANCE] For you, great King,
   I would not from your love make such a stray
   To match you where I hate; therefore beseech you
   To avert your liking a more worthier way
   Than on a wretch whom nature is ashamed 210

STAGE DIRECTION *Flourish:* trumpet fanfare, used to announce the arrival or departure of monarchs or other distinguished persons.
193. **tender:** offer, with ironic echo of "untender" in l. 104.
196. **aught:** anything.   **little-seeming:** i.e., inferior.
202. **Dowered:** endowed, with ironic sense of relieved of her dowry.   **strangered:** made a
stranger, i.e., disinherited.
204. **Election makes not up:** i.e., choice is impossible.
209. **avert:** turn away.

Almost t'acknowledge hers.

FRANCE   This is most strange,
That she—whom even but now was your object,
The argument of your praise, balm of your age,
The best, the dearest—should in this trice of time
Commit a thing so monstrous to dismantle   215
So many folds of favor. Sure, her offence
Must be of such unnatural degree
That monsters it, or your fore-vouched affection
Fall into taint; which to believe of her
Must be a faith that reason without miracle   220
Should never plant in me.

CORDELIA   I yet beseech your majesty—
If for I want that glib and oily art,
To speak and purpose not, since what I well intend
I'll do't before I speak—that you make known   225
It is no vicious blot, murder, or foulness,
No unchaste action or dishonored step,
That hath deprived me of your grace and favor,
But even for want of that for which I am richer:
A still-soliciting eye and such a tongue   230
That I am glad I have not; though not to have it
Hath lost me in your liking.

LEAR   Better thou hadst
Not been born than not t'have pleased me better.

FRANCE   Is it but this: a tardiness in nature,
Which often leaves the history unspoke   235
That it intends to do? My lord of Burgundy,
What say you to the lady? Love's not love
When it is mingled with regards that stands
Aloof from the entire point. Will you have her?
She is herself a dowry.

BURGUNDY   Royal King,   240
Give but that portion which yourself proposed,
And here I take Cordelia by the hand,
Duchess of Burgundy.

LEAR   Nothing, I have sworn, I am firm.

BURGUNDY   I am sorry then you have so lost a father   245

213. **balm:** soother.
218. **fore-vouched:** previously pledged.
219. **taint:** disgrace.
223. **oily:** obsequious.
230. **still-soliciting:** always begging.
235. **unspoke:** unspoken.
239. **Aloof:** detached, outside of.
244. **Nothing:** ironic echo of l. 85.

That you must lose a husband.

CORDELIA   Peace be with Burgundy.
　　Since that respect and fortunes are his love,
　　I shall not be his wife.

FRANCE   Fairest Cordelia, that art most rich being poor,   250
　　Most choice forsaken, and most loved despised,
　　Thee and thy virtues here I seize upon.
　　Be it lawful, I take up what's cast away.
　　Gods, gods! 'Tis strange, that from their cold'st neglect
　　My love should kindle to inflamed respect.   255
　　Thy dowerless daughter, King, thrown to my chance,
　　Is queen of us, of ours, and our fair France.
　　Not all the dukes of wat'rish Burgundy
　　Can buy this unprized precious maid of me.
　　Bid them farewell, Cordelia, though unkind;   260
　　Thou losest here a better where to find.

LEAR   Thou hast her, France, let her be thine, for we
　　Have no such daughter, nor shall ever see
　　That face of hers again. Therefore, be gone,
　　Without our grace, our love, our benison.   265
　　Come, noble Burgundy.

　　　　Flourish. Exeunt [LEAR, BURGUNDY, ALBANY, CORNWALL,
　　　　GLOUCESTER, EDMUND, *and* ATTENDANTS]

FRANCE   Bid farewell to your sisters.

CORDELIA   The jewels of our father, with washed eyes
　　Cordelia leaves you. I know you what you are,
　　And like a sister am most loath to call   270
　　Your faults as they are named. Love well our father:
　　To your professèd bosoms I commit him.
　　But yet, alas, stood I within his grace,
　　I would prefer him to a better place.
　　So farewell to you both.   275

GONERIL   Prescribe not us our duty.

REGAN　　　　　　　　　　　　　Let your study
　　Be to content your lord, who hath received you
　　At fortune's alms. You have obedience scanted,
　　And well are worth the want that you have wanted.

CORDELIA   Time shall unfold what plighted cunning hides;   280

---

258. wat'rish: waterish, i.e., diluted or inferior (reduced to two syllables to fit the meter).
261. where: i.e., place.
265. benison: blessing.
278. fortune's alms: i.e., as a charity case.
279. And . . . wanted: i.e., deserve your lack of favor and dowry.
280. plighted: (1) pledged (used ironically); (2) folded, i.e., obscured.

Who covers faults, at last with shame derides.
Well may you prosper.

FRANCE   Come, fair Cordelia.

Exeunt FRANCE *and* CORDELIA

GONERIL   Sister, it is not a little I have to say of what most
nearly appertains to us both. I think our father will hence
tonight.   285

REGAN   That's most certain, and with you; next month with
us.

GONERIL   You see how full of changes his age is; the observation we have made of it hath not been little. He always loved
our sister most, and with what poor judgment he hath now   290
cast her off appears too grossly.

REGAN   'Tis the infirmity of his age; yet he hath ever but slen-
derly known himself.

GONERIL   The best and soundest of his time hath been but
rash. Then must we look from his age to receive not alone   295
the imperfections of long-engrafted condition, but there-
withal the unruly waywardness that infirm and choleric
years bring with them.

REGAN   Such unconstant starts are we like to have from him
as this of Kent's banishment.   300

GONERIL   There is further compliment of leave-taking between France and him. Pray you, let's hit together. If our father carry authority with such disposition as he bears, this
last surrender of his will but offend us.

REGAN   We shall further think of it.   305

GONERIL   We must do something, and i'th'heat.   *Exeunt*

Act 1, Scene 2

Enter EDMUND

EDMUND   Thou, Nature, art my goddess; to thy law
My services are bound. Wherefore should I
Stand in the plague of custom and permit

281. **shame derides:** i.e., will be derided by shame.
284. **hence:** go hence.
291. **grossly:** obviously.
294. **time:** i.e., time of his life.
296. **long-engrafted:** i.e., a long time.
297. **choleric:** i.e., hot-tempered.
299. **unconstant:** changeable.
302. **France:** i.e., the King of France.
306. **i'th'heat:** in the heat, i.e., while excited about something.
1.2. **Location:** The Earl of Gloucester's castle.
3. **custom:** customary beliefs or laws.

The curiosity of nations to deprive me?
For that I am some twelve or fourteen moonshines   5
Lag of a brother? Why "bastard"? Wherefore "base"
When my dimensions are as well compact
My mind as generous, and my shape as true
As honest madam's issue? Why brand they us
With "base", with "baseness", "bastardy"? Base? Base?   10
Who in the lusty stealth of nature take
More composition and fierce quality
Than doth within a dull, stale, tired bed
Go to th'creating a whole tribe of fops
Got 'tween a sleep and wake? Well, then,   15
Legitimate Edgar, I must have your land.
Our father's love is to the bastard Edmund
As to the legitimate. Fine word, "legitimate"!
Well, my legitimate, [*takes out a letter*] if this letter speed
And my invention thrive, Edmund the base   20
Shall to th'legitimate. I grow, I prosper.
Now gods, stand up for bastards!

    Enter GLOUCESTER

GLOUCESTER Kent banished thus? And France in choler
  parted?
And the king gone tonight? Prescribed his power,
Confined to exhibition? All this done   25
Upon the gad? Edmund, how now? What news?
EDMUND So please your lordship, none. [*Puts up the letter.*]
GLOUCESTER Why so earnestly seek you to put up that letter?
EDMUND I know no news, my lord.
GLOUCESTER What paper were you reading?   30
EDMUND Nothing, my lord.
GLOUCESTER No? What needed then that terrible dispatch of
  it into your pocket? The quality of nothing hath not such
  need to hide itself. Let's see. Come, if it be nothing, I shall
  not need spectacles.   35

4. **curiosity:** undue preciseness. **deprive me:** i.e., deprive me of an inheritance because
I'm illegitimate.
5–6. **moonshines / Lag:** i.e., months younger than.
6. **base:** (1) illegitimate; (2) of a low rank.
7. **compact:** compacted, or made up of.
9. **honest madam's:** i.e., married woman's.
9–15. **Why brand . . . and wake:** Edmund argues that children conceived by passionate
lovers are better than those conceived by bored, married couples.
14. **fops:** fools.
19. **speed:** succeed.
23. **choler:** anger.
25. **exhibition:** show.
33. **nothing:** ironic echo of l. 85.

EDMUND   I beseech you, sir, pardon me. It is a letter from my
  brother that I have not all o'erread; and for so much as I
  have perused, I find it not fit for your o'erlooking.
GLOUCESTER   Give me the letter, sir.
EDMUND   I shall offend either to detain or give it. The con-   40
  tents, as in part I understand them, are to blame.
GLOUCESTER   Let's see, let's see.
EDMUND   I hope, for my brother's justification, he wrote this
  but as an essay or taste of my virtue.   [*Gives him the letter.*]
GLOUCESTER [*Reads*]   "This policy and reverence of age makes   45
  the world bitter to the best of our times, keeps our fortunes
  from us till our oldness cannot relish them. I begin to find
  an idle and fond bondage in the oppression of aged tyranny,
  who sways not as it hath power, but as it is suffered. Come
  to me, that of this I may speak more. If our father would   50
  sleep till I waked him, you should enjoy half his revenue forever and live the beloved of your brother. Edgar." Hum?
  Conspiracy? "Sleep till I waked him, you should enjoy half
  his revenue." My son Edgar, had he a hand to write this, a
  heart and brain to breed it in? When came this to you? Who   55
  brought it?
EDMUND   It was not brought me, my lord; there's the cunning
  of it. I found it thrown in at the casement of my closet.
GLOUCESTER   You know the character to be your brother's?
EDMUND   If the matter were good, my lord, I durst swear it   60
  were his: but in respect of that, I would fain think it were
  not.
GLOUCESTER   It is his?
EDMUND   It is his hand, my lord, but I hope his heart is not in
  the contents.   65
GLOUCESTER   Has he never before sounded you in this business?
EDMUND   Never, my lord. But I have heard him oft maintain
  it to be fit that, sons at perfect age and fathers declined, the
  father should be as ward to the son, and the son manage his   70
  revenue.
GLOUCESTER   O villain, villain! His very opinion in the letter!

---

44. **essay or taste:** test or trial.
49. **sways:** (1) moves; (2) rules.
55. **breed:** grow.
58. **casement of my closet:** window of my room.
59. **character:** handwriting, with ironic pun on "personality."
61. **fain:** enjoy, with pun on "feign," i.e., deceive.
64. **hand:** handwriting.
66. **sounded you:** sounded you out.
69. **declined:** enfeebled.
70. **ward:** guardian.

Abhorred villain, unnatural, detested, brutish villain! Worse
than brutish! Go, sirrah, seek him; I'll apprehend him!
Abominable villain, where is he?   75

EDMUND   I do not well know, my lord. If it shall please you to
suspend your indignation against my brother till you can derive from him better testimony of his intent, you should run
a certain course; where if you violently proceed against him,
mistaking his purpose, it would make a great gap in your   80
own honor and shake in pieces the heart of his obedience. I
dare pawn down my life for him, he hath writ this to feel my
affection to your honor and to no other pretense of danger.

GLOUCESTER   Think you so?

EDMUND   If your honor judge it meet, I will place you where   85
you shall hear us confer of this and by an auricular assurance have your satisfaction, and that without any further
delay than this very evening.

GLOUCESTER   He cannot be such a monster.

EDMUND   Nor is not, sure.   90

GLOUCESTER   To his father, that so tenderly and entirely loves
him. Heaven and earth! Edmund, seek him out, wind me
into him. I pray you, frame the business after your own wisdom. I would unstate myself to be in a due resolution.

EDMUND   I will seek him, sir, presently, convey the business   95
as I shall find means, and acquaint you withal.

GLOUCESTER   These late eclipses in the sun and moon portend no good to us. Though the wisdom of Nature can reason it thus and thus, yet nature finds itself scourged by the
sequent effects. Love cools, friendship falls off, brothers di-   100
vide; in cities, mutinies, in countries, discords; in palaces,
treason; and the bond cracked 'twixt son and father. This
villain of mine comes under the prediction: there's son
against father. The king falls from bias of nature, there's father against child. We have seen the best of our time.   105

73. **villain:** evil-doer, with secondary meaning of "low-born," which ironically puns on Edmund's obsessions with being illegitimate.
82. **pawn down:** pledge.
86. **auricular:** audible.
92–93. **wind me into him:** get wind of, or smell him out for me (OED); Gloucester will
need to "smell" his way to Dover after 3.7.92–93.
93. **frame:** shape.
93–94. **wisdom:** judgment.
96. **means:** opportunity.
96. **withal:** therewith.
97. **late eclipses:** lunar and solar eclipses occurred in England in September and October
1605, and this allusion is used to date the composition of the play to no earlier than September 1605.
97–98. **portend:** foretell.
100. **sequent:** resulting.
105. **best:** happiest period.

Machinations, hollowness, treachery, and all ruinous disorders follow us disquietly to our graves. Find out this villain,
Edmund, it shall lose thee nothing. Do it carefully. And the
noble and true-hearted Kent banished, his offence—hon-
esty. 'Tis strange!   *Exit*   110

EDMUND   This is the excellent foppery of the world, that
when we are sick in fortune, often the surfeits of our own
behavior, we make guilty of our disasters the sun, the moon,
and the stars; as if we were villains on necessity, fools by
heavenly compulsion, knaves, thieves, and treacherers by   115
spherical predominance, drunkards, liars, and adulterers by
an enforced obedience of planetary influence; and all that
we are evil in, by a divine thrusting on. An admirable eva-
sion of whoremaster man, to lay his goatish disposition on
the charge of a star! My father compounded with my mother   120
under the Dragon's tail, and my nativity was under Ursa
Major, so that it follows I am rough and lecherous. Fut! I
should have been that I am had the maidenliest star in the
firmament twinkled on my bastardizing.

     Enter EDGAR

[*Aside*] Pat, he comes, like the catastrophe of the old com-   125
     edy. My cue is villainous melancholy, with a sigh like Tom
     of Bedlam! [*To* EDGAR] Oh, these eclipses do portend
     these divisions. [*Sings*] Fa, sol, la, mi.

EDGAR   How now, brother Edmund, what serious contempla-
tion are you in?   130

106. **Machinations:** evil plots.
111–124. **This is . . . my bastardizing:** Edmund satirizes the belief that human behavior
is predetermined by astrological events, rather than determined by the exercise of free will.
He may be holding a book in his hand and referring to a passage in it during this speech.
111. **foppery:** foolishness.
115. **treacherers:** traitors.
116. **spherical:** i.e., astrological.
118. **thrusting:** forcing, with sexual pun.
119. **whoremaster:** i.e., lecherous.   **goatish:** lustful.
120. **compounded:** (1) united in sexual intercourse; (2) produced a compounded, or com-
posite, product (Edmund).
121. **Dragon's tail:** descending node of the moon's orbit (*OED*).   **nativity:** birth.
121–22. **Ursa Major:** northern constellation (also known as the Great Bear, a symbol of
lechery).
122. **Fut:** "God's foot" (an oath).   **that:** i.e., what.   **maidenliest:** most virginal.
125. **catastrophe:** i.e., calamity that serves as a theatrical denouement.
126. **cue:** Edmund sees himself as an actor here; Shakespeare frequently reminded his audiences of the artificiality of theatrical productions by having characters reflect on the art of
acting.
126–127. **Tom of Bedlam:** This appears in *F* but not *Q*, which has instead "them of Bedlam"; Bedlam alludes to Bethlehem Hospital, London, which housed the insane. This variant, with its ironic foreshadowing of Edgar's disguise as Tom of Bedlam in Acts 3 and 4,
almost certainly represents an authorial revision, made sometime after the composition,
and probably after early performances, of the play.
128. **Fa . . . mi:** notes on the scale of C major.

EDMUND   I am thinking, brother, of a prediction I read this
other day, what should follow these eclipses.

EDGAR   Do you busy yourself with that?

EDMUND   I promise you, the effects he writes of succeed un-
happily, as of unnaturalness between the child and the par-   135
ent, death, dearth, dissolutions of ancient amities, divisions
in state, menaces and maledictions against king and nobles,
needless diffidences, banishment of friends, dissipation of
cohorts, nuptial breaches, and I know not what.

EDGAR   How long have you been a sectary astronomical?   140

EDMUND   Come, come. When saw you my father last?

EDGAR   The night gone by.

EDMUND   Spake you with him?

EDGAR   Ay, two hours together.

EDMUND   Parted you in good terms? Found you no displea-   145
sure in him by word nor countenance?

EDGAR   None at all.

EDMUND   Bethink yourself wherein you may have offended
him, and at my entreaty forbear his presence until some little time hath qualified the heat of his displeasure, which at   150
this instant so rageth in him that with the mischief of your
person it would scarcely allay.

EDGAR   Some villain hath done me wrong.

EDMUND   That's my fear. I pray you have a continent forbearance till the speed of his rage goes slower; and as I say, re-   155
tire with me to my lodging, from whence I will fitly bring
you to hear my lord speak. Pray ye, go; there's my key. If you
do stir abroad, go armed.

EDGAR   Armed, brother?

EDMUND   Brother, I advise you to the best, go armed. I am no   160
honest man, if there be any good meaning toward you. I
have told you what I have seen and heard but faintly, nothing like the image and horror of it. Pray you, away!

EDGAR   Shall I hear from you anon?

EDMUND   I do serve you in this business.   *Exit* EDGAR   165

---

134. he writes of: This may signal that Edmund is showing Edgar the book he had in his
hands in ll. 111–118.
136. amities: friendships.
137. maledictions: slanders.
138. diffidences: distrust.
138–39. dissipation of cohorts: dispersal of supporters.
139. nuptial: wedding.
140. sectary astronomical: faithful follower of astrology.
146. countenance: behavior.
149. forbear: avoid.
154–55. continent forbearance: self-restrained control.
156. fitly: at the appropriate time.
158. stir abroad: i.e., go out.
164. anon: at once.

A credulous father and a brother noble,
Whose nature is so far from doing harms
That he suspects none; on whose foolish honesty
My practices ride easy. I see the business.
Let me, if not by birth, have lands by wit.   170
All with me's meet that I can fashion fit.   *Exit*

Act 1, Scene 3

Enter GONERIL *and* [*her*] *steward* OSWALD

GONERIL   Did my father strike my gentleman for chiding of
his fool?
OSWALD   Ay, madam.
GONERIL   By day and night, he wrongs me; every hour
He flashes into one gross crime or other   5
That sets us all at odds. I'll not endure it.
His knights grow riotous, and himself upbraids us
On every trifle. When he returns from hunting,
I will not speak with him. Say I am sick.
If you come slack of former services,   10
You shall do well; the fault of it I'll answer.   [*Horns within*]
OSWALD   He's coming, madam, I hear him.
GONERIL   Put on what weary negligence you please,
You and your fellows. I'd have it come to question.
If he distaste it, let him to my sister,   15
Whose mind and mine I know in that are one,
Not to be overruled. Idle old man,
That still would manage those authorities
That he hath given away! Now, by my life,
Old fools are babes again, and must be used   20
With checks as flatteries when they are seen abused.
Remember what I have said.
OSWALD   Well, madam.
GONERIL   And let his knights have colder looks among you;
What grows of it no matter. Advise your fellows so.

---

171. **meet:** just.
STAGE DIRECTION *steward:* official who controls the domestic affairs of a household
(*OED*).
1.3. Location: The Duke of Albany's castle.
10. **come slack:** become negligent.
STAGE DIRECTION *Horns within:* flourish of trumpets offstage to announce Lear's arrival.
14. **come to question:** become an issue.
15. **distaste:** dislike.
20. **babes:** babies.
21. **checks . . . abused:** reprimands as much as flatters when they misbehave.
24. **grows:** comes.

I would breed from hence occasions, and I shall,   25
That I may speak. I'll write straight to my sister
To hold my course. Prepare for dinner.   *Exeunt*

Act 1, Scene 4

Enter KENT [*disguised as* CAIUS]

KENT   If but as well I other accents borrow
That can my speech defuse, my good intent
May carry through itself to that full issue
For which I razed my likeness. Now, banished Kent,
If thou canst serve where thou dost stand condemned,   5
So may it come, thy master, whom thou lov'st,
Shall find thee full of labors.

Horns within. Enter LEAR, [KNIGHTS], *and* ATTENDANTS

LEAR   Let me not stay a jot for dinner. Go, get it ready.
                    [*Exit* FIRST KNIGHT]
[*To* KENT] How now, what art thou?
KENT   A man, sir.   10
LEAR   What dost thou profess? What wouldst thou with
    us?
KENT   I do profess to be no less than I seem, to serve him
    truly that will put me in trust, to love him that is honest,
    to converse with him that is wise and says little, to fear   15
    judgment, to fight when I cannot choose, and to eat no
    fish.
LEAR   What art thou?
KENT   A very honest-hearted fellow, and as poor as the
    king.   20
LEAR   If thou be'st as poor for a subject as he's for a king,
    thou art poor enough. What wouldst thou?

---

25. breed from hence occasions: i.e., grow productive from future occurrences of his
misbehavior (see Lear's curse in 1.4.258–72 that Goneril not be allowed to breed, or produce children).
27. hold my course: keep to my plan.
1.4. Location: The Duke of Albany's castle.
1–2. accents borrow . . . speech defuse: The banished Kent will adopt a regional or
lower-class accent (and the shabby clothes of a servant, named Caius), in order to "defuse"
his voice and appearance and thereby conceal his identity.
3. issue: matter.
4. razed: erased through cutting out (used figuratively).
8. a jot: even the smallest amount of time; Lear enters hungry and impatient here, as well
anxious for the arrival of his Fool.
16–17. eat no fish: adheres to some (unexplained) strict principle (possibly signaling that
he refuses to eat fish on Fridays, as Catholics must do in order to abstain from meat).

KENT   Service.

LEAR   Who wouldst thou serve?

KENT   You.   25

LEAR   Dost thou know me, fellow?

KENT   No, sir, but you have that in your countenance
which I would fain call master.

LEAR   What's that?

KENT   Authority.   30

LEAR   What services canst thou do?

KENT   I can keep honest counsel, ride, run, mar a curious
tale in telling it, and deliver a plain message bluntly. That
which ordinary men are fit for, I am qualified in, and the
best of me is diligence.   35

LEAR   How old art thou?

KENT   Not so young, sir, to love a woman for singing, nor
so old to dote on her for anything. I have years on my
back forty-eight.

LEAR   Follow me; thou shalt serve me, if I like thee no   40
worse after dinner. I will not part from thee yet. Dinner,
ho, dinner! Where's my knave, my Fool? Go you and call
my Fool hither.   [*Exit* SECOND KNIGHT]

    Enter OSWALD

You, you, sirrah, where's my daughter?

OSWALD   So please you—   *Exit*   45

LEAR   What says the fellow there? Call the clotpoll back.
                         [*Exit* THIRD KNIGHT]

Where's my Fool? Ho, I think the world's asleep!

    [*Enter* KNIGHT]

How now? Where's that mongrel?

[THIRD] KNIGHT   He says, my lord, your daughter is not well.

LEAR   Why came not the slave back to me when I called him?   50

[THIRD KNIGHT]   Sir, he answered me in the roundest manner,
he would not.

---

35. diligence: earnest willingness to undertake an action, i.e., he will steadfastly obey
Lear's commands.

42. knave: boy or servant, here used affectionately.   **Fool:** jester or clown, in this case,
employed by Lear to amuse him; traditionally dressed in "motley" (multicolored clothes)
with a "coxcomb" hat resembling a rooster's comb, carrying a *marotte*, a baton with a deco-
ration at the end. In Shakespeare's time, the actor playing the role of Cordelia may have
doubled the role of the Fool.

44. sirrah: contemptuous form of address, frequently used to denigrate servants or inferi-
ors; the term is inappropriate for a steward such as Oswald, who oversees servants and in-
feriors.

46. clotpoll: blockhead; the *OED* credits Shakespeare with the first use of this word.

48. mongrel: cross-bred dog, hence inferior.

51. roundest: circuitously, hence deliberately obscure.

LEAR   He would not?

[THIRD] KNIGHT   My lord, I know not what the matter is, but
to my judgment your highness is not entertained with that   55
ceremonious affection as you were wont. There's a great
abatement of kindness appears as well in the general dependents as in the duke himself also, and your daughter.

LEAR   Ha? Say'st thou so?

[THIRD] KNIGHT   I beseech you pardon me, my lord, if I be   60
mistaken, for my duty cannot be silent when I think your
highness wronged.

LEAR   Thou but remember'st me of mine own conception. I
have perceived a most faint neglect of late, which I have
rather blamed as mine own jealous curiosity than as a very   65
pretence and purpose of unkindness. I will look further into't. But where's my Fool? I have not seen him this two days.

[THIRD] KNIGHT   Since my young lady's going into France, sir,
the Fool hath much pined away.

LEAR   No more of that, I have noted it well. Go you and tell   70
my daughter I would speak with her.   [Exit THIRD KNIGHT]
Go you, call hither my Fool.   [Exit FOURTH KNIGHT]

        Enter OSWALD

O you, sir, you, come you hither. Who am I, sir?

OSWALD   My lady's father.

LEAR   "My lady's father"? My lord's knave, you whoreson dog,   75
you slave, you cur!

OSWALD   I am none of these, my lord, I beseech your pardon.

LEAR   Do you bandy looks with me, you rascal?

                                                [Strikes him]

OSWALD   I'll not be strucken, my lord.

KENT   Nor tripped neither, you base football player.   80

                                                [Trips him]

LEAR   I thank thee, fellow. Thou serv'st me, and I'll love thee.

KENT   Come, sir, arise, away. I'll teach you differences. Away,

---

56. **wont:** accustomed.
57. **abatement:** decrease.
57–58. **dependents:** i.e., servants.
58. **duke:** i.e., Albany.
60. **beseech:** entreat.
63. **conception:** understanding.
68. **young lady's:** i.e., Cordelia's.
75. **"My lady's father":** Lear's anger here stems from his assumption that Oswald should refer to him instead as "the king."   **cur:** dog, i.e., surly person.
78. **bandy looks:** exchange words (on an equal footing); Lear is shocked at Oswald's lack of subservience to a monarch.
79. **strucken:** struck.
80. **base football:** i.e., player of a lower-class sport.
82. **differences:** distinctions between social ranks.

away! If you will measure your lubber's length again, tarry;
but away, go to, you have wisdom, so.

[*Exit* OSWALD]

LEAR   Now, my friendly knave, I thank thee; there's earnest of   85
thy service.

[*Gives* KENT *money*]

Enter FOOL

FOOL   Let me hire him, too; here's my coxcomb.   [*Offers*
KENT *his fool's cap.*]
LEAR   How now, my pretty knave, how dost thou?
FOOL [*To* KENT]   Sirrah, you were best take my coxcomb.
KENT   Why, my boy?   90
FOOL   Why? For taking one's part that's out of favor. Nay, and
thou canst not smile as the wind sits, thou'lt catch cold
shortly. There, take my coxcomb. Why, this fellow has ban-
ished two on's daughters and did the third a blessing against
his will. If thou follow him, thou must needs wear my cox-   95
comb. How now, nuncle, would I had two coxcombs and
two daughters.
LEAR   Why, my boy?
FOOL   If I gave them any living, I'd keep my coxcombs myself.
There's mine; beg another of thy daughters.   100
LEAR   Take heed, sirrah, the whip.
FOOL   Truth's a dog that must to kennel. He must be whipped
out, when the Lady Brach may stand by the fire and stink.
LEAR   A pestilent gall to me.
FOOL   Sirrah, I'll teach thee a speech.   105
LEAR   Do.
FOOL   Mark it, uncle:
Have more than thou showest,
Speak less than thou knowest,
Lend less than thou owest,   110

83. **measure your lubber's length:** i.e., show off your loutish behavior. **go to:** come,
come, i.e., stop.
85. **earnest:** earnest money (payment in advance).
87. **coxcomb:** see l. 42.
94. **on's:** contraction of "of his" (the fool frequently speaks in slang, as well as colloquial
and proverbial expressions, in contrast to Lear's more formal language).
96. **nuncle:** contraction of "mine uncle," a term of endearment; Lear's surrogate father-
son relationship with the Fool is in contrast to his relationships with his real children.
101. **the whip:** Lear threatens the Fool that further mockery could result in his being
whipped.
102. **must to kennel:** must go to kennel (i.e., be restrained).
103. **Lady Brach:** i.e., contemptible female dog.
104. **pestilent gall:** infectious or foul bitterness.

Ride more than thou goest,
Learn more than thou trowest,
Set less than thou throwest,
Leave thy drink and thy whore,
And keep in-a-door,   115
And thou shalt have more,
Than two tens to a score.

LEAR   This is nothing, Fool.

FOOL   Then, 'tis like the breath of an unfeed lawyer, you gave
me nothing for't. Can you make no use of nothing, nuncle?   120

LEAR   Why, no, boy; nothing can be made out of nothing.

FOOL [To KENT]   Prithee, tell him so much the rent of his
land comes to; he will not believe a Fool.

LEAR   A bitter Fool.

FOOL   Dost know the difference, my boy, between a bitter   125
Fool and a sweet one?

LEAR   No, lad, teach me.

FOOL   That lord that counseled thee to give away thy land,
Come place him here by me; do thou for him stand,
The sweet and bitter Fool will presently appear,   130
The one in motley here, the other found out there.

LEAR   Dost thou call me Fool, boy?

FOOL   All thy other titles thou hast given away; that thou
wast born with.

KENT   This is not altogether fool, my lord.   135

FOOL   No, faith, lords and great men will not let me. If I had
a monopoly out, they would have part on't; and lords too,
they will not let me have all the Fool to myself; they'll be
snatching. Nuncle, give me an egg, and I'll give thee two
crowns.   140

LEAR   What two crowns shall they be?

FOOL   Why, after I have cut the egg i'th'middle and eat up the
meat, the two crowns of the egg. When thou clovest thy
crown i'th'middle and gavest away both parts, thou borest
thine ass on thy back o'er the dirt. Thou hadst little wit in   145

112. trowest: believe.
115. in-a-door: indoors.
118–21. nothing: ironic echo of 1.1.85.
119. unfeed: unpaid, hence unproductive.
122. Prithee: pray you (contraction of "pray thee").
125. my boy: the Fool is the only character that Lear allows to treat him subserviently.
128–31. That lord . . . out there: this passage appears in Q but not F.
131. motley: see 1. 42.
136–40. No, faith . . . two crowns: The Fool is satirically lamenting that he does not have
a monopoly on acting foolishly, as lords and great men (such as Lear) can also do so.
140. crowns: (1) five shilling coins; (2) royal crowns (i.e., headgear); (3) heads that wear
royal crowns (OED); (4) heads; (5) rings or circles.
143. clovest: divided.   borest: bore, i.e., carried.

thy bald crown when thou gav'st thy golden one away. If I
speak like myself in this, let him be whipped that first finds
it so.

      [*Sings*] Fools had ne'er less grace in a year,
         For wise men are grown foppish,   150
      And know not how their wits to wear,
         Their manners are so apish.

LEAR   When were you wont to be so full of songs, sirrah?

FOOL   I have used it, nuncle, e'er since thou mad'st thy
daughters thy mothers; for when thou gav'st them the rod   155
and put'st down thine own breeches.

      [*Sings*] Then they for sudden joy did weep,
         And I for sorrow sung,
      That such a king should play bo-peep,
         And go the Fool among.   160
Prithee, nuncle, keep a schoolmaster that can teach thy
Fool to lie. I would fain learn to lie.

LEAR   And you lie, sirrah, we'll have you whipped.

FOOL   I marvel what kin thou and thy daughters are: they'll
have me whipped for speaking true, thou'lt have me   165
whipped for lying, and sometimes I am whipped for holding
my peace. I had rather be any kind o'thing than a Fool, and
yet I would not be thee, nuncle. Thou hast pared thy wit
o'both sides and left nothing i'th'middle. Here comes one
o'the parings.   170

      Enter GONERIL

LEAR   How now, daughter! What makes that frontlet on? You
are too much of late i'th'frown.

FOOL   Thou wast a pretty fellow when thou hadst no need to
care for her frowning. Now thou art an O without a figure. I
am better than thou art now. I am a Fool, thou art nothing.   175
      [*To* GONERIL] Yes, forsooth, I will hold my tongue, so your

150. **foppish:** foolish.
152. **apish:** ape-like.
153. **wont:** accustomed.
155. **rod:** used for whipping on the buttocks.
156. **breeches:** knee-length trousers.
159. **bo-peep:** child's game of hiding.
162. **fain:** enjoy, with pun on "feign," i.e., deceive.
164. **kin:** relatives.
166–67. **holding my peace:** keeping silent.
168. **pared:** trimmed.
171. **frontlet:** forehead ornament or bandage, possibly ironic, as such a bandage was
sometimes worn to prevent wrinkles (*OED*).
172. **i'th'frown:** frowning, i.e., bad-tempered.
174. **O without a figure:** zero, without a number before it, or "nothing," and punning on
one meaning of "crown" as circle, and possibly to "O" as a slang term for female genitalia.
176–77. **your face bids me:** i.e., Goneril is looking at the Fool contemptuously.

face bids me, though you say nothing. Mum, mum!
　　He that keeps neither crust nor crumb,
　　Weary of all, shall want some.
[*Pointing at* LEAR] That's a shelled peasecod.   180
GONERIL　Not only, sir, this, your all-licensed Fool,
　　But other of your insolent retinue
　　Do hourly carp and quarrel, breaking forth
　　In rank and not-to-be-endured riots. Sir,
　　I had thought by making this well known unto you   185
　　To have found a safe redress, but now grow fearful,
　　By what yourself too late have spoke and done,
　　That you protect this course, and put it on
　　By your allowance; which if you should, the fault
　　Would not 'scape censure, nor the redresses sleep;   190
　　Which in the tender of a wholesome weal
　　Might in their working do you that offence
　　Which else were shame, that then necessity
　　Will call discreet proceeding.
FOOL　For, you know, nuncle,   195
　　The hedge-sparrow fed the cuckoo so long,
　　That it's had it head bit off by it young.
So out went the candle, and we were left darkling.
LEAR　Are you our daughter?
GONERIL　I would you would make use of that good wisdom,   200
　　Whereof I know you are fraught, and put away
　　These dispositions that of late transport you
　　From what you rightly are.

177.　**Mum, mum:** words used to signal silence (closed lips).
180.　**shelled peasecod:** shelled pea-pod (which contains peas), hence nothing, as the peas will scatter without the pod, used ironically to mean an emasculated or impotent man.
181.　**all-licensed:** i.e., carrying Lear's license to do anything.
182.　**insolent retinue:** offensive retainers, i.e., followers.
183.　**carp:** bicker.
184.　**rank:** rebellious.
186.　**redress:** i.e., reprimand.
188.　**course:** i.e., rowdy behavior.
189.　**allowance:** permission.
190.　**'scape censure:** escape being censured, or condemned.　**redresses sleep:** i.e., reprimands avoided.
191.　**tender:** offer.　**wholesome weal:** general well-being of society.
193–94.　**Which in . . . discreet proceeding:** Goneril suggests that Lear be seen as wielding "discreet proceeding" or discreet correction, of the riotous behavior of his followers, rather than suffer the "shame" of letting it continue.
197:　This line varies slightly in *Q* and *F* (see Textual Variants), but both versions are grammatically incorrect; this *F* version probably represents a proverbial rendering of the expression.
198.　**darkling:** (1) dark; (2) in the dark, hence helpless.
199.　**our:** Here Lear ironically questions whether Goneril is behaving both as a loving daughter and a loyal subject.
201.　**fraught:** filled.
202.　**dispositions:** i.e., current riotous situation.

FOOL   May not an ass know when the cart draws the horse?
   Whoop, Jug, I love thee!   205
LEAR   Does any here know me?
   This is not Lear.
   Does Lear walk thus, speak thus? Where are his eyes?
   Either his notion weakens, his discernings
   Are lethargied. Ha! Waking? 'Tis not so.   210
   Who is it that can tell me who I am?
FOOL   Lear's shadow.
LEAR   I would learn that, for by the marks
   Of sovereignty, knowledge, and reason,
   I should be false persuaded I had daughters.   215
FOOL   Which they will make an obedient father.
LEAR [To GONERIL]   Your name, fair gentlewoman?
GONERIL   This admiration, sir, is much o'th'savor
   Of other your new pranks. I do beseech you
   To understand my purposes aright,   220
   As you are old and reverend, should be wise.
   Here do you keep a hundred knights and squires,
   Men so disordered, so debauched and bold,
   That this our court, infected with their manners,
   Shows like a riotous inn; epicurism and lust   225
   Makes it more like a tavern or a brothel
   Than a graced palace. The shame itself doth speak
   For instant remedy. Be then desired
   By her, that else will take the thing she begs,
   A little to disquantity your train,   230
   And the remainders that shall still depend
   To be such men as may besort your age,
   Which know themselves and you.

---

205. Jug: pet name for a woman, here used disparagingly; the Fool may be singing a line from a song.
209. notion: intellect or understanding.   **discernings:** comprehension.
210. lethargied: slow or weakened.   **Waking:** Lear questions whether he is dreaming or actually experiencing this response from Goneril.
212. shadow: (1) image of the body cast by light; (2) actor (see *A Midsummer Night's Dream*, Epilogue, l. 1). This line is given to the Fool in *F* and to Lear in *Q*.
213. marks: outward signs.
217: Lear is being sarcastic, suggesting that Goneril is so changed in her behavior that he cannot recognize her.
218. o'th'savor: of the savor, or of the same taste.
220. aright: correctly.
223. debauched: the *F* spelling of "debosh'd" suggests "debauched"; *Q* has "deboyst."
225. epicurism: Epicureanism, the pursuit of pleasure and sensuality, usually excessive, as practiced by the Greek philosopher Epicuris (born c. 341 B.C.E.).
227. speak: ask.
230. disquantity your train: reduce the number of your followers.
232. besort: befit.

LEAR   Darkness and devils!
  Saddle my horses, call my train together!
  Degenerate bastard, I'll not trouble thee.   235
  Yet have I left a daughter.
GONERIL   You strike my people, and your disordered rabble
  Make servants of their betters.

        Enter ALBANY

LEAR   Woe that too late repents! O, sir, are you come?
  Is it your will—speak, sir. Prepare my horses.   240
  Ingratitude! Thou marble-hearted fiend,
  More hideous when thou show'st thee in a child
  Than the sea-monster.
ALBANY   Pray, sir, be patient.
LEAR [*To* GONERIL]   Detested kite, thou liest!   245
  My train are men of choice and rarest parts,
  That all particulars of duty know,
  And in the most exact regard support
  The worships of their name. O most small fault,
  How ugly didst thou in Cordelia show,   250
  Which, like an engine, wrenched my frame of nature
  From the fixed place, drew from my heart all love,
  And added to the gall. O Lear, Lear, Lear!
  [*Taps his head*] Beat at this gate that let thy folly in
  And thy dear judgment out. Go, go, my people!   255
ALBANY   My lord, I am guiltless as I am ignorant
  Of what hath moved you.
LEAR   It may be so, my lord.
  Hear, Nature, hear dear goddess, hear
  Suspend thy purpose, if thou didst intend
  To make this creature fruitful.   260
  Into her womb convey sterility,
  Dry up in her the organs of increase,
  And from her derogate body never spring

---

235. bastard: Lear accuses Goneril of being another man's child; this anxiety about the
true paternity of children began with Gloucester's complaints about Edmund at 1.1.6.
241. marble-hearted: i.e., cold-hearted or unyielding.
245. kite: bird of prey, hence a term of contempt.
249. worships of their name: i.e., the dignity of their elevated position.
253. gall: bitterness.
254. gate: i.e., his head.
256: Albany's name recalls "Albion" (the Celtic name for Britain, or more specifically England, due to its white cliffs), as used by the Romans (Albion links to "Albus" or "white" in
Latin). Albany begins to be delineated here from his wife and the other characters endan-
gering Lear and the kingdom.
262. increase: reproduction.
263. derogate: debased.

A babe to honour her. If she must teem,
Create her child of spleen, that it may live   265
And be a thwart disnatured torment to her.
Let it stamp wrinkles in her brow of youth,
With cadent tears fret channels in her cheeks,
Turn all her mother's pains and benefits
To laughter and contempt, that she may feel   270
How sharper than a serpent's tooth it is
To have a thankless child. Away, away!

    Exeunt [LEAR, KENT, EDMUND, KNIGHTS, *and* ATTENDANTS]

ALBANY   Now, gods that we adore, whereof comes this?
GONERIL   Never afflict yourself to know more of it,
  But let his disposition have that scope   275
  As dotage gives it.

    Enter LEAR

LEAR   What, fifty of my followers at a clap?
  Within a fortnight?
ALBANY   What's the matter, sir?
LEAR   I'll tell thee. [*To* GONERIL] Life and death! I am
    ashamed
  That thou hast power to shake my manhood thus,   280
  That these hot tears which break from me perforce
  Should make thee worth them.
  Blasts and fogs upon thee!
  Th'untented woundings of a father's curse
  Pierce every sense about thee! Old fond eyes,   285
  Beweep this cause again, I'll pluck ye out
  And cast you with the waters that you loose
  To temper clay. Ha! Let it be so.
  I have another daughter,
  Who I am sure is kind and comfortable.   290
  When she shall hear this of thee, with her nails
  She'll flay thy wolvish visage. Thou shalt find

---

264. **teem:** give birth.
265. **child of spleen:** ill-natured or disagreeable child.
266. **thwart:** perverse or obstinate. **disnatured:** made unnatural.
268. **cadent:** falling.   **fret:** form by wearing away.
275. **disposition:** behavior.
276. **dotage:** old age.
277. **clap:** sudden stroke.
283. **Blasts:** strong winds.
284. **Th'untented:** the unprobed.
286. **Beweep:** weep for.   **pluck ye out:** ironic foreshadowing of the actions of 3.7.
288. **temper:** mix with the earth.
292. **flay:** strip the skin off.   **visage:** face.

That I'll resume the shape which thou dost think
I have cast off forever! Thou shalt, I warrant thee!   *Exit*
GONERIL   Do you mark that?   295
ALBANY   I cannot be so partial, Goneril,
To the great love I bear you—
GONERIL   Pray you, content. What Oswald, hoa?
    [*To* FOOL]   You, sir, more knave than Fool, after your
        master!
FOOL   Nuncle Lear, Nuncle Lear, tarry, and take the Fool   300
with thee.
            A fox, when one has caught her,
            And such a daughter,
            Should sure to the slaughter,
            If my cap would buy a halter;   305
            So the Fool follows after.   *Exit*
GONERIL   This man hath had good counsel! A hundred
    knights?
'Tis politic and safe to let him keep
At point a hundred knights? Yes, that on every dream,
Each buzz, each fancy, each complaint, dislike,   310
He may enguard his dotage with their powers
And hold our lives in mercy. Oswald, I say!
ALBANY   Well, you may fear too far.
GONERIL   Safer than trust too far.
Let me still take away the harms I fear,   315
Not fear still to be taken. I know his heart.
What he hath uttered I have writ my sister;
If she sustain him and his hundred knights
When I have showed th'unfitness—

        Enter OSWALD

How now, Oswald?   320
What, have you writ that letter to my sister?
OSWALD   Ay, madam.
GONERIL   Take you some company and away to horse.
Inform her full of my particular fear,
And thereto add such reasons of your own   325
As may compact it more. Get you gone,
And hasten your return.   [*Exit* OSWALD]
                No, no, my lord,

298. **hoa:** exclamation of surprise or used to attract attention.
307. **good counsel:** used ironically.
309. **At point:** in readiness.
311. **enguard his dotage:** guard his old age (and feeble-mindedness).
326. **compact:** make up.

This milky gentleness and course of yours,
Though I condemn not, yet under pardon
Y'are much more at task for want of wisdom,   330
Than praised for harmful mildness.
ALBANY   How far your eyes may pierce I cannot tell;
   Striving to better, oft we mar what's well.
GONERIL   Nay then—
ALBANY   Well, well, the event.   *Exeunt*   335

Act 1, Scene 5

Enter LEAR, KENT [*disguised as* CAIUS], GENTLEMAN, *and*
FOOL

LEAR   Go you before to Gloucester with these letters. Acquaint my daughter no further with anything you know than
   comes from her demand out of the letter. If your diligence
   be not speedy, I shall be there afore you.
KENT   I will not sleep, my lord, till I have delivered your letter.   5
                                                        Exit

FOOL   If a man's brains were in his heels, were't not in danger
   of kibes?
LEAR   Ay, boy.
FOOL   Then, I prithee, be merry; thy wit shall not go slipshod.
LEAR   Ha, ha, ha.   10
FOOL   Shalt see thy other daughter will use thee kindly, for
   though she's as like this as a crab's like an apple, yet I can
   tell what I can tell.
LEAR   What canst thou tell, boy?
FOOL   She will taste as like this as a crab does to a crab. Thou   15
   canst tell why one's nose stands i'th'middle on's face?
LEAR   No.
FOOL   Why, to keep one's eyes of either side's nose, that what
   a man cannot smell out, he may spy into.
LEAR   I did her wrong.   20
FOOL   Canst tell how an oyster makes his shell?
LEAR   No.

328. **milky:** weak.
330. **Y'are:** archaic contraction of "you are."
335. **the event:** i.e., to the matter.
1.5 **Location:** Outside the Duke of Albany's castle.
3. **diligence:** Lear adopts Kent's description of himself (at 1.4.35).
7. **kibes:** chapped chilblain (or blister) on the heel.
9. **slipshod:** in badly fitting shoes (ironically meaning "down at heel" or poor).
12. **crab's:** crab-apple's (a type of sour apple).
16. **on's:** of his.
20. **her:** probably referring to Cordelia, but Shakespeare leaves it ambiguous.

FOOL   Nor I neither; but I can tell why a snail has a house.

LEAR   Why?

FOOL   Why, to put's head in, not to give it away to his daugh-   25
ters, and leave his horns without a case.

LEAR   I will forget my nature. So kind a father! Be my horses
ready?

FOOL   Thy asses are gone about 'em. The reason why the
seven stars are no more than seven is a pretty reason.   30

LEAR   Because they are not eight.

FOOL   Yes, indeed, thou wouldst make a good Fool.

LEAR   To take't again perforce. Monster ingratitude!

FOOL   If thou wert my Fool, nuncle, I'd have thee beaten for
being old before thy time.   35

LEAR   How's that?

FOOL   Thou shouldst not have been old till thou hadst been
wise.

LEAR   O let me not be mad, not mad, sweet heaven! Keep me
in temper; I would not be mad!   40

        [*Enter* SERVANT]

How now, are the horses ready?

SERVANT   Ready, my lord.

LEAR   Come, boy.   *Exeunt* [LEAR *and* SOLDIERS]

FOOL   She that's a maid now, and laughs at my departure,
Shall not be a maid long, unless things be cut shorter.   45

                                        Exit

Act 2, Scene 1

Enter EDMUND *and* CURAN, *severally*

EDMUND   'Save thee, Curan.

CURAN   And you, sir. I have been with your father and given
him notice that the Duke of Cornwall and Regan his
duchess will be here with him this night.

EDMUND   How comes that?   5

25. put's: put his.
29. asses: ironically used of Lear's followers.
33. perforce: by force.
40. in temper: sane.
44. maid: virgin.
45. things: i.e., his penis; the Fool may be miming here by inserting his *marotte*, or fool's-
stick, between his legs.
2.1. Location: The Earl of Gloucester's castle.
STAGE DIRECTION *severally*: at different doors; the Globe theatre had at least two, and
possibly three, doors upstage.
1. 'Save: a contraction of "God save you," a greeting.

CURAN   Nay, I know not. You have heard of the news abroad?
I mean the whispered ones, for they are yet but ear-kissing
arguments.
EDMUND   Not I; pray you, what are they?
CURAN   Have you heard of no likely wars toward, 'twixt the   10
dukes of Cornwall and Albany?
EDMUND   Not a word.
CURAN   You may do then, in time. Fare you well, sir.   *Exit*
EDMUND   The duke be here tonight! The better—best!
This weaves itself perforce into my business.   15
My father hath set guard to take my brother,
And I have one thing of a queasy question
Which I must act. Briefness and fortune work!

        Enter EDGAR

Brother, a word, descend; brother, I say!
My father watches. O, sir, fly this place!   20
Intelligence is given where you are hid.
You have now the good advantage of the night.
Have you not spoken 'gainst the Duke of Cornwall?
He's coming hither, now i'th'night, i'th'haste,
And Regan with him. Have you nothing said   25
Upon his party against the Duke of Albany?
Advise yourself.
EDGAR   I am sure on't, not a word.
EDMUND   I hear my father coming. Pardon me,
In cunning, I must draw my sword upon you.
Draw, seem to defend yourself. Now, quit you well.   30
[*Shouts*] Yield! Come before my father! Light here, hoa, here!—
[*To* EDGAR] Fly, brother!—[*Shouts*] Torches, torches!—[*To*
    EDGAR] So, farewell.   *Exit* EDGAR
Some blood drawn on me would beget opinion
Of my more fierce endeavor [*wounds his arm*]. I have   35
    seen drunkards

7. **ear-kissing arguments:** i.e., rumors.
10. **likely wars:** this is the first indication that Lear's division of the kingdoms between Goneril and Regan (and their husbands) may produce civil war.
14. **better—best:** i.e., things are going better than Edmund had planned.
15. **perforce:** (1) by force; (2) inevitably.
17. **queasy:** hazardous.
19. **descend:** Edgar makes his entrance from the balcony above and comes down a flight of stairs.
21. **Intelligence:** information provided by spies.
27. **on't:** on it.
29. **cunning:** deceit, used ironically.
30. **quit you:** (1) acquit yourself; (2) leave.
32. **Fly:** flee.
34. **beget opinion:** i.e., add to his story that Edgar attacked him.

Do more than this in sport. Father, father!
Stop, stop! No help?

Enter GLOUCESTER, *and* SERVANTS *with Torches*

GLOUCESTER   Now, Edmund, where's the villain?
EDMUND   Here stood he in the dark, his sharp sword out,
Mumbling of wicked charms, conjuring the moon   40
To stand auspicious mistress.
GLOUCESTER   But where is he?
EDMUND   Look, sir, I bleed.
GLOUCESTER   Where is the villain, Edmund?
EDMUND   Fled this way, sir, when by no means he could—
GLOUCESTER   Pursue him, ho, go after!   [*Exeunt* SERVANTS]
                         "By no means" what?
EDMUND   Persuade me to the murder of your lordship,   45
But that I told him the revenging gods
'Gainst parricides did all their thunder bend,
Spoke with how manifold and strong a bond
The child was bound to'th'father; sir, in fine,
Seeing how loathly opposite I stood   50
To his unnatural purpose, in fell motion
With his prepared sword he charges home
My unprovided body, latched mine arm.
And when he saw my best alarumed spirits
Bold in the quarrel's right, roused to th'encounter,   55
Or whether ghasted by the noise I made,
Full suddenly he fled.
GLOUCESTER   Let him fly far,
Not in this land shall he remain uncaught;
And found, dispatch. The noble duke my master,
My worthy arch and patron, comes tonight.   60

40–41. Mumbling . . . mistress: Edmund's suggestion that Edgar has become a disciple
of darkness, worshipping the moon as an "auspicious mistress," or favoring goddess (compare *All's Well That Ends Well*, 3.3.8), foreshadows Edgar's "mumbling of wicked charms"
as Tom of Bedlam.
47. parricides: patricides, the murdering of parents by children.
48. manifold: variable or multifaced.
49. in fine: in brief.
51. fell: vicious.
53. unprovided: i.e., lacking armor or protection; in 5.3, Edgar and Edmund will fight in
full armor.   **latched:** struck.
54. alarumed spirits: i.e., eagerness to fight.
56. ghasted: frightened.
59. dispatch: be dispatched, i.e., killed (compare *Coriolanus* 3.1.286).
60. arch: chief, i.e., his employer.

By his authority I will proclaim it,
That he which finds him shall deserve our thanks,
Bringing the murderous coward to the stake;
He that conceals him, death.

EDMUND   When I dissuaded him from his intent   65
And found him pight to do it, with cursed speech
I threatened to discover him. He replied,
"Thou unpossessing bastard, dost thou think,
If I would stand against thee, would the reposal
Of any trust, virtue, or worth in thee   70
Make thy words faithed? No; what should I deny—
As this I would, though thou didst produce
My very character—I'd turn it all
To thy suggestion, plot, and damned practice;
And thou must make a dullard of the world,   75
If they not thought the profits of my death
Were very pregnant and potential spirits
To make thee seek it."   *Tucket within*

GLOUCESTER   O strange and fastened villain!
Would he deny his letter, said he? I never got him.
Hark, the duke's trumpets. I know not where he comes. 80
All ports I'll bar, the villain shall not 'scape;
The duke must grant me that. Besides, his picture
I will send far and near, that all the kingdom
May have due note of him; and of my land,
Loyal and natural boy, I'll work the means   85
To make thee capable.

Enter CORNWALL, REGAN, *and* ATTENDANTS

CORNWALL   How now, my noble friend, since I came hither,
Which I can call but now, I have heard strange news.

---

62. **he:** i.e., whoever   **him:** i.e., Edgar
63. **to the stake:** i.e., burned at the stake.
64. **He:** i.e., whoever.
66. **pight:** resolved.
68. **unpossessing:** i.e., unable to possess his father's land due to his illegitimacy, but with possible pun on another meaning of "unprejudiced," or innocent, as Edgar will be proven to be.
69. **reposal:** placement of trust in.
71. **faithed:** i.e., spoken in faith or truth.
75. **dullard:** stupid person.
77. **pregnant:** productive.
STAGE DIRECTION *Tucket within:* trumpet flourish, offstage.
78. **fastened:** firmly committed.
79. **got:** begot, i.e., fathered.
81. **ports:** seaports, i.e., borders.
82. **his picture:** i.e., description of his face (or his portrait?).
85. **natural:** (1) kind; (2) illegitimate; (3) not deceptive.
86. **capable:** capable of inheriting.

REGAN   If it be true, all vengeance comes too short
  Which can pursue the offender. How dost, my lord?   90
GLOUCESTER   O Madam, my old heart is cracked, it's cracked.
REGAN   What, did my father's godson seek your life?
  He whom my father named, your Edgar?
GLOUCESTER   O lady, lady, shame would have it hid.
REGAN   Was he not companion with the riotous knights   95
  That tended upon my father?
GLOUCESTER   I know not, madam; 'tis too bad, too bad.
EDMUND   Yes, madam, he was of that consort.
REGAN   No marvel, then, though he were ill affected.
  'Tis they have put him on the old man's death,   100
  To have th'expense and waste of his revenues.
  I have this present evening from my sister
  Been well informed of them, and with such cautions,
  That if they come to sojourn at my house,
  I'll not be there.
CORNWALL   Nor I, assure thee, Regan.   105
  Edmund, I hear that you have shown your father
  A child-like office.
EDMUND   It was my duty, sir.
GLOUCESTER   He did bewray his practice, and received
  This hurt you see, striving to apprehend him.
CORNWALL   Is he pursued?   110
GLOUCESTER   Ay, my good lord.
CORNWALL   If he be taken, he shall never more
  Be feared of doing harm. Make your own purpose
  How in my strength you please. For you, Edmund,
  Whose virtue and obedience doth this instant   115
  So much commend itself, you shall be ours;
  Nature's of such deep trust we shall much need;
  You we first seize on.
EDMUND   I shall serve you, sir, truly, however else.
GLOUCESTER   For him I thank your grace.   120
CORNWALL   You know not why we came to visit you?

---

92. my father's godson: This surrogate father-son relationship of Lear and Edgar will be ironically played out in Acts 3 and 4.
98. consort: group of companions; Edmund's lie here suits his purposes as well as Regan's.
100. put him on: put him onto, i.e., encouraged him about.
101. th'expense: the spending.
104. sojourn: temporary stay; compare Lear's use of the word in 1.1.37.
107. child-like office: filial and loving service.
108. He did bewray his practice: i.e., Edmund exposed Edgar's treacherous practices.
113. Make your own purpose: i.e., use whatever methods necessary.
116. ours: i.e., under our patronage and in our service.
117. much need: i.e., need many in our service.

REGAN   Thus out of season, threading dark-eyed night
　　Occasions, noble Gloucester, of some prize,
　　Wherein we must have use of your advice.
　　Our father he hath writ, so hath our sister,   125
　　Of differences, which I best thought it fit
　　To answer from our home. The several messengers
　　From hence attend dispatch. Our good old friend,
　　Lay comforts to your bosom and bestow
　　Your needful counsel to our businesses,   130
　　Which craves the instant use.
GLOUCESTER   I serve you, madam;
　　Your graces are right welcome.   *Exeunt. Flourish.*

Act 2, Scene 2

Enter KENT [*disguised as* CAIUS], *and* OSWALD, *severally*

OSWALD   Good dawning to thee, friend. Art of this house?
KENT   Ay.
OSWALD   Where may we set our horses?
KENT   I'th'mire.
OSWALD   Prithee, if thou lov'st me, tell me.   5
KENT   I love thee not.
OSWALD   Why, then I care not for thee.
KENT   If I had thee in Lipsbury pinfold, I would make thee
　　care for me.
OSWALD   Why dost thou use me thus? I know thee not.   10
KENT   Fellow, I know thee.
OSWALD   What dost thou know me for?
KENT   A knave, a rascal, an eater of broken meats, a base,
　　proud, shallow, beggarly, three-suited, hundred-pound, filthy
　　worsted-stocking knave; a lily-livered, action-taking, whore-   15
　　son, glass-gazing, super-serviceable, finical rogue; one-
　　trunk-inheriting slave; one that wouldst be a bawd in way of

---

122. **out of season:** i.e., not at the usual time.
128. **attend dispatch:** are waiting to be sent.
131. **craves:** desires.
2.2. **Location:** Outside the Earl of Gloucester's castle.
1. **dawning:** i.e., the beginning of dawn.
8. **Lipsbury pinfold:** i.e., enclosed between my lips (a "pinfold" is a livestock enclosure).
9. **care for me:** i.e., care about what I would do to you.
13. **broken:** leftover.
14. **three-suited, hundred-pound:** a slur on Oswald's limited wardrobe and its cost, typical for a steward.
15. **worsted-stocking:** woolen-stocking (rather than finer stockings made of silk).
16. **glass-gazing, super-serviceable, finical:** mirror-gazing (hence, vain), officious (or un-principled and willing to serve anyone), affected.   **one-trunk-inheriting:** poor enough to inherit only one trunk of possessions.
17. **bawd:** sexual procurer.

good service, and art nothing but the composition of a
knave, beggar, coward, pander, and the son and heir of a
mongrel bitch, one whom I will beat into clamorous whin-   20
ing if thou deniest the least syllable of thy addition.

OSWALD   Why, what a monstrous fellow art thou, thus to rail
on one that's neither known of thee nor knows thee!

KENT   What a brazen-faced varlet art thou to deny thou
knowest me! Is it two days since I tripped up thy heels and   25
beat thee before the king? Draw, you rogue! For though it be
night, yet the moon shines. I'll make a sop o'th'moonshine
of you. [*Draws his sword*]   You whoreson, cullionly barber-
monger, draw!

OSWALD   Away, I have nothing to do with thee.   30

KENT   Draw, you rascal! You come with letters against the
king, and take Vanity the puppet's part against the royalty of
her father.   [*Threatens him with sword*] Draw, you rogue, or
I'll so carbonado your shanks—draw, you rascal, come your
ways!   35

OSWALD   Help, hoa! Murder! Murder!

KENT   Strike, you slave! Stand, rogue! Stand, you neat slave,
strike!

OSWALD   Help, ho! Murder! Murder!

Enter EDMUND *with his rapier drawn,* CORNWALL, REGAN,
GLOUCESTER [*and*] SERVANTS

EDMUND   How now, what's the matter? Part!   40

KENT   With you, goodman boy, if you please. Come, I'll flesh
ye. Come on, young master.

GLOUCESTER   Weapons? Arms? What's the matter here?

CORNWALL   Keep peace, upon your lives! He dies that strikes
again. What is the matter?   45

REGAN   The messengers from our sister and the king?

CORNWALL   What is your difference? Speak!

OSWALD   I am scarce in breath, my lord.

19. **pander:** pimp.
20. **clamorous:** noisy.
21. **addition:** i.e., character.
22. **rail on:** complain about.
24. **brazen-faced varlet:** shameless rogue or knave.
27. **sop:** pieced of soaked bread, i.e., a fool.
28–29. **cullionly barber-monger:** rascally frequenter of the barber; Kent, previously a
courtier, now in disguise as a more lowly man, primarily attacks Oswald's pretentious attire,
which cannot elevate him from the position of a mere steward.
32. **Vanity the puppet's part:** i.e., Goneril; "puppet" is a contemptuous term for a woman.
34. **carbonado:** slash and hack.   **shanks:** i.e., legs.
41. **goodman:** term used for a man below the rank of gentleman (*OED*).
41–42. **flesh ye:** plunge a sword into you.
47. **difference:** i.e., argument

KENT   No marvel, you have so bestirred your valor. You cowardly rascal, nature disclaims in thee: a tailor made thee.   50

CORNWALL   Thou art a strange fellow—a tailor make a man?

KENT   A tailor, sir, a stone-cutter or a painter could not have
made him so ill, though they had been but two years o'th'-
trade.

CORNWALL   Speak yet, how grew your quarrel?   55

OSWALD   This ancient ruffian, sir, whose life I have spared at
suit of his grey beard—

KENT   Thou whoreson zed, thou unnecessary letter! My lord,
if you will give me leave, I will tread this unbolted villain
into mortar and daub the wall of a jakes with him. Spare my   60
grey beard, you wagtail?

CORNWALL   Peace, sirrah. You beastly knave, have you no reverence?

KENT   Yes, sir, but anger hath a privilege.

CORNWALL   Why art thou angry?   65

KENT   That such a slave as this should wear a sword,
Who wears no honesty. Such smiling rogues as these,
Like rats, oft bite the holy cords atwain,
Which are too too intrince t'unloose; smooth every passion
That in the natures of their lords rebel,   70
Bring oil to fire, snow to their colder moods,
Revenge, affirm, and turn their halcyon beaks
With every gall and vary of their masters,
Knowing naught, like dogs, but following.
A plague upon your epileptic visage!   75
Smoile you my speeches, as I were a fool?

---

50. **a tailor made thee:** you are unnatural (with secondary mocking again of Oswald's pretentious attire).
53–54. **two years o'th'trade:** i.e., served only the first two years of a seven-year appren-
ticeship.
56. **ancient ruffian:** aged, violent man.
58. **zed:** the letter "Z," unnecessary because its sound can be rendered with an "s."
59. **unbolted:** unfastened.
60. **mortar:** builder's paste of sand, lime, and water.   **daub:** cover.   **jakes:** privy, i.e.,
toilet.
61. **wagtail:** contemptuous term for a young man.
62. **sirrah:** contemptuous term for servant or inferior.
68. **holy cords:** i.e., familial bonds.
69. **intrince:** intricate.
72. **halcyon:** patient, calm.
73. **gall and vary:** bitterness and variable moods.
74. **naught:** nothing.
75. **epileptic visage:** i.e., contorted face.
76. **Smoile:** smile at.

Goose, if I had you upon Sarum Plain,
I'd drive ye cackling home to Camelot.
CORNWALL   What, art thou mad, old fellow?
GLOUCESTER   How fell you out? Say that.   80
KENT   No contraries hold more antipathy,
Than I and such a knave.
CORNWALL   Why dost thou call him knave? What is his fault?
KENT   His countenance likes me not.
CORNWALL   No more perchance does mine, nor his, nor hers.   85
KENT   Sir, 'tis my occupation to be plain.
I have seen better faces in my time
Than stands on any shoulder that I see
Before me at this instant.
CORNWALL   This is some fellow
Who, having been praised for bluntness, doth affect   90
A saucy roughness, and constrains the garb
Quite from his nature. He cannot flatter, he;
An honest man and plain, he must speak truth.
And they will take it so; if not, he's plain.
These kind of knaves I know, which in this plainness   95
Harbour more craft and more corrupter ends
Than twenty silly-ducking observants
That stretch their duties nicely.
KENT   Sir, in good faith, in sincere verity,
Under the allowance of your great aspect,   100
Whose influence like the wreath of radiant fire
On flickering Phoebus' front—
CORNWALL   What mean'st thou by this?
KENT   To go out of my dialect, which you discommend so
much. I know, sir, I am no flatterer. He that beguiled you in
a plain accent was a plain knave, which for my part I will not   105
be, though I should win your displeasure to entreat me to't.
CORNWALL [To OSWALD]   What was the offence you gave him?

77. **Goose:** fool.
77–78. **Sarum . . . Camelot:** Sarum Plain is outside Salisbury (the location of Camelot, the home of King Arthur); Kent appears to be saying he'd drive Oswald "cackling," or crying like a goose, away, but the reference to Sarum and Camelot is unexplained.
84. **countenance:** behavior or demeanor.   **likes:** pleases.
85. **perchance:** by chance.
86. **occupation:** habit.   **plain:** plain in speech, blunt.
91. **saucy:** rude.   **garb:** behavior.
97. **silly-ducking:** constantly ducking up and down (bowing).
98. **stretch their duties nicely:** perform their duties fussily.
99. **verity:** truth.
102. **Phoebus' front:** the forehead of Phoebus (Apollo as the sun-god).
103. **dialect:** i.e., his usual bluntness.   **discommend:** disapprove of.

OSWALD   I never gave him any.
　　It pleased the king his master very late
　　To strike at me upon his misconstruction,   110
　　When he, compact, and flattering his displeasure,
　　Tripped me behind; being down, insulted, railed,
　　And put upon him such a deal of man that
　　That worthied him, got praises of the king
　　For him attempting who was self-subdued,   115
　　And in the fleshment of this dread exploit
　　Drew on me here again.
KENT   None of these rogues and cowards
　　But Ajax is their Fool.
CORNWALL   Fetch forth the stocks!
　　You stubborn, ancient knave, you reverent braggart,
　　We'll teach you.
KENT   Sir, I am too old to learn: 120
　　Call not your stocks for me. I serve the king,
　　On whose employment I was sent to you.
　　You should do small respect, show too bold malice
　　Against the grace and person of my master,
　　Stocking his messenger.
CORNWALL   Fetch forth the stocks!   125
　　As I have life and honor, there shall he sit till noon.
REGAN   Till noon? Till night, my lord, and all night too.
KENT   Why, madam, if I were your father's dog,
　　You should not use me so.
REGAN   Sir, being his knave, I will.
CORNWALL   This is a fellow of the selfsame color   130
　　Our sister speaks of. Come, bring away the stocks!
                                        Stocks brought out
GLOUCESTER   Let me beseech your grace not to do so.
　　His fault is much, and the king, his master,
　　Will check him for't. Your purposed low correction
　　Is such as basest and 'temned'st wretches   135
　　For pilf'rings and most common trespasses

110. **misconstruction:** misinterpretation.
111. **he:** i.e., Kent.   **compact:** made up of.
115. **who was self-subdued:** i.e., Oswald had already been tripped up and beaten.
116. **fleshment:** excitement as a result of his success.
118. **Ajax:** Greek warrior renowned for his strength and ridiculed for his stupidity; the term also was slang for "a jakes," or privy (*OED*).   **stocks:** a wooden instrument of punishment, in which a person was forced to sit down, with legs (and sometimes hands) locked between planks.
119. **reverent:** used ironically to mean "irreverent" or disrespectful.
130. **color:** i.e., rude behavior.
134. **check:** reprimand.
135. **'temnest:** contraction of "contemnest," or scorns
136. **pilf'rings:** pilferings, or thefts.

Are punished with. The king must take it ill
That he, so slightly valued in his messenger,
Should have him thus restrained.

CORNWALL   I'll answer that.

REGAN   My sister may receive it much more worse   140
  To have her gentlemen abused, assaulted,
  For following her affairs. Put in his legs.

                          [KENT *is put in the stocks.*]
  Come, my lord, away!

                  [*Exeunt all but* GLOUCESTER *and* KENT]

GLOUCESTER   I am sorry for thee, friend. 'Tis the duke's plea-
  sure,
  Whose disposition all the world well knows   145
  Will not be rubbed nor stopped. I'll entreat for thee.

KENT   Pray do not, sir. I have watched and travailed hard.
  Some time I shall sleep out, the rest I'll whistle.
  A good man's fortune may grow out at heels.
  Give you good morrow.   150

GLOUCESTER   The duke's to blame in this; 'twill be ill taken.

                                                            Exit

KENT   Good king, that must approve the common saw,
  Thou out of heaven's benediction com'st
  To the warm sun.   [*He takes out a letter.*]
  Approach, thou beacon, to this under globe,   155
  That by thy comfortable beams I may
  Peruse this letter. Nothing almost sees miracles
  But misery. I know 'tis from Cordelia,
  Who hath most fortunately been informed
  Of my obscurèd course, and shall find time   160
  From this enormous state, seeking to give
  Losses their remedies. All weary and o'erwatched,
  Take vantage, heavy eyes, not to behold
  This shameful lodging. Fortune, goodnight;
  Smile; once more turn thy wheel.   *Sleeps*   165

139. **answer:** answer for.
145. **disposition:** behavior or character.
147. **travailed:** (1) travelled; (2) labored.
149. **out at heels:** in distress (Kent is pointing to his stocked feet).
152. **saw:** command.
153. **benediction:** blessing.
155. **beacon:** i.e., the sun.   **under globe:** this place (on the earth); with pun on the
"Globe" theatre, the venue for the play's performance.
160. **obscurèd course:** i.e., his service to Lear in disguise.
163. **vantage:** advantage.
164–65. **Fortune . . . wheel:** The goddess Fortune spun a wheel to determine a person's
fortune, i.e., destiny.
STAGE DIRECTION *Sleeps:* This stage direction appears in *Q* but not *F*, which does not
give an exit direction for Kent. Neither *Q* nor *F* indicates that a new scene begins after
Kent's speech, and *F*, which uses regularized scene notations (unlike *Q* which lacks such no-

Act 2, Scene 3

Enter EDGAR

EDGAR   I heard myself proclaimed,
And by the happy hollow of a tree
Escaped the hunt. No port is free, no place
That guard and most unusual vigilance
Does not attend my taking. Whiles I may 'scape   5
I will preserve myself, and am bethought
To take the basest and most poorest shape
That ever penury in contempt of man
Brought near to beast. My face I'll grime with filth,
Blanket my loins, elf all my hair in knots,   10
And with presented nakedness outface
The winds and persecutions of the sky.
The country gives me proof and precedent
Of Bedlam beggars, who with roaring voices
Strike in their numbed and mortified arms,   15
Pins, wooden pricks, nails, sprigs of rosemary;
And with this horrible object, from low farms,
Poor pelting villages, sheep-cotes, and mills,
Sometime with lunatic bans, sometime with prayers,
Enforce their charity. "Poor Turlygod! Poor Tom!"   20
That's something yet. Edgar I nothing am.   *Exit*

---

tations), does not offer another scene break in Act 2. However, editors since the eighteenth century have introduced a scene break here and another after Edgar's soliloquy in order to keep Act 2, Scene 2, from being so long.
2.3. Location: Outside the Earl of Gloucester's castle.
1: Edgar does not notice the sleeping Kent, who has remained onstage.   **proclaimed:** i.e., proclaimed as a criminal.
3. port: seaport (following from his father's command to bar the "ports" to him at 2.1.81).
8. penury: poverty.
10. elf: tangle.
11. outface: stand up to.
14. Bedlam beggars: wandering beggars from Bethlehem hospital for the insane, who, as Edgar notes, committed self-harm due to their madness.
18. sheep-cotes: shelters for sheep.
19. bans: angry curses.
20. Poor Turlygod! Poor Tom: William Warburton (editor, *Shakespeare's Works*, 1747) conjectured that "Turlygod" was a corruption of "Turlupin," a beggar; "Poor Tom" is a proverbial name for a madman.

Act 2, Scene 4

Enter LEAR, FOOL, *and* [a] GENTLEMAN

LEAR 'Tis strange that they should so depart from home
And not send back my messengers.
GENTLEMAN   As I learned,
The night before there was no purpose in them
Of this remove.
KENT [*Waking*]   Hail to thee, noble master!
LEAR Ha? Mak'st thou this shame thy pastime?   5
KENT No, my lord.
FOOL Ha, ha, he wears cruel garters. Horses are tied by the
heads, dogs and bears by'th'neck, monkeys by th'loins, and
men by'th'legs. When a man's overlusty at legs, then he
wears wooden nether-stocks.   10
LEAR What's he that hath so much thy place mistook
To set thee here?
KENT   It is both he and she,
Your son and daughter.
LEAR No.
KENT Yes.   15
LEAR No, I say.
KENT I say, yea.
LEAR No, no, they would not.
KENT Yes, they have.
LEAR By Jupiter, I swear no.   20
KENT By Juno, I swear aye.
LEAR   They durst not do't;
They could not, would not do't. 'Tis worse than murder,
To do upon respect such violent outrage.

2.4 **Location:** Outside the Earl of Gloucester's castle.
4: see note on 2.2.165.
4. remove: i.e., traveling to Gloucester's home.
7. cruel garters: A garter is a band used to keep stockings up (with pun on "crewel" or woolen); the Fool mocks Kent's legs being enclosed in the stocks.
8. th'loins: i.e., around the hips.
9. overlusty at legs: eager to run away (with pun on being promiscuous).
10. nether-stocks: stockings below, with pun on the stocks around Kent's legs.
11. place: position or rank (i.e., as Lear's attendant).
20–21: These lines are found in *F*, but not *Q*, and were probably added to intensify this encounter.
20. Jupiter: king of the Roman gods.
21. Juno: queen of the Roman gods.

Resolve me with all modest haste which way
Thou mightst deserve or they impose this usage,   25
Coming from us.
KENT   My lord, when at their home
I did commend your highness' letters to them,
Ere I was risen from the place that showed
My duty kneeling, came there a reeking post,
Stewed in his haste, half breathless, panting forth   30
From Goneril, his mistress, salutations,
Delivered letters spite of intermission,
Which presently they read; on those contents
They summoned up their meiney, straight took horse,
Commanded me to follow and attend   35
The leisure of their answer, gave me cold looks;
And meeting here the other messenger,
Whose welcome I perceived had poisoned mine—
Being the very fellow which of late
Displayed so saucily against your highness—   40
Having more man than wit about me, drew.
He raised the house with loud and coward cries.
Your son and daughter found this trespass worth
This shame which here it suffers.
FOOL   Winter's not gone yet, if the wild geese fly that way.   45
        Fathers that wear rags
            Do make their children blind,
        But fathers that bear bags
            Shall see their children kind.
        Fortune, that arrant whore,   50
            Ne'er turns the key to th'poor.
But for all this, thou shalt have as many dolors for thy
daughters as thou canst tell in a year.

---

25. usage: treatment (i.e., stocking Kent).
26–36. My lord . . . cold looks: Kent's narration of the way he was treated before he en-
countered Oswald (which the audience is not allowed to see staged) may be embellished
here, thereby discounting his commitment to being truthful; if his account is true, it may
somewhat excuse his inappropriate and rude behavior to the royal Regan and Cornwall.
27. commend: deliver.
29. reeking post: heated or sweating messenger.
30. stewed: (1) dripping; (2) drunk; (3) having partaken of the stews, i.e., brothels.
31. salutations: greetings.
32. spite: in spite of.
34. meiney: group of attendants.
37. other messenger: i.e., Oswald.
40. saucily: rudely.
47. blind: i.e., blind to his condition.
48. bags: bags of money.
51. turns the key: allows access to.
52. dolors: (1) sorrows; (2) money (from "dollar," a Spanish coin).

LEAR   O, how this mother swells up toward my heart!
   Hysterica passio, down thou climbing sorrow,   55
   Thy element's below. Where is this daughter?
KENT   With the earl, sir, here within.
LEAR   Follow me not, stay there!   *Exit*
KNIGHT   Made you no more offence but what you speak of?
KENT   None. How chance the king comes with so small a   60
   number?
FOOL   And thou hadst been set i'th'stocks for that question,
   thou'st well deserved it.
KENT   Why, Fool?
FOOL   We'll set thee to school to an ant, to teach thee there's   65
   no laboring i'th'winter. All that follow their noses are led by
   their eyes but blind men, and there's not a nose among
   twenty but can smell him that's stinking. Let go thy hold
   when a great wheel runs down a hill, lest it break thy neck
   with following it. But the great one that goes upward, let   70
   him draw thee after. When a wise man gives thee better
   counsel, give me mine again. I would have none but knaves
   follow it, since a Fool gives it.
       That sir which serves and seeks for gain
          And follows but for form,   75
       Will pack when it begins to rain
          And leave thee in the storm.
       But I will tarry, the Fool will stay,
          And let the wise man fly;
       The knave turns Fool that runs away,   80
          The Fool no knave, perdy.
KENT   Where learned you this, Fool?
FOOL   Not i'th'stocks, Fool.

    Enter LEAR *and* GLOUCESTER

LEAR   Deny to speak with me?
   They are sick, they are weary,
   They have travailed all the night? Mere fetches,   85
   The images of revolt and flying off.
   Fetch me a better answer.

54–55. **mother . . . /** *Hysterica passio*: the latter, Latin, term, means "the suffocation of
the mother," and this female "hysteria" was thought to derive from disorders of the uterus
or womb ("*hysterikus*" in Greek).
56. **element's:** position (i.e., lower in his body).
61. **number:** number of attendants.
62. **And:** if.
81. **perdy:** contraction of "par Dieu" (by God), i.e., without doubt.
85. **travailed:** (1) travelled; (2) labored.   **fetches:** excuses.
86. **flying off:** i.e., they have avoided him.

GLOUCESTER   My dear lord,
  You know the fiery quality of the duke,
  How unremovable and fixed he is
  In his own course.
LEAR   Vengeance, plague, death, confusion!   90
  "Fiery?" What "quality"? Why Gloucester, Gloucester,
  I'd speak with the Duke of Cornwall and his wife.
GLOUCESTER   Well, my good lord, I have informed them so.
LEAR   "Informed them"? Dost thou understand me, man?
GLOUCESTER   Ay, my good lord.   95
LEAR   The king would speak with Cornwall, the dear father
  Would with his daughter speak, commands, tends service.
  Are they informed of this? My breath and blood—
  "Fiery"? "The fiery duke"—Tell the hot duke that—
  No, but not yet; maybe he is not well.   100
  Infirmity doth still neglect all office
  Whereto our health is bound. We are not ourselves
  When nature, being oppressed, commands the mind
  To suffer with the body. I'll forbear,
  And am fallen out with my more headier will,   105
  To take the indisposed and sickly fit
  For the sound man. Death on my state! Wherefore
  Should he sit here? This act persuades me
  That this remotion of the duke and her
  Is practice only. Give me my servant forth.   110
  Go tell the duke and's wife I'd speak with them,
  Now, presently. Bid them come forth and hear me,
  Or at their chamber door I'll beat the drum
  Till it cry sleep to death.
GLOUCESTER   I would have all well betwixt you.   *Exit*   115
LEAR   O, me, my heart, my rising heart! But down—
FOOL   Cry to it, nuncle, as the cockney did to the eels when

---

88. **fiery:** hot-tempered.
89. **unremovable:** impossible to move.
97. **tends:** expects.
101. **office:** position of authority.
105. **headier:** more impetuous.
106. **fit:** struggle.
107. **sound:** sane, healthy.   **Death:** the figure of Death.
109. **remotion:** removal from their house, as well as their remoteness (in refusing to see Lear).
110. **practice:** an exercise, i.e., without meaning.
111. **and's:** and his.
112. **presently:** immediately.
114. **cry sleep to death:** i.e., keeps all from sleeping due to the noise.
117. **cockney:** i.e., a squeamish woman.
117–19. **eels . . . down:** The cockney has indeed been too squeamish to kill the eels (by "knapping" or hitting them on the "coxcombs," or heads), and they are rising out of the pie, covered with pastry, in which she put them.

she put 'em i'th'paste alive. She knapt 'em o'th'coxcombs
with a stick and cried, "Down, wantons, down!" 'Twas her
brother that in pure kindness to his horse buttered his hay.   120

      Enter CORNWALL, REGAN, GLOUCESTER, [*and*] SERVANTS

LEAR   Good morrow to you both.
CORNWALL   Hail to your grace.
                        KENT *here set at liberty*
REGAN   I am glad to see your highness.
LEAR   Regan, I think you are. I know what reason
I have to think so. If thou shouldst not be glad,
I would divorce me from thy mother's tomb,   125
Sepulch'ring an adultress.   [*To* KENT] Oh, are you free?
Some other time for that. Belovèd Regan,
Thy sister's naught. O, Regan, she hath tied
Sharp-toothed unkindness like a vulture here.
I can scarce speak to thee, thou'lt not believe   130
With how depraved a quality—O Regan!
REGAN   I pray you, sir, take patience. I have hope
You less know how to value her dessert
Than she to scant her duty.
LEAR   Say? How is that?   135
REGAN   I cannot think my sister in the least
Would fail her obligation. If, sir, perchance
She have restrained the riots of your fellows,
'Tis on such ground, and to such wholesome end
As clears her from all blame.   140
LEAR   My curses on her!
REGAN   O sir, you are old.
Nature in you stands on the very verge
Of her confine. You should be ruled and led
By some discretion that discerns your state
Better than you yourself. Therefore I pray you   145
That to our sister you do make return;
Say you have wronged her.

---

120. **buttered his hay:** i.e., acted the fool.
126. **Sepulch'ring an adultress:** Lear, once again anxious about the paternity of his children, tells Regan that her behavior suggests that his wife was unfaithful to him and produced Regan through an adulterous affair.
128. **naught:** (1) nothing; (2) wicked (as in "naughty").
129. **here:** Lear is pointing to his heart.
133. **dessert:** i.e., what she deserves.
134. **scant:** make little of.
137. **obligation:** Regan is equivocal here; she clearly thinks that she and Goneril are no
longer obliged to obey Lear.
142–43. **very verge / Of her confine:** i.e., has reached the end of life.

LEAR   Ask her forgiveness?
    Do you but mark how this becomes the house?
    [*Kneels*] "Dear daughter, I confess that I am old;
    Age is unnecessary: on my knees I beg   150
    That you'll vouchsafe me raiment, bed, and food."
REGAN   Good sir, no more. These are unsightly tricks.
    Return you to my sister.
LEAR   [*Rises*] Never, Regan.
    She hath abated me of half my train,
    Looked black upon me, struck me with her tongue   155
    Most serpent-like upon the very heart.
    All the stored vengeances of heaven fall
    On her ingrateful top! Strike her young bones,
    You taking airs, with lameness.
CORNWALL   Fie, sir, fie.
LEAR   You nimble lightnings, dart your blinding flames   160
    Into her scornful eyes! Infect her beauty,
    You fen-sucked fogs, drawn by the powerful sun
    To fall and blister!
REGAN   O the blest gods!
    So will you wish on me, when the rash mood is on.
LEAR   No, Regan, thou shalt never have my curse.   165
    Thy tender-hefted nature shall not give
    Thee o'er to harshness. Her eyes are fierce, but thine
    Do comfort and not burn. 'Tis not in thee
    To grudge my pleasures, to cut off my train,
    To bandy hasty words, to scant my sizes,   170
    And in conclusion, to oppose the bolt
    Against my coming in. Thou better know'st
    The offices of nature, bond of childhood,
    Effects of courtesy, dues of gratitude.
    Thy half o'th'kingdom hast thou not forgot   175
    Wherein I thee endowed.
REGAN   Good sir, to th'purpose.
LEAR   Who put my main i'th'stocks?   *Tucket within*

        Enter OSWALD

151. **raiment:** clothing.
152. **unsightly:** inappropriate.
154. **abated:** reduced.
158. **top:** head.
159. **taking airs:** vicious winds.   **Fie:** i.e., shame on you.
162. **fen-sucked:** sucked from the marshes.
166. **tender-hefted:** remaining tender.
170. **bandy:** exchange.   **scant my sizes:** i.e., ignore my "assizes," or commands.
171. **oppose the bolt:** i.e., bolt the door.
176. **to th'purpose:** i.e., get to the point.

CORNWALL   What trumpet's that?
REGAN   I know't, my sister's. This approves her letter
  That she would soon be here. Is your lady come?
LEAR   This is a slave whose easy-borrowed pride   180
  Dwells in the fickle grace of her he follows.
  Out, varlet, from my sight!
CORNWALL   What means your grace?

        Enter GONERIL

LEAR   Who stocked my servant? Regan, I have good hope
  Thou didst not know on't.
  Who comes here? O heavens!   185
  If you do love old men, if your sweet sway
  Allow obedience, if you yourselves are old,
  Make it your cause, send down and take my part.
  [*To* GONERIL] Art not ashamed to look upon this beard?
  O Regan, will you take her by the hand?   190
GONERIL   Why not by the hand, sir? How have I offended?
  All's not offence that indiscretion finds,
  And dotage terms so.
LEAR   O sides, you are too tough!
  Will you yet hold? How came my man i'th'stocks?
CORNWALL   I set him there, sir, but his own disorders   195
  Deserved much less advancement.
LEAR   You, did you?
REGAN   I pray you, father, being weak, seem so.
  If till the expiration of your month
  You will return and sojourn with my sister,
  Dismissing half your train, come then to me.   200
  I am now from home and out of that provision
  Which shall be needful for your entertainment.
LEAR   Return to her, and fifty men dismissed?
  No, rather I abjure all roofs and choose
  To wage against the enmity o'th'air,   205
  To be a comrade with the wolf and owl,
  Necessity's sharp pinch. Return with her?

178. **approves:** commands.
181. **fickle:** changeable.
182. **varlet:** rogue.
184. **on't:** on, or of, it.
186. **sway:** rule.
190. **hand:** i.e., Regan and Goneril hold hands here to put up a united front against Lear.
192. **indiscretion finds:** lack of discretion, or discernment, misjudges.
193. **dotage:** old age.
199. **sojourn:** see note on 2.1.104.
204–206. These lines ironically foreshadow Lear's existence on the heath in Act 3.
204. **abjure:** renounce, repudiate.

Why, the hot-blooded in France, that dowerless took
Our youngest born—I could as well be brought
To knee his throne and, squire-like, pension beg   210
To keep base life afoot. Return with her?
Persuade me rather to be slave and sumpter
To this detested groom.
GONERIL   At your choice, sir.
LEAR   I prithee, daughter, do not make me mad.
I will not trouble thee, my child. Farewell.   215
We'll no more meet, no more see one another.
But yet thou art my flesh, my blood, my daughter,
Or rather a disease that's in my flesh,
Which I must needs call mine. Thou art a boil,
A plague-sore, or embossed carbuncle   220
In my corrupted blood. But I'll not chide thee.
Let shame come when it will, I do not call it.
I do not bid the thunder-bearer shoot,
Nor tell tales of thee to high-judging Jove.
Mend when thou canst, be better at thy leisure.   225
I can be patient, I can stay with Regan,
I and my hundred knights.
REGAN   Not altogether so.
I looked not for you yet, nor am provided
For your fit welcome. Give ear, sir, to my sister,
For those that mingle reason with your passion   230
Must be content to think you old, and so—
But she knows what she does.
LEAR   Is this well spoken now?
REGAN   I dare avouch it, sir. What, fifty followers?
Is it not well? What should you need of more?
Yea, or so many, sith that both charge and danger   235
Speak 'gainst so great a number? How in one house
Should many people under two commands
Hold amity? 'Tis hard, almost impossible.

208. **hot-blooded in France:** i.e., the King of France.
210. **squire-like:** i.e., like a squire, an attendant on a knight, i.e. like a servant.
212. **sumpter:** a beast of burden.
213. **groom:** Lear is pointing to Oswald.
214. **make me mad:** Lear seems to understand that he is losing his sanity, although he believes that others make him mad; Shakespeare leaves it ambiguous as to whether Lear already suffered from madness at the beginning of the play.
220. **embossed carbuncle:** raised tumor or sore.
221. **chide:** scold.
223. **thunder-bearer:** i.e., Jupiter, king of the Roman gods, as shooter of thunderbolts.
224. **Jove:** poetic name for Jupiter, here as a judge.
229. **fit:** appropriate.
233. **avouch:** affirm.
235. **sith:** since.
238. **amity:** friendship.

GONERIL   Why might not you, my lord, receive attendance
  From those that she calls servants, or from mine?   240
REGAN   Why not, my lord? If then they chanced to slack ye,
  We could control them. If you will come to me—
  For now I spy a danger—I entreat you
  To bring but five and twenty; to no more
  Will I give place or notice.   245
LEAR   I gave you all.
REGAN   And in good time you gave it.
LEAR   Made you my guardians, my depositaries,
  But kept a reservation to be followed
  With such a number. What, must I come to you
  With five and twenty, Regan, said you so?   250
REGAN   And speak't again, my lord. No more with me.
LEAR   Those wicked creatures yet do look well-favored
  When others are more wicked. Not being the worst
  Stands in some rank of praise.   [*To* GONERIL] I'll go with
    thee.
  Thy fifty yet doth double five-and-twenty,   255
  And thou art twice her love.
GONERIL   Hear me, my lord.
  What need you five-and-twenty? Ten? Or five?
  To follow in a house where twice so many
  Have a command to tend you?
REGAN   What need one?
LEAR   Oh, reason not the need! Our basest beggars   260
  Are in the poorest thing superfluous.
  Allow not nature more than nature needs,
  Man's life is cheap as beast's. Thou art a lady;
  If only to go warm were gorgeous,
  Why Nature needs not what thou gorgeous wearest,   265
  Which scarcely keeps thee warm. But for true need—
  You heavens, give me that patience, patience I need.

---

239. receive attendance: be served by.
241. slack: i.e., neglect or ignore; at 1.3.10 Goneril had encouraged Oswald to "become slack" in his service to Lear.
242. This line begins Lear's verbal bargaining for the number of his attendants with Regan and Goneril; he uses the same words of measurement ("all," "nothing," "more," "less," etc.) as in the similar bargaining in the love-test in 1.1, when he divided the kingdom.
246. And . . . it: In the source play, *King Leir*, the two sisters begin as evil, but state to each other the reasons for their anger toward their father and youngest sister; Shakespeare leaves Goneril and Regan without such obvious, or stated, motives for their cruelty.
247. depositaries: trustees.
260. reason: i.e., question (reason is used as a verb, not a noun).
261. poorest thing superfluous: i.e., have an excess, even though poor.
264. to go warm were gorgeous: i.e., a person derived beauty from being warm rather than simply wearing beautiful attire. Lear reasons here that to measure everything by need alone, rather than desire, leaves humans stripped of dignity and self-worth; in 4.6.159 he will decide that "robes and furred gowns hide all," including evil.

You see me here, you gods, a poor old man,
As full of grief as age, wretched in both.
If it be you that stirs these daughters' hearts   270
Against their father, fool me not so much
To bear it tamely. Touch me with noble anger!
And let not women's weapons, water-drops,
Stain my man's cheeks! No, you unnatural hags,

} misogyny!

I will have such revenges on you both   275
That all the world shall—I will do such things—
What they are, yet I know not, but they shall be
The terrors of the earth! You think I'll weep.
No, I'll not weep, I have full cause of weeping,

                              Storm and tempest

But this heart shall break into a hundred thousand flaws   280
Or ere I'll weep. O Fool, I shall go mad.

            Exeunt LEAR, [GLOUCESTER], KENT, [KNIGHT], *and* FOOL

CORNWALL   Let us withdraw; 'twill be a storm.
REGAN   This house is little. The old man and's people
    Cannot be well bestowed.
GONERIL   'Tis his own blame hath put himself from rest,
    And must needs taste his folly.   285
REGAN   For his particular, I'll receive him gladly,
    But not one follower.
GONERIL   So am I purposed.
    Where is my lord of Gloucester?
CORNWALL   Followed the old man forth.

        Enter GLOUCESTER

                            He is returned.   290
GLOUCESTER   The king is in high rage.
CORNWALL   Whither is he going?
GLOUCESTER   He calls to horse, but will I know not whither.
CORNWALL   'Tis best to give him way; he leads himself.
GONERIL   My lord, entreat him by no means to stay.   295
GLOUCESTER   Alack, the night comes on, and the high winds
    Do sorely rustle; for many miles about
    There's scarce a bush.

273. **women's weapons, water-drops:** i.e., tears.
STAGE DIRECTION Storm and tempest: this is an original stage effect in Shakespeare's
time: for thunder, most likely clashing noises (made by striking a drum or metal instrument); for lightning, flashes of light (from fireworks using gunpowder); and for rain, water
poured or sprinkled from above.
283. **and's:** and his.
284. **bestowed:** i.e., accomodated in the house.
288. **purposed:** decided.
293. **to horse:** for a horse.
298. **a bush:** i.e., any natural shelter.

REGAN   O sir, to willful men,
  The injuries that they themselves procure
  Must be their schoolmasters. Shut up your doors.   300
  He is attended with a desperate train,
  And what they may incense him to, being apt
  To have his ear abused, wisdom bids fear.
CORNWALL   Shut up your doors, my lord. 'Tis a wild night,
  My Regan counsels well. Come out o'th'storm.   *Exeunt* 305

Act 3, Scene 1

Storm still. Enter KENT [*disguised as* CAIUS] *and a* GEN-
TLEMAN, *severally*

KENT   Who's there, besides foul weather?
GENTLEMAN   One minded like the weather, most unquietly.
KENT   I know you. Where's the king?
GENTLEMAN   Contending with the fretful elements;
  Bids the wind blow the earth into the sea,   5
  Or swell the curlèd waters 'bove the main,
  That things might change or cease; tears his white hair,
  Which the impetuous blasts with eyeless rage
  Catch in their fury and make nothing of;
  Strives in his little world of man to outscorn   10
  The to-and-fro conflicting wind and rain.
  This night, wherein the cub-drawn bear would couch,
  The lion and the belly-pinched wolf
  Keep their fur dry, unbonneted he runs,
  And bids what will take all.
KENT   But who is with him?   15
GENTLEMAN   None but the Fool, who labors to out-jest
  His heart-struck injuries.
KENT   Sir, I do know you,
  And dare upon the warrant of my note
  Commend a dear thing to you. There is division,

3.1. **Location:** The heath.
6. **main:** i.e., the land.
7–15. **tears . . . all:** These lines appear in *Q* but not *F*; this scene has undergone careful revision, with numerous other cuts and additions, sometimes awkwardly done. These and other well-known and much-analyzed Q-only lines have been interpolated into this *F*-based edition.
10. **outscorn:** outdo in scorning.
12. **cub-drawn bear:** bear drawn by its young.
13. **belly-pinched:** hungry, i.e. even the most hungry and desperate animal would take shelter rather than stay out in the storm, as Lear is doing.
14. **unbonneted:** hatless.
16. **out-jest:** overcome by jesting or being amusing.
18. **warrant of my note:** promise to fulfill my task.
19. **dear:** i.e., secret.

Although as yet the face of it be covered   20
With mutual cunning, 'twixt Albany and Cornwall.
Who have—as who have not, that their great stars
Throned and set high?—servants, who seem no less,
Which are to France the spies and speculations
Intelligent of our state. What hath been seen,   25
Either in snuffs and packings of the dukes,
Or the hard rein which both of them hath borne
Against the old kind king; or something deeper,
Whereof, perchance, these are but furnishings.
But true it is, from France there comes a power   30
Into this scattered kingdom, who already
Wise in our negligence, have secret feet
In some of our best ports, and are at point
To show their open banner. Now to you:
If on my credit you dare build so far   35
To make your speed to Dover, you shall find
Some that will thank you, making just report
Of how unnatural and bemadding sorrow
The king hath cause to plain.
I am a gentleman of blood and breeding,   40
And from some knowledge and assurance offer
This office to you.
GENTLEMAN   I will talk further with you.
KENT   No, do not.
For confirmation that I am much more
Than my out-wall, open this purse and take   45
What it contains. If you shall see Cordelia—
As fear not but you shall—show her this ring,

---

20. **covered**: hidden.
22–29. **Who . . . furnishings**: These lines appear in F but not Q, intensifying the anxiety
about possible civil war between Albany and Cornwall. However, that Q's variant passage
(at ll. 30–42) focuses on the anxiety about foreign war (an invasion by the French forces of
Cordelia and her husband) does not mean that in later revision Shakespeare eliminated references to a French invasion; many other passages on the subject were not replaced in F. In
terms of continuity, Kent discusses here the contents of the letter from Cordelia that he
read (at 2.2.158) while stocked, so the Q-only passage is still relevant. The Q-only and F-
only passages can co-exist, as both recount the type of dangerous gossip that has become
prevalent in the kingdom. As the play's final battle in Act 5 is indeed a result of this foreign
invasion rather than a civil war, the Q-only lines have been interpolated into this F-based
edition.
26. **snuffs and packings**: resentments and conspiracies.
32. **Wise in our negligence**: aware of the neglected state of the kingdom due to the
squabbling between Lear and his daughters.
34. **open banner**: i.e., flags set out to announce war.
38. **bemadding sorrow**: sorrow that causes madness.
39. **plain**: complain.
40. **blood and breeding**: i.e., holding rank from birth and upbringing
42. **office**: duty.
45. **out-wall**: outward appearance (i.e., his rough disguise as Caius).

And she will tell you who that fellow is
That yet you do not know. Fie on this storm!
I will go seek the king.   50
GENTLEMAN   Give me your hand. Have you no more to say?
KENT   Few words, but to effect more than all yet:
That when we have found the king, in which your pain,
That way, I'll this. He that first lights on him
Holla the other.   *Exeunt*   55

Act 3, Scene 2

Storm still. Enter LEAR *and* FOOL

LEAR   Blow, wind, and crack your cheeks! Rage, blow,
You cataracts and hurricanos, spout
Till you have drenched our steeples, drowned the cocks!
You sulph'rous and thought-executing fires,
Vaunt-couriers of oak-cleaving thunderbolts,   5
Singe my white head. And thou all-shaking thunder,
Strike flat the thick rotundity o'th'world,
Crack nature's moulds, all germens spill at once
That makes ingrateful man.
FOOL   O nuncle, court holy-water in a dry house is better   10
than this rain-water out o'door. Good nuncle, in, and ask
thy daughters' blessing. Here's a night pities neither wise
man nor Fools.
LEAR   Rumble thy bellyful; spit, fire; spout, rain!
Nor rain, wind, thunder, fire are my daughters.   15
I tax not you, you elements, with unkindness.
I never gave you kingdom, called you children.
You owe me no subscription. Then, let fall
Your horrible pleasure. Here I stand your slave,
A poor, infirm, weak, and despised old man.   20

48. **that fellow:** i.e., Kent.
53. **in which your pain:** i.e., which is your mission or duty.
54. **That way, I'll this:** i.e. each of us will go in an opposite direction.
55. **Holla:** i.e., call out to.
3.2. **Location:** The heath.
2. **STAGE DIRECTION Storm still:** see note on 2.4.279.
2. **cataracts and hurricanos:** heavenly downpours and hurricanes.
3. **cocks:** weathercocks (i.e., weathervanes), which included the symbol of a bird, usually found atop a church-steeple (an anachronism for this play, set in pre-Christian Britain).
5. **Vaunt-couriers:** messengers who come ahead.
7. **rotundity:** roundness or fullness.
8. **germens:** seeds.
10. **court holy-water:** i.e., to flatter (proverbial).
18. **subscription:** allegiance or service.

But yet I call you servile ministers,
That will with two pernicious daughters join
Your high-engendered battles 'gainst a head
So old and white as this. Oh, ho, 'tis foul.

FOOL   He that has a house to put's head in has a good head-   25
piece.
   [*Sings*] The codpiece that will house
    Before the head has any,
   The head and he shall louse;
    So beggars marry many.   30
   The man that makes his toe
    What he his heart should make,
   Shall of a corn cry woe,
    And turn his sleep to wake.
For there was never yet fair woman but she made mouths in   35
a glass.

   Enter KENT, [*disguised as* CAIUS]

LEAR   No, I will be the pattern of all patience. I will say nothing.

KENT   Who's there?

FOOL   Marry, here's grace and a codpiece; that's a wise man   40
and a Fool.

KENT   Alas, sir, are you here? Things that love night
Love not such nights as these. The wrathful skies
Gallow the very wanderers of the dark
And make them keep their caves. Since I was man,   45
Such sheets of fire, such bursts of horrid thunder,
Such groans of roaring wind and rain I never
Remember to have heard. Man's nature cannot carry
Th'affliction nor the fear.

---

21. **servile ministers:** enslaved attendants (i.e., of the gods on whom Lear calls).
22. **pernicious:** harmful.
23. **high-engendered:** begotten or conceived by the heavens.
25. **put's:** put his.   **head-piece:** head.
27. **codpiece:** "a bagged appendage to the front of the close-fitting hose or breeches worn by men" (*OED*), and slang for male genitalia.   **house:** i.e., have sexual intercourse.
28. **any:** i.e., shelter.
29. **louse:** be covered by lice.
30. **beggars marry many:** i.e., make even more beggars.
31–32. **The man . . . make:** i.e., the man who kicks out (with his toe) or banishes what his heart values (including Cordelia and Kent).
33. **corn:** painful sore on foot.
34. **sleep to wake:** i.e., not be able to sleep.
35–36. **made mouths in a glass:** i.e., vainly admired herself in the mirror.
40. **grace:** a graced or favored person.   **codpiece:** see note on 1.27.
44. **Gallow:** hang on a gallows (a crossed piece of wood used for execution).   **wanderers:** nocturnal animals.
45. **keep:** stay in.   **man:** i.e., an adult.

LEAR   Let the great gods,
  That keep this dreadful pudder o'er our heads,   50
  Find out their enemies now. Tremble, thou wretch,
  That hast within thee undivulged crimes
  Unwhipped of justice. Hide thee, thou bloody hand,
  Thou perjured and thou simular of virtue
  That art incestuous. Caitiff, to pieces shake,   55
  That under covert and convenient seeming
  Has practiced on man's life. Close pent-up guilts,
  Rive your concealing continents and cry
  These dreadful summoners grace. I am a man
  More sinned against than sinning.
KENT   Alack, bare-headed?   60
  Gracious my lord, hard by here is a hovel.
  Some friendship will it lend you 'gainst the tempest.
  Repose you there, while I to this hard house—
  More harder than is the stones whereof 'tis raised,
  Which even but now, demanding after you,   65
  Denied me to come in—return and force
  Their scanted courtesy.
LEAR   My wits begin to turn.
  Come on, my boy. How dost, my boy? Art cold?
  I am cold myself. Where is this straw, my fellow?
  The art of our necessities is strange   70
  And can make vile things precious. Come, your hovel.
  Poor Fool and knave, I have one part in my heart
  That's sorry yet for thee.
FOOL [Sings]   He that has and a little tiny wit,
    With heigh-ho, the wind and the rain,   75
    Must make content with his fortunes fit,
    Though the rain it raineth every day.

50. **pudder:** puddle, i.e., downpour.
53. **Unwhipped of:** unpunished by.
54. **simular:** one who simulates or fakes.
55. **Caitiff:** vile or miserable figure.
56. **covert:** hidden. **seeming:** falseness.
58. **Rive:** tear forth from. **continents:** containment.
58–59. **cry / These dreadful summoners grace:** suspend the actions of these horrible summoners (who officially commanded people to appear in civil or ecclesiastical court).
60. **More sinned against than sinning:** Lear's claim here can be judged against his words and actions in the previous two acts of the play.
60. **bare-headed:** i.e., out in the storm without any head covering; Kent recognizes that both Lear's physical body (and head) and his powers of reasoning have become vulnerable.
61. **hard by here is a hovel:** nearby is a shed, or poor form of shelter.
63. **hard:** cruel, unyielding.
67. **scanted:** i.e., stingy. **wits:** abilities to reason. **turn:** change for the worse.
69. **straw:** i.e., only form of shelter.
71. **Come:** i.e., let's go to.
74–77. Adapted from a melancholy song sung by Feste at the conclusion of *Twelfth Night*.

LEAR   True, boy. Come, bring us to this hovel.
                                    Exeunt [all but the FOOL]
FOOL   This is a brave night to cool a courtesan. I'll speak a
       prophecy ere I go: 80
         When priests are more in word than matter;
         When brewers mar their malt with water;
         When nobles are their tailors' tutors,
         No heretics burned, but wenches' suitors,
         When every case in law is right;   85
         No squire in debt, nor no poor knight;
         When slanders do not live in tongues,
         Nor cutpurses come not to throngs;
         When usurers tell their gold i'th'field,
         And bawds and whores do churches build,   90
         Then shall the realm of Albion come to great confusion.
         Then comes the time, who lives to see't,
         That going shall be used with feet.
       This prophecy Merlin shall make, for I live before his time.
                                                        Exit

Act 3, Scene 3

Enter GLOUCESTER *and* EDMUND *with lights*

GLOUCESTER   Alack, alack Edmund, I like not this unnatural
       dealing. When I desired their leave that I might pity him,
       they took from me the use of mine own house, charged me
       on pain of perpetual displeasure neither to speak of him, en-
       treat for him, or any way sustain him.   5
EDMUND   Most savage and unnatural!

79–94. The Fool's prophecy appears in *F* but not in *Q*; it may have been added later
in revision (although it may simply have been cut from *Q* during the original composition), perhaps to intensify James I's English subjects' anxiety about the chaos to
which the country could be subject.
82. malt: i.e., alcohol.
84. wenches: i.e., sexually promiscuous women.
86. in debt: squires and their superiors, knights, were usually in debt due to the costs of
serving their masters.
88. cutpurses come to thongs: pickpockets prey on crowds.
89. usurers: money-lenders.   tell . . . i'th'field: i.e., count out in the open.
90. bawds: sexual procurer.
91. Albion: ancient name for Britain which embodied its mythical greatness.
94. Merlin: the great magician of King Arthur's time; chronicle historians dated Leir's rule
in the 8th c. B.C.E., and Arthur's in the 6th c. C.E.; Merlin, known for his mystical prophecies, is invoked ironically by the Fool, whose prophecies spring not from mysticism but simple observance of human behavior.
3.1. Location: The Earl of Gloucester's castle.
1. Alack: an exclamation of pity or dissatisfaction.   unnatural dealing: unkind and unnatural treatment of Lear by his daughters.
2. leave: permission.

GLOUCESTER   Go to, say you nothing. There's a division between the dukes, and a worse matter than that. I have received a letter this night—'tis dangerous to be spoken—I
have locked the letter in my closet. These injuries the king   10
now bears will be revenged home. There is part of a power
already footed. We must incline to the king. I will seek him
and privily relieve him. Go you and maintain talk with the
duke, that my charity be not of him perceived. If he ask for
me, I am ill and gone to bed. If I die for't—as no less is   15
threatened me—the king my old master must be relieved.
There is strange things toward. Edmund, pray you be careful.   *Exit*
EDMUND   This courtesy, forbid thee, shall the duke
Instantly know, and of that letter too.   20
This seems a fair deserving, and must draw me
That which my father loses: no less than all.
The younger rises when the old doth fall.   *Exit*

Act 3, Scene 4

Enter LEAR, KENT [*disguised as* CAIUS], *and* FOOL

KENT   Here is the place, my lord. Good my lord, enter.
The tyranny of the open night's too rough
For nature to endure.   *Storm still*
LEAR   Let me alone.
KENT   Good my lord, enter here.
LEAR   Wilt break my heart?
KENT   I had rather break mine own. Good my lord, enter.   5
LEAR   Thou think'st 'tis much that this contentious storm
Invades us to the skin: so 'tis to thee.
But where the greater malady is fixed,
The lesser is scarce felt. Thou'dst shun a bear,
But if thy flight lay toward the roaring sea,   10
Thou'dst meet the bear i'th'mouth. When the mind's free,
The body's delicate. The tempest in my mind
Doth from my senses take all feeling else,
Save what beats there: filial ingratitude.
Is it not as this mouth should tear this hand   15

---

7. **Go to:** i.e., come, come.
9. **letter:** i.e., from Cordelia or her supporter.
10. **closet:** room.
12. **footed:** i.e., landed in the kingdom.
13. **privily:** privately or secretly.
3.4. **Location:** The heath, near a hovel.
11. **i'th'mouth:** face-to-face.

For lifting food to't? But I will punish home.
No, I will weep no more. In such a night,
To shut me out? Pour on, I will endure
In such a night as this! O Regan, Goneril,
Your old kind father, whose frank heart gave all—   20
O that way madness lies. Let me shun that,
No more of that.
KENT   Good my lord, enter here.
LEAR   Prithee, go in thyself, seek thine own ease.
This tempest will not give me leave to ponder
On things would hurt me more; but I'll go in.   25
[*To the* FOOL]   In, boy, go first. You houseless poverty—
Nay get thee in. I'll pray and then I'll sleep.   [*Exit* FOOL]
[*Kneels in prayer*]   Poor naked wretches, wheresoe'er you
     are
That bide the pelting of this pitiless storm,
How shall your houseless heads and unfed sides,   30
Your looped and windowed raggedness defend you
From seasons such as these? O I have ta'en
Too little care of this. Take physic, pomp,
Expose thyself to feel what wretches feel,
That thou mayst shake the superflux to them   35
And show the heavens more just.

          Enter FOOL

EDGAR   [*Within*]   Fathom and half; fathom and half; poor
     Tom!
FOOL   Come not in here, nuncle! Here's a spirit! Help me,
     help me!
KENT   Give me thy hand. Who's there?   40
FOOL   A spirit, a spirit. He says his name's Poor Tom.
KENT   What art thou that dost grumble there i'th'straw?
     Come forth!

          Enter EDGAR [*disguised as* POOR TOM]

EDGAR   Away, the foul fiend follows me. Through the sharp
     hawthorn blows the winds. Hum, go to thy cold bed and   45
     warm thee.

16. **punish home:** punish it directly.
20. **frank:** unrestrained.
29. **bide:** abide, i.e., endure.
30. **sides:** i.e., bodies.
31. **looped and windowed:** full of holes, i.e., inadequately dressed.
33. **physic, pomp:** medicinal curative (or purge) and excessive food.
35. **superflux:** (1) surplus; (2) discharge from the bowels.
37. **Fathom:** measurement equaling about five feet.
38. **spirit:** ghost.
42. **Poor Tom:** See note on 2.3.20.
45. **Hum:** i.e., Ha!

LEAR   Didst thou give all to thy daughters, and art thou come
    to this?

EDGAR   Who gives anything to Poor Tom, whom the foul
    fiend hath led through fire and through flame, through   50
    sword, and whirlpool, o'er bog and quagmire; that hath laid
    knives under his pillow and halters in his pew; set ratsbane
    by his porridge; made him proud of heart to ride on a bay
    trotting-horse over four-inched bridges, to course his own
    shadow for a traitor. Bless thy five wits, Tom's a-cold! O do,   55
    de, do, de, do, de! Bless thee from whirlwinds, star-blasting,
    and taking. Do Poor Tom some charity, whom the foul fiend
    vexes. There could I have him now, and there, and there,
    and there again, and there!   *Storm still*

LEAR   Has his daughters brought him to this pass?   60
    Couldst thou save nothing? Wouldst thou give 'em all?

FOOL   Nay, he reserved a blanket, else we had been all
    shamed.

LEAR   Now all the plagues that in the pendulous air
    Hang fated o'er men's faults, light on thy daughters!   65

KENT   He hath no daughters, sir.

LEAR   Death, traitor! Nothing could have subdued nature
    To such a lowness but his unkind daughters.
    Is it the fashion that discarded fathers
    Should have thus little mercy on their flesh?   70
    Judicious punishment: 'twas this flesh begot
    Those pelican daughters.

EDGAR   Pillicock sat on Pillicock hill;
        Alow, alow, loo, loo

FOOL   This cold night will turn us all to Fools and madmen.   75

EDGAR   Take heed o'th'foul fiend, obey thy parents, keep thy
    words justly, swear not, commit not with man's sworn
    spouse, set not thy sweet heart on proud array. Tom's a-cold.

---

49. Shakespeare borrows much of Poor Tom's vocabulary, including his invocation of numerous devils, or "foul fiends," from Samuel Harsnett's *A Declaration of Egregious Popish Impostures* (1603).
51. quagmire: soggy ground.
52. ratsbane: rat poison.
54. course: pursue.
56. star-blasting: the pernicious influence of malign stars (*OED*).   **taking:** (1) being seized; (2) having a seizure.
62. reserved a blanket: i.e., Tom is clothed only in a filthy blanket.
64. pendulous: floating.
65. light: land on.
72. pelican: i.e., unnatural or cannibalistic (pelicans were thought to use their own blood to feed their young); compare 1.1.07.
73. Pillicock: penis.   **Pillicock hill:** female genitalia.
74. Alow . . . loo: word used to incite dogs to the hunt.
77. man's: i.e., another man's.
78. on proud array: in ostentatious, or improper, dress.

LEAR   What hast thou been?

EDGAR   A servingman, proud in heart and mind, that curled   80
my hair, wore gloves in my cap, served the lust of my mistress' heart, and did the act of darkness with her. Swore as
many oaths as I spake words, and broke them in the sweet
face of heaven. One that slept in the contriving of lust and
waked to do it. Wine loved I deeply, dice dearly, and in   85
woman out-paramoured the Turk. False of heart, light of
ear, bloody of hand; hog in sloth, fox in stealth, wolf in
greediness, dog in madness, lion in prey. Let not the creak-
ing of shoes nor the rustlings of silks betray thy poor heart
to woman. Keep thy foot out of brothels, thy hand out of   90
plackets, thy pen from lenders' books, and defy the foul
fiend. Still through the hawthorn blows the cold wind. Says
suum, mun, nonny. Dolphin, my boy, my boy! *Cessez!* Let
him trot by.   *Storm still*

LEAR   Thou wert better in a grave than to answer with thy un-   95
covered body this extremity of the skies. Is man no more
than this? Consider him well. Thou owest the worm no silk,
the beast no hide, the sheep no wool, the cat no perfume.
Ha? Here's three on's are sophisticated, thou art the thing
itself. Unaccommodated man is no more but such a poor,   100
bare, forked animal as thou art. Off, off, you lendings!
Come, unbutton here!   [LEAR *begins to undress.*]

Enter GLOUCESTER, *with a torch*

FOOL [*Stops* LEAR *from undressing*]   Prithee, nuncle, be contented. 'Tis a naughty night to swim in. Now a little fire in a
wild field were like an old lecher's heart—a small spark, all   105
the rest on's body cold. Look, here comes a walking fire.

EDGAR   This is the foul fiend Flibbertigibbet. He begins at
curfew and walks at first cock. He gives the web and the

82. **did the act of darkness:** had sexual intercourse.
83. **spake:** spoke.
86. **out-paramoured the Turk:** had more lovers than a sultan with a harem.
87. **sloth:** laziness.
91. **plackets:** openings of a woman's underskirt (hence slang for "vagina").
93. **suum, mun, nonny:** nonsense words.   **Dolphin:** i.e., Edgar is calling for his horse
(the word is also slang for "dauphin," the French term for the male heir to the throne).
Cessez: Cease (French).
98. **cat no perfume:** musky perfume was produced from the secretion of civets (large
African cats).   **on's:** on his.
100. **Unaccommodated:** (1) undressed; (2) unaccompanied; (3) ignored; (4) rejected or
banished (with ironic pun on Lear's banishment of Cordelia and Kent in 1.1).
101. **forked:** having two legs.   **lendings:** borrowings, i.e., clothes.
106. **cold:** i.e., sexually impotent.
107. **Flibbertigibbet:** name of a devil borrowed from Harsnett (see note on 1.49).   **curfew:** i.e., dusk.
108. **first cock:** i.e., dawn.
108–109. **web and the pin:** diseases of the eye (i.e., cataracts).

pin, squints the eye, and makes the harelip; mildews the
white wheat, and hurts the poor creature of earth.   110
  Swithold footed thrice the old,
  He met the night-mare and her nine-fold;
  Bid her alight and her troth plight,
  And aroint thee, witch, aroint thee!

KENT How fares your grace?   115

LEAR [*Pointing to* GLOUCESTER] What's he?

KENT Who's there? What is't you seek?

GLOUCESTER What are you there? Your names?

EDGAR Poor Tom, that eats the swimming frog, the toad, the
tadpole, the wall-newt, and the water; that in the fury of his   120
heart, when the foul fiend rages, eats cow-dung for salads,
swallows the old rat and the ditch-dog, drinks the green
mantle of the standing pool; who is whipped from tithing to
tithing, and stock-punished and imprisoned; who hath three
suits to his back, six shirts to his body.   125
  Horse to ride, and weapon to wear;
  But mice and rats and such small deer
  Have been Tom's food for seven long year.
Beware my follower! Peace, Smulkin; peace, thou fiend!

GLOUCESTER What, hath your grace no better company?   130

EDGAR The Prince of Darkness is a gentleman. Modo he's
called, and Mahu—

GLOUCESTER Our flesh and blood, my lord, is grown so vile
That it doth hate what gets it.

EDGAR Poor Tom's a-cold.   135

GLOUCESTER Go in with me. My duty cannot suffer
To obey in all your daughters' hard commands.
Though their injunction be to bar my doors
And let this tyrannous night take hold upon you,
Yet have I ventured to come seek you out   140
And bring you where both fire and food is ready.

LEAR First let me talk with this philosopher.
  [*To* EDGAR] What is the cause of thunder?

---

109. **harelip:** misshapen, or cleft, palate (mouth).
112. **night-mare and her nine-fold:** (1) mare and her nine foals; (2) demon and her nine
companions.
113. **troth plight:** pledged marriage.
114. **aroint thee:** be gone!
122–23. **green mantle:** algae.
123. **standing:** stagnant.
123–24. **tithing to tithing:** from one parish to another, to which tithes, or taxes, were paid
(i.e., Edgar claims he has been whipped for vagrancy).
124–125. **three suits:** Kent mocked Oswald in 2.2.12–14 for being "three-suited," or
lowly.
129. **Smulkin:** devil mentioned by Harsnett (see note on 1.49).
131–32. **Modo . . . Mahu:** from Harsnett.

KENT   Good my lord, take his offer, go into th'house.
LEAR   I'll talk a word with this same learned Theban.   145
   What is your study?
EDGAR   How to prevent the fiend, and to kill vermin.
LEAR   Let me ask you one word in private.

                                 [They speak apart]

KENT   Importune him once more to go, my lord.
   His wits begin t'unsettle.
GLOUCESTER   Canst thou blame him?   150

                                 Storm still

   His daughters seek his death. Ah, that good Kent,
   He said it would be thus, poor banished man!
   Thou sayest the king grows mad. I'll tell thee, friend,
   I am almost mad myself. I had a son,
   Now outlawed from my blood; he sought my life   155
   But lately, very late. I loved him, friend,
   No father his son dearer. True to tell thee,
   The grief hath crazed my wits. What a night's this!
   I do beseech your grace—
LEAR   O, cry you mercy, sir!
   [To EDGAR*]*   Noble philosopher, your company.   160
EDGAR   Tom's a-cold.
GLOUCESTER   In, fellow, there, into th'hovel; keep thee warm.
LEAR   Come, let's in all.
KENT   This way, my lord.
LEAR   With him!
   I will keep still with my philosopher.
KENT   Good my lord, soothe him; let him take the fellow.   165
GLOUCESTER   Take him you on.
KENT   Sirrah, come on. Go along with us.
LEAR   Come, good Athenian.
GLOUCESTER   No words, no words. Hush.
EDGAR   Childe Roland to the dark tower came.   170
   His word was still "Fie, fo, and fum;
   I smell the blood of a British man."   *Exeunt*

---

145. Theban: i.e., philosopher.
168. Athenian: see note on 1. 123.
170. Childe Roland: allusion to *Le Chanson de Roland*, a medieval poem about the warrior Roland, who served Charlemagne.
171–72. Fie . . . British man: the refrain of the giant killed by Jack in the fairy tale "Jack the Giant Killer" (i.e., "Jack and the Beanstalk").

Act 3, Scene 5

Enter CORNWALL *and* EDMUND

CORNWALL   I will have my revenge ere I depart his house.

EDMUND   How, my lord, I may be censured, that nature thus gives way to loyalty, something fears me to think of.

CORNWALL   I now perceive it was not altogether your brother's evil disposition made him seek his death, but a provoking merit set a-work by a reprovable badness in himself. 5

EDMUND   How malicious is my fortune, that I must repent to be just! This is the letter which he spoke of, which approves him an intelligent party to the advantages of France. O heavens, that this treason were not, or not I the detector! 10

CORNWALL   Go with me to the duchess.

EDMUND   If the matter of this paper be certain, you have mighty business in hand.

CORNWALL   True or false, it hath made thee Earl of Gloucester. Seek out where thy father is, that he may be ready for our apprehension. 15

EDMUND   [*Aside*] If I find him comforting the king, it will stuff his suspicion more fully.   [*To* CORNWALL] I will persevere in my course of loyalty, though the conflict be sore between that and my blood. 20

CORNWALL   I will lay trust upon thee, and thou shalt find a dearer father in my love.   *Exeunt*

Act 3, Scene 6

Enter KENT [*disguised as* CAIUS] and GLOUCESTER

GLOUCESTER   Here is better than the open air. Take it thankfully. I will piece out the comfort with what addition I can. I will not be long from you.

KENT   All the power of his wits have given way to his impatience. The gods reward your kindness!   *Exit* [GLOUCESTER] 5

Enter LEAR, EDGAR *and the* FOOL

3.5. **Location:** The Earl of Gloucester's castle.
6. **reprovable:** reprehensible.
19. **stuff:** fill out.
22. **upon:** in.
3.6. **Location:** A hovel on the heath.

EDGAR   Frateretto calls me, and tells me Nero is an angler in
the lake of darkness. Pray, innocent, and beware the foul
fiend.

FOOL   Prithee, nuncle, tell me whether a madman be a gentleman or a yeoman.   10

LEAR   A king, a king!

FOOL   No, he's a yeoman that has a gentleman to his son; for
he's a mad yeoman that sees his son a gentleman before
him.

LEAR   To have a thousand with red burning spits come hizzing   15
in upon 'em!

EDGAR   The foul fiend bites my back.

FOOL   He's mad that trusts in the tameness of a wolf, a
horse's health, a boy's love, or a whore's oath.

LEAR   It shall be done. I will arraign them straight. [*To*   20
EDGAR] Come, sit thou here, most learned justice.   [*To the*
FOOL] Thou, sapient sir, sit here.   [*To the air*] No, you she-
foxes—

EDGAR   Look where he stands and glares! Want'st thou eyes at
trial, madam?   25
    [*Sings*] Come o'er the bourn, Bessy, to me.

FOOL [*Sings*]   Her boat hath a leak
    And she must not speak
    Why she dares not come over to thee.

EDGAR   The foul fiend haunts poor Tom in the voice of a   30
nightingale. Hoppedance cries in Tom's belly for two white
herring. Croak not, black angel! I have no food for thee.

KENT [*To* LEAR]   How do you, sir? Stand you not so amazed.
Will you lie down and rest upon the cushions?

LEAR   I'll see their trial first. Bring in their evidence.   35

---

6. Frateretto: a devil named by Harsnett (see note on 3.4.49).   **Nero:** Roman emperor
renowned for his debauchery and corruption.
7. lake of darkness: i.e., the River Styx, upon which the dead were ferried by Charon to
Hades, or the underworld, according to Greek mythology.
10. yeoman: a freeholder, or commoner, hence inferior to a "gentleman" who is a member
of the gentry.
15. hizzing: hissing.
20–56. This "mock-trial," as it has come to be called, appears in Q but not F; it was evidently cut from F, for a variety of reasons, including possible self-censorship. Shakespeare
and his acting company may have come to see it as distracting from the theatrical power of
the treatment of Gloucester in the next scene. Due to the way in which this scene has become so ingrained in cultural consciousness (and in Shakespearean criticism since the
eighteenth century), it has been interpolated here into this F-based edition.
20. I . . . straight: ironically echoing the type of trial, or love-test, to which Lear forced his
three daughters to submit in 1.1.
22. The presence of Goneril and Regan in this scene is imagined only.
26. Come . . . me: lines from a contemporary song.
31. Hoppedance: another devil mentioned by Harsnett.
31. white: fresh or salted, but unsmoked.
32. Croak: cry out.

[*To* EDGAR]   Thou robed man of justice, take thy place.
[*To the* FOOL]   And thou, his yoke-fellow of equity,
Bench by his side.   [*To* KENT] You are o'th'commission;
Sit you too.

EDGAR   Let us deal justly.   40
     Sleepest or wakest, thou, jolly shepherd?
       Thy sheep be in the corn;
     And for one blast of thy minikin mouth
       Thy sheep shall take no harm.
Purr, the cat, is grey.   45

LEAR   Arraign her first: 'tis Goneril—I here take my oath before this honorable assembly—kicked the poor king her father.

FOOL [*To the air*]   Come hither, mistress. Is your name
Goneril?   50

LEAR   She cannot deny it.

FOOL   Cry you mercy, I took you for a joint-stool.

LEAR   And here's another whose warped looks proclaim
What store her heart is made on. Stop her there!
Arms, arms, sword, fire! Corruption in the place!   55
False justicer, why hast thou let her 'scape?

EDGAR   Bless thy five wits.

KENT   O pity! Sir, where is the patience now
That you so oft have boasted to retain?

EDGAR [*Aside*]   My tears begin to take his part so much   60
They mar my counterfeiting.

LEAR   The little dogs and all,
Trey, Blanch, and Sweetheart—see, they bark at me.

EDGAR   Tom will throw his head at them. Avaunt, you curs!
     Be thy mouth or black or white,   65
       Tooth that poisons if it bite,
     Mastiff, greyhound, mongrel grim,
     Hound or spaniel, brach or him,

---

36. robed man of justice: i.e., judge in robes.
37. yoke-fellow of equity: i.e., fellow judge in the court of equity (a type of law court).
38. commission: i.e., the judges' panel.
41–42. Sleepst . . . corn: i.e., while the shepherd was sleeping, his unwatched flock of sheep had gotten into a corn field where they are gorging themselves and becoming sick.
43. blast of thy minikin: cry of thy shrill.
47. kicked: (1) struck with a foot; (2) defied; (3) forced out; (4) tried to kill (?).
52. took you for a joint-stool: i.e., the Fool ironically uses a proverbial expression to note that the figure that Lear takes to be Goneril is instead a stool (made by a joiner, or carpenter, hence "joint-stool").
53. warped: contorted.
61. counterfeiting: disguise.
64. Avaunt you curs: Begone you dogs (or vicious things).
67. mongrel: mixed-breed dog
68. brach: female dog.

Or bobtail tyke or trundle-tail,
Tom will make them weep and wail;   70
For with throwing thus my head,
Dogs leapt the hatch, and all are fled.
Do, de, de, de. *Cessez!* Come, march to wakes and fairs and
market towns. Poor Tom, thy horn is dry.

LEAR   Then let them anatomize Regan; see what breeds about   75
her heart. Is there any cause in nature that makes these
hard hearts?   [*To* EDGAR] You, sir, I entertain you for one of
my hundred, only I do not like the fashion of your garments.
You'll say they are Persian; but let them be changed.

KENT   Now, good my lord, lie here, and rest awhile.   80

LEAR   Make no noise, make no noise. Draw the curtains. So,
so. We'll go to supper i'th'morning.   [*He sleeps*]

FOOL   And I'll go to bed at noon.

Enter GLOUCESTER

GLOUCESTER   Come hither, friend. Where is the king my master?   85

KENT   Here, sir, but trouble him not; his wits are gone.

GLOUCESTER   Good friend, I prithee take him in thy arms.
I have o'erheard a plot of death upon him.
There is a litter ready. Lay him in't
And drive toward Dover, friend, where thou shalt meet   90
Both welcome and protection. Take up thy master,
If thou shouldst dally half an hour, his life
With thine and all that offer to defend him
Stand in assured loss. Take up, take up,
And follow me that will to some provision   95
Give thee quick conduct.

69. **bobtail tyke or trundle-tail:** bobbed-tail mongrel or curly-tailed mongrel.
72. **hatch:** i.e., kennel door.
73. *Cessez:* cease (French).
74. **horn:** i.e., voice.
75. **anatomize:** dissect.   **breeds:** grows.
76–77. **Is . . . hearts:** This serves as the seminal question in the play: that is, do "hard hearts," i.e., cruelty, derive from a natural source (such as the body at birth) or from circumstances, surroundings, or upbringing? Shakespeare, unlike the author of the source play *King Leir*, does not provide the audience with the history of Lear's interactions with his children before the love-test. Thus Shakespeare does not provide clear motivation for the stubbornness of Cordelia in 1.1 or the subsequent malice of Goneril and Regan. **breeds:** grows.
78. **hundred:** i.e., the hundred knights (or "century") he announced he would allow himself when he divided the kingdom in 1.1, and which Goneril and Regan tried to barter down to nothing in 2.4.259.
79. **Persian:** i.e., luxurious.
87. **take him in thy arms:** i.e., pick him up and carry him away.
89. **litter:** i.e., stretcher or bed to carry him on.
90. **Dover:** This town, with its white cliffs, symbolizes the glory of Britain as a whole.
92. **dally:** linger.
94. **Take up:** i.e., pick up Lear.

KENT   Oppressed nature sleeps.
    This rest might yet have balmed thy broken sinews
    Which, if convenience will not allow,
    Stand in hard cure.   [To FOOL] Come, help to bear thy
        master;
    Thou must not stay behind.
GLOUCESTER   Come, come away.   100

        Exeunt [all but EDGAR]

EDGAR   When we our betters see bearing our woes,
    We scarcely think our miseries our foes.
    Who alone suffers, suffers most i'th'mind,
    Leaving free things and happy shows behind.
    But then the mind much sufferance doth o'erskip,   105
    When grief hath mates, and bearing, fellowship.
    How light and portable my pain seems now,
    When that which makes me bend makes the king bow.
    He childed as I fathered. Tom, away!
    Mark the high noises, and thyself bewray   110
    When false opinion, whose wrong thoughts defile thee,
    In thy just proof repeals and reconciles thee.
    What will hap more tonight, safe 'scape the king!
    Lurk, lurk!   [Exit]

                    Act 3, Scene 7

        Enter CORNWALL, REGAN, GONERIL, EDMUND, and SER-
        VANTS

CORNWALL [To GONERIL]   Post speedily to my lord your hus-
    band; show him this letter. The army of France is landed.
    [To SERVANTS] Seek out the traitor Gloucester.
                              [Exeunt some SERVANTS]
REGAN   Hang him instantly!
GONERIL   Pluck out his eyes!   5

97. **balmed:** healed.   **sinews:** tendons, i.e., his body.
101–14. **When . . . lurk:** This passage appears in Q but not F; as Acts 1 and 2 are unusu-
ally long, most of the apparent cuts in F, which occur from Act 3, shorten the play and
speed up its conclusion.
108. **bow:** bend over (i.e., collapse).
109. **childed as I fathered:** acted like a child (i.e., became weak and dependent) as I
acted like a father (i.e., matured).
110. **bewray:** expose.
113. **hap:** happen.   **safe:** safely.
3.7. **Location:** The Earl of Gloucester's castle.
1. **Post:** send.
5. **Pluck out his eyes:** Goneril suggests this form of punishment, but leaves before it is in-
flicted. At 1.4.286 Lear cursed her cruelty by threatening to "pluck" out his own eyes rather
than allowing her to see him reduced to tears.

CORNWALL   Leave him to my displeasure. Edmund, keep you
   our sister company. The revenges we are bound to take upon
   your traitorous father are not fit for your beholding. Advise
   the duke, where you are going, to a most festinate preparation. We are bound to the like. Our posts shall be swift and   10
   intelligent betwixt us. Farewell, dear sister; farewell, my lord
   of Gloucester.

        Enter OSWALD

   How now, where's the king?
OSWALD   My lord of Gloucester hath conveyed him hence.
   Some five or six and thirty of his knights,   15
   Hot questrists after him, met him at gate,
   Who, with some other of the lord's dependents,
   Are gone with him towards Dover, where they boast
   To have well-armed friends.
CORNWALL   Get horses for your mistress.   [*Exit* OSWALD]   20
GONERIL   Farewell, sweet lord, and sister.
CORNWALL   Edmund, farewell.
                              [*Exeunt*] GONERIL *and* EDMUND
                              Go seek the traitor Gloucester.
   Pinion him like a thief; bring him before us.
                              [*Exeunt two or three* SERVANTS]
   Though well we may not pass upon his life
   Without the form of justice, yet our power   25
   Shall do a curt'sy to our wrath, which men
   May blame but not control. Who's there? The traitor?

        Enter GLOUCESTER, *brought in by two or three* [SERVANTS]

REGAN   Ingrateful fox! 'tis he.
CORNWALL   Bind fast his corky arms.
GLOUCESTER   What means your graces? Good my friends,   30
   consider
   You are my guests. Do me no foul play, friends.
CORNWALL   Bind him, I say!
REGAN   Hard, hard! O filthy traitor!
GLOUCESTER   Unmerciful lady as you are, I'm none.
CORNWALL   To this chair bind him. Villain, thou shalt find—

---

8. **beholding:** witnessing.
9. **festinate:** hasty.
10. **to the like:** i.e., to do the same.   **posts:** messages sent by post.
16. **questrists:** those in search of others.
19. **well-armed:** well supplied with weapons.
23. **Pinion:** bind, tie up.
26. **curt'sy:** courtesy (contracted to preserve the pentameter).
29. **corky:** withered.

[REGAN *plucks* GLOUCESTER's *beard*]

GLOUCESTER   By the kind gods, 'tis most ignobly done,   35
  To pluck me by the beard.
REGAN   So white, and such a traitor?
GLOUCESTER   Naughty lady,
  These hairs which thou dost ravish from my chin
  Will quicken and accuse thee. I am your host.
  With robbers' hands my hospitable favors   40
  You should not ruffle thus. What will you do?
CORNWALL   Come, sir, what letters had you late from France?
REGAN   Be simple answered, for we know the truth.
CORNWALL   And what confederacy have you with the traitors
  Late footed in the kingdom?
REGAN   To whose hands   45
  You have sent the lunatic king. Speak.
GLOUCESTER   I have a letter guessingly set down,
  Which came from one that's of a neutral heart,
  And not from one opposed.
CORNWALL   Cunning.
REGAN   And false.
CORNWALL   Where hast thou sent the king?
GLOUCESTER   To Dover.   50
REGAN   Wherefore to Dover? Wast thou not charged at
    peril—
CORNWALL   Wherefore to Dover? Let him first answer that!
GLOUCESTER   I am tied to th'stake, and I must stand the
    course.
REGAN   Wherefore to Dover?
GLOUCESTER   Because I would not see thy cruel nails   55
  Pluck out his poor old eyes, nor thy fierce sister
  In his anointed flesh stick boarish fangs.
  The sea, with such a storm as his bare head
  In hell-black night endured, would have buoyed up
  And quenched the stellèd fires.   60

---

38. ravish: (1) seize; (2) rape.
42. late: lately.
44. confederacy: conspiracy.
45. footed: landed; Cornwall repeats Gloucester's own report to Edmund at 3.3.12.
47. guessingly: by conjecture (i.e., Gloucester claims that the letter is unclear).
51. Wherefore: Why.
53. tied to th'stake: i.e., tied like a bear to a stake, and hence left to fight off a pack hungry dogs during a "bear-baiting" event or "course," a form of entertainment common in Shakespeare's age.
56. pluck out his poor old eyes: ironic foreshadowing as well as echo (see note on l. 5).
57. anointed: i.e., consecrated by God   **boarish:** boar-like, hence cruel.
60. stellèd: starry.

Yet, poor old heart, he holp the heavens to rain.
If wolves had at thy gate howled that stern time,
Thou shouldst have said, "Good porter, turn the key:
All cruels else subscribe." But I shall see
The winged vengeance overtake such children.   65
CORNWALL   See't shalt thou never. Fellows, hold the chair.
    Upon these eyes of thine I'll set my foot.
GLOUCESTER   He that will think to live till he be old,
    Give me some help!   [CORNWALL *puts out one of* GLOUCES-
    TER*'s eyes*]   O cruel! O you gods!
REGAN   One side will mock another: th'other, too.   70
CORNWALL   If you see vengeance—
[FIRST] SERVANT   Hold your hand, my lord.
    I have served you ever since I was a child,
    But better service have I never done you
    Than now to bid you hold.
REGAN   How now, you dog!
[FIRST] SERVANT   If you did wear a beard upon your chin   75
    I'd shake it on this quarrel. What do you mean?
CORNWALL   My villein!
[FIRST] SERVANT   Why then, come on, and take the chance of
    anger.

        [*They*] *draw and fight*

REGAN   [*To another* SERVANT] Give me thy sword. A peasant
    stand up thus!

        She takes a sword and runs at [*the* FIRST SERVANT *from*]
        behind

[FIRST] SERVANT   Oh, I am slain. My lord, you have one eye
    left   80
    To see some mischief on him. Oh!   [*dies*]
CORNWALL   Lest it see more, prevent it. Out vile jelly!

        [*He puts out* GLOUCESTER*'s other eye*]

    Where is thy luster now?
GLOUCESTER   All dark and comfortless. Where's my son Ed-
    mund?

---

61. **holp:** helped.
63. **porter:** servant responsible for opening a door and allowing access.
64. **cruels else subscribe:** cruelties otherwise allow.
65. **winged:** i.e., sent by the gods.
70. **mock:** (1) jest at; (2) tempt; (3) make faces at.
77. **villein:** peasant or servant, with pun on "villain" or scoundrel.
79. **stand up:** confront me.

Edmund, enkindle all the sparks of nature   85
  To quit this horrid act.
REGAN   Out, treacherous villain!
  Thou call'st on him that hates thee. It was he
  That made the overture of thy treasons to us,
  Who is too good to pity thee.
GLOUCESTER   O my follies! Then Edgar was abused.   90
  Kind gods, forgive me that, and prosper him.
REGAN   Go thrust him out at gates, and let him smell
  His way to Dover.   *Exit* [*a* SERVANT] *with* GLOUCESTER
                    How is't, my lord? How look you?
CORNWALL   I have received a hurt. Follow me, lady.
  [*To* SERVANTS]   Turn out that eyeless villain. Throw this
    slave   95
  Upon the dunghill. Regan, I bleed apace.
  Untimely comes this hurt. Give me your arm.
                          Exeunt [CORNWALL *and* REGAN]
[SECOND] SERVANT   I'll never care what wickedness I do,
  If this man come to good.
[THIRD] SERVANT   If she live long
  And in the end meet the old course of death,   100
  Women will all turn monsters.
[SECOND] SERVANT   Let's follow the old earl and get the Bed-
    lam
  To lead him where he would. His roguish madness
  Allows itself to anything.
[THIRD SERVANT]   Go thou. I'll fetch some flax and whites of
    eggs   105
  To apply to his bleeding face. Now, heaven help him.
                          Exeunt [*severally*]

---

85. **enkindle:** illuminate, bring to light.
88. **overture:** approached the subject of.
95. **slave:** i.e., the First Servant.
96. **dunghill:** hill composed or dung or rubbish.   **apace:** quickly, copiously.
97. **Untimely:** prematurely (i.e. fatally).
102. **the Bedlam:** i.e., Poor Tom.
105. **flax:** i.e., a bandage made of flax (a type of natural fiber).

Act 4, Scene 1

Enter EDGAR [*as* POOR TOM]

EDGAR   Yet better thus, and known to be condemned,
Than still condemned and flattered. To be worst,
The lowest and most dejected thing of fortune,
Stands still in esperance, lives not in fear.
The lamentable change is from the best;   5
The worst returns to laughter. Welcome, then,
Thou unsubstantial air that I embrace:
The wretch that thou hast blown unto the worst
Owes nothing to thy blasts.

Enter GLOUCESTER *led by an* OLD MAN

But who comes here? My father, poorly led?   10
World, world, O world!
But that thy strange mutations make us hate thee,
Life would not yield to age.
OLD MAN   O my good lord,
I have been your tenant and your father's tenant
These fourscore years.   15
GLOUCESTER   Away, get thee away! Good friend, be gone.
Thy comforts can do me no good at all;
Thee they may hurt.
OLD MAN   You cannot see your way.
GLOUCESTER   I have no way, and therefore want no eyes.
I stumbled when I saw. Full oft 'tis seen   20
Our means secure us, and our mere defects
Prove our commodities. O dear son Edgar,
The food of thy abusèd father's wrath,
Might I but live to see thee in my touch,
I'd say I had eyes again.
OLD MAN   How now? Who's there?   25
EDGAR [*Aside*]   O gods! Who is't can say "I am at the worst"?
I am worse than e'er I was!
OLD MAN   'Tis poor mad Tom.
EDGAR [*Aside*]   And worse I may be yet. The worst is not
So long as we can say, "This is the worst."

4.1. Location: Countryside near Dover.
4. esperance: hope.
10. poorly: in poverty or distress (and led by a poor man).
19. want: (1) need; (2) desire.
22. commodities: needs or advantages.
24. see thee in my touch: i.e., feel you.

OLD MAN   Fellow, where goest?

GLOUCESTER   Is it a beggar man?   30

OLD MAN   Madman and beggar too.

GLOUCESTER   He has some reason, else he could not beg.
I'th'last night's storm I such a fellow saw,
Which made me think a man a worm. My son
Came then into my mind, and yet my mind   35
Was then scarce friends with him. I have heard more since.
As flies to wanton boys are we to th'gods;
They kill us for their sport.

EDGAR   [Aside] How should this be?
Bad is the trade that must play Fool to sorrow,
Ang'ring itself and others.—Bless thee, master.   40

GLOUCESTER   Is that the naked fellow?

OLD MAN   Ay, my lord.

GLOUCESTER   Get thee away. If for my sake
Thou wilt o'ertake us hence a mile or twain
I'th'way toward Dover, do it for ancient love,
And bring some covering for this naked soul,   45
Which I'll entreat to lead me.

OLD MAN   Alack, sir, he is mad.

GLOUCESTER   'Tis the time's plague when madmen lead the blind.
Do as I bid thee; or rather do thy pleasure.
Above the rest, be gone.   50

OLD MAN   I'll bring him the best 'parel that I have,
Come on't what will.   Exit

GLOUCESTER   Sirrah, naked fellow—

EDGAR   Poor Tom's a-cold. [Aside]   I cannot daub it farther.

GLOUCESTER   Come hither, fellow.   55

EDGAR [Aside]   And yet I must. [To GLOUCESTER] Bless thy
sweet eyes, they bleed.

GLOUCESTER   Know'st thou the way to Dover?

EDGAR   Both stile and gate, horse-way and footpath. Poor
Tom hath been scared out of his good wits. Bless thee, good
man's son, from the foul fiend. Five fiends have been in   60
poor Tom at once: of lust, as Obidicut; Hobbididence,
prince of dumbness; Mahu, of stealing; Modo, of murder;
Flibbertigibbet, of Mobing, and Mohing, who since pos-

---

37. **wanton:** naughty, uncontrollable.
43. **twain:** two.
50. **Above:** as to.
51. **'parel:** apparel.
54. **daub:** pretend.
58. **stile:** steps allowing a walker to cross over a fence.
60–63. Tom names a number of Harsnett's devils here (see note on 3.4.49).
63–64. **possesses:** (1) demonically inhabits; (2) has sexual intercourse with.

sesses chambermaids and waiting-women. So, bless thee,
master.   65
GLOUCESTER   Here, take this purse, you whom the heavens'
plagues
Have humbled to all strokes. That I am wretched
Makes thee the happier. Heavens deal so still.
Let the superfluous and lust-dieted man
That slaves your ordinance, that will not see   70
Because he does not feel, feel your power quickly.
So distribution should undo excess,
And each man have enough. Dost thou know Dover?
EDGAR   Ay, master.
GLOUCESTER   There is a cliff whose high and bending head   75
Looks fearfully in the confinèd deep.
Bring me but to the very brim of it,
And I'll repair the misery thou dost bear
With something rich about me. From that place
I shall no leading need.
EDGAR   Give me thy arm.   80
Poor Tom shall lead thee.   *Exeunt*

Act 4, Scene 2

Enter GONERIL, EDMUND *and* OSWALD

GONERIL   Welcome, my lord. I marvel our mild husband
Not met us on the way.   [*To* OSWALD] Now, where's your
master?
OSWALD   Madam, within, but never man so changed.
I told him of the army that was landed;
He smiled at it. I told him you were coming;   5
His answer was, "The worse." Of Gloucester's treachery,
And of the loyal service of his son
When I informed him, then he called me sot,
And told me I had turned the wrong side out.
What most he should dislike seems pleasant to him,   10
What like, offensive.

---

64. **waiting-women:** women in service of a noblewoman or monarch.
67. **strokes:** blows or attacks.
69. **superfluous and lust-dieted:** excessive and consumed with lust.
70. **slaves your ordinance:** makes a slave of your commands (to suit himself).
72. **distribution:** division.
76. **confinèd deep:** i.e., from the English Channel.
4.2. **Location:** Outside the Duke of Albany's castle.
1. **mild:** (1) overly sensitive or gentle; (2) cowardly.
8. **sot:** fool.

GONERIL   [*To* EDMUND]   Then shall you go no further.
  It is the cowish terror of his spirit
  That dares not undertake. He'll not feel wrongs
  Which tie him to an answer. Our wishes on the way
  May prove effects. Back, Edmund, to my brother.   15
  Hasten his musters and conduct his powers.
  I must change names at home and give the distaff
  Into my husband's hands. This trusty servant
  Shall pass between us. Ere long you are like to hear—
  If you dare venture in your own behalf—   20
  A mistress's command [*Gives him a token*]   Wear this; spare
    speech.
  Decline your head. This kiss, if it durst speak,
  Would stretch thy spirits up into the air.
  Conceive, and fare thee well.
EDMUND   Yours in the ranks of death.
GONERIL   My most dear Gloucester, 25
  Oh, the difference of man and man
  To thee a woman's services are due;
  My Fool usurps my body.   *Exit* [EDMUND]
OSWALD   Madam, here comes my lord.   *Exit*

        Enter ALBANY

GONERIL   I have been worth the whistling.
ALBANY   O Goneril,   30
  You are not worth the dust which the rude wind
  Blows in your face. I fear your disposition.
  That nature which condemns its origin
  Cannot be bordered certain in itself.
  She that herself will sliver and disbranch   35

---

12. **cowish:** cowardly.
15. **effects:** i.e., effective.   **brother:** i.e., brother-in-law Cornwall
16. **Hasten his musters and conduct his powers:** i.e., tell him to quickly gather his men
and bring his troops.
17. **change names:** exchange roles.   **distaff:** spool on which to wind flax (i.e., a house-
wife's role).
21. **spare speech:** i.e., don't speak.
23. **stretch thy spirits up into the air:** sexually arouse you.
24. **Conceive:** (1) succeed; (2) conceive a child with me.
25. **in the ranks:** until.
27. **services:** sexuality.
28. **My Fool:** i.e., Albany, envisioned here as similar to Lear's Fool.   **usurps:** appropriates,
sexually uses.
29. **worth the whistling:** i.e., worth his attention or calling out to (proverbial).
32. **disposition:** behavior, character.
33. **origin:** father (i.e., Lear).
34. **bordered certain:** remain within moral borders or compass.
35–37: Albany complains that Goneril cuts herself off from her own origins (i.e., her family tree).

From her material sap, perforce must wither
And come to deadly use.

GONERIL   No more, the text is foolish.

ALBANY   Wisdom and goodness to the vile seem vile;
Filths savor but themselves. What have you done?
Tigers, not daughters, what have you performed?   40
A father and a gracious, aged man,
Whose reverence even the head-lugged bear would lick,
Most barbarous, most degenerate, have you madded.
Could my good brother suffer you to do it?
A man, a prince, by him so benefited?   45
If that the heavens do not their visible spirits
Send quickly down to tame the vile offences,
It will come.
Humanity must perforce prey on itself
Like monsters of the deep.

GONERIL   Milk-livered man,   50
That bear'st a cheek for blows, a head for wrongs,
Who hast not in thy brows an eye discerning
Thine honor from thy suffering, that not know'st
Fools do those villains pity who are punished
Ere they have done their mischief. Where's thy drum?   55
France spreads his banners in our noiseless land,
With plumèd helm thy state begins thereat,
Whilst thou, a moral fool, sits still and cries
"Alack, why does he so?"

ALBANY   See thyself, devil:
Proper deformity shows not in the fiend   60
So horrid as in woman.

GONERIL   O vain fool!

---

37. **text:** i.e., his moral lecture to her.
40. **Tigers:** i.e., predators.
42. **head-lugged:** pulled at the head.
43. **madded:** made mad or insane.
44. **brother:** i.e., Cornwall.
50. **Milk-livered:** effeminate, cowardly; compare 1.4.327.
55. **drum:** i.e., to announce the arrival of troops.
56. **noiseless:** silent, and unprepared for war.
57. **plumèd helm:** feather-covered helmet.   **thereat:** there, at that point; some editors amend this word to "threats," as in *Q1* and *Q2* (reprinted from *Q1*); however, corrected *Q1* uses "thereat" which seems logical here. In any case, this line is part of three passages that appear in the *Q* texts but not *F* (see Textual Variants) and thus underwent revision, probably on more than one occasion.
58. **moral fool:** (1) a jester concerned with being moral, not usually a jester's subject; (2) foolish man unable to understand how the world works; both senses are ironic, given that Lear's Fool, played by the actor who doubled the role of Cordelia, frequently provides the play's moral conscience.

ALBANY   Thou changèd and self-covered thing, for shame,
     Be-monster not thy feature. Were't my fitness
     To let these hands obey my blood,
     They are apt enough to dislocate and tear   65
     Thy flesh and bones. Howe'er thou art a fiend,
     A woman's shape doth shield thee.
GONERIL   Marry, your manhood, mew!

          Enter a MESSENGER

ALBANY   What news?
MESSENGER   O my good lord, the Duke of Cornwall's dead,   70
     Slain by his servant going to put out
     The other eye of Gloucester.
ALBANY   Gloucester's eyes?
MESSENGER   A servant that he bred, thrilled with remorse,
     Opposed against the act, bending his sword
     To his great master; who, thereat enraged,   75
     Flew on him and amongst them felled him dead,
     But not without that harmful stroke which since
     Hath plucked him after.
ALBANY   This shows you are above,
     You justices, that these our nether crimes
     So speedily can venge. But O, poor Gloucester!   80
     Lost he his other eye?
MESSENGER   Both, both, my lord.
     This letter, madam, craves a speedy answer:
     'Tis from your sister.
GONERIL   [*Aside*] One way I like this well;
     But being widow, and my Gloucester with her,
     May all the building in my fancy pluck   85
     Upon my hateful life. Another way
     The news is not so tart. [*To* MESSENGER]   I'll read, and
          answer.   *Exit*

---

62. **self-covered thing**: disguised object, rather than a truthful woman.
63. **Be-monster**: turn into a monster.
68. **Marry**: by Mary, an interjection of surprise or contempt.   **mew**: meow, an interjection of derision.
73. **bred**: brought up.   **thrilled with**: full of.
75. **thereat**: there, at that point.
76. **felled**: struck.
78. **plucked**: killed (with ironic echo of the plucking out of Gloucester's eyes).
79. **justices**: just or fair gods.   **nether**: lower, i.e., earthly.
80. **venge**: avenge.
83–87: With her husband dead, Regan can pursue Edmund, the man Goneril names as "my Gloucester" (i.e., the new Duke of Gloucester, as his father has been stripped of his title), leaving Goneril's fancy (or sexual fantasy) plucked (or pulled out, used ironically; see note on 1. 78), resulting in a "hateful life." However, the death of Cornwall also means that Regan now lacks support to fight Goneril, to whom this news is, then, not so "tart" or bitter.

ALBANY   Where was his son when they did take his eyes?
MESSENGER   Come with my lady hither.
ALBANY   He is not here.
MESSENGER   No, my good lord; I met him back again.   90
ALBANY   Knows he the wickedness?
MESSENGER   Ay, my good lord; 'twas he informed against him
  And quit the house on purpose that their punishment
  Might have the freer course.
ALBANY   Gloucester, I live
  To thank thee for the love thou showed'st the king,   95
  And to revenge thine eyes. [*To* MESSENGER]   Come hither,
    friend.
  Tell me what more thou know'st.   *Exeunt*

Act 4, Scene 3

Enter KENT [*disguised as* CAIUS] *and a* GENTLEMAN.

KENT   Why the King of France is so suddenly gone back,
  know you no reason?
GENTLEMAN   Something he left imperfect in the state which
  since his coming forth is thought of, which imports to the
  kingdom so much fear and danger that his personal return   5
  was most required and necessary.
KENT   Who hath he left behind him general?
GENTLEMAN   The Marshal of France, Monsieur La Far.
KENT   Did your letters pierce the queen to any demonstration
  of grief?   10
GENTLEMAN   Ay, sir. She took them, read them in my pres-
    ence,
  And now and then an ample tear trilled down
  Her delicate cheek. It seemed she was a queen
  Over her passion, who most rebel-like
  Sought to be king o'er her.

---

93. **quit:** left.
94. **have the freer course:** proceed without restriction.
4.3. **Location:** The French camp, near Dover.
3. This scene appears in *Q* but not *F*; it was clearly cut, probably to speed up the action of
Act 4, particularly as this scene consists of narration of events that have happened offstage.
But as Cordelia once again figures largely here in being absent (as in the various remorse-
ful comments about her from Lear, Kent, and the Fool from 1.3. to 3.6), the scene seems
consistent with the *F* text as a whole. In fact, 4.3 serves to reintroduce the audience to
Cordelia, who has been offstage since Lear's banishment of her in 1.1; whether the audience comes to see her as significantly changed (and softened) since then or as misinter-
preted in 1.1 (as harsh and stubborn) is left open. The *Q* scene is interpolated here into this
F-based edition.
4. **imports:** suggests, or carries.
9. **pierce:** move deeply.
12. **ample:** large.

KENT   O, then it moved her?   15
GENTLEMAN   Not to a rage, patience and sorrow stream.
  Who should express her goodliest, you have seen
  Sunshine and rain at once; her smiles and tears
  Were like a better way. Those happy smilets
  That played on her ripe lip seemed not to know   20
  What guests were in her eyes; which parted thence
  As pearls from diamonds dropped. In brief,
  Sorrow would be a rarity most beloved
  If all could so become it.
KENT   Made she no verbal question?   25
GENTLEMAN   Faith, once or twice she heaved the name of fa-
  ther
  Pantingly forth, as if it pressed her heart;
  Cried, "Sisters, sisters! Shame of ladies! Sisters!
  Kent! Father! Sisters! What, i'th'storm? I'th'night?
  Let pity not be believed!" There she shook   30
  The holy water from her heavenly eyes,
  And clamor moistened. Then away she started
  To deal with grief alone.
KENT   It is the stars,
  The stars above us, govern our conditions,
  Else one self mate and make could not beget   35
  Such different issues. You spoke not with her since?
GENTLEMAN   No.
KENT   Was this before the king returned?
GENTLEMAN   No, since.
KENT   Well, sir, the poor distressed Lear's i'th'town,
  Who sometime in his better tune remembers   40
  What we are come about and by no means
  Will yield to see his daughter.
GENTLEMAN   Why, good sir?
KENT   A sovereign shame so elbows him. His own unkindness
  That stripped her from his benediction, turned her

---

19. **smilets:** small smiles.
26. **heaved the name of father:** At 1.1.89, Cordelia insisted to Lear that she could not "heave" her heart "into her mouth" and accede to his love-test; here she indeed heaves her heart into her mouth, at least according to the Gentleman's report.
31. **holy water:** i.e., tears.
33–34. **It is the stars . . . govern our conditions:** Edmund rejected the same belief at 1.2.111–20.
35. **mate and make:** husband and father.
36. **issues:** children.
40. **tune:** reason.
43. **sovereign:** (1) great or overpowering; (2) royal; (3) husband-like (used ironically to mean "paternal."
44. **benediction:** blessing.

To foreign casualties, gave her dear rights   45
To his dog-hearted daughters—these things sting
His mind so venomously that burning shame
Detains him from Cordelia.
GENTLEMAN   Alack, poor gentleman!
KENT   Of Albany's and Cornwall's powers you heard not?
GENTLEMAN   'Tis so. They are afoot.   50
KENT   Well, sir, I'll bring you to our master, Lear,
And leave you to attend him. Some dear cause
Will in concealment wrap me up awhile.
When I am known aright, you shall not grieve
Lending me this acquaintance. I pray you, go   55
Along with me.   *Exeunt*

Act 4, Scene 4

Enter with Drum and Colors, CORDELIA, GENTLEMEN *and*
SOLDIERS

CORDELIA   Alack, 'tis he. Why, he was met even now,
As mad as the vexed sea, singing aloud,
Crowned with rank fumitor and furrow-weeds,
With burdocks, hemlock, nettles, cuckoo-flowers,
Darnel, and all the idle weeds that grow   5
In our sustaining corn. A century send forth.
Search every acre in the high-grown field,
And bring him to our eye.   [*Exit a* GENTLEMAN]
                    What can man's wisdom
In the restoring his bereavèd sense?
He that helps him, take all my outward worth.   10
GENTLEMAN   There is means, madam.
Our foster-nurse of nature is repose,
The which he lacks. That to provoke in him
Are many simples operative, whose power
Will close the eye of anguish.

---

45. **casualties:** i.e., persons of only casual acquaintance, including her husband.
54. **aright:** i.e., as my true self of Kent, rather than Caius.
4.4. **Location:** The French camp, near Dover.
4. **STAGE DIRECTION** *Colors:* banners or flags carried by the troops to signify their nationality or allegiance.
2. **vexed:** distressed.
3–5. **fumitor . . . weeds:** Fumitory and the other plants listed are varieties of herbs, flowers and weeds.
6. **century:** a troop of one hundred soldiers.
10. **outward:** material.
11. **means:** i.e., means to heal him.
12. **foster-nurse:** woman who takes care of children.
14. **simples operative:** useful, simple remedies.

CORDELIA   All blest secrets,   15
   All you unpublished virtues of the earth,
   Spring with my tears; be aidant and remediate
   In the good man's desires. Seek, seek for him,
   Lest his ungoverned rage dissolve the life
   That wants the means to lead it.

    Enter MESSENGER.

MESSENGER   News, madam.   20
   The British powers are marching hitherward.
CORDELIA   'Tis known before. Our preparation stands
   In expectation of them. O dear father,
   It is thy business that I go about.
   Therefore great France   25
   My mourning and importuned tears hath pitied.
   No blown ambition doth our arms incite,
   But love, dear love, and our aged father's right.
   Soon may I hear and see him.   *Exeunt*

Act 4, Scene 5

    Enter REGAN *and* OSWALD.

REGAN   But are my brother's powers set forth?
OSWALD   Ay, madam.
REGAN   Himself in person there?
OSWALD   Madam, with much ado. Your sister is the better soldier.
REGAN   Lord Edmund spake not with your lord at home?   5
OSWALD   No, madam.
REGAN   What might import my sister's letters to him?
OSWALD   I know not, lady.
REGAN   Faith, he is posted hence on serious matter.
   It was great ignorance, Gloucester's eyes being out,   10
   To let him live. Where he arrives he moves
   All hearts against us. Edmund, I think, is gone,

17. **aidant:** helpful.   **remediate:** act as remedies.
20. **wants:** lacks.
24. **It . . . about:** Biblical allusion to the twelve-year-old Christ's words to his worried mother Mary, after he spent three days in the temple discussing theology with the rabbis, "wist [i.e., know] ye not that I must be about my Father's [i.e., God's] business" (Luke 2.49).
25. **France:** the King of France.
4.5. **Location:** The Earl of Gloucester's castle.
1. **powers set forth:** i.e., army already on the move.
5. **spake:** spoke.
7. **import:** (1) mean; (2) bring.
9. **posted:** has quickly left on horseback.

In pity of his misery, to dispatch
His nighted life, moreover to descry
The strength o'th'enemy.   15
OSWALD   I must needs after him, madam, with my letters.
REGAN   Our troops set forth tomorrow. Stay with us.
The ways are dangerous.
OSWALD   I may not, madam.
My lady charged my duty in this business.
REGAN   Why should she write to Edmund? Might not you   20
Transport her purposes by word? Belike—
Some things—I know not what. I'll love thee much:
Let me unseal the letter.
OSWALD   Madam, I had rather—
REGAN   I know your lady does not love her husband.
I am sure of that; and at her late being here   25
She gave strange oeillades and most speaking looks
To noble Edmund. I know you are of her bosom.
OSWALD   I, madam?
REGAN   I speak in understanding; y'are, I know't.
Therefore I do advise you take this note.   30
My lord is dead. Edmund and I have talked,
And more convenient is he for my hand
Than for your lady's. You may gather more.
If you do find him, pray you give him this.
And when your mistress hears thus much from you,   35
I pray desire her call her wisdom to her.
So, fare you well.
If you do chance to hear of that blind traitor,
Preferment falls on him that cuts him off.
OSWALD   Would I could meet him, madam. I should show   40
What party I do follow.
REGAN   Fare thee well.   *Exeunt*

---

13. **dispatch:** be rid of.
14. **nighted:** darkened or unhappy.   **descry:** (1) discover; (2) make known.
16. **must needs:** must go.
18. **ways:** roads.
19. **charged my duty in:** i.e., ordered me to do.
21. **Transport her purposes by word:** i.e., carry her message verbally rather than by letter.
25. **late:** lately.
26. **oeillades:** loving glances.   **speaking:** significant, meaningful.
27. **of her bosom:** i.e., loyal to her.
32. **convenient:** suitable, appropriate.
36. **call her wisdom to her:** act wisely.
39. **Preferment:** advancement or promotion.
41. **party:** side or group.

Act 4, Scene 6

Enter GLOUCESTER *and* EDGAR *[dressed like a peasant]*

GLOUCESTER   When shall I come to th'top of that same hill?
EDGAR   You do climb up it now. Look how we labor!
GLOUCESTER   Methinks the ground is even.
EDGAR   Horrible steep.
  Hark, do you hear the sea?
GLOUCESTER   No, truly.
EDGAR   Why, then your other senses grow imperfect   5
  By your eyes' anguish.
GLOUCESTER   So may it be indeed.
  Methinks thy voice is altered, and thou speakst
  In better phrase and matter than thou didst.
EDGAR   Y'are much deceived. In nothing am I changed
  But in my garments.   10
GLOUCESTER   Methinks y'are better spoken.
EDGAR   Come on, sir, here's the place. Stand still. How fearful
  And dizzy 'tis to cast one's eyes so low!
  The crows and choughs that wing the midway air
  Show scarce so gross as beetles. Halfway down   15
  Hangs one that gathers samphire, dreadful trade!
  Methinks he seems no bigger than his head.
  The fishermen that walked upon the beach
  Appear like mice, and yond tall anchoring barque
  Diminished to her cock, her cock a buoy   20
  Almost too small for sight. The murmuring surge
  That on the unnumbered idle pebble chafes
  Cannot be heard so high. I'll look no more,
  Lest my brain turn and the deficient sight
  Topple down headlong.

4.6. Location: Countryside near Dover.
6. STAGE DIRECTION *peasant:* Edgar later wields a baton or staff against Oswald (l. 230), and probably enters with this stage property.
3. even: flat.
8. in better phrase and matter: i.e., Edgar has evidently forgotten to use Poor Tom's voice and manner of speaking, and Gloucester questions if he is indeed Poor Tom, who took charge of him in 4.1.56.
11: Edgar tries hard here to convince Gloucester that he has been led to the top of the Dover Cliffs, where he plans to commit suicide; in fact, Edgar has led his father to flat, safe ground where he will not be able to injure himself (Gloucester's desire to commit suicide appears in the source material, *The Aracdia*; see pp. 153–156).
14. choughs: jackdaws, a type of chattering crows.
15. gross: large.
16. samphire: plant that grows on sea rocks.   **trade:** occupation or habit.
19. barque: small ship.
20. cock: boat belonging to the barque.   **buoy:** floating object that signals an underwater hazard.
22. chafes: rubs.
25. Topple: fall over from dizziness at such a great height.

GLOUCESTER   Set me where you stand.   25
EDGAR   Give me your hand. You are now within a foot
  Of th'extreme verge. For all beneath the moon
  Would I not leap upright.
GLOUCESTER   Let go my hand.
  Here, friend, 's another purse: in it a jewel
  Well worth a poor man's taking. Fairies and gods   30
  Prosper it with thee. Go thou further off.
  Bid me farewell, and let me hear thee going.
EDGAR   Now fare ye well, good sir.
GLOUCESTER   With all my heart.
EDGAR [*Aside*]   Why I do trifle thus with his despair
  Is done to cure it.
GLOUCESTER   [*He kneels*]   O you mighty gods!   35
  This world I do renounce, and in your sights
  Shake patiently my great affliction off.
  If I could bear it longer and not fall
  To quarrel with your great opposeless wills,
  My snuff and loathèd part of nature should   40
  Burn itself out. If Edgar live, O bless him—
  Now, fellow, fare thee well.   *He falls*
EDGAR   Gone, sir; farewell.
  [*Aside*] And yet I know not how conceit may rob
  The treasury of life when life itself
  Yields to the theft. Had he been where he thought,   45
  By this had thought been past. Alive or dead?
  Hoa, you, sir! Friend? Hear you, sir? Speak!—
  Thus might he pass indeed. Yet he revives.—
  What are you, sir?
GLOUCESTER   Away, and let me die.   50

27. **verge:** edge of the cliff.   **all beneath the moon:** everything on earth.
29. **'s:** is.
34. **trifle:** play.
39. **opposeless:** unable to be opposed.
40. **snuff:** resentment, bitterness.
42. **STAGE DIRECTION** *He falls:* Gloucester falls forward, assuming that he is falling off a cliff; instead he falls onto the flat surface (of the stage).
43. **conceit:** i.e., Gloucester's firm belief (in attempting suicide).
45. **Yields:** gives up; i.e., Edgar fears that Gloucester so wishes to die that he may succeed, even if the slight fall forward did not injure him.
47. Edgar adopts the accent of a peasant here, so he will not be discovered by Gloucester to be the same person as Poor Tom.
48. **pass:** pass away, die.
49. **What:** who.

EDGAR   Hadst thou been aught but goss'mer, feathers, air,
   So many fathom down precipitating,
   Thou'dst shivered like an egg. But thou dost breathe,
   Hast heavy substance, bleed'st not, speak'st, art sound.
   Ten masts at each make not the altitude   55
   Which thou hast perpendicularly fell.
   Thy life's a miracle. Speak yet again.
GLOUCESTER   But have I fallen or no?
EDGAR   From the dread summit of this chalky bourn.
   Look up a-height: the shrill-gorged lark so far   60
   Cannot be seen or heard; do but look up.
GLOUCESTER   Alack, I have no eyes.
   Is wretchedness deprived that benefit
   To end itself by death? 'Twas yet some comfort
   When misery could beguile the tyrant's rage   65
   And frustrate his proud will.
EDGAR   Give me your arm.
   Up; so. How is't? Feel you your legs? You stand.
GLOUCESTER   Too well, too well.
EDGAR   This is above all strangeness.
   Upon the crown o'th'cliff, what thing was that
   Which parted from you?
GLOUCESTER   A poor unfortunate beggar.   70
EDGAR   As I stood here below, methought his eyes
   Were two full moons. He had a thousand noses,
   Horns whelked and waved like the enragèd sea.
   It was some fiend. Therefore, thou happy father,
   Think that the clearest gods, who make their honors   75
   Of men's impossibilities, have preserved thee.
GLOUCESTER   I do remember now. Henceforth I'll bear
   Affliction till it do cry out itself
   "Enough, enough," and die. That thing you speak of,
   I took it for a man. Often 'twould say   80
   "The fiend, the fiend!" He led me to that place.

---

51. **aught:** anything. **goss'mer:** gossamer:
52. **fathom down precipitating:** measures (of five feet) falling down so quickly.
53. **shivered:** shattered.
54. **heavy:** solid, intact. **sound:** well.
55. **Ten masts at each:** i.e., the height of ten ships' masts put together.
56. **perpendicularly:** vertically.
59. **chalky bourn:** white area (from the "white cliffs of Dover").
60. **shrill-gorged:** shrill-throated or voiced.
65. **beguile:** overcome.
67. **Up; so:** Gloucester has remained on the ground since falling over.
69. **thing:** i.e., person.
73. **whelked:** twisted like a whelk (a mollusk).

EDGAR   Bear free and patient thoughts.

Enter LEAR, *mad.*

But who comes here?
The safer sense will ne'er accommodate
His master thus.

LEAR   No, they cannot touch me for coining. I am the king   85
himself.

EDGAR   O thou side-piercing sight!

LEAR   Nature's above art in that respect. There's your press-
money. That fellow handles his bow like a crow-keeper.
Draw me a clothier's yard. Look, look, a mouse! Peace,   90
peace, this piece of toasted cheese will do't. There's my
gauntlet. I'll prove it on a giant. Bring up the brown bills. O
well flown, bird, i'th'clout, i'th'clout! Hewgh! Give the word!

EDGAR   Sweet marjoram.

LEAR   Pass.   95

GLOUCESTER   I know that voice.

LEAR   Ha! Goneril with a white beard! Ha, Regan! They flattered me like a dog and told me I had the white hairs in my
beard ere the black ones were there. To say "ay" and "no" to
everything that I said "ay" and "no" to was no good divinity.   100
When the rain came to wet me once and the wind to make
me chatter, when the thunder would not peace at my bid-

---

82. free: i.e., calm.   **STAGE DIRECTION mad:** Lear enters here crowned with the kind of herbs, flowers, and weeds described at 4.4.3–5.

83. safer sense: sane mind.

84. master: person or body; i.e., a man with a same mind would never behave or appear thus.

85. touch me for coining: lay hands on, or apprehend, me for making coins (monarchs only enjoyed the privilege of minting or producing coins); "coining" appears in Q only, as F has "crying"; the interpolation of "coining" into an edition set from F is now standard among editors.

87. side-piercing: An allusion to Christ being pierced in the side by a soldier after having been crucified (John 19.34), i.e., even when a man thinks he has suffered the most pain possible, more suffering can occur.

88. Nature's . . . respect: Lear (referring to his words "I am the king himself" in 1.85–86) claims that a king made by nature is more genuine than one made by artifice.

88–89. press-money: (1) loan to a sovereign in an emergency (*OED*); (2) payment made to a man being pressed, or enlisted, into military service (Lear thinks he is building an army, hence his complaint about the poor archer in 1.89). His true madness can be compared to the feigned madness of Edgar (as Poor Tom) in 3.4 and 3.6.

89. handles . . . crow-keeper: handles his bow and arrow like a scarecrow (i.e., ineptly).

90. Draw . . . yard: draw the bow out to its full position.

91. do't: do it, here used to mean "catch the mouse"; Lear's *non-sequiturs* suggest his irrationality.

92. gauntlet: i.e., Lear has thrown down his gauntlet, or glove, as a sign that he is challenging the mouse to a duel; this is an ironic foreshadowing of Albany throwing down his gauntlet to Edmund in 5.2, and the duel between Edgar and Edmund in 5.3.

92. prove it on a giant: repeat the challenge even to a giant.

92. bills: weapons combining a spear and battle-ax (*OED*).

93. i'th'clout: in the clout, or target-center (for an archer).

100. divinity: (1) divine, or royal, quality; (2) ability to be adored.

102. peace: i.e., stop.

ding, there I found 'em, there I smelt 'em out. Go to, they
are not men of their words. They told me I was everything.
'Tis a lie; I am not ague-proof.   105
GLOUCESTER   The trick of that voice I do well remember.
Is't not the king?
LEAR   Ay, every inch a king!
When I do stare, see how the subject quakes.
I pardon that man's life. What was thy cause?
Adultery? Thou shalt not die! Die for adultery?   110
No, the wren goes to't, and the small gilded fly
Does lecher in my sight. Let copulation thrive,
For Gloucester's bastard son was kinder to his father
Than my daughters got 'tween the lawful sheets.
To't, luxury, pell-mell, for I lack soldiers.   115
Behold yon simp'ring dame,
Whose face between her forks presages snow,
That minces virtue, and does shake the head
To hear of pleasure's name.
The fitchew nor the soilèd horse goes to't   120
With a more riotous appetite.
Down from the waist they are centaurs,
Though women all above.
But to the girdle do the gods inherit;
Beneath is all the fiend's. There's hell, there's darkness,   125
There is the sulphurous pit, burning, scalding,
Stench, consumption. Fie, fie, fie! Pah, pah!
Give me an ounce of civet. Good apothecary,
Sweeten my imagination. There's money for thee.
GLOUCESTER   O, let me kiss that hand!   130
LEAR   Let me wipe it first; it smells of mortality.

105. **ague-proof:** immune from fever or flu, i.e., omnipotent.
106. **trick:** i.e., familiar sound.
110. **adultery:** implied by the play to be Gloucester's sin in producing Edmund.
111. **wren:** small bird.
112. **lecher:** act lecherously, or sexually promiscuously.
114. **got . . . sheets:** begotten, or conceived, in legal marriage.
115. **To't:** go to it, i.e., copulate.   **pell-mell:** (1) in any possible combination; (2) collectively, in a mass.   **lack soldiers:** need soldiers to be conceived.
116. **simp'ring:** simpering, i.e., flirtatious.
117. **forks:** legs.   **presages snow:** foretells chastity (or coldness).
118. **minces virtue:** i.e., pretends to be chaste. Lear is preoccupied in these lines with the woman who pretends to be sexually chaste (putting her face between her "forks" or legs, so as to prevent men access to her genitals) but is in fact promiscuous.
120. **fitchew:** polecat.   **soilèd:** defiled.
121. **riotous:** unrestrained; in 1.4. Goneril complained repeatedly about Lear's "riotous" knights.
122. **centaurs:** mythological creatures with the head, arms, and upper body of a man and lower body and legs of a horse (and thus are lusty).
124. **girdle:** a woman's belt.
128. **civet:** perfume.   **apothecary:** preparer and seller of drugs and medicines.

GLOUCESTER   O ruined piece of nature! This great world
  Shall so wear out to naught. Dost thou know me?
LEAR   I remember thine eyes well enough. Dost thou squiny
  at me?
  No, do thy worst, blind Cupid, I'll not love.   135
  Read thou this challenge, mark but the penning of it.
GLOUCESTER   Were all thy letters suns, I could not see one.
EDGAR [*Aside*]   I would not take this from report; it is,
  And my heart breaks at it.
LEAR   Read.   140
GLOUCESTER   What? With the case of eyes?
LEAR   O ho, are you there with me? No eyes in your head, nor
  no money in your purse? Your eyes are in a heavy case, your
  purse in a light; yet you see how this world goes.
GLOUCESTER   I see it feelingly.   145
LEAR   What, art mad? A man may see how this world goes
  with no eyes; look with thine ears. See how yond justice
  rails upon yond simple thief. Hark in thine ear: change
  places and handy-dandy, which is the Justice, which is the
  thief? Thou hast seen a farmer's dog bark at a beggar?   150
GLOUCESTER   Ay, sir.
LEAR   And the creature run from the cur? There thou mightst
  behold the great image of authority. A dog's obeyed in office.
  Thou rascal beadle, hold thy bloody hand.
  Why dost thou lash that whore? Strip thy own back.   155
  Thou hotly lusts to use her in that kind
  For which thou whip'st her. The usurer hangs the cozener.
  Thorough tattered clothes great vices do appear:
  Robes and furred gowns hide all. Plate sin with gold,
  And the strong lance of justice hurtless breaks;   160
  Arm it in rags, a pygmy's straw does pierce it.
  None does offend, none, I say none. I'll able 'em.
  Take that of me, my friend, who have the power

---

133. **naught:** nothing, the central measurement on which the play's characters have
focused thus far.
134. **squiny:** squint.
135. **blind Cupid:** in Roman mythology, Cupid, the god of love, shot his darts of love
while blind or blindfolded, so that love could rise indiscriminately and randomly.
136. **Read thou:** Lear hands them a real or imagined letter, which the blinded Gloucester
would not be able to read.
138. **take this from report:** believe this if it was reported to me; but "it is" real.
145. **feelingly:** (1) too much; (2) through feeling or touch.
148. **change:** exchange.
149. **handy-dandy:** a child's game involving changing places.
154. **beadle:** a low-ranking officer of the law.
156. **kind:** way.
157. **usurer:** money-lender.   **cozener:** cheater.
159. **Robes . . . all:** This is the lesson Lear learned on the heath at 3.4.96–101 (compare
3.6.36).   **Plate:** cover.

To seal th'accuser's lips. Get thee glass eyes,
And, like a scurvy politician, seem   165
To see the things thou dost not. Now, now, now, now.
Pull off my boots. Harder, harder! So.

EDGAR [*Aside*]   O matter and impertinency mixed,
Reason in madness.

LEAR   If thou wilt weep my fortunes, take my eyes.   170
I know thee well enough. Thy name is Gloucester.
Thou must be patient. We came crying hither.
Thou know'st the first time that we smell the air
We wail and cry. I will preach to thee. Mark.

GLOUCESTER   Alack, alack the day.   175

LEAR   When we are born, we cry that we are come
To this great stage of fools. This a good block.
It were a delicate stratagem to shoe
A troop of horse with felt, I'll put't in proof.
And when I have stole upon these son-in-laws,   180
Then kill, kill, kill, kill, kill, kill!

     Enter three GENTLEMEN

[FIRST] GENTLEMAN [*To* LEAR]   O here he is: lay hands upon
   him. Sir,
Your most dear daughter—

LEAR   No rescue? What, a prisoner? I am e'en
The natural fool of fortune. Use me well.   185
You shall have ransom. Let me have surgeons,
I am cut to'th'brains.

[FIRST] GENTLEMAN   You shall have anything.

LEAR   No seconds? All myself?
Why, this would make a man a man of salt,
To use his eyes for garden water-pots   190
Ay, and laying autumn's dust.

[FIRST] GENTLEMAN   Good sir—

LEAR   I will die bravely,
Like a smug bridegroom. What? I will be jovial.
Come, come, I am a king, masters, know you that?

---

165. **scurvy:** worthless, or diseased.
168. **matter and impertinency:** i.e., significant and irrelevant matters.
174. **Mark:** i.e., pay attention.
177. **block:** scheme or contrivance.
178. **stratagem:** trick.
179. **felt:** soft woolen material, hence inappropriate to serve as horseshoes (usually made of iron).
185. **fool of fortune:** Lear still sees himself as subject to fate (here, the goddess Fortune) rather than as able to exercise free will.
188. **seconds:** attendants (at a duel).
189. **salt:** crying salty tears.
192. **die:** This word carried a second meaning of "to reach sexual climax," hence the "smug" or satisfied bridegroom in l. 193.

[FIRST] GENTLEMAN   You are a royal one, and we obey you.   195
LEAR   Then there's life in't. Come, and you get it;
    You shall get it by running. Sa', sa', sa', sa'!

Exit LEAR *running [pursued by two* GENTLEMEN]

[FIRST] GENTLEMAN   A sight most pitiful in the meanest
    wretch,
    Past speaking of in a king. Thou hast a daughter
    Who redeems nature from the general curse   200
    Which twain have brought her to.
EDGAR   Hail, gentle sir.
[FIRST] GENTLEMAN   Sir, speed you: what's your will?
EDGAR   Do you hear aught, sir, of a battle toward?
[FIRST] GENTLEMAN   Most sure and vulgar: everyone hears that,
    Which can distinguish sound.
EDGAR   But, by your favor,   205
    How near's the other army?
[FIRST] GENTLEMAN   Near and on speedy foot. The main de-
    scry
    Stands on the hourly thought.
EDGAR   I thank you, sir. That's all.
[FIRST] GENTLEMAN   Though that the queen on special cause
    is here,   210
    Her army is moved on.
EDGAR   I thank you, sir.   *Exit* [GENTLEMEN]
GLOUCESTER   You ever gentle gods, take my breath from me.
    Let not my worser spirit tempt me again
    To die before you please.
EDGAR   Well pray you, father.
GLOUCESTER   Now, good sir, what are you?   215
EDGAR   A most poor man, made tame to fortune's blows,
    Who by the art of known and feeling sorrows
    Am pregnant to good pity. Give me your hand;
    I'll lead you to some biding.

---

197. **Sa'**: contraction of "save" (*OED*), as in "God save me"; most editors assume instead that the word reflects some form of hunting cry or challenge.
199. **Past**: beyond.
200. **general curse**: i.e., original sin, the Biblical fall of Adam and Eve in the Garden of Eden (Genesis 1–3) through temptation by the devil, with the further implication that women were then "cursed" by God to suffer pain through childbirth (and thus from sexuality).
201. **twain**: (1) Adam and Eve; (2) Cordelia's two sisters.
202. **speed**: contraction of "God save you," a gracious greeting.
207. **descry**: discover or announcement.
208. **hourly thought**: i.e., constantly.
218. **pregnant to**: full of.

GLOUCESTER   Hearty thanks;
The bounty and the benison of heaven   220
To boot, to boot.

    Enter OSWALD

OSWALD   A proclaimed prize! Most happy!
That eyeless head of thine was first framed flesh
To raise my fortunes. Thou old unhappy traitor,
Briefly thyself remember: the sword is out
That must destroy thee.
GLOUCESTER   Now let thy friendly hand   225
Put strength enough to't.
OSWALD   Wherefore, bold peasant,
Dar'st thou support a published traitor? Hence,
Lest the infection of his fortune take
Like hold on thee. Let go his arm!
EDGAR [*In a West Country accent*]   Chi'll not let go, zir, with-   230
out vurther 'casion.
OSWALD   Let go slave, or thou diest.
EDGAR   Good gentleman, go your gait, and let poor volk pass.
And ch'ud ha'bin zwaggered out of my life, 'twould not ha'
bin zo long as 'tis by a vortnight. Nay, come not near th'old   235
man. Keep out, che vor'ye, or I'ce try whether your costard
or my ballow be the harder; chi'll be plain with you.
OSWALD [*Draw his sword*]   Out, dunghill!   *They fight*
EDGAR   Chi'll pick your teeth, zir. Come, no matter vor your
foins.   [EDGAR *wounds* OSWALD]   240
OSWALD   Slave, thou hast slain me. Villain, take my purse.
If ever thou wilt thrive, bury my body,
And give the letters which thou find'st about me

---

220. benison: blessing.
221. To boot: (1) in addition; (2) to your advantage.
222. A proclaimed prize: i.e., Goneril and Regan promised a reward to anyone who cap-
tured Gloucester.
225. friendly: desired, i.e., Gloucester is still suicidal.
230. STAGE DIRECTION West Country accent: Conventionally, English West Country
accents were used on stage to represent a country bumpkin or clown. Edgar thus pro-
nounces "I'll" as "Ch'ill," "for" as "vor," etc; F intensifies this accent by providing the pho-
netic spelling used here.   **'casion:** i.e., occasion.
234. And ch'ud ha'bin: i.e., If I could have been.   **zwaggered:** blustered, bragged.
235. by a vortnight: i.e., Edgar claims that if Oswald could have hurt him with so much
verbal abuse, it would have happened already (i.e., before a fortnight, or two weeks, had
passed).
236. che vor'ye: i.e., I warn thee.   **I'ce:** i.e., I shall.   **costard:** i.e., head.
237. ballow: baton or staff.
238. dunghill: hill of dung or rubbish.
239. pick your teeth: i.e., with his weapon.
240. foins: clumsy jabs by a sword.

To Edmund, Earl of Gloucester: seek him out
Upon the English party. O untimely death! Death!   245

                    He dies

EDGAR   I know thee well—a serviceable villain,
   As duteous to the vices of thy mistress
   As badness would desire.
GLOUCESTER   What, is he dead?
EDGAR   Sit you down, father; rest you.
   Let's see these pockets. The letters that he speaks of   250
   May be my friends. He's dead. I am only sorry
   He had no other deaths-man. Let us see.
   Leave, gentle wax, and manners, blame us not.
   To know our enemies' minds, we rip their hearts;
   Their papers is more lawful.   255
   [*Reads the letter*] "Let our reciprocal vows be remembered.
   You have many opportunities to cut him off. If your will
   want not, time and place will be fruitfully offered. There is
   nothing done, if he return the conqueror; then am I the
   prisoner, and his bed my jail from the loathed warmth   260
   whereof, deliver me, and supply the place for your labor.
   Your wife (so I would say), your affectionate servant, and
   for you her own for venture, Goneril."
   O indistinguished space of woman's will!
   A plot upon her virtuous husband's life,   265
   And the exchange my brother!—Here in the sands
   Thee I'll rake up, the post unsanctified
   Of murderous lechers, and in the mature time
   With this ungracious paper strike the sight
   Of the death-practiced duke. For him 'tis well   270
   That of thy death and business I can tell.

                    [*Exit, dragging out* OSWALD's *body*]

GLOUCESTER   The king is mad. How stiff is my vile sense,
   That I stand up and have ingenious feeling
   Of my huge sorrows! Better I were distract,
   So should my thoughts be severed from my griefs,   275

---

246. **serviceable:** i.e., willing to serve anyone (see Kent's application of this term to Oswald at 2.2.16).
252. **deaths-man:** (1) executioner; (2) companion at his death.
253. **leave gentle wax:** i.e., he is ripping open the letter, sealed by wax.
257. **him:** i.e., Albany.
261. **labor:** i.e., sexual enjoyment.
264. **will:** (1) command or desire; (2) genitalia.
267. **post:** place.
268. **mature:** later, and more appropriate.
270. **death-practiced:** experienced at murder.
274. **distract:** distracted, mad.

And woes by wrong imaginations lose
The knowledge of themselves.

     A drum afar off. [*Enter* EDGAR]

EDGAR   Give me your hand.
Far of methinks I hear the beaten drum.
Come, father, I'll bestow you with a friend.   *Exeunt*

Act 4, Scene 7.

    Enter CORDELIA, KENT [*disguised as* CAIUS], *and* GENTLE-
MAN

CORDELIA   O thou good Kent, how shall I live and work
To match thy goodness? My life will be too short,
And every measure fail me.
KENT   To be acknowledged, madam, is o'erpaid.
All my reports go with the modest truth,   5
Nor more, nor clipped, but so.
CORDELIA   Be better suited:
These weeds are memories of those worser hours.
I prithee, put them off.
KENT   Pardon, dear madam.
Yet to be known shortens my made intent.
My boon I make it that you know me not   10
Till time and I think meet.
CORDELIA   Then be't so, my good lord.—How does the king?
GENTLEMAN   Madam, sleeps still.
CORDELIA   O you kind gods,
Cure this great breach in his abusèd nature;   15
The untuned and jarring senses, O, wind up
Of this child-changèd father!
GENTLEMAN   So please your majesty,
That we may wake the king? He hath slept long.

278. **drum:** i.e., of an approaching army.
279. **bestow you with:** place you in the care of.
4.7. **Location:** The French camp, near Dover.
3. **measure:** attempt.
6. **Nor more, nor clipped, but so:** not more or less (i.e., cut short), but just so or even,
reminiscent of Cordelia's measurement of love for Lear at 1.1.91.
7. **weeds:** i.e., Caius's attire.
9. **to be known . . . intent:** i.e., to reveal myself as Kent would upset my plan.
10. **boon:** request.   **know me not:** i.e., reveal me to be Kent.
13. **GENTLEMAN:** While Q presents both a Doctor and a Gentleman as attendants on
Lear, F condenses the characters into one Gentleman, who speaks the lines of both Q characters. This revision undoubtedly was done to cut one actor from the scene.
15. **breach:** break.
17. **child-changèd:** (1) changed into a child; (2) changed (into madness) by his children.

CORDELIA   Be governed by your knowledge and proceed
  I'th'sway of your own will. Is he arrayed?   20

  Enter LEAR *[asleep] in a chair carried by* SERVANTS

GENTLEMAN   Ay, madam. In the heaviness of sleep
  We put fresh garments on him.
  Be by, good madam, when we do awake him;
  I doubt of his temperance.
CORDELIA   Very well.
GENTLEMAN   Please you, draw near. [*Music within*]—Louder
  the music there!   25
CORDELIA   O my dear father, restoration hang
  Thy medicine on my lips, and let this kiss
  Repair those violent harms that my two sisters
  Have in thy reverence made.
KENT   Kind and dear princess!
CORDELIA   Had you not been their father, these white flakes 30
  Did challenge pity of them. Was this a face
  To be opposed against the warring winds?
  To stand against the deep dread-bolted thunder?
  In the most terrible and nimble stroke
  Of quick cross lightning? To watch, poor perdu,   35
  With this thin helm? Mine enemy's dog,
  Though he had bit me, should have stood that night
  Against my fire. And wast thou fain, poor father,
  To hovel thee with swine and rogues forlorn
  In short and musty straw? Alack, alack,   40
  'Tis wonder that thy life and wits at once
  Had not concluded all. [*To the* GENTLEMAN] He wakes.
    Speak to him.
GENTLEMAN   Madam, do you; 'tis fittest.
CORDELIA   How does my royal lord? How fares your majesty?
LEAR   You do me wrong to take me out o'th'grave.   45
  Thou art a soul in bliss, but I am bound

20. **I'th'sway:** in the rule.   **arrayed:** dressed appropriately (as a king).
24. **temperance:** i.e., sanity.
29. **reverence:** respect and veneration.
30. **flakes:** i.e., his thin hair.
31. **Did challenge:** i.e., should have provoked.
35. **perdu:** lost one.
38. **Against:** next to.   **fain:** obliged.
42. **concluded all:** i.e., caused your death.
44. Cordelia treats Lear as her father first and her king second.
46. **soul in bliss:** i.e., spirit in heaven.

Upon a wheel of fire, that mine own tears
Do scald like molten lead.

CORDELIA   Sir, do you know me?

LEAR   You are a spirit, I know. Where did you die?   50

CORDELIA   Still, still far wide.

GENTLEMAN   He's scarce awake. Let him alone a while.

LEAR   Where have I been? Where am I? Fair daylight?
I am mightily abused. I should e'en die with pity
To see another thus. I know not what to say.   55
I will not swear these are my hands. Let's see:
I feel this pin prick. Would I were assured
Of my condition.

CORDELIA   Oh look upon me, sir,
And hold your hand in benediction o'er me.
No, sir, you must not kneel.

LEAR   Pray do not mock me.   60
I am a very foolish, fond old man,
Fourscore and upward,
Not an hour more, nor less,
And to deal plainly,
I fear I am not in my perfect mind.   65
Methinks I should know you and know this man;
Yet I am doubtful, for I am mainly ignorant
What place this is, and all the skill I have
Remembers not these garments, nor I know not
Where I did lodge last night. Do not laugh at me,   70
For, as I am a man, I think this lady
To be my child Cordelia.

CORDELIA   And so I am, I am.

LEAR   Be your tears wet? Yes, faith. I pray, weep not.
If you have poison for me, I will drink it.
I know you do not love me; for your sisters   75
Have, as I do remember, done me wrong.
You have some cause; they have not.

CORDELIA   No cause, no cause.

LEAR   Am I in France?

---

47. **wheel of fire:** This metaphor embodies both pagan and Christian images of suffering from and expiation of sin; once again Lear sees himself as being victimized by external forces rather than his own actions.
48. **molten:** liquefied by burning.
51. **far wide:** i.e., far from sane.
58. **condition:** i.e., being alive.
62. **Fourscore:** eighty.
63. **Not an hour more, nor less:** see note on 1.6.
71. **as I am a man:** Lear sees himself, for the first time, as a man, subject to physical and psychological suffering, rather than a monarch, the same type of "unaccommodated" man he discovered in Poor Tom at 3.4.100.
77. **No cause, no cause:** an ironic echo of "Nothing" (1.1.85).

KENT   In your own kingdom, sir.

LEAR   Do not abuse me.

GENTLEMAN   Be comforted, good madam. The great rage   80
You see is killed in him, and yet it is danger
To make him even o'er the time he has lost.
Desire him to go in. Trouble him no more
Till further settling.

CORDELIA   Will't please your highness walk?

LEAR   You must bear with me. Pray you now, forget   85
And forgive. I am old and foolish.

                         Exeunt. Manet KENT *and* GENTLEMAN

GENTLEMAN   Holds it true, sir, that the Duke of Cornwall was
so slain?

KENT   Most certain, sir.

GENTLEMAN   Who is conductor of his people?   90

KENT   As 'tis said, the bastard son of Gloucester.

GENTLEMAN   They say Edgar, his banished son, is with the
Earl of Kent in Germany.

KENT   Report is changeable. 'Tis time to look about. The powers of the kingdom approach apace.   95

GENTLEMAN   The arbitrement is like to be bloody. Fare you
well, sir.   [*Exit*]

KENT   My point and period will be throughly wrought
Or well or ill as this day's battle's fought.   *Exit*

Act 5, Scene 1

Enter with drum and colors, EDMUND, REGAN, GENTLE-
MEN *and* SOLDIERS

EDMUND [*To a* GENTLEMAN]   Know of the duke if his last pur-
pose hold,
Or whether since he is advised by aught
To change the course? He's full of alteration

---

79. **abuse:** mislead.
84. **settling:** i.e., settling down or resting.
86. **STAGE DIRECTION Manet:** remaining.
87–99: These lines appear in Q but not F and were probably cut to save time, as they nar-
rate, rather than show, action.
90. **conductor:** leader.
94. **Report is changeable:** i.e., rumors are unreliable.
95. **apace:** quickly.
96. **arbitrement:** result.
98. **My point . . . wrought:** i.e., my commitment and time will be thoroughly used.
5.1. **Location:** The British camp near Dover.
1. **STAGE DIRECTION drum and colors:** drummers marching with flag-bearers, representing the combined troops of Edmund and Regan.
1–2. **last purpose:** most recent decision, i.e., to join the troops of Edmund and Regan
against the French.
3. **the course:** his decision to fight.

And self-reproving. Bring his constant pleasure.

                              [Exit GENTLEMAN]

REGAN   Our sister's man is certainly miscarried.   5

EDMUND   'Tis to be doubted, madam.

REGAN   Now, sweet lord,

  You know the goodness I intend upon you.

  Tell me but truly, but then speak the truth,

  Do you not love my sister?

EDMUND   In honored love.

REGAN   But have you never found my brother's way   10

  To the forfended place?

EDMUND   That thought abuses you.

REGAN   I am doubtful that you have been conjunct

  And bosomed with her, as far as we call hers.

EDMUND   No, by mine honor, madam.

REGAN   I never shall endure her. Dear my lord,   15

  Be not familiar with her.

EDMUND   Fear me not.

  She and the duke her husband—

        Enter with drum and colors, ALBANY, GONERIL, [*and*]
        SOLDIERS

GONERIL [*Aside*]   I had rather lose the battle than that sister

  Should loosen him and me.

ALBANY   Our very loving sister, well bemet.   20

  Sir, this I heard: the king is come to his daughter,

  With others whom the rigor of our state

  Forced to cry out. Where I could not be honest,

  I never yet was valiant. For this business,

  It touches us as France invades our land,   25

  Not bolds the king with others whom I fear

  Most just and heavy causes make oppose.

---

4. **Bring his constant pleasure:** bring news of his current decision as to whether to fight.
5. **man:** i.e., Oswald.   **miscarried:** i.e., failed or gotten into some trouble.
6. **doubted:** assumed or feared.
9. **honored:** i.e., chaste and dignified.
11. **forfended place:** Goneril's bed (and her body).   **abuses:** degrades.
12–13. **conjunct / And bosomed:** i.e., sexually joined and intimate.
13. **hers:** hers in every way.
15. **endure her:** put up with her (and any involvement with Edmund).
16. **familiar:** intimate.
19. **loosen:** split apart.
20. **bemet:** met.
22–23: **others . . . cry out:** i.e., Cordelia's French troops have been joined by English soldiers who have rebelled, or cried out, against the harshness, or "rigor," in the kingdom since
Lear's abdication. These and the following lines make clear that the French foreign war co-
exists with the civil threat, even in the *F* text, which appears to cut systematically references
to the French invasion (see note on 3.1.22–29).
25–27. **touches . . . oppose:** i.e., Albany is willing to join Edmund and Regan in battle
against the French although he recognizes that the English soldiers who have joined Lear
are "just," or justified, in their rebellion.

EDMUND   Sir, you speak nobly.

REGAN   Why is this reasoned?

GONERIL   Combine together 'gainst the enemy;
  For these domestic and particular broils   30
  Are not the question here.

ALBANY   Let us then determine with th'ancient of war
  On our proceeding.

EDMUND   I shall attend you presently at your tent.   [*Exit*]

REGAN   Sister, you'll go with us?   35

GONERIL   No.

REGAN   'Tis most convenient. Pray you, go with us.

GONERIL [*Aside*]   O ho, I know the riddle! I will go.

Enter EDGAR [*disguised as a peasant*]

EDGAR [*To* ALBANY]   If e'er your grace had speech with man so
    poor,
  Hear me one word.

ALBANY [*To the others*]   I'll overtake you.

Exeunt [GONERIL, REGAN], *and both the armies*

                              Speak.   40

EDGAR   Before you fight the battle, ope this letter.
  If you have victory, let the trumpet sound
  For him that brought it. Wretched though I seem,
  I can produce a champion that will prove
  What is avouchèd there. If you miscarry,   45
  Your business of the world hath so an end,
  And machination ceases. Fortune loves you.

ALBANY   Stay till I have read the letter.

EDGAR   I was forbid it.
  When time shall serve, let but the herald cry,   50
  And I'll appear again.   *Exit*

ALBANY   Why, fare thee well. I will o'erlook thy paper.

Enter EDMUND

EDMUND   The enemy's in view; draw up your powers.
  [*Gives him a letter*] Here is the guess of their true strength
    and forces

---

30. **domestic and particular broils:** civil and specific quarrels.
32. **th'ancient of war:** senior officer or commander, thus experienced in war.
38. **riddle:** i.e., trick.
39. **poor:** poorly attired.
41. **ope:** open.
45. **avouchèd:** affirmed;   **miscarry:** fail.
47. **machination:** plotting, conspiracy; compare 1.2.106.
50. **herald cry:** trumpeter sound.
52. **o'erlook:** read over.
54. **guess:** estimate.

By diligent discovery; but your haste   55
Is now urged on you.
ALBANY   We will greet the time.   *Exit*
EDMUND   To both these sisters have I sworn my love,
Each jealous of the other as the stung
Are of the adder. Which of them shall I take?
Both? One? Or neither? Neither can be enjoyed   60
If both remain alive. To take the widow
Exasperates, makes mad her sister Goneril,
And hardly shall I carry out my side,
Her husband being alive. Now then, we'll use
His countenance for the battle, which being done,   65
Let her that would be rid of him devise
His speedy taking off. As for the mercy
Which he intends to Lear and to Cordelia,
The battle done, and they within our power,
Shall never see his pardon; for my state   70
Stands on me to defend, not to debate.   *Exit*

Act 5, Scene 2

Alarum within. Enter with drum and colors, LEAR,
CORDELIA, *and* SOLDIERS, *over the stage, and exeunt. Enter* EDGAR *and* GLOUCESTER

EDGAR   Here, father, take the shadow of this tree
For your good host. Pray that the right may thrive.
If ever I return to you again
I'll bring you comfort.
GLOUCESTER   Grace go with you, sir.   *Exit*

Alarum and retreat within. Enter EDGAR

EDGAR   Away, old man! Give me thy hand; away!   5
King Lear hath lost, he and his daughter ta'en.
Give me thy hand. Come on.

---

56. greet the time: deal with it immediately.
59. adder: poisonous snake.
63. side: plan.
65. countenance: position, authority.
67. taking off: death.
5.2. Location: Near the battlefield.
1. father: old man (with ironic use of its real meaning of "parent").
2. good host: i.e., stand by for protection.
4. STAGE DIRECTION *Alarum and retreat within:* i.e., noises of battle and withdrawal
of an army offstage (usually staged by characters shouting or running in the wings or upstage).
6. ta'en: taken.

GLOUCESTER   No further, sir; a man may rot even here.

EDGAR   What, in ill thoughts again? Men must endure
Their going hence even as their coming hither: / 10
Ripeness is all. Come on.

GLOUCESTER   And that's true too.   *Exeunt*

Act 5, Scene 3

Enter in conquest with drum and colors EDMUND,
[with] LEAR *and* CORDELIA, *as prisoners*; SOLDIERS, CAP-
TAIN

EDMUND   Some officers take them away: good guard,
Until their greater pleasures first be known
That are to censure them.

CORDELIA   We are not the first
Who with best meaning have incurred the worst.
For thee, oppressèd king, am I cast down,   5
Myself could else out-frown false fortune's frown.
Shall we not see these daughters and these sisters?

LEAR   No, no, no, no. Come, let's away to prison.
We two alone will sing like birds i'th'cage.
When thou dost ask me blessing, I'll kneel down   10
And ask of thee forgiveness: so we'll live,
And pray, and sing, and tell old tales, and laugh
At gilded butterflies, and hear poor rogues
Talk of court news, and we'll talk with them too—
Who loses and who wins; who's in, who's out—   15
And take upon 's the mystery of things,
As if we were God's spies; and we'll wear out

---

10. **going hence**: death   **coming hither**: birth.
11. **Ripeness is all**: readiness, or the appropriate time, is everything (i.e., nothing should
be done before the appropriate time).
5.3. **Location**: The scene continues.
1. **good guard**: i.e., guard them securely.
2. **their**: i.e., referring to Regan, Goneril, and Albany.
3. **censure them**: punish Lear and Cordelia.
4. **best meaning**: the best, or most noble or just, intentions.
5. **cast down**: distressed (with ironic meaning of "banished" or "reduced in circumstances").
6. **out-frown false fortune's frown**: overcome the false-hearted displeasure of the goddess
Fortune.
7. **these**: used contemptuously, and pitiably, in place of "our," to stress the unnatural unkindness and lack of kinship of Goneril and Regan.
8. **away**: go away.
13. **gilded butterflies**: (1) butterflies that are gold-plated, hence used unnaturally for dec-
orative display; (2) ingratiating courtiers, dressed in gaudy clothing (*OED*).
16. **'s**: us.
17. **God's spies**: spies employed by God, or the gods (gods' spies), hence doing divine service.

In a walled prison packs and sects of great ones
That ebb and flow by th'moon.

EDMUND   Take them away.

LEAR   Upon such sacrifices, my Cordelia,   20
The gods themselves throw incense. Have I caught thee?
He that parts us shall bring a brand from heaven
And fire us hence like foxes. Wipe thine eyes.
The good years shall devour them, flesh and fell.
Ere they shall make us weep,   25
We'll see 'em starved first. Come.

                    [Exeunt LEAR and CORDELIA, guarded]

EDMUND   Come hither, Captain. Hark:
Take thou this note. Go follow them to prison.
One step I have advanced thee; if thou dost
As this instructs thee, thou dost make thy way   30
To noble fortunes. Know thou this: that men
Are as the time is; to be tender-minded
Does not become a sword. Thy great employment
Will not bear question: either say thou'lt do't,
Or thrive by other means.

CAPTAIN   I'll do't, my lord.   35

EDMUND   About it, and write 'happy' when thou hast don't.
Mark, I say, instantly, and carry it so
As I have set it down.

CAPTAIN   I cannot draw a cart nor eat dried oats;
If it be man's work, I'll do it.   *Exit*   40

        Flourish. Enter ALBANY, GONERIL, REGAN, SOLDIERS

ALBANY   Sir, you have showed today your valiant strain,
And fortune led you well. You have the captives
Who were the opposites of this day's strife.
I do require them of you, so to use them

---

18. **packs and sects:** groups of predatory people (drawn from the sense of "packs" of dogs roaming around for food) and cliques (exclusive social group).
21. **gods . . . incense:** i.e., the gods approve of the sacrifice, done in their service.
22. **brand:** hot, smoking iron (used to flush foxes out of their holes).
24. **fell:** hair.
25. **they:** those imprisoning Lear and Cordelia.
26. **Come:** In a sense, Lear has accomplished what he set out to do in 1.1, i.e., to lay his "rest," or retirement, on Cordelia's "kind nursery" (1.1.122), or care; their imprisonment like two "birds i'th cage" will ensure this exclusive partnership.
29. **step:** rank.
31–32. **men / Are as the time is:** Ironic echoing of Edgar's statement that "ripeness is all" (5.2.11).
39. **draw . . . oats:** i.e., I'm a man who can freely choose, not a beast of burden, subject to others' commands; this comment is an ironic mocking of the kinds of statements made throughout the play by Lear, who sees himself as subject to Fortune's commands.
43. **opposites . . . strife:** i.e., the enemy.

As we shall find their merits and our safety   45
  May equally determine
EDMUND   Sir, I thought it fit
  To send the old and miserable king
  To some retention and appointed guard,
  Whose age had charms in it, whose title more,
  To pluck the common bosom on his side   50
  And turn our impressed lances in our eyes
  Which do command them. With him I sent the queen—
  My reason all the same—and they are ready
  Tomorrow, or at further space, t'appear
  Where you shall hold your session. At this time   55
  We sweat and bleed. The friend hath lost his friend,
  And the best quarrels in the heat are cursed
  By those that feel their sharpness.
  The question of Cordelia and her father
  Requires a fitter place.
ALBANY   Sir, by your patience,   60
  I hold you but a subject of this war,
  Not as a brother.
REGAN   That's as we list to grace him.
  Methinks our pleasure might have been demanded
  Ere you had spoke so far. He led our powers,
  Bore the commission of my place and person,   65
  The which immediacy may well stand up
  And call itself your brother.
GONERIL   Not so hot.
  In his own grace he doth exalt himself
  More than in your addition.
REGAN   In my rights,
  By me invested, he compeers the best.   70
GONERIL   That were the most if he should husband you.

45–46. **their merits . . . equally determine:** i.e., we will make us of them as their merits
and our safety require. **fit:** appropriate.
48. **retention and appointed guard:** imprisonment and specially appointed guards.
49–52. **Whose age . . . command them:** i.e., Edmund claims to be worried that Lear's title and nobility would charm, and win over, guards and attract the support of the common
people; thus Edmund has had him specially sequestered.
55. **session:** law court.
59. **Cordelia and her father:** Edmund reduces Cordelia to a woman, rather than the
Queen of France, and Lear to an old man being led, rather than the King of Britain.
61. **subject:** i.e., subject to my command.
62. **list:** wish.
63. **demanded:** inquired about.
65. **Bore:** carried the authority of.
66. **immediacy:** urgency of.
67. **hot:** angry, impassioned.
69. **addition:** i.e., the additional qualities or power which you give him.
70. **compeers:** is the equal of.
71. **husband:** (1) rule; (2) become the husband of.

REGAN   Jesters do oft prove prophets.

GONERIL   Holla, holla!
That eye that told you so, looked but asquint.

REGAN   Lady, I am not well, else I should answer
From a full-flowing stomach. [*To* EDMUND] General,   75
Take thou my soldiers, prisoners, patrimony.
Dispose of them, of me, the walls is thine
Witness the world that I create thee here
My lord and master.

GONERIL   Mean you to enjoy him?

ALBANY   The let-alone lies not in your good will.   80

EDMUND   Nor in thine, lord.

ALBANY   Half-blooded fellow, yes.

REGAN   Let the drum strike, and prove my title thine.

ALBANY   Stay yet, hear reason. Edmund, I arrest thee
On capital treason, and in thine attaint
This gilded serpent. [*To* REGAN] For your claim, fair sister,   85
I bar it in the interest of my wife.
'Tis she is subcontracted to this lord,
And I, her husband, contradict your banns.
If you will marry, make your love to me;
My lady is bespoke.

GONERIL   An interlude!   90

ALBANY   Thou art armed, Gloucester.
Let the trumpet sound.
If none appear to prove upon thy person
Thy heinous, manifest, and many treasons,
There is my pledge. [*Throws down a glove*] I'll make it on
    thy heart,   95
Ere I taste bread, thou art in nothing less
Than I have here proclaimed thee.

---

72. Holla: Term of contempt.
73. asquint: (1) sideways or unclearly; (2) unfavorably; both senses ironically mock the necessity of Gloucester having to "squiny" (4.6.134), or squint, since his blinding by Regan and Cornwall in 3.7.
75. From a full-flowing stomach: i.e., (1) with full anger: (2) in no uncertain terms.
76. Take thou: i.e., take me as if I were your plunder in battle.   **patrimony:** inheritance.
77. the walls: i.e., my boundaries (as a woman and as a piece of plunder).
80. let-alone: letting alone, i.e., ability to stop it.
81. Half-blooded: i.e., illegitimate.
84. capital treason: treachery against the state.   **attaint:** i.e., the charge of dishonor against you.
85. gilded serpent: snake disguised by golden covering; compare Lear's desire that he and Cordelia live like "gilded butterflies" (l. 13).   **fair sister:** lovely (used ironically) sister-in-law.
88. banns: i.e., declared intention to be married.
90. bespoke: spoken for.   **interlude:** comic play or farce.
94. heinous, manifest: horrible, revealed.
96. nothing: another ironic echo of the central word in the play.

REGAN   Sick, O sick!
GONERIL [*Aside*]   If not, I'll ne'er trust medicine.
EDMUND   There's my exchange! [*Throws down a glove*] What
   in the world he is
  That names me traitor, villain-like he lies.   100
  Call by thy trumpet: he that dares, approach;
  On him, on you—who not?—I will maintain
  My truth and honor firmly.
ALBANY   A herald, ho!

    Enter a HERALD

  Trust to thy single virtue, for thy soldiers,
  All levied in my name, have in my name   105
  Took their discharge.
REGAN   My sickness grows upon me.
ALBANY   She is not well. Convey her to my tent.
                     [*Exit* REGAN, *led by a* SOLDIER]
  Come hither, herald. Let the trumpet sound,
  And read out this.   *A trumpet sounds*
HERALD [*Reads*]   "If any man of quality or degree within the   110
  lists of the army will maintain upon Edmund, supposed Earl
  of Gloucester, that he is a manifold traitor, let him appear
  by the third sound of the trumpet. He is bold in his de-
  fence."   *First trumpet*
  Again!   *Second trumpet*   115
  Again!   *Third trumpet*

    Trumpet answers within. Enter EDGAR, *armed*

ALBANY   Ask him his purposes, why he appears
  Upon this call o'th'trumpet.
HERALD   What are you?
  Your name, your quality, and why you answer
  This present summons?

---

98. **medicine:** poison, deliberately altered from "poison" in Q, perhaps to echo ironically
the medicines that have healed Lear in Act 4.
103–116. This entrance of the Herald and Edgar has been altered slightly but significantly
between Q and F, largely in incorporating as set-off stage directions in F the many directions given as dialogue in Q (see Textual Variants).
STAGE DIRECTION HERALD: trumpeter, who fulfills a formal function in heraldry of
"announcing and ushering in with pomp and ceremony" (OED).
105. Albany has discharged, or sent away, his soldiers, removing them from the army commanded by Edmund.
110. **quality or degree:** nobility (by birth) or rank.
111. **lists:** register of names.
112. **manifold:** many-sided; compare 2.1.48.
113–14. **He is bold in his defense:** i.e., the challenger will be bold, or courageous, in his
own defense of the charge against Edmund.

EDGAR   Know, my name is lost,   120
   By treason's tooth bare-gnawn and canker-bit.
   Yet am I noble, as the adversary
   I come to cope.
ALBANY   Which is that adversary?
EDGAR   What's he that speaks for Edmund, Earl of Gloucester?
EDMUND   Himself. What sayst thou to him?
EDGAR   Draw thy sword,   125
   That if my speech offend a noble heart
   Thy arm may do thee justice. Here is mine.
   Behold, it is my privilege,
   The privilege of mine honors,
   My oath, and my profession. I protest,   130
   Maugre thy strength, place, youth, and eminence,
   Despite thy victor-sword and fire-new fortune,
   Thy valor and thy heart, thou art a traitor:
   False to thy gods, thy brother, and thy father,
   Conspirant 'gainst this high illustrious prince,   135
   And from th'extremest upward of thy head
   To the descent and dust below thy foot,
   A most toad-spotted traitor. Say thou no,
   This sword, this arm, and my best spirits are bent
   To prove upon thy heart, whereto I speak,   140
   Thou liest.
EDMUND   In wisdom I should ask thy name,
   But since thy outside looks so fair and warlike,
   And that thy tongue, some say, of breeding breathes,
   What safe and nicely I might well delay
   By right of knighthood I disdain and spurn.   145
   Here do I toss those treasons to thy head,
   With the hell-hated lie o'erwhelm thy head,
   Which, for they yet glance by and scarcely bruise,
   This sword of mine shall give them instant way
   Where they shall rest for ever. Trumpets, speak!   150

         Alarums. [*They*] *fight.* [EDMUND *falls*]

---

121. bare-gnawn and canker-bit: gnawed bare and worm-eaten; Edmund's claim suggests
that he is remembering his days as Poor Tom, subject to the decay caused by the predatory
natural world.
123. cope: (1) contend in a duel with; (2) handle or touch.
131. Maugre: in spite of.
132. fire-new: created from the flames of battle.
138. toad-spotted: i.e., loathsome as a toad.
142. outside: outward appearance (Edgar is dressed in embellished armor and is unrecog-
nizable).
143. tongue: language.   **breeding:** a noble upbringing (compare Gloucester's comment
at 1.1.8 that Edmund's "breeding" has been at his charge).

ALBANY   Save him, save him.

GONERIL   This is practice, Gloucester;
By the law of war thou wast not bound to answer
An unknown opposite. Thou art not vanquished,
But cozened and beguiled.

ALBANY   Stop your mouth, dame,   155
Or with this paper shall I stop it. [*To* EDMUND] Hold, sir,
Thou worse than any name, read thine own evil.
[*To* GONERIL] No tearing, lady. I perceive you know it.

GONERIL   Say if I do; the laws are mine, not thine.
Who can arraign me for't?   *Exit*

ALBANY   Most monstrous!   160
Oh, know'st thou this paper?

EDMUND   Ask me not what I know.

ALBANY   Go after her, she's desperate, govern her.

[*Exit a* SOLDIER]

EDMUND   What you have charged me with, that have I done,
And more, much more; the time will bring it out.
'Tis past, and so am I. But what art thou   165
That hast this fortune on me? If thou'rt noble,
I do forgive thee.

EDGAR   Let's exchange charity.
I am no less in blood than thou art, Edmund.
If more, the more th'hast wronged me.
My name is Edgar, and thy father's son.   170
The gods are just, and of our pleasant vices
Make instruments to plague us.
The dark and vicious place where thee he got
Cost him his eyes.

EDMUND   Th'hast spoken right, 'tis true.
The wheel is come full circle; I am here.   175

---

152. **practice:** a trick.
155. **cozened:** tricked.
158. **No tearing:** i.e., of the letter (Goneril has attempted to wrestle the letter away
from Albany).
160. **arraign me:** charge me with a criminal offense.
161. **EDMUND:** As with a few other lines in this scene, this one has been reassigned in *F*
(see Textual Variants); in *Q* it is assigned to Goneril, who defiantly exits by silencing herself.
In revision, the line is given in *F* to Edmund, who speaks it remorsefully, not defiantly, for
two lines later he willingly confesses all.
162. **govern:** control.
167. **exchange charity:** offer each other forgiveness.
173. **The dark . . . he got:** the sexual lust in which Gloucester begot, or produced you.
Edgar repeats Edmund's own claims in 1.2 that because he was conceived in lust he must
be evil.
175. **wheel is come full circle:** i.e., Fortune's wheel has turned completely, going from
low to high to low; compare Kent's belief in this concept (2.2.164), and Lear's complaint
that he is "bound unto a wheel of fire" (4.7.47).

ALBANY   Methought thy very gait did prophesy
  A royal nobleness. I must embrace thee.
  Let sorrow split my heart if ever I
  Did hate thee or thy father.
EDGAR   Worthy prince, I know't.
ALBANY   Where have you hid yourself?   180
  How have you known the miseries of your father?
EDGAR   By nursing them, my lord. List a brief tale,
  And when 'tis told, O that my heart would burst!
  The bloody proclamation to escape
  That followed me so near—O, our lives' sweetness,   185
  That we the pain of death would hourly die
  Rather than die at once!—taught me to shift
  Into a madman's rags, to assume a semblance
  That very dogs disdained; and in this habit
  Met I my father with his bleeding rings,   190
  Their precious stones new-lost; became his guide,
  Led him, begged for him, saved him from despair,
  Never—O fault!—revealed myself unto him
  Until some half hour past, when I was armed.
  Not sure, though hoping of this good success,   195
  I asked his blessing, and from first to last
  Told him our pilgrimage; but his flawed heart—
  Alack, too weak the conflict to support—
  'Twixt two extremes of passion, joy and grief,
  Burst smilingly.
EDMUND   This speech of yours hath moved me,   200
  And shall perchance do good. But speak you on,
  You look as you had something more to say.
ALBANY   If there be more, more woeful, hold it in,
  For I am almost ready to dissolve,
  Hearing of this.   205
EDGAR   This would have seemed a period to such
  As love not sorrow; but another, to amplify too much,
  Would make much more and top extremity.
  Whilst I was big in clamor, came there in a man

176. **Methought:** I thought. **gait:** way of walking.
182. **List:** listen to.
187. **shift:** change.
190. **rings:** eye sockets.
191. **stones:** eyes.
193. **revealed myself unto him:** The audience does not see this reconciliation between father and son.
197. **pilgrimage:** religious quest.
204. **dissolve:** emotionally collapse.
208. **top:** go over the top of.
209. **big in clamor:** i.e., shouting and crying.

Who, having seen me in my worst estate,   210
Shunned my abhorred society. But then, finding
Who 'twas that so endured, with his strong arms
He fastened on my neck and bellowed out
As he'd burst heaven threw him on my father
Told the most piteous tale of Lear and him   215
That ever ear received; which in recounting
His grief grew puissant and the strings of life
Began to crack. Twice then the trumpets sounded,
And there I left him 'tranced.
ALBANY   But who was this?
EDGAR   Kent, sir, the banished Kent, who in disguise   220
Followed his enemy king and did him service
Improper for a slave.

Enter a GENTLEMAN, *with a bloody knife*

GENTLEMAN   Help, help! Oh, help!
EDGAR   What kind of help?
ALBANY   Speak
man!
EDGAR   What means this bloody knife?
GENTLEMAN   'Tis hot, it smokes;
It came even from the heart of—Oh, she's dead!   225
ALBANY   Who dead? Speak, man!
GENTLEMAN   Your lady, sir, your lady; and her sister
By her is poisoned: she confesses it.
EDMUND   I was contracted to them both; all three
Now marry in an instant.
EDGAR   Here comes Kent.   230

Enter KENT [*as himself*]

ALBANY   Produce the bodies, be they alive or dead.

GONERIL's *and* REGAN's *bodies brought out.*

This judgment of the heavens that makes us tremble,
Touches us not with pity. O, is this he?
[*To* KENT] The time will not allow the compliment
Which very manners urges.
KENT   I am come   235
To bid my king and master aye good night.
Is he not here?

217. **puissant:** powerful.
219. **'tranced:** entranced, or unconsious.
229. **contracted to:** (1) engaged to; (2) in league or conspiracy with.
234. **compliment:** i.e., courteous greeting.
236. **aye:** forever or always.

ALBANY   Great thing of us forgot!
  Speak, Edmund; where's the king, and where's Cordelia?
  Seest thou this object, Kent?
KENT   Alack, why thus?
EDMUND   Yet Edmund was beloved.   240
  The one the other poisoned for my sake,
  And after slew herself.
ALBANY   Even so. Cover their faces.
EDMUND   I pant for life. Some good I mean to do,
  Despite of mine own nature. Quickly send—
  Be brief in it—to th'castle; for my writ   245
  Is on the life of Lear and on Cordelia.
  Nay, send in time.
ALBANY   Run, run, O run!
EDGAR   To who, my lord?—Who has the office?
  Send thy token of reprieve.
EDMUND   Well thought on. Take my sword. The captain,   250
  Give it the captain!
EDGAR   Haste thee for thy life.
                                        [*Exit* GENTLEMAN]
EDMUND   He hath commission from thy wife and me
  To hang Cordelia in the prison and
  To lay the blame upon her own despair,
  That she fordid herself.   255
ALBANY   The gods defend her. Bear him hence a while.
                                  [EDMUND *is carried off*]

  Enter LEAR *with* CORDELIA *in his arms* [*and the* GENTLE-
  MAN *following*]

LEAR   Howl, howl, howl, howl! O, you are men of stones.
  Had I your tongues and eyes, I would use them so,
  That heaven's vault should crack. She's gone for ever.

237. **thing**: matter.
245. **writ**: written command.
248. **office**: charge or command.
255. **fordid herself**: committed suicide. In the chronicle histories and numerous other
sources for the Lear story, Cordelia and her father defeat, rather than are defeated by, the
English troops, he is returned to the throne, and after his death she rules as queen for a few
years, until being deposed by her nephews and sent to prison, where she commits suicide.
Shakespeare's main source, the play *King Leir*, ends with Cordelia and Lear triumphant in
battle; however the anticipation of Cordelia's suicide in prison some years later would probably have been familiar to audience members.
256. **Bear him hence**: carry him away.
257. **Howl**: The play repeatedly uses images of "curs," or dogs, to represent the basest in-
stincts and behaviors of human beings, and given Lear's comprehension on the heath of
man as "a poor, bare, forked animal" (3.4.101), he may be howling himself, or ordering others to do so. Compare Gloucester's rebuke to Regan and Cornwall of their treatment of
Lear on the heath, "If wolves had at thy gate howled that stern time, / Thou shouldst have
said, 'Good porter, turn the key: / All cruels else subscribe'" (3.7.62–64); their response is to
blind Gloucester.

I know when one is dead and when one lives.   260
She's dead as earth. [*He lays her down*] Lend me a looking-
    glass;
If that her breath will mist or stain the stone,
Why then she lives.
KENT   Is this the promised end?
EDGAR   Or image of that horror?
ALBANY   Fall and cease.
LEAR   This feather stirs, she lives: if it be so,   265
It is a chance which does redeem all sorrows
That ever I have felt.
KENT   Oh, my good master!
LEAR   Prithee away!
EDGAR   'Tis noble Kent, your friend.
LEAR   A plague upon you, murderers, traitors all.
I might have saved her; now she's gone for ever.   270
Cordelia, Cordelia, stay a little. Ha?
What is't thou sayst?—Her voice was ever soft,
Gentle, and low, an excellent thing in woman.—
I killed the slave that was a-hanging thee.
CAPTAIN   'Tis true, my lords, he did.
LEAR   Did I not, fellow?   275
I have seen the day with my good biting falchion
I would have made him skip. I am old now,
And these same crosses spoil me. [*To* KENT] Who are you?
Mine eyes are not o'the best, I'll tell you straight.
KENT   If fortune brag of two she loved and hated,   280
One of them we behold.
LEAR   This is a dull sight. Are you not Kent?
KENT   The same,
Your servant Kent. Where is your servant Caius?
LEAR   He's a good fellow, I can tell you that.
He'll strike, and quickly too. He's dead and rotten.   285

---

261. looking-glass: mirror.
263. promised end: (1) end of the world, or doom, prophesied in the Bible (Revelation);
(2) what inevitably occurs due to the course of action in the play; (3) death; Kent leaves this
statement ambiguous here.
265. This feather stirs: i.e., Lear has now placed a feather under Cordelia's nose.
266–67. sorrows . . . ever I have felt: The self-centered Lear of 1.1 is still present here,
seeing Cordelia's death as his own tragedy, rather than hers or that of others.
276. good biting falchion: sword able to inflict strong and damaging blows.
277. skip: run away in fear.
278. crosses: (1) emotional blows or burdens (as in Christian references to the cross on
which Christ was crucified); (2) physical blows (as from a sword, following l. 276).   **spoil:**
harm or defeat.
281. One: i.e., the hated one.
282. dull sight: unclear vision, playing on the physical and emotional blindness throughout the play.

KENT   No, my good lord, I am the very man—
LEAR   I'll see that straight.
KENT   That from your first of difference and decay
   Have followed your sad steps.
LEAR   You are welcome hither.
KENT   Nor no man else. All's cheerless, dark, and deadly.   290
   Your eldest daughters have fordone themselves
   And desperately are dead.
LEAR   Ay, so I think.
ALBANY   He knows not what he says, and vain it is
   That we present us to him.
EDGAR   Very bootless.

     Enter a MESSENGER

MESSENGER   Edmund is dead, my lord.
ALBANY   That's but a trifle here.   295
   You lords and noble friends, know our intent.
   What comfort to this great decay may come
   Shall be applied. For us, we will resign
   During the life of this old majesty
   To him our absolute power. [*To* EDGAR *and* KENT] You, to
     your rights,   300
   With boot, and such addition as your honors
   Have more than merited. All friends shall taste
   The wages of their virtue, and all foes
   The cup of their deservings. O see, see!
LEAR   And my poor fool is hanged. No, no! No life?   305
   Why should a dog, a horse, a rat have life,
   And thou no breath at all? Thou'lt come no more,
   Never, never, never, never, never!
   Pray you, undo this button. Thank you, sir.
   O, O, O, O.   310

---

288. difference: i.e., different, or declining, circumstances.
290. All's cheerless, dark, and deadly: ironic echo of Gloucester's statement after his
blinding: "All dark and comfortless" (3.7.83).
291. fordone: killed.
292. desperately: in desperation.
294. bootless: useless, profitless.
295. trifle: trifling or unimportant thing.
298–300. resign . . . power: i.e., Albany will resign the rule of the kingdom and return it
to Lear.
301. boot: advantage.
305. my poor fool is hanged: The Fool's disappearance from the play after 3.6 is never
fully explained, however, this statement does not mean, as some have interpreted (and
staged) it, that the Fool has also been hanged.
310. This line appears in Q but not F; F replaces it with the two lines at 311–12. In addition, Lear is assigned l. 314 in Q (it is assigned to Kent in F) and dies in Q immediately after it, his heart burst by his knowledge that Cordelia is dead. In F he dies after l. 312,
believing that he sees her lips move in breathing and is thus still alive.

Do you see this? Look on her! Look, her lips!
Look there, look there!

EDGAR   He faints. My lord, my lord!

LEAR   Break, heart, I prithee break.   *He dies.*

EDGAR   Look up, my lord.

KENT   Vex not his ghost. Oh, let him pass. He hates him   315
That would upon the rack of this tough world
Stretch him out longer.

EDGAR   He is gone indeed.

KENT   The wonder is he hath endured so long.
He but usurped his life.

ALBANY   Bear them from hence. Our present business   320
Is general woe. [*To* KENT *and* EDGER] Friends of my soul,
   you twain
Rule in this realm and the gored state sustain.

KENT   I have a journey, sir, shortly to go:
My master calls me; I must not say no.

EDGAR   The weight of this sad time we must obey,   325
Speak what we feel, not what we ought to say.
The oldest have borne most; we that are young
Shall never see so much, nor live so long.

                         Exeunt with a dead march

FINIS

---

316. rack: frame on which a person was stretched out and tortured when the frame was expanded.
319. usurped: (1) appropriated or used without authority; (2) kept longer than allowed.
321. twain: two.
322. gored state: i.e., kingdom pierced with disorder and chaos.
323. journey: i.e., journey toward death.
324. master: (1) Lear; (2) God.
325–28. These lines are assigned to Albany in *Q* and to Edgar in *F*; as Albany has already abdicated in favor of Lear (at f. 298) and has just asked Kent and Edgar to share the rule of the kingdom (which Kent then refuses), it is logical and consistent for Edgar to speak these lines. Yet, Albany, but not Edgar, was present in J. J when Goneril and Regan spoke what they "ought" to say (i.e., empty flattery) to Lear while Cordelia spoke what she felt (i.e., the truth), and thus Albany seems to bring the play full circle if he speaks these lines. However, Edgar, and not Albany, has suffered and felt the full effects from speech that is empty of truth and feeling, making him a more experienced moral spokesman for the play. In any event, this apparent authorial revision adds immeasurably to the play's complexity and power.
328. a dead march: solemn music appropriate for a funeral march.

A Note on the Text

King Lear was entered in the Register of the Stationer's Company in November 1607, and first printed in 1608 in quarto form, most likely typeset from Shakespeare's "foul papers," or original draft, of the play. Both the Stationer's Register and the title page of this Quarto 1 suggest that the play had been performed in 1606 on St. Stephen's Night (December 26) before King James I at Whitehall Palace. Quarto 1 was reprinted in 1619 by Thomas Pavier, with a false date of 1608. Although an unauthorized edition, the 1619 Quarto 2 was evidently used in collation with the theatrical manuscript used to print the next edition of the play, in the 1623 First Folio of Shakespeare's plays. Thus, there are two texts of the play, Quarto 1 and Folio (each of which underwent minor correction during printing) that are considered authoritative, that is, typeset from manuscripts used by Shakespeare and his acting company, of which he was a sharer.

Quarto 1 (which even when corrected still contains numerous obvious errors) contains about 300 lines that do not appear in the Folio text, and the Folio contains about 100 lines that do not appear in Quarto 1. The texts vary substantively in other ways, including in the reshaping of various characters' roles and in the focus on foreign versus civil war. Some of the variants between Quarto 1 and Folio show a regularization of the text as in lineation (in order to highlight split lines), stage directions and speech-prefixes, as well as the correction of inconsistencies and errors. However, the most significant of the variants, including the replacement in the Folio of so much Quarto 1 material, strongly suggests that Shakespeare revised his original text of the play (as represented by Quarto 1), probably after it had been in performance for some years or months. The Folio text, then, represents a later revision, and an alternate text, or "version," of the play. Whether Shakespeare himself considered the Folio text to be an "improvement" on the Quarto 1 text can never be resolved. Most likely, Shakespeare revised the play to suit changing theatrical conditions and/or cultural or political circumstances, or to suit his own artistic vision, or for a combination of reasons.

This Norton Critical Edition uses the Folio text as copy-text, as the Folio almost certainly represents Shakespeare's reshaping of the play and because it lacks the copious authorial and compositorial errors found in Quarto 1. However, as so many Quarto 1-only passages (including the "mock-trial" in Act 3, Scene 6) have for four hundred years engaged critics, students, actors, directors, as well as reading and theatrical audiences around the world, these passages (when not replaced in the Folio by revisions) have been interpolated into the text of this edition. Thus, this is a "conflated" edition.

These textual notes record substantive variants primarily between Quarto 1 and Folio; corrections made to either text during printing are also noted, and occasional emendations from Quarto 2 are also noted. However, accidental variants (such as simple contractions of "he is" to "he's" or "them" to " 'em") are not recorded, nor are changes in lineation (especially from verse to prose or prose to verse). Stage directions use the original wording of the Folio, or Quarto 1, except when generic names (including "Bastard" and "Steward") have been regularized to the character names given in the dialogue. Emendations or additions to the stage directions are marked by brackets; however, *Exit* has been emended to *Exeunt* when necessary without the use of brackets.

Historical collations are only noted in cases in which an earlier editor's emendation has since become standard for editors. An entire scene (Act 4, Scene 3) in Quarto 1, which does not appear in the Folio, has been interpolated into this edition; for this reason, the Folio's numbering of scenes in Act 4 has not been followed. In addition, this text adopts George Steevens's break up of Act 2, Scene 2 into two additional scenes.

Abbreviations used: *Q*: Quarto 1; *Q uncorr.*: Quarto 1 uncorrected; *Q corr.*: Quarto 1 corrected; *Q2*: Quarto 2; *F*: Folio 1; *F uncorr.*: Folio 1 uncorrected; *F corr.*: Folio 1 corrected; SD: stage directions; SP: speech prefix. Editions cited: *Rowe* (1709); *Theobald* (1733); *Hanmer* (1743–44); *Capell* (1767–68); and *Steevens* (1778).

Textual Variants

Dramatis Personae] not in Q or F
KING LEAR] THE TRAGEDIE OF / KING LEAR *F*; M. William Shak-speare / *HIS* / True Chronicle Historie of the life and death of King LEAR and his three / Daughters. / *With the vnfortunate life of* Edgar, *sonne* / and heire to the Earle of Gloster, and his / sullen and assumed humor of / TOM of Bedlam *Q*
Act 1, Scene 1] *Actus Primus. Scena Prima F*; *not in Q*   0 SD EDMUND] *Edmond F*; *Bastard Q* [*throughout scene*]   4 kingdom]

F; kingdoms *Q*   5 qualities] *F*; equalities *Q*   13 a son, sir] *F*; sir a
sonne   20 to] *F*; into *Q*   24 SP EDMUND] *Edm. F*; *Bast. Q*
[*throughout the scene*]   31 SD *Sennet*] *F*; *Sound a Sennet Q   En-
ter one bearing a coronet, then* LEAR] *Q*; *Enter King Lear F*;
CORNWALL, ALBANY, GONERIL, REGAN, CORDELIA, *and*
ATTENDANTS] *F*; *then the Dukes of Albany, and Cornwall, next
Gonorill, Regan, Cordelia, with followers Q*   33 SD *Exit*] *F*; *not in
Q*   34 shall] *F*; will *Q*   purpose] *F*; purposes *Q* 35 Give me] *F*;
not in Q   that] *F*; *not in Q*   36 fast] *F*; first *Q* 37 from our age]
F; of our state *Q*   38 Conferring] *F*; Confirming *Q*   strengths]
F; yeares *Q*   38–43 while . . . now] *F*; *not in Q*   43 princes] *F*; two
 great Princes *Q*   47–48 Since . . . state] *F*; *not in Q*   51 with
merit challenge] *F*; most challenge it *Q*   53 word] *F*; words *Q*   54
and] *F*; or *Q*   57 as] *F*; a *Q*   found] *F*; friend *Q*   60 speak] *F*;
doe *Q*   62 shadowy] *F*; shady *Q*   and . . . rivers] *F*; *not in Q*   64
issues] *F*; issue *Q*   66 of] *F*; to *Q*   Speak] *Q*: *not in F*   67 that
self-mettle as my sister] *F*; the self same mettle that my sister is *Q*
70 comes too] *F*; came *Q*   72 possesses] *Q*; professes *F*   76 pon-
derous] *F*; richer *Q*   80 conferred] *F*; confirm'd *Q*   Now] *F*; but
now *Q*   81 our last and least] *F*; the last, not least in our deere
loue *Q*   81–83 to . . . interest] *F*; *not in Q*   83 draw] *F*; win *Q*
84 Speak] *F*; *not in Q*   86–87 LEAR Nothing? CORDELIA Nothing.] *F*; *not in Q*   88 Nothing will] *F*; How, nothing can *Q*   91
no] *F*; nor *Q*   92 How, how Cordelia] *F*; goe to, goe to *Q*   93 you]
F; it *Q*   102 To . . . all] *Q*; *not in F*   103 thy heart with this] *F*;
this with they heart *Q*   106 Let] *F*; Well let *Q*   108 mysteries]
F2; mistresse *Q*; miseries *F*   night] *F*; might *Q*   116 to my
bosom] *F*; *not in Q*   126 dowers] *F*; dower *Q*   the] *F*; this *Q*
128 with] *F*; in *Q*   134 addition] *F*; additions *Q*   137 between]
F; betwixt *Q*   144 mad] *F*; man *Q*   wouldst] wouldest *F*; wilt *Q*
147 falls] *F*; stoops *Q*   Reserve thy state] *F*; Reuerse thy doome
Q   151–52 sounds / Reverb] *F*; sound / Reuerbs *Q*   153 a pawn]
Q; pawn *F1*   154 thine] *F*; thy *Q*   155 motive] *F*; the motive *Q*
160 Miscreant] *F*; recreant *Q*   ALBANY . . . forbear.] *F*; *not in
Q* 161 Kill] *F*; Doe, kill *Q*   thy] *F*; the *Q*   162 gift] *F*; doome *Q*
165 recreant] *F*; *not in Q*   thine] *F*; thy *Q*   166 That] *F*; Since
Q   vows] *F*; vow *Q*   167 strained] *F*; straied *Q*   168 betwixt] *F*;
betweene *Q1*   sentences] *F corr.*; sentence *Q, F*   171 Five] *F*;
foure *Q*   172 disasters] *F*; diseases *Q*   173 sixth] sixt *F*; fift *Q*
178 since] *Q*; sith *F*   179 Freedom] *F*; Friendship *Q*   181 justly
thinkst] *F*; rightly thinks *Q*   rightly] *F*; iustly *Q*   185 SD *Exit*] *F*;
not in Q   SD *Flourish. Enter* GLOUCESTER with FRANCE *and*
BURGUNDY [*and*] ATTENDANTS] *F*; *Ener France and Burgundie
with Gloster Q*   188 toward] *F*; towards *Q*   this] *F*; a *Q*   191
Most] *F*; *not in Q*   200 Will] *F*; Sir will *Q*   202 Dowered] *F*;

Couered *Q*   204 in] *F*; on *Q*   212 she] *F*; *not in Q*   object] *F*;
best obiect *Q*   213 The] *F*; most *Q* the] *F*; most *Q*   218 your
fore-vouched affection] *F*; you for voucht affections *Q* 221 Should]
F; Could *Q*   224 well] *Q*; will *F*   225 make known] *F*; may know
Q   232 Better] *F*; Goe to, goe to, better *Q*   234 but] *F*; no more
but *Q*   235 Which] *F*; That *Q*   238 regards] *F*; respects *Q*   240
a dowry] *F*; and dowre *Q*   244 I am firm] *F*; *not in Q*   248 respect and fortunes] *F*; respects / Of fortune *Q*   254 cold'st] *F*;
couldst *Q*   256 my] *F*; thy *Q*   258 of] *F*; in *Q*   259 Can] *F*;
Shall *Q*   266 SD *Flourish. Exeunt*] *F*; *Exit Lear and Burgundie Q*
271 Love] *F*; use *Q*   276 duty] *F*; duties *Q*   279 worth the want]
worth the worth *Q*   280 plighted] *F*; pleated *Q*   281 with shame]
F; shame them *Q*   289 not] *Q*; *not in F*   291 grossly] *F*; grosse *Q*
295 from his age to receive] *F*; to receiue from his age *Q*   296 im-
perfections] *F*; imperfection *Q*   302 let's hit] *Q*; let us sit *F*   dis-
position] *F*; dispositions *Q*   305 of it] *F*; on't *Q*
Act 1, Scene 2] *Scena Secunda F*; *not in Q*   0SD EDMUND] *F*
(Bastard); *Bastard Solus Q*; 1 SP EDMUND] *This edition*; Bast Q, *F*
(*throughout the scene*)   10 with "baseness", "bastardy"? Base?
Base?] *F*; base bastardie *Q*   13 dull, stale, tired] *F*; stale dull lyed
Q   15 then] *F*; the *Q*   18–21 Fine word, "legitimate"] *F*; *not in Q*
24 Prescribed] *F*; subscribed *Q*   32 needed] *F*; needes *Q*   37
and] *F*; *not in Q*   44 SD [*Gives him the letter.*]] *This edition*; A Let-
ter Q; not in *F*   45 SP GLOUCESTER [*Reads*]] *F* (*Glou reads.*);
not in Q   45 and reverence] *F*; *not in Q*   51 sleep] *F*; slept *Q*
wake] *F*; wakt *Q*   66 Has] *F*; Hath *Q*   68 heard him oft] *F*; often
heard him *Q*   69 declined] *F*; delining *Q*   the] *F*; his *Q*   70 his]
F; the *Q*   74 sirrah] *F*; sir *Q*   I'll] *F*; I *Q*   78 his] *F*; this *Q*   82
writ] *F*; wrote *Q*   83 other] *F*; further *Q*   90–91 EDMUND Nor
is not, sure. / GLOUCESTER To . . . earth] *Q*; *not in F*   93 the] *F*;
your *Q*   95 will] *F*; shall *Q*   96 find] *F*; see *Q*   101 in palaces] *F*
Pallaces *Q*   102 and the] *F* the *Q*   102–07 This . . . graves] *F*; *not
in Q*   109–10 honesty] *F*; honest *Q*   110 'Tis] *F*; strange *Q*   SD
Exit] *F*; *not in Q*   112 surfeits] *F*; surfeit *Q*   114 on] *F*; by *Q*
115 treacherers] *Q1*; Treachers *F*   116 spherical] *F*; spirituall *Q*
119 on] *F*; to *Q*   120 a star] *F*; Starres *Q*   122 Fut!] *Q*; *not in F*
123 in] *F*; of *Q*   124 bastardizing] *F*; bastardy *Q*   125 Pat] *F*;
Edgar; and out *Q*   126 My cue] *F*; mine *Q*   126 sigh] *F*; sith *Q*
Tom] *F*; them of *Q*   128 Fa . . . mi] *F*; *not in Q*   133 with] *F*;
about *Q*   134 writes] *F*; writ *Q*   135–41 as . . . come] *Q*; *not in F*
142 The] *F*; Why, the *Q*   144 Ay] *F*; *not in Q*   146 nor] *F*; or *Q*
149 until] *F*; till *Q*   152 person] *F*; parson *Q*   154–60 I . . . ED-
MUND] *F*; *not in Q* 160 go armed] *Q*; not in *F*   161 toward] *F*;
towards *Q*   165 SD *Exit* EDGAR] *Q*; *Exit F* (after l. 164)
Act 1, Scene 3] *Scena Tertia F*; *not in Q*   0 SD *Enter* GONERIL

and [*her*] *steward* OSWALD] F (*Enter Goneril, and Steward*); *Enter Goneril and Gentleman* Q   3 SP OSWALD] *Ste.* F (*throughout the scene*); *Gent.* Q (*throughout the scene*)   3 Ay] F; Yes Q   7 up-braids] F; obrayds Q   14 fellows] F; fellow seruants Q   to] F; in Q   15 distaste] F; dislike Q   my] F; our Q   17–21 Not . . . abused] Q; *not in F*   22 have said] F; tell you Q   Well] F; Very well 25–26 I would . . . speak] Q; *not in F*   27 course] F; very course, goe Q   27 SD *Exeunt*] F; *Exit* Q

Act 1, Scene 4] F(*Scena Quarta*); *not in Q*   1 well] Q; will F   7 labors] F; labour Q   7 SD *Horns within. Enter* LEAR, [KNIGHTS], *and* ATTENDANTS] F; *Enter Lear* Q   31 thou] F; *not in Q*   37 sir] F; *not in Q*   44 You, you] F; you Q   45 SP OS-WALD] Steward F (*throughout the scene*); *Stew.* Q (*throughout the scene*) SD *Exit*] F; not in Q   49 SP [THIRD] KNIGHT] *Knigh.* F; *Kent* Q   51 SP [THIRD] KNIGHT] *Knigh* (or *Knight*) F (*throughout the scene*); *seruant* Q (*throughout the scene*)   53 He] F; A Q   57 of kindness appears] F; appeer's Q   66 purpose] F; purport Q   67 my] F; this Q   70 well] F; *not in Q*   72 SD *Enter* OSWALD] F (*Enter Steward*); *not in Q*   73 sir, you] F; sir, you sir Q   77 these] F; this Q   your pardon] F; you pardon me Q   79 strucken] F; struck Q   82 arise, away] F; *not in Q*   84 go to] F; *not in Q*   you have] Q; have you F   so] F; *not in Q*   85 my] F; *not in Q*   90 my boy] F; Foole Q   93 has] F; hath Q   94 did] F; done Q   103 the Lady] F; Ladie oth'e Q   104 gall] F; gull Q   119 'tis] F; *not in Q*   120 nuncle] F; vncle Q   126 one] F; foole Q   128–139 That . . . snatching] Q; *not in F*   139 Nuncle, give me an egg] F; giue me an egge Nuncle Q   145 thine] F; thy Q   on thy] F; at'h Q   149 grace] F; wit Q   151 And] F; They Q   to] F; do Q   160 Fool] F; fooles Q   161 Prithee] Q (prethe); Pry'thy F   162 to] F; Q *corr.*; *not in Q uncorr.*   165 thou'lt] F; thou wilt Q   166 sometimes] F; sometime Q   169 o'both] F; a both Q   171 You] F; Me thinks you Q   172 of late] F; alate Q   174 frowning] F; frowne Q *corr.*, Q *uncorr.*   Now] F, Q *corr.*; Q *uncorr.*   188 it] F; *not in Q*   191 Which] F; that Q   194 Will] F; must Q   proceeding] F; proceed-ings Q   195 know] F; trow Q   197 it's] F; it Q   by] F; be Q   200 I] F; Come sir, I Q   202 transport] F; transforme Q   206 Does] F; Doth Q   207 This] F; why this Q   208 Does] F; doth Q   209 weakens] F; weaknes Q   his] F; or his Q   210 lethargied. Ha! Waking] F; lethergie, sleeping or wakeing; ha! sure Q   212 SP FOOL] F; *not in Q*   213–16 LEAR I . . . father] Q; *not in F*   218 This] F; Come sir, this Q   220 To] F; *not in Q*   223 debauched] F (debosh'd); deboyst Q   226 Makes it] F; make Q   a] F; *not in Q*   227 graced] F; great Q   231 remainders] F; remainder Q   233 Which] F; that Q   238 SD *Enter* ALBANY] F; *Enter Duke* Q   239 Woe] F; We Q   O . . . come] Q; *not in F*   240 speak, sir] F;

that we *Q*   my] *F*; any *Q*   244–45 ALBANY Pray . . . LEAR] *F*;
not in Q   245 liest] *F*; list *Q*   246 are] *F*; and *Q*   251 Which] *F*;
that *Q*   253 Lear, Lear, Lear!] *F*; Lear. Lear! *Q*   256 SP AL-
BANY] *F*; *Duke Q* (*throughout the scene*)   257 Of . . . you] *F*; *not
in Q*   258 Hear] *F*; harke *Q*   goddess, hear] *F*; Goddesse *Q*   266
thwart disnatured] *F*; thourt disuetur'd *Q*   268 cadent] *F*; accent
Q   272 Away! Away] *F*; goe, goe, my people *Q*   272 SD [*Exeunt*
LEAR . . . ATTENDANTS]] *Exit F*; *not in Q*   274 more of it] *F*;
the cause *Q*   276 As] *F*; that *Q*   276 SD *Enter* LEAR] *F*; *not in Q*
281 which] *F*; that *Q*   282 thee worth them.] *F*; the worst *Q*
283–84 thee / Th'untented] *F*; the untender *Q*   285 Pierce] *F*; peruse *Q*   thee] *F*; the *Q*   287 loose] *F*; make *Q*   288–89 Ha? Let
it be so. / I have] *F*; yea, is't come to this? yet have I left *Q*   290
Who] *F*; whom *Q*   292–94 Thou . . . thee] *Q*; *not in F*   294 SD
Exit] *F*; *not in Q*   295 that] *F*; that my lord *Q*   298 Pray . . . hoa]
F; *not in Q*   299 You, sir] *F*; Come sir no more, you *Q*   301 thee]
F; *not in Q*   305 SD *Exit*] *F*; *not in Q*   307–12 This . . . mercy] *F*;
not in Q   312 Oswald, I say] *F*; What *Oswald*, ho *Q* 313–19 AL-
BANY Well . . . unfitness] *F*; *not in Q*   319 *Enter* OSWALD] *En-
ter Steward F*; *not in Q*   320 How now, Oswald] *F*; *Oswald.* Here
Madam, *Q*   321 that] *F*; this *Q*   322 Ay] *F*; Yes *Q*   324 fear] *F*;
feares *Q*   327 hasten] *F, Q corr.*; after *Q uncorr.*   No, no] *F*; now
Q   328 milky] *F, Q corr.*; mildie *Q uncorr.*   329 condemn] *F*; dislike *Q*   330 Y'are] *Q*; your are *F*   at task for] *F*; attaskt for *Q corr.*;
alapt *Q uncorr.*   331 praised] *F*; praise *Q*   333 better, oft] *F*; better ought *Q*   335 the event] *Q*; the'uent *F*

Act 1, Scene 5] *Scena Quinta F*; *not in Q*   0 SD *Enter* LEAR . . .
FOOL] *F*; *Enter Lear Q*   4 afore] *F*; before *Q*   6 not] *F*; nere *Q*
12–13 yet I can tell] *F*; yet I con *Q*   14 What canst tell boy] *F*;
Why what canst thou tell my boy *Q*   15 She will] *F*; Sheel *Q*
does] *F*; doth *Q*   18 one's] *F*; his *Q*   19 he] *F*; a *Q*   25 put's] *F*;
put his *Q*   25–26 daughters] *F*; daughter *Q*   32 indeed] *F*; *not in
Q*   39 mad, not mad, sweet heaven] *F*; O mad sweet heaven! I
would not be mad *Q*   41 How now] *F*; *not in Q*   43 Exeunt] *F*
exit *Q*; *not in F*   44 that's a] *F*; that is *Q* 45 unless] *F*; except *Q*
45 SD *Exit Q*; *Exeunt F*

Act 2, Scene 1] *F* (*Actus Secundus. Scena Prima*); *not in Q*   0 SD
Enter Edmund and Curran, severally] *F* (*Enter Bastard, and Curran,
seuerally*); *Enter Bast. And Curan meeting Q*   1 SP EDMUND]
This edition; *Bast. F, Q* (*throughout the scene*)   3 Regan] *F*; *not in
Q*   4 this night] *F*; to night *Q*   7 ear-kissing] *F*; ear-bussing *Q*
10 toward] *F*; towards *Q*   11 dukes] *F*; two Dukes *Q*   13 do] *F*;
not in Q 13 SD *Exit*] *F*; *not in Q*   18 I must act] *F*; must aske *Q*
work] *F*; helpe *Q*   18 SD *Enter Edgar*] *F*; *Q* (*at line 15*)   20 sir]
F; *not in Q*   23 Cornwall] *F*; Cornwall ought *Q*   24 i'th'night] *F*;

in the night *Q*   27 yourself] *F*; your—*Q*   29 cunning] *F*; crauing
Q   30 Draw] *F*; *not in Q*   31 hoa] *F*; here *Q*   32 brother] *F*;
brother flie *Q*   33 SD *Exit Edgar*] *F*; *not in Q*   37 SD *Enter . . .
Torches*] *F*; *Enter Glost. Q*   40 Mumbling] *F*; warbling *Q*   41
stand] *F*; stand's *Q*   44 ho] *F*; *not in Q*   46 revenging] *F*;
reuengiue *Q*   48 manifold] *F*; many fould *Q*   49 to'th'father] *F*;
to the father *Q*   51 in] *F*; with *Q*   53 latched] *F*; lancht *Q*   54
And] *F*; but *Q*   55 quarrel's right] *F*; quarrels, rights *Q*   57 Full]
F; but *Q*   63 coward] *F*; caytife *Q*   69 would the reposal] *F*;
could the reposure *Q*   71 should I] *F*; I should *Q*   74 practice] *F*;
pretence *Q*   77 spirits] *F*; spurres *Q*   78 SD *Tucket within*] *F*; *not
in Q*   78 O] *F*; *not in Q*   79 said he] *F*; *not in Q*   I never got
him] *Q*; *not in F*   80 where] *F*; why *Q* 86 SD *Enter* CORNWALL,
REGAN, *and* ATTENDANTS] *F*; *Enter the Duke of Cornwall Q*
88 strange news] *Q*; strangenesse *F*   91 O] *F*; *not in Q*   it's] *F*; is
Q   94 O] *F*; *not in Q*   96 tended] *F*; tends *Q*   98 of that con-
sort] *F*; *not in Q*   101 th'expense and waste] *F*; the wast and
spoyle *Q corr.*; these—and wast *Q uncorr.*   105 SP CORNWALL]
F; *Duke Q* (*throughout the scene from this point*)   106 hear] *F*;
heard *Q*   107 It was] *F*; Twas *Q*   108 bewray] *F*; betray *Q*   122
threading] *F*; threatening *Q*   123 prize] *F, Q uncorr.*; poyse *Q corr.*
126 differences] *F*; *Q corr.*; defences *Q uncorr.*   best] *F, Q uncorr.*;
lest *Q corr.*   127 home] *F*; *Q corr.*; hand *Q uncorr.*   130 busi-
nesses] *F*; business *Q*   132 SD *Flourish*] *F*; *not in Q*

Act 2, Scene 2] *Scena Secunda F*; *not in Q*   0 SD *Enter* KENT
. . . severally] *F* (*Enter Kent, and Steward seuerally*); *Enter Kent, and
Steward Q*   1 SP OSWALD] This edition; *Steward F, Q* (*throughout the scene*)   1 dawning] *F*; euen *Q corr.*; deuen *Q uncorr.*
this] *F*; the *Q corr., Q uncorr.*   5 lov'st] *F*; love *Q*   14 three-
suited] *F*; three shewted *Q corr.*; three snyted *Q uncorr.*   15
worsted-stocking] woosted-stocking *F*; worsted-stocken *Q corr.*;
wosted stocken *Q uncorr.*   action-taking] *F*; action taking knaue *Q
corr., Q uncorr.*   16 super-serviceable, finical] *F*; superfinicall *Q*
20 one] *F*; *not in Q*   clamorous] *Q corr., Q uncorr.* (clamorous);
clamours *F*   21 deniest] *F*; denie *Q corr., Q uncorr.*   thy] *F*; the *Q*
22 Why] *F*; *not in Q*   25–26 days since I tripped up thy heels and
beat thee] *F*; days agoe since I beat thee, and tript vp thy heeles *Q*
27 yet] *F*; *not in Q*   27–28 o'th'moonshine of you] *F*; of the
moone-shine a'you *Q*   31 come with] *F*; bring *Q*   36 hoa, Murder! Murder] *F*; ho, murther, helpe *Q*   39 SD *Enter* EDMUND
with his rapier drawn] *Q*; *Enter Bastard F* SD CORNWALL *. . .*
SERVANTS] *F*; *Gloster the Duke and Dutchesse Q*   40 SD ED-
MUND] *This edition*; *Bast. F, Q* (*throughout the scene*)   Part] *F*;
not in Q   41 if] *F*; and *Q*   42 ye] *F*; you *Q*   44 SP CORN-
WALL] *F*; *Duke Q* (*throughout the scene*)   52 A] *F*; I, a *Q*   53

they] *F*; he *Q* 53–54 years o'th'trade] *F*; houres at the trade *Q*
60 wall] *F*; walles *Q* 62 sirrah] *F*; sir *Q* 64 hath] *F*; has *Q* 68
holy] *F* (*corrected*); holly *F* (*uncorrected*); *not in Q* atwain] *F*; in
twaine *Q* 69 too intrince t'unloose] *Capell*; t'intrince t'vnloose *F*;
to intrench, to inloose *Q* 71 fire] *F*; stir *Q* their] *Q*; the *F* 72
Revenge] *F*; Reneag *Q* 74 dogs] *F*; dayes *Q* 78 drive ye] *F*; send
you *Q* 83 What is his fault] *F*; what's his offence *Q* 85 nor his,
nor hers] *F*; or his, or hers *Q* 88 Than] *F* (Then); That *Q* 89
some] *F*; a *Q* 91 roughness] *F*; ruffines *Q* 93 An . . . plain] *F*;
not in Q 99 faith] *F*; sooth *Q* in] *F*; or in *Q* 100 great] *F*;
graund *Q* 102 On] *F*; In *Q* flickering] *Q*; flicking thou] *Q*; not
in *F* 103 dialect] *F*; dialogue *Q* 111 compact] *F*; coniunct *Q*
116 dread] *Q*; dead *F* 118 Fetch] *F*; Bring *Q* stocks] *F*; *not in
Q* 119 ancient] *F*; miscreant *Q corr.*; ausrent *Q uncorr.*; 120 Sir]
F; *F*; *not in Q* 122 employment] *F*; imployments *Q* 123 respect]
Q corr., Q uncorr.; respects *F* 125 Stocking] *F*; Stopping *Q corr.*;
Stobing *Q uncorr.* 126 sit] *F, Q corr.*; set *Q uncorr.* 129 should]
F; could *Q* 130 color] *F*; nature *Q* 131 SD *Stocks brought out*] *F*;
not in Q 133 His . . . and] *Q*; *not in F* king] *F*; good king *Q*
134–37 Will . . . will] *Q*; *not in F* 135 basest and 'temned'st] *Q
corr.*; belest and contaned *Q uncorr.* 142 For . . . legs] *Q*; *not in F*
143 my] *F*; my good *Q* SD *Exeunt . . . KENT*] *F* (*Exit*); *not in Q*
147 Pray] *F*; Pray you *Q* 148 out] *F*; ont *Q* 151 taken] *F*; tooke
Q SD *Exit*] *F*; *not in Q* 152 saw] *F*; *Q corr.*; say *Q uncorr.* 157
miracles] *F*; my wracke *Q corr.*; my rackles *Q uncorr.* 159 most]
F, Q corr.; not *Q uncorr.* 162 their] *F, Q corr.*; and *Q uncorr.*
o'erwatched] *F*; ouerwatch *Q corr., Q uncorr.* 163 Take] *F, Q
corr.*; Late *Q uncorr.* 165 SD *Sleeps*] *Q*; *not in F*

Act 2, Scene 3] *Steevens*; *not in F, Q* 5 Whiles] *F*; while *Q* 10
elf] *F* (elfe); else *Q* 12–13 winds and persecutions] *F*; wind, and
persecution *Q* 15 numbed and mortified arms] *F*; numb'd and
mortified bare arms *Q corr.*; numb'd mortified bare *Q uncorr.* 16
Pins] *F, Q corr.*; Pies *Q uncorr.* 17 from low farms] *F*; from low
seruice *Q corr.*; frame low seruice *Q uncorr.* 19 Sometime] *Q*;
Sometimes *F* 20 Tulygod] *F, Q corr.*; Tuelygod *Q uncorr.*

Act 2, Scene 4] *Steevens*; *not in F, Q* 0 SD *Enter* LEAR . . .
GENTLEMAN] *F* (*corrected*); *Enter Lear, Foole and Gentlemaa F*
(*uncorrected*); *Enter King Q* 1 home] *F*; hence *Q* 2 messengers]
F; messenger *Q* 2 SP GENTLEMAN] *F* (*Gent.*); *Knight Q*
(*throughout the scene*) 5 thy] *Q*; ahy *F* 6 KENT No my lord] *F*;
not in Q 7 Ha, ha] *F*; ha ha, looke *Q* cruel] *F*; crewell *Q* 8
heads] *F*; heeles *Q* by th'loins] *F*; bit'h loynes *Q* 9 man's] *Q*
(mans); man *F* 18–19 LEAR No . . . have] *Q*; *not in F* 21
KENT By . . . ay. LEAR] *F*; *not in Q* 22 could not, would] *F*;
would not, could *Q* 25 might'st] *F*; may'st *Q* impose] *F*; purpose

Q   30 panting] *Q*; painting *F*   33 those] *F*; whose *Q*   34 meiney] *F*; men *Q*   45 FOOL Winters . . . year] *F*; *not in Q*   57 here] *F*; *not in Q*   58 SD *Exit*] *F*; *not in Q*   59 but] *F*; then *Q* 61 number] *F*; traine *Q*   62 i'th'stocks] *F*; in the stockes *Q*   66 i'th'winter] *F*; in the winter *Q*   68 twenty] *F*; 100. *Q*   69 lest] *F*, *Q* (least)   70 upward] *F*; up the hill *Q*   71 gives] *F corr.*, *Q*; giue *F uncorr.*   74 which] *F*; that *Q*   and seeks] *F*; *not in Q*   76 begins] *F*; begin *Q*   82 SD *Enter* LEAR and GLOUCESTER] *Q*; *at line 81 in F*   84 They are sick, they are] *F*; th'are sicke, th'are *Q* 85 have travailed]: haue trauail'd *F corr.*, *F uncorr.*; traueled *Q*   all the] *F corr.*, *F uncorr.*; hard to *Q*   fetches] *F corr.*, *F uncorr.*; Iustice *Q*   86 The] *F*; I the *Q*   90 plague, death] *F*; death, plague *Q* 91 Fiery? What] *F*; what fierie *Q*   93–94 GLOUCESTER Well . . . . man] *F*; *not in Q*   96 father] *F*, *Q corr.*; fate *Q uncorr.*   97 his] *F*, *Q corr.*; the *Q uncorr.*   commands, tends] *F*, commands her *Q corr.*; come and tends *Q uncorr.*   98 Are . . . blood] *F*; *not in Q*   99 Fiery? The] *F*; The *Q uncorr.*; *not in Q corr.*   100 No] *F*, *Q corr.*; Mo *Q uncorr.*   103 commands] *F*; command *Q*   110 practice only. Give] *F*; practice, only giue *Q*   111 Go] *F*; *not in Q* 115 SD *Exit*] *F*; *not in Q*   116 my rising . . . down] *F*; *not in Q* 118   'em   i'th'paste]   *F*;   vm   it'h   past   *Q*   *uncorr.*, *Q corr.*   knapt 'em o'th'coxcombs] *F*; rapt vm ath coxcombs *Q uncorr.*, *Q corr.*   120 SD *Enter* CORNWALL . . . SERVANTS] *F*; *Enter Duke and Regan Q*   121 SP CORNWALL] *F*; *Duke Q (throughout the scene)*   SD KENT *here set at liberty*] *F*; *not in Q* 125 divorce me from thy mother's tomb] *Q corr.*; Mother Tombe *F*; deuose me from they mothers fruit *Q uncorr.*   126 Oh] *F*; yea *Q* 128 sister's] *F* (Sisters); sister is *Q*   131 depraved] *F*; depriued *Q uncorr.*, deptoued *Q corr.*   135–40 LEAR Say . . . blame] *F*; *not in Q*   143 her] *Q*; his *F*   145 you] *F*; *not in Q*   147 her] *F*; her Sir *Q*   148 but] *F*; *not in Q*   153 Never] *F*; No *Q*   159 sir, fie] *F*; fie sir *Q*   163 blister] *F*; blast her pride *Q*   164 is on] *F*; *not in Q* 166 tender-hefted] *F*; tender hested *Q*   167 Thee] *F*; thy *Q*   175 o'th'kingdom] *F*; of the kingdome *Q*   177 SD *Tucket within*] *F*; *not in Q*   *Enter Oswald*] *F*; *after* that? *in Q*   181 fickle] *Q uncorr.*, *Q corr.*; sickly *F*   he] *F*; a *Q uncorr.*, *Q corr.*   183 stocked] *F*; struck *Q*   184 on't] *F*; ant *Q*   186 your] *F*; you *Q uncorr.*, *Q corr.*   187 you] *F*; *not in Q*   190 by the hand] *Q*; by'th'hand *F*   205 o'th'air] *F*; of the air *Q*   208 hot-blooded] *F*; bloodied *F corr.*, hot bloud in *Q uncorr.*   210 beg] *F*; bag *Q*   214 I] *F*; Now I *Q*   218 that's in] *F*; that lies within *Q*   219 boil] *F* (byle); bile *Q*   220 or] *F*; an *Q* 222 call it] *F*, *Q corr.*, callit *Q uncorr.*   227 so] *F*; so sir *Q*   228 looked] *F*; looke *Q*   231 you] *F*; you are *Q*   232 spoken] *F*; spoken now *Q*   236 Speak] *F*; Speakes *Q*   one] *F*; a *Q*   241 ye] *F*;

you *Q*   252 look] *F*; seem *Q*   259 need] *F*; needes *Q*   262 na-
ture] *F* (*corrected*), *Q*; Nattue *F* (*uncorrected*)   263 is] *F*; as *Q*
268 man] *F*; fellow *Q*   270 daughters' hearts] (dauthers hearts) *F*
corr., Q; Daughte shearts *F uncorr.*   272 tamely] *F*; lamely *Q*
273 And] *F*; O *Q*   278 I'll weep] *F* (*corrected*), *Q*; ile, weep *F*
279 SD *Storm and tempest*] *F*; *not in Q*   280 into] *F*; in *Q*   281
mad] *F* (*corrected*), *Q*; mads *F*   SD *Exeunt* LEAR . . . FOOL] *Q*;
Exeunt F   283 and's] *F*; and his *Q*   288 SP GONERIL] *F*; *Duke.*
Q   290 CORNWALL] *F*; *Reg. Q*   292–93 CORNWALL Whither
. . . horse] *F*; *not in Q* 293 but] *F*; & *Q*   294 SP CORNWALL] *F*;
Re. Q   best] *F*; good *Q*   296 high] *F*; bleak *Q*   298 scarce] *F*;
not *Q*   305 Regan] *F*; *Reg Q*   o'th'storm] *F*; at'h storm *Q*
Act 3, Scene 1] *F* (*Actus Tertius, Scena Prima*); *not in Q*   0 SD
Storm still] *F*; *not in Q* SD *severally*] *F*; *at seuerall doores F*   1
Who's] *F*; *Whats Q*   besides] *F*; beside *Q*   4 elements] *F*; element
Q   7–15 tears . . . all] *Q*; *not in F*   14 fur] *Q corr.*; surre *Q un-*
corr.   18 note] *F*; art *Q*   19 is] *F*; be *Q*   22–29 Who . . . furnish-
ings] *F*; *not in Q* 30–42 But . . . you] *Q*; *not in F*   43 further] *F*;
farther *Q*   44 am] *F*; *not in Q*   45 out-wall] *F, Q corr.*; outwall *Q*
uncorr.   48 that] *F*; your *Q*   53–54 in which your pain,/That way,
I'll this] *F*; Ile this way, you that *Q*   55 Holla] *F*; hollow *Q*
Act 3, Scene 2] *F* (*Scena Secunda*); *not in Q*   0 SD *Storm still*] *F*;
not in Q 2 cataracts] *F*; caterickes *Q*   3 our] *F*; the *Q*   7 Strike]
F; smite *Q*   o'th'world] *F*; of the world *Q*   8 moulds] *F*; mold *Q*
9 makes] *F*; make *Q*   10 holy] *F, Q corr.*; holly *Q uncorr.*   11
o'door] *F*; a doore *Q*   13 Fools] *F*; foole *Q*   16 tax] *F*; taske *Q*
18 Then] *F*; why then *Q*   22 will] *F*; haue *Q*   join] *F*; ioin'd
Q   23 battles] *F*; battel *Q*   24 ho!] *F*; *not in Q*   25 put's] *F*; put
his *Q*   33 of] *F*; have *Q*   35 but] *F*; *Q corr.*; hut *Q uncorr.*   36
SD *Enter Kent*] *F*; *not in Q*   40 codpiece] *F*; codpis, *Q*   42 are] *F*;
sit *Q*   44 wanderers] *F*; wanderer *Q*   45 make] *F*; make *Q*   46
Such . . . fire] *Q*; *not in F*   47 never] *F*; ne're *Q*   50 pudder] *F*;
Powther *Q*   54 simular] *F*; simular man *Q*   55 to] *F*; in *Q*   57
Has] *F* (ha's); hast *Q*   58 concealing continents] *F*; concealed cen-
ters *Q*   60 than] *F*; their *Q*   63 while] *F*; whilst *Q*   64 the] *F*;
not in Q 65 you] *F*; me *Q*   67 wits begin] *F*; wit begins *Q*   71
And] *F*; that *Q*   your] *F*; you *Q*   72 in] *F*; of *Q*   73 That's sorry]
F; That sorrowes *Q*   74 and] *F*; *not in Q*   77 Though] *F*; for *Q*
78 boy] *F*; my good *Q*   SD *Exeunt* [*all but the* FOOL]] *F* (*Exit*);
not in Q   79–94 FOOL This . . . time *Exit*] *F*; *not in Q*
Act 3, Scene 3] *Scena Tertia*] *F*; *not in Q* 0 SD *Enter* GLOUCES-
TER *and* EDMUND *with lights*] *Q* (*Enter Gloster and the Bastard*
with lights; Enter Gloster, and Edmund F   3 took] *F*; tooke me *Q*
4 perpetual] *F*; their *Q*   5 or] *F*; nor *Q*   6 EDMUND] *This edi-*

tion; Bast. F, Q   7–8 between] F; betwixt Q   12 footed] F; landed
Q   seek] Q; looke F   14 If] F; Though Q   17 strange things] F;
some strange thing Q   23 The] F; then Q   doth] F; for Q
Act 3, Scene 4] *Scena Quarta* F; *not in* Q   2 The] F, Q *corr.;* the
the Q *uncorr.*   3 *Storm still*] F; *not in* Q   6 contentious] F; tem-
pestious Q *corr.;* cruelentious Q *uncorr.*   7 skin: so F *corr.;* skin. so
F *uncorr.;* skin, so Q   10 thy] Q *corr.,* Q *uncorr.;* they F   roaring]
F; Q *corr.;* raging Q *uncorr.*   12 The tempest] F, Q *uncorr.;* this
tempest Q *corr.;*   14 beats there: filial] F *corr.* (beates there, fil-
liall); beates there filiall; F, Q *corr.;* beares their filiall Q *uncorr.*
16 home] F; sure Q   17–18 In . . . endure] F; *not in* Q   20 gave]
F; gave you Q   21 lies] F *corr.,* Q; lie F *uncorr.*   22 here] F; *not in*
Q   23 thine own] F; thy one Q   26–27 In . . . sleep] F; *not in* Q
29 storm] F; night Q   31 looped] Q (loopt); lop'd F   36 SD *Enter*
FOOL] *Enter Edgar, and Foole* F   37 EDGAR Fathom . . . Tom] F;
not in Q   37 fathom and] F *corr.;* Fathomand F *uncorr.*   38 spirit,
a spirit] F; spirit Q   42 i'th'straw] F; in the straw Q   45 winds]
F; cold wind Q   Hum] F; *not in* Q   47 Didst] F; Hast Q   give] F;
giuen Q   50–51 flame, through sword] F; foord Q   51 hath] F;
has Q   55 Bless thy] Q; Blisse thy F   55–56 O . . . de] F; *not in*
Q   Bless] Q; Blisse F   56 star-blasting] F; star-blusting Q   59
SD *Storm still*] F; *not in* Q   60 Has] F; What Q   53 Wouldst] F;
didst Q   73 Pillicock hill] F; pelicocks hill Q   74 Alow, alow, loo,
loo] F; a lo lo lo Q   76 o'th'foul] F; at'h foule Q   77 justly] Q; Iustice F   85 I deeply] Q; I deerely F   86 woman] F; women Q   90
brothels] F; brothell Q   91 plackets] F; placket Q   books] F;
booke Q   92–93 Says suum, mun, nonny] F; hay no on ny Q   93
Cessez] F (*Sesey*); caese Q   95 Thou] F; Why thou Q   a] F; thy Q
96–97 more than] F; more, but Q   99 Ha] F; *not in* Q   101 lend-
ings] leadings F, Q *corr.;* leadings Q *uncorr.*   102 unbutton here]
F; bee true Q *uncorr.;* on Q *corr.*   102 SD *Enter* GLOUCESTER
. . . *torch*] F; *Enter Gloster* Q (after 106)   103–04 contented, 'tis]
F; content, this is Q   106 on's] F; in Q   107 Flibbertigibbet] F;
fliberdegibek Q *corr.;* Striberdegibit Q *uncorr.*   107 at] F; till the Q
corr., leadings Q *uncorr.*   108 gives] F, Q *corr.;* gins Q *uncorr.*
108–09 and the pin, squints] leadings F; & the pin, squemes Q
corr.; the pin-queues leadings Q *uncorr.*   109 harelip] F, Q *uncorr.;*
harte lip Q *uncorr.*   112 He met the night-mare] F, Q *corr.;* a
nellthu night more Q *uncorr.*   113 alight] F; O light Q *corr.,* Q *uncorr.*   114 arount thee witch, aroint] F; arint thee, witch arint thee
Q *corr.;* arint thee, with arint thee Q *uncorr.*   120 wall-newt] F, Q
corr.; dall-wort Q *uncorr.*   129 Smulkin] F; snulbug Q   133 my
lord, is grown so vile] F; is growne so vild my Lord Q   140 ven-
tured] F; venter'd Q   141 fire and food] F; food and fire Q   144
Good my lord] F; My good Lord Q   145 same] F; most Q   149

once more] *F*; *not in Q*   150 SD *Storm still*] *F*; *not in Q*   151 Ah]
F; O *Q*   155 he] *F*; a *Q*   159 sir] *F*; *not in Q*   162 into th'hovel]
F; in't houell *Q*   170 tower] *F*; towne *Q*   172 SD *Exeunt*] *F*; *not
in Q*

Act 3, Scene 5] *Scena Quinta F*; *not in Q*   0 SD EDMUND] *F*;
Bastard Q   1 his] *F*; the *Q*   2 SP EDMUND] *This edition*; *Bast.
F, Q* (*throughout the scene*)   9 which] *F*; *not in Q*   11 were not]
F; were *Q*   19–20 persevere] *Q*; perseuer *F*   23 dearer] *Q*; deere
F   SD *Exeunt*] *F*; *not in Q*

Act 3, Scene 6] *Scena Sexta F*; *not in Q*   0 SD *Enter* KENT *and*
GLOUCESTER] *F*; *Enter Gloster and Lear, Kent, Foole, and Tom Q*
4 his] *F*; not *in Q*   5 reward] *Q*; deserue *F*   5 SD *Exit*] *F* (*after l.
3*); *not in Q*   SD *Enter* LEAR, EDGAR *and* FOOL] *F*; *not in Q*   6
Frateretto] *F*; *Fretereto Q*   7 and] *F*; *not in Q*   12–15 FOOL No . . .
LEAR] *F*; *not in Q*   16–57 EDGAR The . . . wits] *Q*; *not in F*
25 trial: *Q2*; tral *Q1*   34 cushions] cushings *Q*   36 robed] *Capell*;
robbed *Q*   52 joint-stool] *Q2*; ioyne stoole *Q1*   54 on] *Capell*; an
Q   61 They] *F*; Theile *Q*   69 Or] *F*; *not in Q*   tyke] *Q*; tight *F*
trundle-tail] *Q*; Troudle taile *F*   70 them] *Q*; him *F*   73 Do, de,
de, de. *Cessez*] *F*; loudla doodla *Q*   76–77 these hard hearts] *F*;
this hardnes *Q*   entertain] *F*; 77 entertaine you *Q*   79 Persian] *F*;
Persian attire *Q*   80 and rest] *F*; *not in Q*   81–82 So, so] *F*; so,
so, so *Q*   82 i'th'morning] *F*; i'th'morning, so, so, so *Q*   83 *Enter*
GLOUCESTER] *Q*; *F* (*after l. 79*)   83 FOOL And . . . noon] *F*;
not in Q   90 toward] *F*; towards *Q*   94 Take up, take up] *F*; Take
vp the King *Q corr.*; Take vp to keepe *Q uncorr.*   96 KENT Oppressed . . . behind] *F*; *not in Q*   100 SD *Exeunt*] *F*; *Exit Q*
101–114 EDGAR When . . . lurk] *Q*; *not in F*

Act 3, Scene 7] *F* (*Scena Septima*); *not in Q*   0 SD *Enter* CORN-
WALL, REGAN, GONERIL, EDMUND, *and* SERVANTS] *F* (*En-
ter Cornwall, Regan, Gonerill, Bastard, and Servants*); *Enter
Cornwall, and Regan, and Gonorill, and Bastard Q*   3 traitor] *F*; vi-
laine *Q*   7 company] *F, Q corr.*; company (*repeated: after l. 5 and
after l. 7*) *Q uncorr.*   7 revenges] *F*; reuenge *Q*   8 Advise] *Q*;
Aduice *F*   9 festinate] *F* (*festiuate*); festuant *Q*   10 posts] *F*; post
Q   12 SD *Enter* OSWALD] *F*; *Q* (*after l. 13*)   16 questrists] *F*;
questrits *Q*   22 SD *Exeunt* [GONERIL *and* EDMUND] *Q* (*Exit
Gon. And Bast*; *after l. 21*); *Exit F* (*after l. 21*)   24 well] *F*; *not in Q*
27 *Enter* GLOUCESTER *brought in by two or three* [SERVANTS]]
Q; *Enter Gloucester, and Seruants F* (*after* control *in l. 27*)   33 I'm
none] *F*; I am true *Q*   50 Dover] *F*; Douer sir *Q*   57 anointed flesh
stick] *F*; annoynted flesh rash *Q corr.*; aurynted flesh rash *Q uncorr.*
58 bare] *F*, lowd *Q corr.*; lou'd *Q uncorr.*   59 buoyed] *F*; bod *Q
corr.*; layd *Q uncorr.*   60 stelled] *F, Q corr.*; steeled *Q uncorr.*   61
holp] *F*; holpt *Q*   rain] *F*; rage *Q*   62 howled that stern] *F*; heard

that dearne *Q*   64 subscribe] *F*; subscrib'd *Q*   69 you] *F*; ye *Q*
70 th'other, too] *F*; tother to *Q*   78 SD [*They*] *draw and fight*] *Q*;
not in F   79 SD *She . . . behind*] *Q*; *killes him F*   80 you have] *F*;
yet haue you *Q*   85 enkindle] *F*; vnbridle *Q* 86 treacherous] *F*; *not
in Q*   93 *Exit . . .* GLOUCESTER] *F*; *not in Q*   96 dunghill] *F*;
dungell *Q*   97 me your] *F*; mey our *Q*   SD *Exeunt*] *F*; *Exit Q*
98–106 [SECOND] SERVANT *. . . Exit*] *Q*; *not in F*   98 SP
[SECOND] SERVANT] *Seruant Q*   99 [THIRD] SERVANT]
2 Seruant Q   102 [SECOND] SERVANT] *1 Ser. Q*   103 roguish]
Q uncorr.; *not in Q corr.*

Act 4, Scene 1] *Actus Quartus. Scena Prima F*; *not in Q*   4 esper-
ance] *F*; experience *Q*   6–9 Welcome . . . OLD MAN] *F*; *not in Q*
10 But who comes] *F*; Who's here *Q corr.*, *Q uncorr.*   poorly led]
F; parti, eyd *Q corr.*; poorlie, leed *Q uncorr.*   13 age] *F*; age. *Enter
Glost. led by an old man Q*   15 years] *F*; *not in Q*   29 So] *F*; As *Q*
32 He] *F*; A *Q*   33 I'th'last] *F*; In the last *Q*   37 to wanton] *F*;
toth'wanton *Q*   39 Fool] *F*; the Fool *Q*   42 Get thee away] *F*;
Then prethee get thee gon *Q*   52 *Exit*] *F*; *not in Q*   56 EDGAR
And . . . must] *F*; *not in Q*   60 man's son] *F*; man *Q*   60–65 Five
. . . master] *Q*; *not in F*   66 you] *F* (yᵘ); thou *Q*   70 slaves] *F*;
stands *Q*   72 undo] *F*; vnder *Q*   76 fearfully] *F*; firmely *Q*   81
Exeunt] *F*; *not in Q*

Act 4, Scene 2] *F* (*Scena Secunda*); *not in Q*   0 SD *Enter*
GONERIL, EDMUND *and* OSWALD] *F* (*Enter Gonerill, Bastard,
and Steward*); *Enter Gonorill and Bastard Q*   3 master] *F*; master?
Enter Steward Q   10 most he should dislike] *F*; hee should most
desire *Q*   12 terror] *F*, *Q corr.*; curre *Q uncorr.*   15 Edmund] *F*;
Edgar Q   17 names] *F*; armes *Q*   21 command] *F*, *Q corr.*;
coward *Q uncorr.*   25 SP EDMUND] *This edition*; *Bast. F*, *Q*
(*throughout the scene*)   26 Oh . . . and man] *F*; *not in Q*   27 a] *F*,
Q corr.; coward *Q uncorr.*   28 My Fool] *F*; A foole *Q corr.*; My
foote *Q uncorr.*   SD *Exit* [EDMUND]] *F* (*after* death in *l.* 25); *not
in Q*   SD *Exit*] *Q* (*Exit Stew.*); *not in F*   SD *Enter* ALBANY] *F*;
not in Q   30 whistling] *Q corr.*; whistle *F*, *Q uncorr.*   32–50 I
. . . deep] *Q*; *not in F*   33 its] *Q2*; ith *Q1 corr.*; it *Q1 uncorr.*   45
benefited] *Q corr.*; beneflicted *Q uncorr.*   47 the] *Q uncorr.*; this
Q corr.   48 will come] *Q uncorr.*; will *Q corr.*   49 Humanity] *Q
corr.*; humanly *Q uncorr.*   52 eye-discerning] *F*; eye deseruing
53–59 that . . . so] *Q*; *not in F*   53 know'st / Fools do] know'st
fools, do *Q uncorr.*; know'st, foolsdo *Q corr.*   56 noiseless] *Q corr.*
(noyseles); noystles *Q uncorr.*   57 state begins thereat] *Q corr.*;
slayer begins threats *Q uncorr.*   58 Whilst] *Q corr.* (noyseles);
Whil's *Q uncorr.*   60 shows] *Q corr.* (shewes); seemes *F*, *Q uncorr.*
62–68 Thou . . . mew] *Q*; *not in F*   68 mew] *Q corr.*; now *Q uncorr.*   SD MESSENGER] *F* (*after l.* 69); *Gentleman Q*   69 AL-

BANY What news] *Q*; *not in F* 73 thrilled] *F*; thrald *Q* 75
threat-enraged] *F*; thereat inragd *Q* 79 You] *F*; *Q corr.*; your *Q*
uncorr. 87 tart] *F*; tooke *Q* SD Exit] *Q*; *not in F* 97 SD *Ex-*
eunt] *F*; *Exit Q*

Act 4, Scene 3] *not in F, Q* 0–56 *Enter . . . Exeunt*] *Q*; *this scene*
is not in F 11 Ay, sir] *Capell*; I say *Q* 20 seemed] *Pope*; seeme *Q*
30 believed] *Q* (beleeft).

Act 4, Scene 4] *F* (*Scena Tertia*); *not in Q* 0 SD *Enter . . .* SOL-
DIERS] *F*; *Enter Cordelia, Doctor and others. Q* 3 fumitor]
Theobald; Fenitar *F*, femiter *Q* 4 burdocks] *Hanmer*; Hardokes *F*,
hor-docks *Q* 6 century] *Q*; Centery *F* send] *F*, is sent *Q* 10
helps] *F*, helpe *Q* 11 SP GENTLEMAN] *F, Doct. Q* 18 desires]
F, distresse *Q* 27 incite] *F*, in sight *Q* 28 right] *Q*; Rite *F* 29
Exeunt] *F*; *Exit Q*

Act 4, Scene 5] *F* (*Scena Quarta*); *not in Q* 0 SD OSWALD]
Steward F, Q 2 SP OSWALD] *Stew. F, Q* (*throughout the scene*)
3 there] *F, not in Q* 5 lord] *F*; Lady *Q* 7 might] *Q*; night *F* 15
o'th'enemy] *F*; at'h army *Q* 16 madam, with my letter] *F*; with my
letters *Q* 17 troops set] *F*; troope set *Q* 22 things] *F*; thing *Q*
26 oeilliades] *F* (eliads); aliads *Q* 29 y'are] *F*; for *Q* 37 fare you
well] *F*; farewell *Q* 40 him] *Q*; *not in F* 41 party] *F*; Lady *Q*
41 *Exeunt*] *F*; *Exit Q*

Act 4, Scene 6] *F* (*Scena Quinta*); *not in Q* 0 SD EDGAR] *F*;
Edmund Q 1 I] *F*; we *Q* 2 up it] *F*; it vp *Q* 8 In] *F*; With *Q*
16 samphire] *Rowe*; Sampire *F*; sampire *Q* 18 walked] *F* (walk'd);
walke *Q* 19 yond] *F*; yon *Q* 23 so high. I'll] *F*; its so high ile *Q*
31 further] *F*; farther *Q* 33 ye] *F*; you *Q* 35 SD *He kneels*] *F*
(*after* gods); *not in F* 40 snuff] *F*; snurff *Q* 41 him] *F*; *not in*
Q 42 SD *He falls*] *Q*; *not in F* 43 may] *F*; my *Q* 47 Hoa] *F*; ho
Q Friend] *F*; *not in Q* 53 breathe] breath *F, Q* 59 summit] *F*
(Somnet); sommons *Q* 67 is't] *F*; *not in Q* 69 o'th'cliff] *F*; of
the cliffe *Q* 70 beggar] *F*; bagger *Q* 73 enragèd] *F*; enridged *Q*
75 make] *F*; made *Q* their] *Q*; them *F* 80 'twould] *F*; would it *Q*
82 SD *Enter Lear, mad*] *Q* (*after l.* 84); *Enter Lear* 85 coining] *F*;
crying *Q* 91 piece of] *F*; *not in Q* 93 i'th'clout, i'th'clout!
Hewgh] *F*; in the ayre, hagh *Q* 97 with a white beard!] *F*; *not in*
Q Ha, Regan] *Q*; *not in F* 98 the white] *Q*; white *Q* 100 that]
Q; *not in F* 103 smelt 'em] *F*; smelt them *Q* 105 ague-proof] *F*;
argue-proof *Q* 110 die! Die] *F*; die *Q* 117 presages] *F*; pre-
sageth *Q* 118 does] *F*; do *Q* 120 The] *F*; to *Q* 126 sul-
phurous] *F*; sulphury *Q* 127 consumption] *F*; consumation *Q*
129 Sweeten] *F*; to sweeten *Q* 133 Dost] *F*; do *Q* 134 thine] *F*;
thy *Q* at] *F*; on *Q* 136 this] *F*; that *Q* but] *F*; *not in Q* 137
thy] *F*; the *Q* one] *Q*; *not in F* 146 this] *F*; the *Q* 147 thine]
F; thy *Q* yond justice] *F*; yon *Q* 148 yond simple] *F*; yon simple

Q   thine] *F*; thy *Q*   148–49 change places and] *F*; *not in Q*
149–50 Justice, which is the thief] *F*; theefe, which is the Iustice
Q   153 dog's obeyed] *F*; dogge, so bade *Q*   155 thy] *F*; thine *Q*
156 Thou] *F*; thy bloud *Q*   158 clothes] *F*; raggs *Q*   great] *F*;
small *Q*   159 hide] *F*; hides *Q*   159–64 Plate . . . lips] *F*; *not in Q*
plate] THEOBALD; Place sinnes *F*   166 Now, now, now, now] *F*; no
now *Q*   170 fortunes] *F*; fortune *Q*   174 wail] *Q*; wawl *F*   Mark]
F; marke me *Q*   178 shoe] *F*; shoot *Q*   179 felt] *F*; fell *Q*   I'll
. . . proof] *F*; *not in Q*   181 SD *three*] *Q*; *a F*   182 hands] *Q*;
hand *F*   sir] *Q*; sirs *F*   183 daughter] *F*; *not in Q*   186 surgeons]
F; a churgion *Q*   187 to'th'brains] *F*; to the *Q*   189 man a man] *F*
a man *Q*   191–92 Ay . . . sir] *Q*; *not in F*   191 SD FIRST] GEN-
TLEMAN Good sir] *Q corr.*; *not in Q uncorr.*   193 smug] *F*; *not in
Q*   196 Come] *F*; nay *Q*   197 by] *F*; with *Q*   sa', sa', sa', sa'] *F*;
not in Q   SD *Exit* LEAR *running*] *Exit King running Q*; *Exit F*
199 a] *F*; one *Q*   201 have] *F*; hath *Q*   203 sir] *F*; *not in Q*   204
hears that/Which] *F*; here's that/That *Q*   205 sound] *F*; sense *Q*
207 descry] *F*; descryes *Q*   208 Stands] *Q*; Standst *F*   thought]
F; thoughts *Q*   211 *Exit*] *Q*; *F* (*after* on)   216 tame to] *Q*; lame
by *F*   220–21 bounty . . . boot, to boot] *F*, *Q corr.*; bornet and
beniz to saue thee *Q uncorr.*   221 OSWALD] *Stew. F*, *Q* (*throughout the scene*) 223 first] *F*, *Q corr.*; *not in Q uncorr.*   223 old] *F*;
most *Q corr.*, *Q uncorr.*   227 Dar'st] *F*; durst *Q*   230 zir] *F*; sir *Q*
231 vurther 'casion] *F*; cagion *Q*   233 and] *F*; *not in Q*   234–35
ha' bin] *F*; haue beene *Q*   235 as 'tis] *F*; *not in Q*   vortnight] *F*, *Q
corr.*, fortnight *Q uncorr.*   236 che vor'ye, or I'ce] *F*; cheuore ye *Q
corr.*, *Q uncorr.*   costard] *F*, *Q corr.*, coster *Q uncorr.*   237 ballow]
F; bat *Q corr.*; batero *Q uncorr.*   ch'ill] *F*; ile *Q*   238 SD *They
fight*] *Q*; *not in F*   239 zir] *F*; sir *Q*   vor] *F*; vor *Q*   244–45 out /
Upon] *F*; out, upon *Q corr.*; out vpon *Q uncorr.*   245 English] *F*;
British *Q corr.*, *Q uncorr.*   SD *He dies*] *F*; *not in Q*   249–50 rest
you./Let's] *F*; rest you, lets *Q corr.*; rest you lets *Q uncorr.*   250
these] *F*; his *Q corr.*, *Q uncorr.*   The] *F*; These British *Q corr.*, *Q
uncorr.*   speakes of] *F*; speakes of, *Q corr.*; speakes of *Q uncorr.*
254 we] *F*; weed *Q corr.*, wee'd *Q uncorr.*   256 SD *Reads the letter*] *F* (*as centered direction after l. 255*); *A letter* (*after l. 255*), *Q
corr.*; *not in Q uncorr.*   256 our] *F*; your *Q*   260 jail] *F* (Gaole), *Q
corr.* (iayle); gayle *Q uncorr.*   262–63 and . . . venture] *Q*; *not in F*
264 will] *F*; wit *Q*   275 severed] *F*; fenc'd *Q*   277 SD *A drum afar
off*] *Q*; *Drum afarre off F* (*after l. 275*)   279 *Exeunt*] *F*; *not in Q*
Act 4, Scene 7] *F* (*Scena Septima*); *not in Q*   0 SD *and* GEN-
TLEMAN] *F* (*corrected*); *Gentleman F* (*uncorrected*); *and Docter Q*
6 more, nor] *Q*; more, not *F*   8 Pardon] *F*; Pardon me *Q*   13 SP
GENTLEMAN] *F*; *Doct. Q* (*throughout the scene*)   16 jarring] *F*;
hurrying *Q*   20 SD *Enter . . .* SERVANTS] *F*; *not in Q*   21 of] *F*;

of his *Q*   23 Be by, good madam] *F*; *Gent.* Good madam be by *Q*
24–25 CORDELIA Very well./GENTLEMAN Please . . . there] *Q*;
not in F   31 Did challenge] *F*; Had challenged *Q*   32 opposed] *F*;
exposd *Q*   warring] *Q*; jarring *Q*   33–36 To . . . helm] *Q*; *not in F*
36 enemy's] *F*; iniurious *Q*   45 o'th'grave] *F*; ath grave *Q*   49 do]
F; *not in Q*   50 You are] *F*; Yar *Q*   59 your hand] *F* (*corrected*);
yours hand *F* (*uncorrected*); your hands *Q*   60 No, sir] *Q*; *not in F*
63 Not . . . less] *F*; *not in Q*   72 am, I am] *Q*; am *F*   81–82 and
. . . lost] *Q*; *not in F*   86 *Manet* KENT *and* GENTLEMAN] *Q*; *not
in F*   87–99 GENTLEMAN Holds . . . fought. *Exit*] *Q*; *not in F*
Act 5, Scene 1] *F* (*Actus Quintus. Scena Prima*); *not in Q*   *Enter
with drum and colors*, EDMUND, REGAN, GENTLEMEN *and*
SOLDIERS] *F*; *Enter Edmund, Regan, and their powers Q*   O SD
EDMUND] *This edition*; *Bast. F, Q* (*throughout the text*)   3 alter-
ation] *F*; *Q corr.*; abdication; *Q uncorr.*   9 In] *F*; I *Q* 11–13 ED-
MUND That . . . hers] *Q*; *not in F*   17 *Enter . . . Soldiers*] *F*; *Enter
Albany and Goneril with troupes Q*   18–19 GONERIL I . . . me]
Q; *not in F*   19 and] *Q corr.*; nd *Q uncorr.*   21 Sir] *F*; For *Q*
23–28 Where . . . nobly] *Q*; *not in F*   30 and particular broils] *F*;
dore particulars *Q*   31 the] *F*; to *Q*   33 proceeding] *F*; proceed-
ings *Q*   34 EDMUND I . . . tent] *Q*; *not in F*   40 *Exeunt . . .
Armies*] *F* (*after l. 38*); *Exeunt   Q*   47 And . . . ceases] *F*; *not in Q*
52 thy] *F*; the *Q*   53 view] *F, Q corr.*; vew *Q uncorr.*   54 guess] *F*;
quesse *Q*   true] *F*; great *Q*   57 sisters] *F*; sister *Q*   58 stung] *F*;
sting *Q*   65 countenance] *F*; countenadce *Q*   the] *F*; his *Q*
Act 5, Scene 2] *F* (*Scena Secunda*); *not in Q*   0 SD Alarum . . .
Exeunt] *F*; *Alarum. Enter the powers of France ouer the stage,
Cordelia with her father in her hand Q*   O SD EDMUND] *This
edition*; *Bast. F, Q* (*throughout the scene*)   1 tree] *F*; bush *Q*   4
SD *Exit*] *F*; *Q* (*After 'comfort'*)   SD *within. Enter Edgar*] *F*; *not in
Q*   8 further] *F*; farther *Q*   11 GLOUCESTER And . . . too *Exeunt*] *F*; not in *Q*
Act 5, Scene 3] *F* (*Scena Tertia*); *not in Q*   0 SD *Enter . . . Captain*] *F*; *Enter, Edmund, with Lear and Cordelia prisoners Q*   3
first] *F*; best *Q*   8 No, no, no, no] *F*; No, no *Q*   19 by'th'moon] *F*;
bith'Moone *Q*   24 years] *F*; *not in Q*   26 starved] *F*; starue *Q*
SD *Exit*] *F*; *not in Q*   29 One] *F, Q Corr.*; And *Q uncorr.*   36
don't] *F* (dont); don *Q*   39–40 CAPTAIN I . . . do't] *Q*; *not in F*
40 SD *Exit*] *F* (*Exit Captaine*); *not in Q*   *Flourish . . .* SOLDIERS]
F; *Enter Duke, the two Ladies, and others Q*   42 well.] *F* (well:);
well, *Q corr.*; well *Q uncorr.*   44 them] *F*; then *Q*   47 send] *F, Q
corr.*; saue *Q uncorr.*   48 and . . . guard] *Q corr.*; *not in F, Q uncorr.*   49 had] *F*; has *Q corr.*; *Q uncorr.*   50 common] *F* (well:), *Q
corr.*; coren *Q uncorr.*   56–60 We . . . place] *Q*; *not in F*   56 We]
Q corr.; meet *Q uncorr.*   58 sharpness] *Q corr.*; shapes *Q uncorr.*

66 immediacy] *F*; immediate *Q*   69 addition] *F*; aduancement *Q*
69 rights] *F*; right *Q*   77 Dispose . . . thine] *F*; *not in Q*   82 SD
REGAN] *F*; *Bast. Q*   thine] *F*; good *Q*   84 thine attaint] *Q*; thy
arrest *Q*   85 sister] *Q*; sisters *F*   88 your] *F*; the *F*   banns]
banes *F, Q*   89 love] *Q*; loves *F*   90 GONERIL An interlude / AL-
BANY] *F*; *not in Q*   92 Let . . . sound] *F*; *not in Q*   93 person] *F*;
head *Q*   98 medicine] *F*; poison *Q*   103 ho,] *F*; ho. *Bast.* A Herald, ho, a Herald. / *Alb. Q*   SD *Enter a Herald*] *F* (*after* firmly); *not
in Q*   109 SD *A trumpet sounds*] *F*; *Cap.* Sound trumpet?   110
SP HERALD (*Reads*)] *F* (*as centered stage direction*); *Her.* (*as
speech prefix*) *Q*   110–11 within the lists] *F*; in the hoast *Q*   113
by] *F*; at *Q*   114 SD *First trumpet*] *F* (*1 Trumpet*); *not in Q*   115
Again] *F* (*Her.* Againe); *Bast.* Sound? *Q*)   SD *Second trumpet*] *F* (*2
Trumpet*); *not in Q*   116 Again] *F* (*Her.* Againe), *Q*   SD *Third
trumpet*] *F* (*3 Trumpet*); *not in Q*   SD *Trumpet . . . armed*] *F*; *Enter Edgar at the third sound, a trumpet before him Q*   119 your
quality] *F*; and quality *Q*   120 Know] *F*; O know *Q*   122 am I noble as] *F*; are I mou't / Where is *Q*   123 cope] *F*; cope with all *Q*
128–129 my privilege,/The . . . honors] *F*; the priuiledge of my
tongue *Q*   131 place, youth] *F*; youth, place *Q*   132 Despite] *Q*;
Despise *F*   victor-sword] *F*; victor, sword *Q*   fortune] *F*; fortun'd
Q   135 Conspirant] *F*; Conspicuate *Q*   137 below thy foot] *F*;
beneath thy feet *Q*   143 tongue] *F*; being *Q*.   144 What . . . de-
lay] *F*; *not in Q*   147 hell-hated lie, o'erwhelm] hell heatedly, ore-
turnd *Q*   150 *Alarums. Fights*] *F*; *not in Q*   153 war] *F*; armes *Q*
wast] *F*; art *Q* 155 Stop] *F*; stople *Q*   156 Hold, sir] *F*; *not in Q*
158 No] *F*; nay no *Q*   160 SD *Exit*] *F*; *Exit Gonorill* (*after l.* 161)
Q   161 Oh] *F*; *not in Q*   SP EDMUND] *F* (*Bast.*); *Gon. Q*   166
thou'rt] *F*; thou bee'st *Q*   171 vices] *F*; vertues *Q*   172 plague] *F*;
scourge *Q*   174 'tis true] *F*; *not in Q*   175 circle] *F*; circled *Q*
186 we] *F*; with *Q*   193 fault] *F*; Father *Q*   197 our] *F*; my *Q*
206–22 EDGAR This . . . slave] *Q*; not in *F*   222 SD *a* GENTLE-
MAN] *F*; *one Q*   SD *with a bloody knife*] *Q*; *not in F*   223 Oh,
help] *F*; *not in Q*   SD EDGAR] *F*; *Alb. Q*   223–24 ALBANY
Speak, man./EDGAR] *F*; *not in Q*   224 this] *F*; *not in Q*   'Tis] *F*;
Its *Q*   225 Oh . . . dead] *F*; *not in Q*   226 dead? Speak, man] *F*;
man, speak *Q*   228 confesses] *F*; hath confest *Q*   230 EDGAR
Here comes Kent. / *Enter* KENT] *F*; *not in Q*   231 SD *Goneril's . . .
out*] *F*; *The bodies of Gonorill and Regan are brought in Q* (*after*
Kent *in l.* 239)   Goneril's] *This edition*; *Goneril F*   232 judgment]
F; Iustice *Q*   233 pity] *F*; *Edg.* Here comes *Kent* sir. / *Alb. Q*   is
this] *F*; tis *Q*   234 Which] *F*; that *Q*   237 ALBANY] *F*; *Duke Q*
(*throughout the rest of the scene*)   244 mine] *F*; my *Q*   248 has]
F; hath *Q*   250 The captain] *Q*; *not in F*   257 Howl howl, howl,
howl,] *Q*; howl, howl, howl *F*   you] *Q*; your *F*   267 Oh] *F*; A *Q*

269 you, murderers] *F*; your murderous *Q*   273 woman] *F*;
women *Q*   277 him] *F*; them *Q*   282 This . . . sight] *F*; *not in Q*
289 You are] *This edition*; Your are *F*; You'r *Q*   292 Ay, so I think]
F; So thinke I too *Q*   293 says] *F*; sees *Q*   294 SD *a* MESSEN-
GER] *F*; *Captaine Q*   295 SP MESSENGER] *F*; *Capt. Q*   301
honors] *F*; honor *Q*   305 no! No life] *F*; no life *Q*   306 have] *F*;
of *Q*   307 thou no] *F corr.*, *Q*; thouno *F uncorr.*   Thou'lt] *F corr.*,
F uncorr.; O thou wilt   308 Never, never, never, never, never] *F*;
neuer, neuer, neuer *Q*   310 O, o, o, o] *F*; *not in Q*   311–12 Do
. . . there. *He dies*] *F*; *not in Q*   311 this? Look] *F corr.*, *F uncorr.*
313 He] *F*; O he *Q*   322 realm] *F*; kingdome *Q*   324 me; I] *F*;
and *Q*   325 SP EDGAR] *F*; *Duke Q*   328 *Exeunt with a dead
march*] *F*; *not in Q*

Lear (Michael Gambon) threatens his Fool (Antony Sher) with whipping (Act 1, Scene 4) in the 1983 Royal Shakespeare Company production of *King Lear*. Joe Cocks Studio Collection.
© Shakespeare Birthplace Trust.

Lear. Hear, Nature, hear; dear goddess, hear!
Suspend thy purpose, if thou didst intend
To make this creature fruitful!   *Act I. Scene IV.*

A nineteenth-century engraving of Lear's condemnation of Goneril
(Act 1, Scene 4). By permission of the Shakespeare Birthplace Trust.

Gloucester (Alan Webb) and Lear (Paul Scofield) observe
'Caius' (Tom Fleming) in the stocks (Act 2, Scene 4) in the
1962 Royal Shakespeare Company production of *King Lear*.
Thos. F. and Mig Holte Theatre Photographic Collection.
© Shakespeare Birthplace Trust.

Mr. Garrick as King Lear.

Blow winds and burst your Cheeks.

Act 3.d Scene 1.st

Terry sculp.t

Publish'd by Harrison & C.o May 1.1779.

Lear (David Garrick) on the heath in an eighteenth-century London
production of Nahum Tate's version of *King Lear*
(Act 3, Scene 1 in Tate's text;
Act 3, Scene 2 in Shakespeare's text).
By permission of the Shakespeare Birthplace Trust.

A nineteenth-century engraving of Lear's reconciliation
with Cordelia (Act 4, Scene 7). By permission of the
Shakespeare Birthplace Trust.

James Barry's late-eighteenth-century engraving of Lear's confrontation with the bodies of his daughters (Act 5, Scene 3), from *Boydell's Shakespeare*. By permission of the Shakespeare Birthplace Trust.

SOURCES

Primary Sources

ANONYMOUS

From The True Chronicle History of King Leir and his three daughters (1605)†

[From Scene 1]

Enter King Leir and Nobles

LEIR   Thus to our griefe the obsequies performd
Of our (too late) deceast and dearest Queen,

* * *

Let us request your grave advice, my Lords,   5
For the disposing of our princely daughters,
For whom our care is specially imployd,
As nature bindeth to advaunce their states,
In royall marriage with some princely mates:
For wanting now their mothers good advice,   10
Under whose government they have receyved
A perfit patterne of a virtuous life.* * *

---

† From *The True Chronicle History of King Leir, and his three daughters, Gonorill, Ragan, and Cordella. As it hath bene divers and sundry times lately acted* (London: Printed by Simon Stafford for John Wright, 1605). According to *Henslowe's Diary*, ed. R. A. Foakes (Cambridge University Press, 2002), a play called "King Lear" was performed by the combined Queen's and Sussex's Men in 1594. Although no specific records about the composition or performance of *King Leir* exist, some scholars have conjectured that the 1594 play was, in fact, the play later printed in 1605 as *King Leir*, and that Shakespeare performed in it as a member of this joint company and was therefore familiar with or had access to its text long before it was finally printed. In any case, Shakespeare closely followed this play in writing his own, although he made several changes, including: omitting Gonorill and Ragan's employment of a murderer to kill Lear (whom Lear and his courtier Perillus frighten away); Lear and Perillus's subsequent escape to France, where they accidentally encounter Cordella and her husband and are there reconciled to them; and, most notably, the defeat by Lear, Cordella, and the King of France of the army led by Gonoril and Ragan, who are allowed to flee without punishment. This and the following sources and other early modern material have been presented in original spelling except in the following cases: *v* in primary position (as in "vnless") has been changed to *u; u* in medial position (as in "gouern") has been changed to *v; i* in primary position (as in "iustice") has been changed to *j*, and contractions used in manuscripts (as in "Sʳ" for "Sir", "yoʳ" for "your") have been spelled out. A fuller account of some of these sources are presented in *Narrative and Dramatic Sources of Shakespeare*, ed. Geoffrey Bullough, Vol. VII (London: Routledge and Kegan Paul, 1973), pp. 269–420.

137

For fathers best do know to governe sonnes;
But daughters steps the mothers counsel turnes.

* * *

One foote already hangeth in the grave,
And age hath made deepe furrowes in my face:
The world of me, I of the world am weary,
And I would fayne resigne these earthly cares,   25
And thinke upon the welfare of my soule:
Which by no better meanes may be effected,
Then by resigning up the Crowne from me,
In equall dowry to my daughters three.

* * *

PERILLUS   Of us & ours, your gracious care, my Lord,
Deserves an everlasting memory,
To be inrol'd in Chronicles of fame,
By never-dying perpetuity: 70
Yet to become so provident a Prince,
Lose not the title of a loving father:
Do not force love, where fancy cannot dwell,
Lest stremes being stopt, above the banks do swell.
LEIR   I am resolv'd, and even now my mind   75
Doth meditate a sudden stratagem,
To try which of my daughters loves me best:
Which till I know, I cannot be in rest.
This graunted, when they joyntly shall contend,
Eche[1] to exceed the other in their love: 80
Then at the vantage will I take *Cordella*,
Even as she doth protest she loves me best,
Ile say, Then, daughter, graunt me one request,
To shew thou lovest me as thy sisters doe,
Accept a husband, whom my selfe will woo.   85
This sayd, she cannot well deny my sute,
Although (poore soule) her sences will be mute:
Then will I tryumph in my policy,
And match her with a King of Brittany.

[*From Scene 2*]

* * *

RAGAN   Now we have fit occasion offred us,
To be reveng'd upon her [i.e., Cordella] unperceyv'd.
GONORILL   Nay, our revenge we will inflict on her,   75
Shall be accounted piety in us:
I will so flatter with my doting father,

1. Each.

As he was ne're so flattred in his life.
Nay, I will say, that if it be his pleasure,
To match me to a begger, I will yield: 80
For why, I know what ever I do say,
He meanes to match me with the Cornwall King.
RAGAN   Ile say the like: for I am well assured,
What e're I say to please the old mans mind,
Who dotes, as if he were a child agayne,   90
I shall injoy the noble Cambrian Prince:
Only, to feed his humour, will suffice
To say, I am content with any one
Whom heele appoint me; this will please him more,
Then e're *Apolloes* musike pleased Jove.   95
GONORILL   I smile to think, in what a wofull plight
Cordella will be, when we answere thus:
For she will rather dye, then give consent
To joyne in marriage with the Irish King:
So will our father think, she loveth him not,   100
Because she will not graunt his desire,
Which we will aggravate in such bitter termes,
That he will soone convert his love to hate:
For he, you know, is alwayes in extremes.
RAGAN   Not all the world could lay a better plot,   105
I long till it be put in practice.

[*From Scene 3*]
                          * * *
        Enter Leir and Perillus with the three daughters.
                          * * *

LEIR   *** Deare *Gonorill*, kind *Ragan*, sweet *Cordella*,   25
Ye florishing branches of a Kingly stocke,
Sprung from a tree that once did flourish greene,
Whose blossomes now are nipt with Winters frost,
And pale grym death doth wayt upon my steps,
And summons me vnto his next Assizes.[2]   30
Therefore, deare daughters, as ye tender the safety
Of him that was the cause of your first being,
Resolve a doubt which much molests my mind,
Which of you three to me would prove most kind;
Which loves me most, and which at my request   35
Will soonest yeeld vnto their fathers hest.
GONORILL   I hope, my gracious father makes no doubt
Of any of his daughters love to him

2. Judgment, i.e., death.

Yet for my part, to shew my zeale to you,
Which cannot be in windy words rehearst,   40
I prize my love to you at such a rate,
I thinke my life inferiour to my love.
Should you injoyne me for to tye a milstone
About my neck, and leape into the Sea,
At your commaund I willingly would doe it: 45
Yea, for to doe you good, I would ascend
The highest Turret in all Brittany,
And from the top leape headlong to the ground:
Nay, more, should you appoynt me for to marry
The meanest vassayle in the spacious world,   50
Without reply I would accomplish it:
In briefe, commaund what ever you desire,
And if I fayle, no favour I require.
LEIR   O, how thy words revive my dying soule!
CORDELLA   O, how I doe abhorre this flattery!   55
LEIR   But what sayth *Ragan* to her fathers will?
RAGAN   O, that my simple utterance could suffice,
    To tell the true intention of my heart,
    Which burnes in zeale of duty to your grace,
    And never can be quench'd, but by desire   60
    To shew the same in outward forwardnesse.
    Oh, that there were some other mayd that durst
    But make a challenge of her love with me;
    Ide make her soone confesse she never loved
    Her father halfe so well as I doe you.   65
    I then, my deeds should prove in playner case,
    How much my zeale aboundeth to your grace:
    But for them all, let this one meane suffice,
    To ratify my love before your eyes:
    I have right noble Suters to my love,   70
    No worse then Kings, and happely I love one:
    Yet, would you have me make my choyce anew,
    Ide bridle fancy, and be rulde by you.
LEIR   Did never *Philomel*[3] sing so sweet a note.
CORDELLA   Did neuer flatterer tell so false a tale.   75
LEIR   Speak now, *Cordella*, make my joyes at full,
    And drop downe Nectar from thy hon[e]y lips.
CORDELLA   I cannot paynt my duty forth in words,
    I hope my deeds shall make report for me:
    But looke what love the child doth owe the father,   80
    The same to you I beare, my gracious Lord.

3. I.e., the nightingale.

GONORILL   Here is an answere answerlesse indeed:
  Were you my daughter, I should scarcely brooke it.
RAGAN   Dost thou not blush, proud Peacock as thou art,
  To make our father such a slight reply?   85
LEIR   Why how now, Minion, are you growne so proud?
  Doth our deare love make you thus peremptory?
  What, is your love become so small to us,
  As that you scorne to tell us what it is?
  Do you love us, as every child doth love   90
  Their father? True indeed, as some,
  Who by disobedience short their fathers dayes,
  And so would you; some are so father-sick,
  That they make meanes to rid them from the world;
  And so would you: some are indifferent,   95
  Whether their aged parents live or dye;
  And so are you. But, didst thou know, proud gyrle,
  What care I had to foster thee to this,
  Ah, then thou wouldst say as thy sisters do:
  Our life is lesse, then love we owe to you.   100
CORDELLA   Deare father, do not so mistake my words,
  Nor my playne meaning be misconstrued;
  My toung[e] was never usde to flattery.
GONORILL   You were not best say I flatter: if you do,
  My deeds shall shew, I flatter not with you.   105
  I love my father better then thou canst.
CORDELLA   The prayse were great, spoke from anothers mouth
  But it should seeme your neighbours dwell far off.
RAGAN   Nay, here is one, that will confirme as much
  As she hath sayd, both for my selfe and her.   110
  I say, thou dost not wish my fathers good.
CORDELLA   Deare father.—
LEIR   Peace, bastard Impe, no issue of King *Leir*,
  I will not heare thee speake one tittle more.
  Call not me father, if thou love thy life,   115
  Nor these thy sisters once presume to name:
  Looke for no helpe henceforth from me nor mine:
  Shift as thou wilt, and trust unto thy selfe:
  My Kingdome will I equally devide
  'Twixt thy two sisters to their royall dowre,   120
  And will bestow them worthy their deserts:
  This done, because thou shalt not have the hope,
  To have a childs part in the time to come,
  I presently will dispossesse my selfe,
  And set up these upon my princely throne.   125
GONORILL   I ever thought that pride would have a fall.

RAGAN   Plaine dealing, sister: your beauty is so sheene,[4]
You need no dowry, to make you be a Queene.

[*From Scene 24*]

>   [*In France*] *Enter the Gallian King and Queene, and Mum-*
>   *ford, with a basket, disguised like Countrey folke.* [*They stand*
>   *aside, unobserved*] * * * *Enter, Leir & Perillus very faintly.*

LEIR   * * * Ah, *Gonorill*, was halfe my Kingdomes gift   50
The cause that thou dist seeke to have my life?
Ah, cruell *Ragan*, did I give thee all,
And all could not suffice without my bloud?
Ah, poore *Cordella*, did I give thee nought,
Nor never shall be able for to give?   55
O, let me warne all ages that insueth,
How they trust flattery, and reject the trueth.
Well, unkind Girles, I here forgive you both,
Yet the just heavens will hardly do the like;
And only crave forgivenesse at the end   60
Of good *Cordella*, and of thee, my friend;
Of God, whose Maiesty I have offended,
By my transgression many thousand wayes:
Of her, deare heart, whom I for no occasion
Turn'd out of all, through flatterers perswasion: 65
Of thee, kind friend, who but for me, I know,
Hadst never come unto this place of wo.
CORDELLA   Alack, that ever I should live to see
My noble father in this misery.
KING   Sweet Love, reveale not what thou art as yet,   70
Until we know the ground of all this ill.

                              * * *

CORDELLA   * * * My selfe a father have a great way hence,
Usde me as ill as ever you did her;
Yet, that his reverend age I once might see,
Ide creepe along, to meet him on my knee.   190
LEIR   O, no mens children are unkind but mine.
CORDELLA   Condemne not all, because of others crime:
But looke, deare father, looke behold and see
Thy loving daughter speaketh unto thee.   *she kneeles.*
LEIR   O, stand thou up, it is my part to kneele,   195
And aske forgivenesse for my former faults.   *he kneeles.*
CORDELLA   O, if you wish I should injoy my breath,
Deare father rise, or I receive my death.   *he riseth.*

4. Sparkling.

LEIR   Then I will rise to satisfy your mind,
  But kneele againe, til pardon be resignd.   *he kneeles.*   200
CORDELLA   I pardon you: the word beseemes not me:
  But I do say so, for to ease your knee.
  You gave me life, you were the cause that I
  Am what I am, who else had never bin.
LEIR   But you gave life to me and to my friend,   205
  Whose dayes had else had an untimely end.
CORDELLA   You brought me up, when as I was but young,
  And far unable for to helpe my selfe.
LEIR   I cast thee forth, when as thou wast but young,
  And far unable for to helpe thy selfe.   210
CORDELLA   God, world and nature say I do you wrong,
  That can indure to see you kneele so long.
PERILLUS   Let me breake off this loving controversy,
  Which doth rejoyce my very soule to see.
  Good father, rise, she is your loving daughter,   *He riseth.*   215
  And honours you with as respective duty,
  As if you were the Monarch of the world.
CORDELLA   But I will never rise from off my knee,   *She kneeles.*
  Until I have your blessing, and your pardon
  Of all my faults committed any way,   220
  From my first birth unto this present day.
LEIR   The blessing, which the God of *Abraham* gaue
  Unto the trybe of *Juda*, light on thee,
  And multiply thy dayes, that thou mayst see
  Thy childrens children prosper after thee.   225
  Thy faults, which are just none that I do know,
  God pardon on high, and I forgive below.   *She riseth.*

[*Scene 32*]

    Alarums and excursions, then sound victory.

    Enter Leir, Perillus, King, Cordella, and Mumford.

KING   Thanks be to God, your foes are overcome,
  And you againe possessed of your right.
LEIR   First to the heavens, next, thanks to you, my sonne,
  By whose good meanes I repossesse the same:
  Which if it please you to accept your selfe,   5
  With all my heart I will resigne to you:
  For it is yours by right, and none of mine.
  First, have you raisd, at your owne charge, a power
  Of valiant Souldiers; (this comes all from you)

Next have you ventured your owne persons scathe.[5]   10
And lastly, (worthy *Gallia* neuer staynd)
My kingly title I by thee have gaynd.
KING   Thank heavens, not me, my zeale to you is such,
    Commaund my utmost, I will never grutch.[6]
CORDELLA   He that with all kind love intreats his Queene,   15
    Will not be to her father unkind scene.
LEIR   Ah, my *Cordella*, now I call to mind,
    The modest answere, which I tooke unkind:
    But now I see, I am no whit beguild,
    Thou lovedst me dearely, and as ought a child.   20
    And thou (*Perillus*) partner once in woe,
    Thee to requite, the best I can, Ile doe:
    Yet all I can, I, were it ne're so much,
    Were not sufficient, thy true love is such.
    Thanks (worthy, *Mumford*) to thee last of all,   25
    Not greeted last, 'cause thy desert was small;
    No, thou hast Lion-like layd on to day,
    Chasing the Cornwall King and Cambria;
    Who with my daughters, daughters did I say?
    To save their lives, the fugitives did play.   30
    Come, sonne and daughter, who did me advaunce,
    Repose with me awhile, and then for Fraunce.

    Sound Drummes and Trumpet. Exeunt.

                        FINIS

JOHN HIGGINS

From The Mirror for Magistrates (1574)†

*Cordila shewes how by despaire when she was in prison she
slue herselfe. the yeare before Christe, 800.*

[Leire] had three daughters, first and eldest hight[1] *Gonerell*:
Next after hir, my sister *Ragan* was begote:
The thirde and last was, I the yongest named *Cordell*,   45

---

5. Hurt.
6. Complain.
† From *The First Part of the Mirror for Magistrates* (London: Thomas Marsh, 1574). Subsequent editions of this poem, including that of 1587, contain revisions, but, as both the 1574 and 1587 editions show particular correspondences to lines in Shakespeare's play (and to his main source, *The Chronicle History of King Leir*), it is unclear if he used only one or both editions.
1. Called.

And of us all, our father *Leire* in age did dote.
So minding her that lov'd him best to note,
Because he had no sonne t'enjoye[2] his lande:
He thought to give, where favoure most he fande.[3]

What though I yongest were, yet men me judgde more wise   50
Then either *Gonorell*, or *Ragan* had more age,
And fayrer farre: wherefore my sisters did despise
My grace, and giftes, and sought my praise t'swage[4]
But yet though vice gainst vertue die with rage,
It cannot keepe her underneath to drowne,   55
But still she flittes above, and reapes renowne.

Yet nathelesse, my father did me not mislike:
But age so simple is, and easye to subdue:
As childhode weake, thats voide of wit and reason quite:
They thincke thers nought you flater fainde, but all is true: 60
Once olde and twice a childe, tis said with you,
Which I affirme by proofe, that was definde:
In age my father had a childishe minde.

He thought to wed us unto nobles three, or Peres:[5]
And unto them and theirs, devide and part the lande: 65
For both my sisters first he sent as first their yeares
Requirde their mindes, and love, and favour t'understand.
(Quod he) all doubtes of duty to abande,[6]
I must assaye and eke[7] your frendships prove:
Now tell me eche how much you do me love.   70

Which when they aunswered, they lovde him wel and more
Then they themselves did love, or any worldly wight:[8]
He praised them and said he would againe therefore,
The loving kindnes they deservde in fine requite:[9]
So found my sisters favour in his sight,   75
By flatery fayre they won their fathers hart:
Which after turned him and mee to smart.[1]

2. To enjoy.
3. Put to the test.
4. To assuage.
5. Peers of the realm.
6. Abandon; *Quod*: said.
7. Also; *assaye*: test.
8. Person.
9. Requital.
1. Hurt.

But not content with this he minded me to prove,
For why he wonted was to love me wonders well:
How much dost thou (quoth he) *Cordile* thy father love?   80
I will (said I) at once my love declare and tell:
I lovde you ever as my father well,
No otherwise, if more to know you crave:
We love you chiefly for the goodes you have.

Thus much I said, the more their flattery to detect,   85
But he me answered therunto again with Ire,
Because thou dost thy fathers aged yeares neglect,
That lovde the more of late then thy desertes require,
Thou never shalt, to any part aspire
Of this my realme, emong thy sisters twayne,[2]   90
But ever shalt undoted ay[3] remayne.

* * *

[Leire marries Gonerell to the King of Albany and Ragan to the Prince of Camber and Cornwall. Ostracized and dowerless, Cordila makes a happy marriage with the King of France]

But while that I these joyes enjoyd, at home in *Fraunce*   120
My father *Leire* in *Britayne* waxed aged olde,
My sisters yet them selves the more aloft t'advaunce,
Thought well they might, be by his leave, or sans so bolde,
To take the realme & rule it as they wold.
They rose as rebels voyde of reason quite,   125
And they deprivde him of his crowne and right.

Then they agreed, it should be into partes equall
Devided: and my father threscore knightes & squires
Should always have, attending on him still at cal.
But in six monthes so much encreasid hateful Ires,   130
That *Gonerell* denyde all his desires,
So halfe his garde she and her husband refte:[4]
And scarce alowde the other halfe they lefte.

Eke[5] as in *Scotlande* thus he lay lamenting fates,
When as his daughter so, sought all his utter spoyle: 135
The meaner upstarte gentiles,[6] thought themselves his mates

2. Two; *emong*: among.
3. Always; *undoted*: unloved.
4. Took away.
5. Also.
6. Gentlemen.

And better eke, see here an aged prince his foyle.
Then was he faine for succoure his, to toyle,
With all his knightes, to *Cornewall* there to lye:
In greatest nede, his *Raganes* love to trye.   140

And when he came to *Cornwall, Ragan* then with ioye,
Received him and eke hir husbande did the lyke:
There he abode a yeare and livde without anoy,[7]
But then they tooke, all his retinue from him quite
Save only ten, and shewde him dayly spite,
Which he bewailde complayning durst not strive,   145
Though in disdayne they laste alowde but five.

On this he deemde him selfe was far that tyme vnwyse,
When from his doughter *Gonerell* to *Ragan* bee
Departed erste[8] yet eache did him poore king despise,   150
Wherfore to *Scotlande* once againe with hir to bee
And bide[9] he went: but beastly cruell shee,
Bereavde him of his servauntes all save one,
Bad[1] him content him self with that or none.

Eke at what time he askte of eache to have his garde,   155
To garde his grace where so he walkte or wente:
They calde him doting foole and all his hestes[2] debarde,
Demaunded if with life he could not be contente.
Then he to late his rigour did repente,
Gainst me and sayde, *Cordila* now adieu: 160
I finde the wordes thou toldste me to to true.

And to be short, to *Fraunce* he came alone to mee,
And tolde me how my sisters him our father usde
Then I besought my king with teares upon my knee,
That he would aide my father thus by them misusde   165
Who nought at all my humble heste[3] refusde:
But sent to every coste of *Fraunce* for ayde,
Wherwith my father home might be conveide.

* * *

This had: I partid with my father from my fere,[4]
We came to *Britayne* with our royall campe to fight:

7. Annoyance.
8. Right away.
9. Abide.
1. Bade.
2. Requests.
3. Request.
4. Husband.

And manly fought so long our enemies vanquisht were
By martiall feates, and force by subjectes sword and might.
The Britishe kinges were fayne[5] to yelde our right,   180
And so my father well this realme did guide,
Three yeares in peace and after that he dide.[6]

RAPHAEL HOLINSHED

From Chronicles (1586)†

From *The Fifth Chapter*

Leir the sonne of Baldud was admitted ruler over the Britaines, in
the yeare of the world 3105, at what time Joas reigned in Juda. This
Leir was a prince of right noble demeanor, governing his land and
subjects in great wealth. He made the towne of Caerleir now called
Leicester, which standeth upon the river of Sore. It is written that
he had by his wife three daughters without other issue, whose
names were Gonorilla, Regan, and Cordeilla, which daughters he
greatly loved, but specially Cordeilla the yoongest farre above the
two elder. When this Leir therefore was come to great yeres, & began to waxe unweldie through age, he thought to understand the
affections of his daughters towards him, and preferre hir whome he
best loved, to the succession over the kingdome. Wherupon he first
asked Gonorilla the eldest, how well she loved him: who calling hir
gods to record, professed that she 'loved him more than hir owne
life, which by right and reason should be most deere unto hir. With
which answer the father being well pleased, turned to the second,
and demanded of hir how well she loved him: who answered (confirming hir saiengs with great othes) that she loved him more than
toong could expresse, and farre above all other creatures of the
world'.

    Then called he his yoongest daughter Cordeilla before him, and
asked of hir what account she made of him, unto whome she made
this answer as followeth: 'Knowing the great love and fatherlie zeale

---

5. Glad.
6. Cordila concludes her story by describing her five-year reign after Leire's death, her
    overthrow by her nephews, and her suicide by stabbing in prison.
† From *The First and Second Volumes of Chronicles* (London, 1586), vol. 1, book 2,
    pp. 12–13 (signature B1r). Shakespeare made frequent use of Holinshed's *Chronicles*,
    the first volume of which was published in 1577, in writing his English history plays and
    tragedies. Although the *Chronicles* were expanded between 1577 and 1586, Holinshed's
    history of Leir, which closely follows Geoffrey's history, remained largely unchanged in
    the later text (the second edition is presented here).

that you have alwaies borne towards me (for the which I maie not answere you otherwise than I thinke, and as my conscience leadeth me) I protest unto you, that I have loved you ever, and will continuallie (while I live) love you as my naturall father. And if you would more understand of the love that I beare you, assertaine your selfe, that so much as you have, so much you are worth, and so much I love you, and no more'. The father being nothing content with this answer, married his two eldest daughters, the one unto Henninus the duke of Cornewall, and the other unto Maglanus the duke of Albania, betwixt whome he willed and ordeined that his land should be divided after his death, and the one halfe thereof immediatelie should be assigned to them in hand: but for the third daughter Cordeilla he reserved nothing.

Nevertheles it fortuned that one of the princes of Gallia (which now is called France) whose name was Aganippus, hearing of the beautie, womanhood, and good conditions of the said Cordeilla, desired to have hir in marriage, and sent over to hir father, requiring that he might have hir to wife: to whome answer was made, that he might have his daughter, but as for anie dower he could have none, for all was promised and assured to hir other sisters alreadie. Aganippus notwithstanding this answer of deniall to receive anie thing by way of dower with Cordeilla, tooke hir to wife, onlie moved thereto (I saie) for respect of hir person and amiable vertues. This Aganippus was one of the twelve kings that ruled Gallia in those daies, as in the British historie it is recorded. But to proceed.

After that Leir was fallen into age, the two dukes that had married his two eldest daughters, thinking it long yer the government of the land did come to their hands, arose against him in armour, and [w]rest from him the governance of the land, upon conditions to be continued for terme of life: by the which he was put to his portion, that is, to live after a rate assigned to him for the maintenance of his estate, which in processe of time was diminished as well by Maglanus as by Henninus. But the greatest griefe that Leir tooke, was to see the unkindnesse of his daughters, which seemed to thinke that all was too much which their father had, the same being never so little: in so much that going from the one to the other, he was brought to that miserie, that scarslie they would allow him one servant to wait upon him.

In the end, such was the unkindnesse, or (as I maie saie) the unnaturalnesse which he found in his two daughters, notwithstanding their faire and pleasant words uttered in time past, that being constreined of necessitie, he fled the land, & sailed into Gallia, there to seeke some comfort of his yongest daughter Cordeilla, whom before time he hated. The ladie Cordeila hearing that he was arrived in poore estate, she first sent to him privilie a certeine summe of

monie to apparell himselfe withall, and to reteine a certeine number of servants that might attend upon him in honorable wise, as
apperteined to the estate which he had borne: and then so accom-
panied, she appointed him to come to the court, which he did, and
was so joifullie, honorablie, and lovinglie received, both by his
sonne in law Aganippus, and also by his daughter Cordeilla, that
his hart was greatlie comforted: for he was no lesse honored, than
if he had beene king of the whole countrie himselfe.

Now when he had informed his sonne in law and his daughter in
what sort he had beene used by his other daughters, Aganippus
caused a mightie armie to be put in a readinesse, and likewise a
great navie of ships to be rigged, to passe over into Britaine with
Leir his father in law, to see him againe restored to his kingdome. It
was accorded, that Cordeilla should also go with him to take possession of the land, the which he promised to leave unto hir, as the
rightfull inheritour after his decesse, notwithstanding any former
grant made to hir sisters or to their husbands in anie manner of
wise.

Hereupon, when this armie and navie of ships were readie, Leir
and his daughter Cordeilla with hir husband tooke the sea, and arriving in Britaine, fought with their enimies, and discomfited them
in battel, in the which Maglanus and Henninus were slaine: and
then was Leir restored to his kingdome, which he ruled after this by
the space of two yeeres, and then died, fortie yeeres after he first
began to reigne. His bodie was buried at Leicester in a vau[l]t vnder
the channell of the river of Sore beneath the towne.

The sixt Chapter

* * * Cordeilla the yoongest daughter of Leir was admitted
Q[ueen] and supreme governesse of Britaine, in the yeere of the
world 3155, before the bylding of Rome 54, Uzia then reigning in
Judea, and Jeroboam ouer Israell.

EDMUND SPENSER

From The Faerie Queene (1590)†

27

Next him king *Leyr* in happie peace long raind,[1]
    But had no issue male him to succeed,
    But three faire daughters, which were well uptraind,[2]
    In all that seemed fit for kingly seed:
    Mongst whom his realme he equally decreed
    To have divided. Tho when feeble age
    Night to his utmost date he saw proceed,
    He cald his daughters; and with speeches sage
Inquyrd, which of them most did love her parentage.

28

The eldest *Gonorill* gan[3] to protest,
    That she much more then her owne life him lov'd:
    And *Regan* greater love to him profest,
    Then all the world, when ever it were proov'd;
    But *Cordeill* said she lov'd him, as behoov'd:
    Whose simple answere, wanting colours faire
    To paint it forth, him to displeasance moov'd,
    That in his crowne he counted her no haire,
But twixt the other twaine[4] his kingdome whole did shaire.

29

So wedded th' one to *Maglan* king of Scots,
    And th'other to the king of *Cambria*,
    And twixt them shayrd his realme by equall lots:
    But without dowre[5] the wise *Cordelia*
    Was sent to *Aganip* of *Celtica*.
    Their aged Syre, thus eased of his crowne,
    A private life led in *Albania*,
    With *Gonorill*, long had in great renowne,
That nought him griev'd to bene from rule deposed downe.

---

† From *The Faerie Queene* (London: William Ponsonbie, 1590), book II, canto X, stanzas 27–33, pp. 332–34. According to Spenser's version, Cordeill hangs herself after her imprisonment by her nephews, probably inspiring Shakespeare to portray her as being executed by hanging; in previous versions she stabs or "slays" herself.
1. Reigned.
2. Brought up.
3. Began.
4. Two.
5. Dowry.

30

But true it is, that when the oyle[6] is spent,
    The light goes out, and weeke is throwne away;
    So when he had resignd his regiment,
    His daughter gan despise his drouping day,
    And wearie waxe[7] of his continuall stay.
    Tho to his daughter *Regan* he repayrd,
    Who him at first well vsed every way;
    But when of his departure she despayrd,
Her bountie she abated, and his cheare empayrd.[8]

31

The wretched man gan then avise[9] too late,
    That love is not, where most it is profest,
    Too truely tryde in his extreamest state;
    At last resolv'd likewise to prove the rest,
    He to *Cordelia* him selfe addrest,
    Who with entire affection him receav'd,
    As for her Syre and king her seemed best;
    And after all an army strong she leav'd,
To war on those, which him had of his realme bereav'd.

32

So to his crowne she him restor'd againe,
    In which he dyde, made ripe for death by eld,[1]
    And after wild, it should to her remaine:
    Who peaceably the same long time did weld:[2]
    And all mens harts in dew obedience held:
    Till that her sisters children, woxen[3] strong
    Through proud ambition, against her rebeld,
    And overcommen kept in prison long,
Till wearie of that wretched life, her selfe she hong.[4]

33

Then gan the bloudie brethren both to raine:
    But fierce *Cundah* gan shortly to envie
    His brother *Morgan*, prickt with proud disdaine,

6. Oil.
7. Grew.
8. Impaired.
9. Learn.
1. Old age.
2. Wield.
3. Grew.
4. Hanged.

To have a pere in part of soveraintie,
And kindling coles of cruell enmitie,
Raisd warre, and him in battell overthrew:
Whence as he to those woodie hils did flie,
Which hight of him *Glamorgan*, there him slew:
Then did he raigne alone, when he none equall knew.

SIR PHILIP SIDNEY

From The Countesse of Pembroke's Arcadia (1590)†

[The two princes Pyrocles and Musidorus encounter] an aged man, and a young, scarcely come to the age of a man, both poorely arrayed, extreamely weather-beaten; the olde man blinde, the young man leading him: and yet through all those miseries, in both these seemed to appeare a kind of noblenesse, not suitable to that affliction. But the first words they heard, were these of the old man. Well *Leonatus* (said he) since I cannot perswade thee to lead me to that which should end my griefe, & thy trouble, let me now entreat thee to leave me: feare not, my miserie cannot be greater then it is, & nothing doth become me but miserie: feare not the danger of my blind steps, I cannot fall worse then I am. . . . Deare father (answered he) doo not take away from me the onely remnant of my happinesse: while I have power to doo your service, I am not wholly miserable. . . . These dolefull speeches, and some others to like purpose (well shewing they had not bene borne to the fortune they were in,) moved the Princes to goe out unto them, and aske the younger what they were? . . .

[Leonatus replied] This old man (whom I leade) was lately rightfull Prince of this countrie of *Paphlagonia*, by the hard-harted ungratefulnes of a sonne of his, deprived, not onely of his kingdome (whereof no forraine[1] forces were ever able to spoyle him) but of his sight, the riches which Nature graunts to the poorest creatures. Whereby, and by other his unnaturall dealings, he hath bin driven to such griefe, as even now he would have had me to have led him to the toppe of this rocke, thence to cast himselfe headlong to death: and so would haue made me (who received my life of him) to be the worker of his destruction. But noble Gentlemen (said he) if either of you have a father, and feele what duetifull affection is engraffed[2] in a sonnes hart, let me intreate you to convey this af-

---

† From *The Countesse of Pembroke's Arcadia* (London: William Ponsonbie, 1590), book 2, chap. 10, pp. 143–44, 146–47.
1. Foreign.
2. I.e., engraved.

flicted Prince to some place of rest and securitie. Amongst your worthie actes it shall be none of the least, that a King, of such might and fame, and so unjustly oppressed, is in any sort by you relieved.

But before they could make him answere, his father began to speake, 'Ah my sonne (said he) how evill an Historian are you, that leave out the chiefe knotte of all the discourse! my wickednes, my wickednes. And if thou doest it to spare my ears, (the onely sense nowe left me proper for knowledge) assure thy selfe thou dost mistake me. And I take witnesse of that Sunne which you see (with that he cast up his blinde eyes, as if he would hunt for light,) and wish my selfe in worse case then I do wish my selfe, which is as evill as may be, if I speake untruely; that nothing is so welcome to my thoughts, as the publishing of my shame. Therefore know you Gentlemen (to whom from my harte I wish that it may not prove ominous foretoken of misfortune to haue mette with such a miser as I am) that whatsoever my sonne (ô God, that trueth binds me to reproch him with the name of my sonne) hath said, is true. But besides those truthes, this also is true, that having had in lawful mariage, of a mother fitte to beare royall children, this sonne (such one as partly you see, and better shall knowe by my shorte declaration) and so injoyed the expectations in the world of him, till he was growen to justifie their expectations (so as I needed envie no father for the chiefe comfort of mortalitie, to leave an other onesselfe after me) I was caried by a bastarde sonne of mine (if at least I be bounde to beleeve the words of that base woman my concubine, his mother) first to mislike, then to hate, lastly to destroy, to doo my best to destroy, this sonne (I thinke you thinke) undeserving destruction. What waies he used to bring me to it, if I should tell you, I should tediously trouble you with as much poysonous hypocrisie, desperate fraude, smoothe malice, hidden ambition, and smiling envie as in any living person could be harbored'.

* * * The blind King (having in the chief cittie of his Realme, set the crowne upon his sonne *Leonatus* head) with many teares (both of joy and sorrow) setting forth to the whole people, his owne fault and his sonnes vertue, after he had kist him, and forst his sonne to accept honour of him (as of his newe-become subject) even in a moment died, as it should seeme: his hart broken with unkindnes and affliction, stretched so farre beyond his limits with this excesse of comfort, as it was able no longer to keep safe his roial spirits. But the new King (having no lesse lovingly performed all duties to him dead, then alive) pursued on the siege of his unnatural brother, as much for the revenge of his father, as for the establishing of his owne quiet. In which siege truly I cannot but acknowledge the prowesse of those two brothers, then whom the Princes never

found in all their travell two men of greater habilitie to performe, nor of habler[3] skill for conduct.

But *Plexirtus* finding, that if nothing els, famin would at last bring him to destruction, thought better by humblenes to creepe, where by pride he could not march. * * * That though no man had lesse goddnes in his soule then he, no man could better find the places whence arguments might grow of goodnesse to another: though no man felt lesse pitie, no man could tel better how to stir pitie: no man more impudent to deny, where proofes were not manifest; no man more ready to confesse with a repenting manner of aggravating his owne evil, where denial would but make the fault fouler. Now he tooke this way, that having gotten a pasport for one (that pretended he would put *Plexirtus* alive into his hands) to speak with the King his brother, he him selfe (though much against the minds of the valiant brothers, who rather wished to die in brave defence) with a rope about his necke, barefooted, came to offer himselfe to the discretion of *Leonatus*. Where what submission he used, how cunningly in making greater the faulte he made the faultiness the lesse, how artificially he could set out the torments of his owne conscience, with the burdensome comber[4] he had found of his ambitious desires, how finely seeming to desire nothing but death, as ashamed to live, he begd life in the refusing it, I am not cunning inough to be able to expresse; but so fell out of it, that though at first sight *Leonatus* saw him with no other eie, then as the murderer of his father; and anger already began to paint revenge in many colours, ere long he had not only gotten pitie, but pardon, and if not an excuse of the fault past, yet an opinion of a future amendment: while the poore villaines (chiefe ministers of his wickednes, now betraied by the author thereof,) were delivered to many cruell sorts of death; he so handling it, that it rather seemed, he had rather come into the defence of an unremediable mischiefe already committed, then that they had done it at first by his consent.

In such sorts the Princes left these reconciled brothers.

3. Abler.
4. Trouble.

JAMES VI OF SCOTLAND
(LATER JAMES I OF BRITAIN)

From The True Law of Free Monarchies (1598)†

By the law of Nature the King becomes a naturall Father to all his Lieges[1] at his Coronation. And as the Father of his fatherly duety is bounde to care for the nourishing, education, and vertuous government of his chilren: even so is the King bounde to care for all his subjects. * * * As the kindly father ought to foresee all inconvenients & dangers that may aryse towardes his children, and though with the hazard of his owne person presse to prevente the same: So ought the King towardes his people. As the Fathers wrath and correction uppon any of his children, that offendeth, ought to be a fatherly chastizement seasoned with pittie, as long as there is any hope of amendment in them: So ought the King towardes any of his lieges that offendes in that measure.

* * * Consider I pray you, what duty his children owe to him, and whether, upon any pretext whatsoeuer, it will not be thoght monstrous and unnaturall to his sonnes to rise up against him, to controll him at their appetite, and when they thinke good to slay him, or to cut him off, and adopt to themselves any other [way] they please in his room. Or can any pretence of wickednes or rigour on his parte be a just excuse for his children to put hand into him? And although we see by the course of nature that love ever useth to descend more then to ascend: in case it were true, that the father hated and wronged the children never so much, will any man endued with the leaste sponke[2] of reason think it lawful for them to meete him with the like?

---

† From *The True Law of Free Monarchies: or the Reciprok[al] dutie betwixt a free King and his naturall subjects* (Edinburgh: Robert Waldegrave, 1598), signatures B4ʳ, B5ʳ, D4ʳ. This treatise, first published in 1598 when James was king of Scotland, was reprinted in 1603 to celebrate his accession to the English throne; it was widely read and analyzed by those anxious about James's political strategy as king of England.
1. Subjects.
2. Amount; *endued*: endowed.

JAMES I

From Basilikon Doron (1603)†

If God send you succession [i.e., children], be carefull for their vertuous education: love them as ye ought, but let them knowe as
much of it, as the gentlenesse of their nature will deserve; contayn-
ing them ever in a reverent love and feare of you. And in case it
please God to provide you to all these three kingdomes, make your
eldest sonne Issac,[1] leaving him all your kingdomes; and provyde
the rest with private possessions. Otherwaies by deviding your kingdomes, ye shall leave the seede of division & discorde among your
posteritie: as befell to this Ile, by the division & assignement
thereof, to the three sonnes of *Brutus, Locrine, Albanact*, and *Camber*.

* * * Embrace true Magnanimitie, not in being vindictive, which
the corrupted judgements of the worlde thinkes to be true Magnanimitie; but by the contrary, in thinking your offender not worthie
of your wrath, empyring[2] over your owne passion, and triumphing
in the commanding of your selfe to forgive. * * * Where ye finde a
notable injury, spare not to give course to the torrents of your
wrath. *The wrath of a King, is like the roaring of a Lyon.*

* * * Tis a true old saying, That a King is as one set on a stage,
whose smallest actions and gestures, all the people gazing lie doe
beholde.

---

† From *Basilikon Doron [The King's Gift]: or His Maiesties Instructions to his dearest sonne,
Henry the Prince* (Edinburgh: Robert Waldegrave, 1603), books 2–3, signatures H1ᵛ-
H2ʳ, H8ʳ, I4ᵛ.
1. Son of the biblical figure Abraham and sole inheritor of his property (to the disadvantage
of Ishmael, Abraham's illegitimate son).
2. Reigning.

SAMUEL HARSNETT

From A Declaration of Egregious Popish Impostures (1603)†

Chapter 10

THE STRANGE NAMES OF THEIR DEVILS

[There were] 5. Captaines, or Commaunders above the rest: Captaine *Pippin, Marwoods* devil, Captaine *Philpot, Trayfords* devil, Captaine *Maho, Saras* devil, Captaine *Modu, Maynies* devil, and Captaine *Soforce*, Anne Smiths devil. * * *

Captaine *Philpot, Trayfords* devil was a Centurion, (as himselfe tells you) and had an hundred under his charge. Mary he was (as seemes) but a white-livered devil, for he was so hastie to be gone out of *Trayford*, for feare of the Exorcist, that hee would scarce give him leave, beeing a bed, to put on his breeches. The names of their punie spirits cast out of *Trayford* were these, *Hilco, Smolkin, Hillio, Hiaclito*, and *Lustie huffe-cap.* * * *

Frateretto, Fliberdigibbet, Hoberdidance, Tocobatto were foure devils of the round, or Morrice, whom *Sara* in her fits, tuned together, in measure and sweet cadence. And least you should conceive, that the devils had no musicke in hell, especially that they would goe a maying without theyr musicke, the Fidler comes in with his Taber, & Pipe, and a whole Morice after him, with motly visards for theyr better grace. These foure had forty assistants under them, as themselves doe confesse.

WILLIAM CAMDEN

From Remaines of a Greater Worke, Concerning Britaine (1606)‡

Ina King of West-Saxons, had three daughters, of whom upon a time he demanded whether they did love him, and so would do during their lives, above all others; the two elder sware deepely they

---

† From *A Declaration of Egregious Popish Impostures* (London: James Roberts, 1603), chap. 10, p. 49.
‡ From *Remaines of a Greater Worke, Concerning Britaine* (London: Printed by G. E. for Simon Waterson, 1605), pp. 182–83.

would; the yongest, but the wisest, told her father without flattery: *That she did love, honour, and reverence him, and so would whilst shee lived, as much as nature and daughterly duty at the uttermost could expect: Yet she did thinke that one day it would come to passe, that she should affect another more fervently, meaning her husband, when she were married: Who being made one flesh with her, as God by commandement had told, and nature had taught hir, she was to cleave fast to, forsaking father and mother, kiffe and kinne.* (Anonymous) One referreth this to the daughters of King *Leir*.

Possible Sources

THE CASE OF CORDELL ANNESLEY AND HER FATHER, BRYAN (1603)

Letter from Sir John Wildegos, Timothy Lawe, and Samuel Lennard to Robert Cecil, Lord Salisbury, October 18, 1603[1]

Accordinge to the tenor of your Lordshipps lettres bearinge date of the 12th of this present, wee repayred unto the howse of Bryan Annesley, of Lee, in the Countie of Kent & Sussex, And findinge him fallen into suche imperfeccion and distemperature of minde and memorye, as we Thought him thereby become altogeather unfit to governe himself or his estate, we indevoured to take a perfect Inventory of such goods and Chattells, as the said Mr Annesley possessed in and about his howse. But Mrs Cordall, his daughter, whoe during the time of all his infirmitie hath taken uponn her the government and the orderinge of him and his affaires, refuseth to suffer anye inventorye to be taken, untill suche tyme as shee hath had conference with some of her freindes, by reason whereof wee could proceede no farther in the execution of your Lordshipps said lettres.

Letter from Cordell Annesley to Robert Cecil, October 23, 1603[2]

I most humbly thanke your Lordship for the sundrye letters that yt hathe pleased your Lordship to directe unto gentlemen of worshippe in these partes, requestinge them to take into their cus-

1. From Cecil Papers, 101/163, reproduced by permission of the most honorable Marquess of Salisbury. Reprinted in *Historical Manuscripts Commission: Report on the Manuscripts of the Earl of Salisbury*, 24 vols. (London: His Majesty's Stationery Office, 1883–1976), 15:262. Hereafter cited as *HMC: Salisbury*.
2. Cecil Papers, 187/119, reproduced by permission of the most honorable Marquess of Salisbury. Reprinted in *HMC: Salisbury*, 15:266.

todies the person and estate of my poore aged and daylye dyinge ffather: But that course so honorable and good for all parties, intended by your Lordship, will by no meanes satisfye Sir John Willgosse, nor can any course else, unless he may have him [i.e., Bryan Annesley] begged for a Lunetike, whose many yeres service to our late dreade Soveraigne Mistris and native Country deserved a better agominaccion,[3] than at his last gaspe to be recorded and regestred a Lunetike, yett fynd no meanes to avoyd so greate an infamy and endlesse blemishe to us and our posteritie, unless yt shall please your Lordship of your honorable disposition, yf he must needes be accompted a Lunetike, to bestowe him upon Sir James Croft, who out of the love he bare unto him in his more happier dayes, and for the good he wysheth unto us his children, is contented upon entreaty to undergoe the burden and care of him and his estate, without intendment to make one penny benefytt to himself by any goodes of his, or ought that maye descend to us his children, as also to prevent any record of Lunacy that may be procured hereafter.

Letter from Sir Thomas Walsingham, James Croftes and Samuel Lennard to Robert Cecil, October 23, 1603[4]

According to the authorytye given us by your Lordshipps lettres, wee repaired to the house of Mr Bryan Annesley, and there in the presence of his two daughters, Lady [Grace] Wildgosse and Mrs Cordell Annesley, have sealed up all such Chestes and Trunkes of Evidence, and other thinges of valewe, as they showed us to be his. And for as much as we were informed that he holdeth divers thinges by lease, which for not payment of the Rent might be in danger to be forfeited, we have therefore requested Sir James Croftes, whome your Lordshipp hath associated to us in this business, to take Care of the payment of such rentes as are reserved upon any lease made to the said Mr Annesley as also for the receipt of such rents as are due to him from any of his tenauntes. But as touching the government of the person and family, though by nature his two daughters may seme fittest to perform this Dutie, yet respecting the absence of Sir John Wildgosse at this tyme, and the present emulation betwene the two gentlewomen we have thought good to refere the determinaccion thereof to your Lordshipp.

3. Reward.
4. Cecil Papers, 101/166, reproduced by permission of the most honorable Marquess of Salisbury. Reprinted in *HMC: Salisbury*, 15:265.

Epitaph on Bryan Annesley[5]

Here lyeth buried the bodyes of Bryan Anslye Esquier, late of Lee
in the country of Kent, and Audry his wife. * * * He had issue by
her one sonne and three daughters, Bryan who died without issue;
Grace married to Sir John Wilgoose, Knight; Christian married to
the Lord Sands; and Cordell married to Sir William Hervey, Knight.
The said Bryan the father died on the Xth of July 1604; he served
Queene Elizabeth as one of the band of Gentlemen Pencioners to
her Majestie the space of XXXtye yeares. The said Awdry died on
the XXVth of Novebeber 1591. Cordell, the youngest daughter, at
her owne proper cost and chardges, in further testimonie of her du-
tifull love unto her father and mother, caused this monument to be
erected for the perpetuall memorie of their names against the nature of oblivious time.

> 'Nec primus, nec ultimus; multi ante,
> Cesserunt, et omnes sequetitur'.[6]

GEOFFREY OF MONMOUTH

From Historia Regum Britanniae (c. 1135)†

*Book II, Chapter XI. Leir, the Son of Bladud, having no Son,
divides his Kingdom among his Daughters.*

After this unhappy Fate of *Bladud, Leir* his Son was advanced to
the Throne, and nobly governed his Country sixty Years. * * * He
was without Male Issue, but had three Daughters whose Names
were *Gonorilla, Regau,* and *Cordeilla,* of whom he was doatingly
fond, but especially of his youngest *Cordeilla.* When he began to

---

5. From J. W. Hales, *Notes and Essays on Shakespeare* (London: George Bell, 1883), from
   an epitaph in a church wall in Lee, Kent. Although Annesley died in 1604, it is not clear
   when the epitaph was put in the church wall, and Hales suggests that Cordell Annesley
   may have been prompted by the play *King Lear* to provide this epitaph; however, it is
   also possible, as Bullough suggests, that the Annesley case served as a source for *King
   Lear.*
6. I.e., "I am neither the first nor the last to die; many precede me; all follow (me)."
† From *The British History . . . of Jeffrey of Monmouth*, ed. Aaron Thompson (London,
   1718), pp. 50–59, based on the Latin manuscript of Geoffrey of Monmouth (also called
   Galfridus Monumetensis), *Historia Regum Britanniae* (*History of the British Kings*),
   book II, c. 1135; this manuscript, which remained unprinted until Thompson's edition,
   was probably not consulted by Shakespeare. Geoffrey of Monmouth was apparently the
   first English historian to relate the history of Lear, and this version was undoubtedly
   used by later historians, whose histories were consulted by authors of other sources used
   directly by Shakespeare.

grow old, he had Thoughts of dividing his Kingdom among them, and of bestowing them on such Husbands, as were fit to be advanced to the Government with them. But to make Tryal who was the worthiest of the best Part of his Kingdom, he went to each of them to ask, which of them loved him most. The Question being proposed, *Gonorilla* the Eldest made Answer, "That she called Heaven to Witness, she loved him more than her own Soul." The Father reply'd, "Since you have preferred my declining Age before your own Life, I will marry you, my dearest Daughter, to whomsoever you shall make Choice of, and give with you the third Part of my Kingdom." Then *Regau*, the second Daughter, willing after the Example of her Sister, to prevail upon her Fathers good Nature, answered with an Oath, "That she could not otherwise express her Thoughts, but that she loved him above all Creatures." The credulous Father upon this made her the same Promise that he did to her elder Sister, that is, the Choice of a Husband, with the third Part of his Kingdom. But *Cordeilla* the youngest, understanding how easily he was satisfied with the flattering Expressions of her Sisters, was desirous to make Tryal of his Affection after a different Manner. "My Father," said she, "Is there any Daughter that can love her Father more than Duty requires? In my Opinion, whoever pretends to it, must disguise her real Sentiments under the Veil of Flattery. I have always loved you as a Father, nor do I yet depart from my purposed Duty; and if you insist to have something more extorted from me, hear now the Greatness of my Affection, which I always bear you, and take this for a short Answer to all your Questions; Look how much you have, so much is your Value, and so much I love you." The Father supposing that she spoke this out of the Abundance of her Heart, was highly provoked, and immediately reply'd; "Since you haue so far despised my Old-age, as not to think me worthy the Love that your Sisters express for me, you shall have from me the like Regard, and shall be excluded from any Share with your Sisters in my Kingdom. Notwithstanding I do not say but that since you are my Daughter, I will marry you to some Foreigner, if Fortune offers you any such Husband; but will never, I do assure you, make it my Business to procure so honourable a Match for you as for your Sisters; because though I have hitherto loved you more than them, you have in Requital thought me less worthy your Affection than they." And without farther Delay, after Consultation with his Nobility, he bestowed his two other Daughters upon the Dukes of *Cornwal* and *Albania*, with half the Island at present, but after his Death, the Inheritance of the whole Monarchy of *Britain*.

It happened after this, that *Aganippus* King of the *Franks*, having heard of the Fame of *Cordeilla*'s Beauty, forthwith sent his Ambas-

sadors to the King to desire *Cordeilla* in Marriage. * * * *Cordeilla*
was sent to *Gaul*, and married to *Aganippus*.

Chapter XII. Leir *finding the Ingratitude of his two eldest
Daughters, betakes himself to his youngest* Cordeilla *in* Gaul.

A long time after this, when *Leir* came to be infirm through Old-
age, the two Dukes, upon whom he had bestowed *Britain* with his
two Daughters, made an Insurrection against him, and deprived
him of his Kingdom, and of all Regal Authority which he had hitherto exercised with great Power and Glory. But at last they came to
an Agreement, and *Maglaunus* Duke of *Albania*, one of his Sons-in-
law, was to allow him and sixty Soldiers, who were to be kept for
State, a Subsistence at his own House. After two Years Stay with his
Son-in-law, his Daughter *Gonorilla* grudged at the Number of his
Men, who began to upbraid the Ministers of the Court with their
scanty Allowance; and having spoke to her Husband about it, gave
Orders that the Number of her Fathers Attendants be reduced to
thirty, and the rest discharged. The Father resenting this Treatment, left *Maglaunus*, and went to *Henuinus*, Duke of *Cornwal*, to
whom he had married his Daughter *Regau*. Here he met with an
honourable Reception, but before the Year was at an End, a Quarrel happened between the two Families, which raised *Regau's* Indignation; so that she commanded her Father to discharge all his
Attendants but five, and to be contented with their Service. This
second Affliction was unsupportable to him, and made him return
again to his former Daughter, with Hopes that the Misery of his
Condition might move in her some Sentiments of Filial Piety, and
that he with his Family might find a Subsistence from her. But she
not forgetting her Resentments, swore by the Gods, He should not
stay with her, unless he would dismiss his Retinue, and be contented with the Attendance of one Man; and with bitter Reproaches, told him how ill his Desire of vain-glorious Pomp suited
with his Old-age and Poverty. When he found that she was by no
Means to be prevailed upon, he was at last forced to comply, and
dismissing the Rest, to take up with one Man. But by this Time he
began to reflect more sensibly with himself upon the Grandeur
from which he had fallen, and the miserable State he was now reduced to, and to enter upon Thoughts of going beyond Sea to his
youngest Daughter. Yet he doubted whether he should be able to
move her Commiseration, whom * * * he had treated so un-
worthily * * * [Leir] took Shipping to *Gaul* * * * with deep Sighs
and Tears he burst forth into the following Complaint.

"O irreversible Decrees of the Fates, that never swerve from your
stated Course!" Why did you ever advance me to an unstable Felic-

ity, since the Punishment of lost Happiness is greater than the Sense of present Misery? The Remembrance of the Time when vast Numbers of Men obsequiously attended me at the taking of Cities and wasting the Enemies Countries, more deeply pierces my Heart, than the View of my present Calamity, which has exposed me to the Derision of those who formerly laid at my Feet. O Rage of Fortune! Shall I ever again see the Day, when I may be able to reward those according their Deserts who have forsaken me in my Distress? How true was thy Answer, *Cordeilla*, when I asked thee concerning thy Love to me, *As much as you have, so much is your Value, and so much I love you?* While I had any Thing to give they valued me, being Friends not to me, but to my Gifts: They loved me then indeed, but my Gifts much more: When my Gifts ceased, my Friends vanished. But with what Face shall I presume to see you my dearest Daughter, since in my Anger I married you upon worse Terms than your Sisters, who, after all the mighty Favours they have received from me, suffer me to be in Banishment and Poverty?" * * * Cordeilla was startled at the News, and wept bitterly [and ordered the reinstatement of his retinue].

Chapter XIII. *He is very honourably received by* Cordeilla, *and the King of* Gaul.

[They] received him honourably, and submitted to his Management the whole Power of *Gaul*.

Chapter XIV. Leir *by the Help of his Son-in-law and* Cordeilla, *being restored to the Kingdom dies.*

* * * *Leir* returned to *Britain* with his Son and Daughter and their Forces they had raised, where he fought with his Sons-in-Law, and routed them. Thus having reduced the whole Kingdom under his Power, he died in the third Year after. *Aganippus* also died; so that *Cordeilla* now obtaining the Government of the Kingdom, buried her Father in a certain Vault, which she ordered to be made for him under the Riuer *Sore* in *Leicester*.[1]

---

1. After reigning for five years, Cordeilla is betrayed by her two nephews and kills herself in prison.

CRITICISM

NAHUM TATE

Preface, *The History of King Lear*†

TO My Esteemed Friend Thomas Boteler, Esq;
SIR,
You have a natural Right to this Piece, since, by your Advice, I attempted the Revival of it with Alterations. Nothing but the Power of your Persuasion, and my Zeal for all the Remains of *Shakespear*, cou'd have wrought me to so bold an Undertaking. I found that the New-modelling of this Story, wou'd force me sometimes on the difficult Task of making the chiefest Persons speak something like their Character, on Matter whereof I had no Ground in my Author. Lear's real, and Edgar's pretended Madness have so much of extravagant Nature (I know not how else to express it) as cou'd never have started but from our Shakespear's Creating Fancy. The Images and Language are so odd and suprizing, and yet so agreeable and prosper, that whilst we grant that none but *Shakespear* cou'd have form'd such Conceptions, yet we are satisfied that they were the only things in the World that ought to be said on those Occasions. I found the whole, to answer your Account of it, a Heap of Jewels, unstrung, and unpolisht; yet so dazling in their Disorder, that I soon perceiv'd I had seiz'd a Treasure. 'Twas my good Fortune to light on one Expedient to rectifie what was wanting in the Regularity and Probability of the Tale, which was to run through the whole, a *Love* betwixt *Edgar* and *Cordelia*; that never chang'd word with each other in the Original. This renders *Cordelia's* Indifference, and her Father's Passion in the first Scene, probable. It likewise gives Countenance to *Edgar's* Disguise, making that a generous Design that was before a poor Shift to save his Life. The Distress of the Story is evidently heightened by it; and it particularly gave Oc-

---

† From Preface, *The History of King Lear, Acted at the Duke's Theatre. Reviv'd with Alterations* (London: Printed for E. Flesher, 1681), signatures A2r-v, A3r. In his revision of the play, which replaced Shakespeare's play from 1681 to 1834, when William Macready returned Shakespeare's version to the London stage, Tate kept most of Shakespeare's original plot, other than the ending; however, Tate changed the play's structure, added or cut characters (including the Fool, who is eliminated), and modernized the language to suit Restoration taste. He retained 3.7, and its blinding of Gloucester by Regan and Cornwall. In his revised ending, Tate has Goneril and Regan poison each other and Albany return the kingdom to Lear, who makes Cordelia queen and betrothes her to Edgar, who has rescued her three times in the play. In the epilogue, Cordelia tells the audience: "Still so many Master-Touches shine / Of that vast Hand that first laid this Design."

casion of a New Scene or Two, of more Success (perhaps) than
Merit. This Method necessarily threw me on making the Tale conclude in a Success to the innocent distrest Persons: Otherwise I
must have incumbered the Stage with dead Bodies, which Conduct
makes many Tragedies conclude with unreasonable Jests. Yet was I
Rackt with no small Fears for so bold a Change, till I found it well
receiv'd by my Audience; and if this will not satisfie the Reader, I
can produce an Authority that questionless will. Neither is it of so
Trivial an Undertaking to make a Tragedy end happily, for 'tis more
difficult to Save than 'tis to Kill. The Dagger and Cup of Poyson are
alwaies in Readiness; but to bring the Action to the last Extremity,
and then by probable Means to recover All, will require the Art and
Judgment of a Writer, and cost him many a Pang in the Performance.

I have one thing more to Apologize for, which is, that I have us'd
less Quaintness of Expression even in the newest Parts of this Play.
I confess 'twas Design in me, partly to comply with my Author's
Style to make the Scenes of a Piece, and partly to give it some Re-
semblance of the Time and Persons here Represented.

SAMUEL JOHNSON

Notes on *King Lear*†

The Tragedy of *Lear* is deservedly celebrated among the dramas of
Shakespeare. There is perhaps no play which keeps the attention so
strongly fixed; which so much agitates our passions and interests
our curiosity. The artful involutions of distinct interests, the striking opposition of contrary characters, the sudden changes of fortune, and the quick succession of events, fill the mind with a
perpetual tumult of indignation, pity, and hope. There is no scene
which does not contribute to the aggravation of the distress or conduct of the action, and scarce a line which does not conduce to the
progress of the scene. So powerful is the current of the poet's imagination, that the mind, which once ventures within it, is hurried
irresistibly along.

On the seeming improbability of *Lear's* conduct it may be observed that he is represented according to histories at that time vul-
garly received as true. And perhaps if we turn our thoughts upon
the barbarity and ignorance of the age to which this story is referred, it will appear not so unlikely as while we estimate *Lear's*

† From *The Plays of William Shakespeare*, ed. Samuel Johnson, vol. 6 (London: J and
R Tonson et al., 1765), pp. 158–59.

manners by our own. Such preference of one daughter to another, or resignation of dominion on such conditions, would yet be credible, if told of a petty prince of *Guinea* or *Madagascar*. *Shakespeare*, indeed, by the mention of his Earls and Dukes, has given us the idea of times more civilised, and of life regulated by softer manners; and the truth is, that though he so nicely discriminates, and so minutely describes the characters of men, he commonly neglects and confounds the characters of ages, by mingling customs ancient and modern, *English* and foreign.

My learned friend Mr *Warton*, who has in the *Adventurer* very minutely criticized this play, remarks, that the instances of cruelty are too savage and shocking, and that the intervention of *Edmund* destroys the simplicity of the story. These objections may, I think, be answered by repeating that the cruelty of the daughters is an historical fact, to which the poet has added little, having only drawn it into a series by dialogue and action. But I am not able to apologize with equal plausibility for the extrusion of *Gloucester's* eyes, which seems an act too horrid to be endured in dramatic exhibition, and such as must always compel the mind to relieve its distress by incredulity. Yet let it be remembered that our author well knew what would please the audience for which he wrote.

The injury done by *Edmund* to the simplicity of the action is abundantly recompensed by the addition of variety, by the art with which he is made to co-operate with the chief design, and the opportunity which he gives the poet of combining perfidy with perfidy, and connecting the wicked son with the wicked daughters, to impress this important moral, that villainy is never at a stop, that crimes lead to crimes and at last terminate in ruin.

But though this moral be incidentally enforced, *Shakespeare* has suffered the virtue of *Cordelia* to perish in a just cause, contrary to the natural ideas of justice, to the hope of the reader, and, what is yet more strange, to the faith of the chronicles. Yet this conduct is justified by the Spectator, who blames *Tate* for giving *Cordelia* success and happiness in his alteration, and declares, that, in his opinion, *the tragedy has lost half its beauty.* * * * A play in which the wicked prosper, and the virtuous miscarry, may doubtless be good, because it is a just representation of the common events of human life: but since all reasonable beings naturally love justice, I cannot easily be persuaded, that the observation of justice makes a play worse; or, that if other excellencies are equal, the audience will not always rise better pleased form the final triumph of persecuted virtue.

In the present case the publick has decided. *Cordelia*, from the time of *Tate*, has always retired with victory and felicity. And, if my sensations could add any thing to the general suffrage, I might re-

late, that I was many years ago so shocked by *Cordelia's* death, that
I know not whether I ever endured to read again the last scenes of
the play till I undertook to revise them as an editor.

There is another controversy among the criticks concerning this
play. It is disputed whether the predominant image in *Lear's* disordered mind be the loss of his kingdom or the cruelty of his daughters. Mr. *Murphy*, a very judicious critick, has evinced by induction
of particular passages, that the cruelty of his daughters is the primary force of his distress, and that the loss of royalty afflicts him
only as a secondary and subordinate evil. He observes with great
justness, that Lear would move our compassion but little, did we
not rather consider the injured father than the degraded king.

CHARLES LAMB

From On the Tragedies of Shakespeare†

So to see Lear acted,—to see an old man tottering about the stage
with a walking-stick, turned out of doors by his daughters in a rainy
night, has nothing in it but what is painful and disgusting. We want
to take him into shelter and relieve him. That is all the feeling
which the acting of Lear ever produced in me. But the Lear of
Shakespeare cannot be acted. The contemptible machinery by
which they mimic the storm which he goes out in, is not more inadequate to represent the horrors of the real elements, than any actor can be to represent Lear: they might more easily propose to
personate the Satan of Milton upon a stage, or one of Michael An-
gelo's terrible figures. The greatness of Lear is not in corporal dimension, but in intellectual: the explosions of his passion are as
terrible as a volcano: they are storms turning up and disclosing to
the bottom of that sea, his mind, with all its vast riches. It is his
mind which is laid bare. This case of flesh and blood seems too insignificant to be thought on; even as he himself neglects it. On the
stage we see nothing but corporal infirmities and weakness, the
impotence of rage while we read it, we see not Lear, but we are
Lear,—we are in his mind, we are sustained by a grandeur which
baffles the malice of daughters and storms; in the aberrations of his
reason, we discover a mighty irregular power of reasoning, immeth-
odized from the ordinary purposes of life, but exerting its powers,
as the wind blows where it listeth, at will upon the corruptions and
abuses of mankind. What have looks, or tones, to do with that sub-

† From *The Works of Charles Lamb in Two Volumes,* ed. Charles Lamb (London: Printed
for C. and J. Ollier, 1818), vol. 2, pp. 25–26.

lime identification of his age with that of the *heavens themselves*, when in his reproaches to them for conniving at the injustice of his children, he reminds them that "they themselves are old". What gesture shall we appropriate to this? What has the voice or the eye to do with such things? But the play is beyond all art, as the tamperings with it shew: it is too hard and stony, it must have love-scenes and a happy ending. It is not enough that Cordelia is a daughter, she must shine as a lover too. Tate has put his hook in the nostrils of this Leviathan, for Garrick and his followers, the showmen of the scene, to draw the mighty beast about more easily. A happy ending!—as if the living martyrdom that Lear had gone through,—the flaying of his feelings alive, did not make a fair dismissal from the stage of life the only decorous thing for him. If he is to live and be happy after, if he could sustain this world's burden after, why all this pudder and preparation, why torment us with all this unnecessary sympathy? As if the childish pleasure of getting his gilt robes and sceptre again could tempt him to act over again his misused station, as if at his years, and with his experience, any thing was left but to die.

Lear is essentially impossible to be represented on a stage.

WILLIAM HAZLITT

From Characters of Shakespeare's Plays: *King Lear†*

We wish that we could pass this play over, and say nothing about it. All that we can say must fall far short of the subject; or even what we ourselves conceive of it. To attempt to give a description of the play itself or of its effect upon the mind, is mere impertinence: yet we must say something. It is then the best of all Shakespeare's plays, for it is the one in which he was the most in earnest. He was here fairly caught in the web of his own imagination. The passion which he has taken as his subject is that which strikes its root deepest into the human heart; of which the bond is the hardest to be unloosed; and the canceling and tearing to pieces of which gives the greatest revulsion to the frame. This depth of nature, this force of passion, this tug and war of the elements of our being, this firm faith in filial piety, and the giddy anarchy and whirling tumult of the thoughts at finding this prop failing it, the contrast between the

---

† From *The Characters of Shakespeare's Plays*, 3rd edition (London: John Templeman, 1838), p. 26. For a modern edition of the text, see *The Complete Works of William Hazlitt*, ed. P. P. Howe (London: J. M. Dent and Sons Ltd., 1930), vol. 4, pp. 257–58, 271–72.

fixed, immoveable basis of natural affection, and the rapid, irregular starts of imagination, suddenly—wrenched from all its accustomed holds and resting-places in the soul, this is what
Shakespeare has given, and what nobody else but he could give. So
we believe.—The mind of Lear, staggering between the weight of
attachment and the hurried movements of passion, is like a tall
ship driven about by the winds, buffetted by the furious waves, but
that still rides above the storm, having its anchor fixed in the bottom of the sea; or it is like the sharp rock circled by the eddying
whirlpool that foams and beats against it, or like the solid promon-
tory pushed from its basis by the force of an earthquake.

The character of Lear itself is very finely conceived for the purpose. It is the only ground on which such a story could be built
with the greatest truth and effect. It is his rash haste, his violent
impetuosity, his blindness to everything but the dictates of his passions or affections, that produces all his misfortunes, that aggra-
vates his impatience of them, that enforces our pity for him.

* * * It has been said, and we think justly, that the third act of
Othello, and the three first acts of LEAR, are Shakspeare's great
master-pieces in the logic of passion: that they contain the highest
examples not only of the force of individual passion, but of its dramatic vicissitudes and striking effects, arising from the different
circumstances and characters of the persons speaking. We see the
ebb and flow of feeling, its pauses and feverish starts, its impatience of opposition, its accumulating force when it has time to
recollect itself of every passing word or gesture, its haste to repel
insinuation, the alternate contraction and dilatation of the soul,
and all "the dazzling fence of controversy" in this mortal combat
with poisoned weapons, aimed at the heart, where each wound is
fatal.

* * * Four things have struck us in reading LEAR:

1. That poetry is an interesting study, for this reason, that it re-
lates to whatever is most interesting in human life. Whoever therefore has a contempt for poetry, has a contempt for himself and
humanity.

2. That the language of poetry is superior to the language of
painting; because the strongest of our recollections relate to feelings, not to faces.

3. That the greatest strength of genius is shown in describing the
strongest passions: for the power of the imagination, in works of invention, must be in proportion to the force of the natural impressions, which are the subject of them.

4. That the circumstance which balances the pleasure against
the pain in tragedy is, that in proportion to the greatness of the evil,
is our sense and desire of the opposite good excited; and that our

sympathy with actual suffering is lost in the strong impulse given to our natural affections, and carried away with the swelling tide of passion, that gushes from and relieves the heart.

A. C. BRADLEY

From Shakespearean Tragedy†

King Lear has again and again been described as Shakespeare's greatest work, the best of his plays, the tragedy in which he exhibits most fully his multitudinous powers; and if we were doomed to lose all his dramas except one, probably the majority of those who know and appreciate him best would pronounce for keeping *King Lear*.

Yet this tragedy is certainly the least popular of the famous four. The 'general reader' reads it less often than the others, and, though he acknowledges its greatness, he will sometimes speak of it with a certain distaste. It is also the least often presented on the stage, and the least successful there. And when we look back on its history after the Restoration, Nahum Tate altered *King Lear* for the stage, giving it a happy ending, and putting Edgar in the place of the king of France as Cordelia's lover. From that time Shakespeare's tragedy in its original form was never seen on the stage for a century and a half. Betterton acted Tate's version; Garrick acted it and Dr. Johnson approved it. Kemble acted it, Kean acted it. In 1823 Kean, 'stimulated by Hazlitt's remonstrances and Charles Lamb's essays', restored the original tragic ending. At last, in 1838,[1] Macready returned to Shakespeare's text throughout.

What is the meaning of these opposite sets of facts? Are the lovers of Shakespeare wholly in the right; and is the general reader and playgoer, were even Tate and Dr. Johnson, altogether in the wrong? I venture to doubt it. When I read *King Lear* two impressions are left on my mind, which seem to answer roughly to the two sets of facts. King Lear seems to me Shakespeare's greatest achievement, but it seems to me *not* his best play. And I find that I tend to consider it from two rather different points of view. When I regard it strictly as a drama, it appears to me, though in certain parts overwhelming, decidedly inferior as a whole to *Hamlet, Othello*, and *Macbeth*.

* * * The stage is the test of strictly dramatic quality, and *King Lear* is too huge for the stage. Of course, I am not denying that it is

---

† From *Shakespearean Tragedy: Lectures on Hamlet, Othello, King Lear, Macbeth* (London: Macmillan and Co., 1904), pp. 234–44.
1. Macready first began to restore the Shakespearean text in 1834 [*Editor*].

a great stage-play. It has scenes immensely effective in the theatre; three of them—the two between Lear and Goneril and between Lear, Goneril and Regan, and the ineffably beautiful scene in the Fourth Act between Lear and Cordelia—lose in the theatre very little of the spell they have for imagination; and the gradual interweaving of the two plots is almost as masterly as in *Much Ado*. But (not to speak of defects due to mere carelessness) that which makes the *peculiar* greatness of *King Lear*,—the immense scope of the work; the mass and varied of intense experience which it contains; the interpenetration of sublime imagination, piercing pathos, and humour almost as moving as the pathos; the vastness of the convulsion both of nature and of human passion; the vagueness of the scene where the action takes place, and of the movements of the figures which cross this scene; the strange atmosphere, cold and dark, which strikes on us as we enter this scene, enfolding these figures and magnifying their dim outlines like a winter mist; the half-realised suggestions of vast universal powers working in the world of individual fates and passions,—all this interferes with dramatic clearness even when the play is read, and in the theatre not only refuses to reveal itself fully through the senses but seems to be almost in contradiction with their reports. This is not so with the other great tragedies. No doubt, as Lamb declared, theatrical representation gives only a part of what we imagine when we read them; but there is no *conflict* between the representation and the imagination, because these tragedies are, in essentials, perfectly dramatic. But *King Lear*, as a whole, is imperfectly dramatic, and there is something in its very essence which is at war with the senses, and demands a purely imaginative realization. It is therefore Shakespeare's greatest work, but it is not what Hazlitt called it, the best of his plays; and its comparative unpopularity is due, not merely to the extreme painfulness of the catastrophe, but in part to its dramatic defects, and in part to a failure in many readers to catch the peculiar effects to which I have referred—a failure which is natural because the appeal is made not so much to dramatic perception as to a rarer and more strictly poetic kind of imagination. For this reason, too, even the best attempts at exposition of *King Lear* are disappointing; they remind us of attempts to reduce to prose the impalpable spirit of the *Tempest*.

JAN KOTT

From Shakespeare Our Contemporary†

The attitude of modern criticism to *King Lear* is ambiguous and somehow embarrassed. Doubtless *King Lear* is still recognized as a masterpiece, beside which even Macbeth and Hamlet seem tame and pedestrian. * * * *King Lear* gives one the impression of a high mountain that everyone admires, yet no one particularly wishes to climb. It is as if the play had lost its power to excite on the stage and in reading; as if it were out of place in our time, or, at any rate, had no place in the modern theatre. But the question is: what is modern theatre?

The apogee of *King Lear's* theatrical history was reached no doubt in the romantic era. To the romantic theatre *King Lear* fitted perfectly; but only conceived as a melodrama, full of horrors, and dealing with a tragic king, deprived of his crown, conspired against by heaven and earth, nature and men. Charles Lamb might well laugh at early nineteenth-century performances in which a miserable old man wandered about the stage bare-headed, stick in hand, in an artificial storm and rain. But the theatre was soon to attain the full power of illusion. Diorama, scene changes effected by means of new stage-machinery, without bringing the curtain down, made it possible suddenly, almost miraculously, to transform a Gothic castle into a mountainous region, or a blood-red sunset into a stormy night. Lightning and thunder, rain and wind, seemed the real thing. * * * The actor's task was to demonstrate the blackest depths of the human soul. Lear's and Gloster's unhappy fate was to arouse pity and terror, to shock the audience. And so it did. Suffering purified Lear and restored his tragic greatness. Shakespeare's King Lear was the 'black theatre' of romanticism.

Then came the turn of the historical, antiquarian and realistic Shakespeare [in Victorian productions]. * * * As a result of the odd marriage between new and perfected theatre techniques with the archaeological reconstruction of a celtic tomb, only the plot remained of Shakespeare's play. In such a theatre Shakespeare was indeed out of place: he was untheatrical.

The turn of the century brought a revolution in Shakespearian studies. For the first time his plays began to be interpreted through the theatre of his time. * * * The return to the so-called 'authentic'

† From *Shakespeare Our Contemporary*, trans. Boleslaw Taborski. Copyright © 1964 by Pantstwowe Wydawnictwo Naukowe and Doubleday, a division of Random House, Inc.

Shakespeare began. From now on the storm was to rage in Lear's and Gloster's breast rather than on the stage. The trouble was, however, that the demented old man, tearing his long white beard, suddenly became ridiculous. He should have been tragic but he no longer was. * * * Producers have found it virtually impossible to cope with the plot of *King Lear*. When realistically treated, Lear and Gloster were too ridiculous to appear tragic heroes. If the exposition was treated as a fairy tale or legend, the cruelty of Shakespeare's world, too, became unreal. Yet the cruelty of *Lear* was to the Elizabethans a contemporary reality, and has remained real since. But it is a philosophical cruelty. Neither the romantic, nor the naturalistic theatre was able to show that sort of cruelty; only the new theatre can. In this new theatre there are no characters, and the tragic element has been superseded by the grotesque. The grotesque is more cruel than tragedy.

* * * A tale of two bad daughters and one good daughter, or a story about the druid king. The opening of *King Lear* compels the producer to make an absurd choice between a fairy tale and a celtic mystery. By being reduced to a fable or to archaeology, *King Lear* had always been deprived of both its great seriousness and its great buffo [i.e., comic] tone. Thus the play used to lose stature at the outset. To my mind, Peter Brook's first discovery consisted in finding an historical situation in which *King Lear* could at last be set; a situation in which it became a history brutal and tragic, serious and grotesque, with real people and real objects taking part.

* * * They were very much alike, those sixteenth-and seventeenth-century nobles, whether in England or in the Ukraine, in Scotland or in Lithuania. Too small, this Lear, to be a king, but his characteristics can easily be found in Border country nobles anywhere. * * * There is in *King Lear*—and Mr Brook was the first to discover it—a combination of madness, passion, pride, folly, imperiousness, anarchy, humanity and awe, which all have their exact place and time in history.

The first three acts almost belong to epic theatre. There are few objects, but every one of them is real and means something: the orb and-the-sword, the map drawn on leather, old Gloster's astrolabe, stocks, even the chain-spoon carried by Oswald as the court steward. *King Lear* is a play about the disintegration of the world. But, in order to show the world disintegrating, one has first to prove that it exists. Until it falls, it has to exist, with its hierarchy of power, with its faiths, rituals and ceremonies, with its mutually entangled relationships of power and family, marriage and adultery, legitimate and illegitimate children, violence and law. To my mind, it was more difficult to show the continued existence of the world in *King Lear* than its disintegration. The disintegration had already been shown by the theatre of the absurd. It sufficed to discover [the playwright Samuel] Beckett in Shakespeare.

The scenes of Lear's madness are like a plummet thrown from a boat to fathom the lowest depths. These people of flesh and blood have now been reduced to trunks, to crippled torsos. Then, from the fourth act onwards, the world slowly begins, as it were, to grow together again. Ceremonies and rituals begin anew, wars are waged somewhere, with someone, for something. But for Lear, for Gloster, those are just the incomprehensible noises of a world which has ceased to exist.

In my conversations with Peter Brook I once tried to persuade him to show how all the characters of this drama descended lower and lower. I wanted the early acts to be performed on a large platform placed high up on the stage and to demonstrate physically, materially, visibly as it were, the disintegration and descent. Brook did not need any of these naïve metaphors. The disintegrated world does not grow together in this production, just as it does not grow together in Shakespeare's play. Human wrecks find their humanity again, but this only means that they refuse to accept suffering, torture and death. They refuse to accept the absurdity of the world in which one lives in order to breed, murder and die.

A brother throws over his shoulder the body of the brother he has killed. This is all there is. There will not be another king. The stage remains empty. Like the world.

PETER BROOK

From The Empty Space†

Shakespeare is a model of theatre that contains [Bertold] Brecht and [Samuel] Beckett, but goes beyond both. Our need in the post-Brecht theatre is to find a way forwards, back to Shakespeare. In Shakespeare the introspection and the metaphysics soften nothing. Quite the reverse. It is through the unreconciled opposition of Rought [i.e., earthly] and Holy, through an atonal screech of absolutely unsympathetic keys that we get the disturbing and the unforgettable impressions of his plays. It is because the contradictions are so strong that they burn on us so deeply.

† From *The Empty Space* (New York: Atheneum, 1968), pp. 91–94. Copyright © 1996 by Peter Brook. Reprinted with the permission of Scribner, an imprint of Simon and Schuster Adult Publishing Group. All rights reserved. Brook discusses here the groundbreaking production he staged for the Royal Shakespeare in 1962 (and subsequently on tour around the world) of *King Lear* with Paul Scofield in the title role (this production was filmed in 1971).

* * * We have at last become aware that the absence of scenery in the Elizabethan theatre was one of its greatest freedoms. In England at least, all productions for quite some time have been influenced by the discovery that Shakespeare's plays were written to be performed continuously, that their cinematic structure of alternating short scenes, plot intercut with subplot, were all part of a total shape. This shape is only revealed dynamically, that is in the uninterrupted sequence of these scenes, and without this their effect and power are lessened as much as would be a film that was projected with breaks and musical interludes between each reel.

* * * Compared with the cinema's mobility, the theatre once seemed ponderous and creaky, but the closer we move towards the true nakedness of theatre, the closer we approach a stage that has a lightness and range far beyond film or television. The power of Shakespeare's plays is that they present man simultaneously in all his aspects: touch for touch, we can identify and withdraw. A primitive situation disturbs us in our subconscious; our intelligence watches, comments, philosophizes.

* * * Experimentally, we can approach Lear not as a linear narrative, but as a cluster of relationships. First, we try to rid ourselves of the notion that because the play is called *King Lear* it is primarily the story of one individual. So we pick an arbitrary point in the vast structure—the death of Cordelia, say, and now instead of looking towards the King we turn instead towards the man who is responsible for her death. We focus on this character, Edmund, and now we begin to pick our way to and fro across the play, sifting the evidence, trying to discover who this Edmund is. He is clearly a villain, whatever our standards, for in killing Cordelia he is responsible for the most gratuitous act of cruelty in the play—yet if we look at our first impression of him in the early scenes, we find he is by far the most attractive character we meet. * * * Not only do we sympathize with Goneril and Regan for falling in love with him, but we tend to side with them in finding Edmund so admirably wicked, because he affirms a life that the sclerosis of the older people seems to deny. Can we keep this same attitude of admiration towards Edmund when he has Cordelia killed? If not, why not? What has changed? Is it Edmund who has changed, through outside events? Or is it just the context that is different? Is a scale of value implied? What are Shakespeare's values? What is the value of a life?

* * * Indeed, it is clearly shown to us in the unfolding of the play that Lear suffers most and 'gets farthest'. Undoubtedly his brief moment of captivity with Cordelia is as a moment of bliss, peace and reconciliation, and Christian commentators often write as though this were the end of the story—a clear tale of the ascent from the inferno through purgation to paradise. Unfortunately for

this neat view the play continues, pitilessly, away from reconciliation.

> 'We that are young
> Shall never see so much, nor live so long.'

The power of Edgar's disturbing statement—a statement that rings
like a half-open question—is that it carries no moral overtones at
all. He does not suggest for one moment that youth or age, seeing
or not seeing, are in any way superior, inferior, more desirable or
less desirable once than the other. In fact we are compelled to face
a play which refuses all moralizing—a play which we begin to see
not as a narrative any longer, but as a vast, complex, coherent poem
designed to study the power and the emptiness of nothing—the
positive and negative aspects latent in the zero. So what does
Shakespeare say? What is he trying to teach us? Does he mean that
suffering has a necessary place in life and is worth cultivating for
the knowledge or inner development it brings? Or does he mean us
to understand that the age of titanic suffering is now over and our
role is that of the eternally young? Wisely, Shakespeare refuses to
answer. But he has given us his play, and its whole field of experience is both question and answer. In this light, the play is directly
related to the most burning themes of our time, the old and the
new in relation to our society, our arts, our notions of progress, our
way of living our lives. If the actors are interested, this is what they
will bring out. If we are interested, that is what we will find. Fancy
dress, then, will be left far behind. The meaning will be for the moment of the performance.

MICHAEL WARREN

Quarto and Folio *King Lear* and the Interpretation of Albany and Edgar†

I

The two texts of *King Lear* present obvious editorial and critical problems. The Quarto of 1608 prints about 283 lines that are not printed
in the 1623 Folio; the Folio prints about 100 that are not printed in
the Quarto.[1] A variation of nearly 400 lines in a text of around 3,300

† From *Shakespeare: Pattern of Excelling Nature* by Michael Warren, pages 95–107.
Reprinted by permission of the University of Delaware Press.
1. I am using the figures cited by Alfred Harbage on p. 1104 of his appendix to his text of
King Lear published in *The Pelican Shakespeare* (Baltimore, 1969), pp. 1104–6.

lines is significant;[2] in addition, there are also a very large number of variant substantive readings. However, far from alarming editors and critics to the delicate problems involved in printing and discussing a single play called *King Lear,* this wealth of material has been treated as an ample blessing from which a "best text" of Shakespeare's *King Lear* may be evolved. Indeed, the standard methods of bibliography and editing—the application of critical principles "to the textual raw material of the authoritative preserved documents in order to approach as nearly as may be to the ideal of the authorial fair copy by whatever necessary process of recovery, independent emendation, or conflation of authorities"[3]—such methods and the accepted assumptions of the origins of each text have led to the editorial habit of establishing and publishing a *King Lear* text that is produced by a process of conflation, by the exercise of a moderate and quasi-scientific eclecticism, and by a studied disregard for the perils of intentionalism.[4] In a recent article Kenneth Muir writes:

> Until the work of bibliographers and textual critics in the present century, editors chose readings from either text, according to taste. It is now generally agreed that, whatever the basis of the Quarto text, the Folio text of *King Lear* is nearer to what Shakespeare wrote; but, even so, editors are still bound to accept a number of readings from the inferior text and, since there were cuts in the prompt-book from which the Folio text was derived, a number of long passages.[5]

This statement reveals certain clear attitudes of editors to their task. It is assumed that there is one primal lost text, an "ideal *King Lear*" that Shakespeare wrote, and that we have two corrupted copies of it. It is hypothesized that F is a less corrupt version of the

---

2. *The Pelican Shakespeare* states that *King Lear* is 3,195 lines long; *The Norton Facsimile: The First Folio of Shakespeare,* ed. Charlton Hinman (New York, 1968), gives *King Lear* 3,301 lines.

3. Fredson Bowers. *Textual and Literary Criticism* (Cambridge, 1966), p. 120.

4. Harbage, "Note on the Text": "In 1608 a version of *King Lear* appeared in a Quarto volume sold by Nathaniel Butter at his shop at the Pied Bull. Its text was reproduced in 1619 in a quarto falsely dated 1608. Various theories have been offered to explain the nature of the Pied Bull text, the most recent being that it represents Shakespeare's rough draft carelessly copied, and corrupted by the faulty memories of actors who were party to the copying. In 1623 a greatly improved though 'cut' version of the play appeared in the first folio, evidently printed from the quarto after it had been carefully collated with the official playhouse manuscript. The present edition follows the folio text, and although it adds in square brackets the passages appearing only in the quarto, and accepts fifty-three quarto readings, it follows the chosen text more closely than do most recent editions. However, deference to the quarto is paid in an appendix, where its alternative readings, both those accepted and those rejected, are listed. Few editorial emendations have been retained, but see. . . ." (p. 1064). See also G. Blakemore Evans, "Note on the Text" of *King Lear,* in *The Riverside Shakespeare* (Boston, 1974), pp. 1295–96, and Kenneth Muir, "Introduction" to *King Lear* (Arden Shakespeare) (Cambridge, Mass., 1959), pp. xix–xx.

5. Kenneth Muir. "King Lear," in Stanley Wells, ed., *Shakespeare: Select Bibliographical Guides* (Oxford, 1973), p. 171.

ideal text than Q, though both preserve features of the ideal original; and that while there is more corruption in Q, some uncor-
rupted elements remain that can mitigate the admittedly lesser
corruption of F. The concept of the "ideal *King Lear*" is problematic
here, first, because its existence cannot be known, and second, because in the absence of such knowledge it is nevertheless further
assumed that all alterations of any nature from that imaginary text
are by hands other than Shakespeare's. Such an assumption is
based on no evidence, and is counter to our experience of authors
and their habits—for example, the modification of texts after first
publication by Jonson, Pope, Yeats, James, and Pinter. Of course, it
is conceivable that this standard hypothesis may indeed be true,
but the confidence with which it is assumed is unwarranted, and
the lack of a constant awareness that it is an assumption leads to
poorly founded judgments. For instance, a statement such as "editors are still bound to accept a number of readings from the inferior
text" is merely an editor's justification of the right to be eclectic; although editors may well be advised at times to adopt readings
where comparison of texts indicates simple misprints or nonsensi-
cal readings, circumspection and wariness are always necessary, for
nonsense may merely be sense we do not yet understand, and further we cannot know that alterations between Q and F are not authorial in origin. Most editors admit that the examination of the
two texts leads to the conclusion that, editing has taken place, and
yet they are generally reluctant to take that editing seriously.

Having asserted the necessity of a decent skepticism in relation
to the concept of the "ideal" text, I wish to argue that in a situation
where statements about textual status are never more than hypotheses based upon the current models of thought about textual
recension, it is not demonstrably erroneous to work with the possibility (a) that there may be no single "ideal play" of *King Lear* (all of
"what Shakespeare wrote"), that there may never have been one,
and that what we create by conflating both texts is merely an invention of editors and scholars; (b) that for all its problems Q is an authoritative version of the play of *King Lear*; and (c) that F may
indeed be a revised version of the play, that its additions and omis-
sions may constitute Shakespeare's considered modification of the
earlier text, and that we certainly cannot know that they are not.[6]

Of course, I am once more introducing, after over fifty years of

---

6. Nor, of course, can we know with absolute confidence that they are, though that is my
   suspicion. The views of four other scholars are notable on this subject of revision. Dr.
   Johnson remarked that "I believe the Folio is printed from Shakespeare's last revision,
   carelessly and hastily performed, with more thought of shortening the scenes than of
   continuing the action," quoted by H. H. Furness, ed., *King Lear* (New Variorum Edition), 9th ed. (London, 1880), p. 215. In *The Pictorial Edition of the Works of Shakespeare*, ed. Charles Knight, 8 vols., (London, [1839]–1843), Knight argued vigorously

relative quiescence, the specter of "continuous copy": not, I would hope, in the confident, fantastic, and disintegrationist mode of Robertson and Dover Wilson, but in a skeptical and conservative way. In his famous lecture *The Disintegration of Shakespeare*, E. K. Chambers dismissed the excesses of his contemporaries as much by the force of ironic rhetoric and an attractive appeal to common sense as by any real proof; but he nowhere succeeded in denying the possibility of authorial reworking. He instanced the few cases of recorded extensive revision as indicative that revision of any kind was rare; and he asserted as follows: "That any substantial revision, as distinct perhaps from a mere abridgement, would entail a fresh application for the Master's allowance must, I think, be taken for granted. The rule was that his hand must be 'at the latter end of the booke they doe play'; and in London, at least, any company seriously departing from the allowed book would run a considerable risk."[7] Which is an interesting hypothesis; but what in this connection would constitute "substantial revision" or "serious departure"? Chambers to the contrary, that same common sense which leads me to praise him in his rejection of disintegrationist excesses leads me nevertheless to believe that a play like *King Lear* may have undergone revision beyond "mere abridgement"—what Chambers, following Henslowe, might classify as "altering"—without the necessity of resubmission to the Master of the Revels.

In putting forward this argument I have ignored many of the complexities of relation that have been the stuff of textual debate for many years. I have done so because they are merely the current working hypotheses of the editing world, and because they are not immediately relevant to my contention. I would maintain that Q and F *King Lear* are sufficiently dissimilar that they should not be conflated, but should be treated as two versions of a single play, both having authority. To substantiate my argument I wish to present three brief studies. In the first I will deal with a short exchange of dialogue to illustrate the impact of conflation on the text as script for the theater; in the second and third I will discuss the varying presentations of Albany and Edgar in Q and F.

---

that the Folio represents an authorial revision of the play (VI,391–93); but he nevertheless included the passages that derive from Q alone in brackets in his published text. In *The Stability of Shakespeare's Texts* (Lincoln, Neb., 1965). E. A. J. Honigmann regards the differences in the texts of *King Lear* as authorial in origin (pp. 121–28), but conceives of them as cases of "authorial 'second thoughts' *before* its [the play's] delivery to the actors. I envisage, in short, two copies of a play, each in the author's hand, disagreeing in both substantive and indifferent readings: the play being regarded as 'finished' by Shakespeare in each version though not therefore beyond the reach of afterthoughts" (p. 2). By contrast, Peter W. M. Blayney (see unnumbered footnote on first page of this essay) informs me in a letter that he believes that Shakespeare's was not the only hand involved in the revision that led to F.

7. E. K. Chambers, *The Disintegration of Shakespeare* ([London], 1924), p. 17.

II

In Act 2 Lear discovers Kent in the stocks; the two texts present the following dialogue (2.4.12–23):[8] first Q:

Lear. Whats he, that hath so much thy place mistooke to set thee here?
Kent. It is both he and shee, your sonne & daugter.
Lear. No.
Kent. Yes.
Lear. No I say.
Kent. I say yea.
Lear. No no, they would not.
Kent. Yes they haue.
Lear. By *Iupiter* I sweare no, they durst not do't,
They would not, could not do't, . . .

then F:

Lear. What's he,
That hath so much thy place mistooke
To set thee heere?
Kent. It is both he and she,
Your Son, and Daughter.
Lear. No.
Kent. Yes.
Lear. No I say.
Kent. I say yea.
Lear. By *Iupiter* I sweare no.
Kent. By *Iuuo*, I sweare I.
Lear. They durst not do't:
They could not, would not do't: . . .

Editors here customarily conflate these texts so that both "No no, they would not / Yes they haue," and Kent's "By *Iuuo*, I sweare I" are retained; in consequence four exchanges are produced where three exist in each of the original texts. Muir's note in the Arden text (p. 83) is concerned with the integrity of the Q lines and critics' opinions of their quality. But the more important issue is that his text (like most others) presents us with a reading that has *no* authority. If F was printed from a copy of Q as is widely and reason-

8. For convenience I shall cite line numberings based on Muir's Arden edition throughout this essay; apparent inconsistencies occasionally result from the Arden relineation. All quotations from Q are from *King Lear, 1608 (Pied Bull Quarto)*: Shakespeare Quarto Facsimiles No. 1, ed. W. W. Greg (Oxford, 1939); all quotations from F are from *The Norton Facsimile: The First Folio of Shakespeare*, ed. Charlton B. Hinman (New York, 1968). The text will normally make clear whether Q or F is being quoted; on occasions when the text is not specified and the lines under discussion appear in both Q and F with only insignificant differences in spelling and punctuation, I quote from F alone.

ably accepted, then one ought to assume that any omission
may have had a purpose: but that assumption is doubly imperative
when new material is included in F that appears to make up for the
omission. However, even if one ignores the standard theory concerning the recension, there is still no case for four exchanges. In
each text the climax on the third exchange is powerful, and sufficient; neither can be proved to be un-Shakespearean—they are
both probably "what Shakespeare wrote"; and so respect for the
theatrical proportions of the play dictates that conflation cannot be
other than textual tinkering, distortion. Either Q or F; *not* both together.

III

As the above passage indicates, the editor, like any other reader
of Shakespeare, must always be conscious that play texts are scripts
for performance; when they are realized on the stage, presence, absence, action, inaction, speech, and silence have far more impact
than when they are noted on the printed page. With this observation in mind I wish to argue that Q and F reveal significant differences in the roles of Albany and Edgar, differences sufficiently
great that one is obliged to interpret their characters differently in
each, and, especially in relation to the alterations in the last scene,
to appreciate a notable contrast in the tone and meaning of the
close of each text. These differences go beyond those which may be
expected when two texts descend in corrupted form from a common original; they indicate that a substantial and consistent recast-
ing of certain aspects of the play has taken place. In brief, the part
of Albany is more developed in Q than in F, and in Q he closes the
play a mature and victorious duke assuming responsibility for
the kingdom; in F he is a weaker character, avoiding responsibility.
The part of Edgar is shorter in F than in Q; however, whereas in Q
he ends the play a young man overwhelmed by his experience, in F
he is a young man who has learned a great deal, and who is emerg-
ing as the new leader of the ravaged society.

In both texts Albany speaks little in the first act. Neither Albany
nor Cornwall speaks in the first scene in Q: their joint exclamation
"Deare Sir forbeare" (1.1.162) appears in F only. In the fourth
scene, which Goneril dominates in both texts, Q lacks two of the
eight brief speeches that F assigns to Albany, and a phrase that com-
pletes a third. Missing are "Pray Sir be patient" (1.4.270) and "Well,
you may feare too farre" (1.4.338), and the phrase "Of what hath
moued you" (1.4.283), which in F succeeds "My Lord, I am guilt-
lesse, as I am ignorant." Albany, who is bewildered and ineffectual in
either text, is more patently so in Q, where he is given no opportu-

nity to urge patience in response to Lear's question—"is it your will that wee prepare any horses" (F "Is it your will, speake Sir? Prepare my Horses") (1.4.267)—and no opportunity to warn Goneril of the unwisdom of her acts. Goneril's part also is smaller in Q than in F—she lacks 1.4.322–43—but she dominates the scene nevertheless.

However, when Albany enters in the fourth act after a period in which he does not ride to Gloucester's house with Goneril and is mentioned only in the context of the always incipient conflict between himself and Cornwall, his reappearance is different in quality in each text. In both texts the scene begins with Oswald reporting Albany's disaffection (4.2.3–11) while Goneril scorns "the Cowish terror of his spirit" (4.2.12). In F Albany's speech on entering is very brief:

> Oh *Gonerill*,
> You are not worth the dust which the rude winde
> Blowes in your face.
>
> (4.2.29–31)

However, Q continues:

>   I feare your disposition
> That nature which contemnes ith origin
> Cannot be bordered certaine in it selfe,
> She that her selfe will sliuer and disbranch
> From her materiall sap, perforce must wither,
> And come to deadly vse.
>
> (4.2.31–36)

And Goneril's prompt dismissal "No more, the text is foolish" leads to a longer speech of powerful moral reproach, likening the sisters to tigers, and reaching its climax in the pious pronouncement that

> If that the heauens doe not their visible spirits
> Send quickly downe to tame this vild offences, it will come
> Humanity must perforce pray on it self like monsters of the deepe.
>
> (4.2.46–50)

The speeches that follow in Q are much reduced in F, and both Albany and Goneril lose lines. The cuts in Goneril's part are largely references to Albany as a "morall foole," statements critical of his mild response to the invasion of France; her stature is not notably diminished by the loss. The reduction of Albany's part, by contrast, severely reduces his theatrical impact. In F he is left with barely six lines between his entrance and that of the messenger, and there is no sense of the new strong position that lines such as the following, even allowing for Goneril's belittling rejection, establish in Q:

Alb. Thou changed, and selfe-couerd thing for shame
Be-monster not thy feature, wer't my fitnes
To let these hands obay my bloud,
They are apt enough to dislecate and teare
Thy flesh and bones, how ere thou art a fiend,
A womans shape doth shield thee.
Gon. Marry your manhood mew . . .

                                        (4.2.62–68)

In Q the succeeding lines of moral outrage at the news of the
blinding of Gloucester present Albany as a man of righteous wrath,
outraged by injustice; the same sequence in F presents Albany as
equally outraged, but because of the brevity of his previous rebukes
he appears more futile in context, less obviously a man capable of
action. The cutting diminishes his stature.

Although Albany does assert himself in the fifth act in both texts,
he is much stronger in Q by virtue of the presence of three passages that are not his in F. At his entrance he asserts control over
the situation in both texts with his first speech; Q reads:

Our very louing sister well be-met
For this I heare the King is come to his daughter
With others, whome the rigour of our state
Forst to crie out, . . .

                                        (5.1.20–23)[9]

The speech continues in Q but not in F:

           where I could not be honest
I neuer yet was valiant, for this busines
It touches vs. as *France* inuades our land
Not bolds the King, with others whome I feare,
Most iust and heauy causes make oppose.

                                        (5.1.23–27)

The inclusion of this passage in Q gives immediate prominence
to the complexity and scrupulousness of Albany's understanding
of the political and moral issues. More important, however, are the
two alterations in the closing moments of the play: 5.3.251 Q assigns to Albany the order "Hast thee for thy life," which F gives to
Edgar; and Q assigns the final four lines to Albany, which again F
gives to Edgar. I shall discuss these changes more fully as I deal
with Edgar, but it is sufficient to point out at this stage that Albany
is in command throughout the last scene in Q, while in F he is con-
siderably effaced at the close.

9. At 5.1.21 F reads "Sir, this I heard," for "For this I heare."

IV

In both Q and F Edgar presents far more complex problems than Albany, not least because he is intrinsically a more complex and difficult character even before textual variations are considered. Edgar's part, which in conflated texts is second only to that of Lear in length,[1] is reduced in size in F, but unlike Albany, Edgar receives some new material which, however it is interpreted, tends to focus attention more precisely upon him.

The differences in Edgar's role between Q and F in the first act are not of major significance: at 1.2.98–100 Q includes and F omits an exchange between Edmund and Gloucester about Edgar that reveals more about Gloucester's character than Edgar's; F omits Edmund's imitative discourse upon the current crisis and Edgar's ironic reply "How long haue you been a sectary Astronomicall?" (1.2.151–57); and F includes a passage not in Q in which Edmund proposes concealing Edgar in his lodging, and recommends going armed, to the surprise of his brother (1.2.172–79). More important variations appear in the third act. At 3.4.37–38 in F (after a stage direction *"Enter Edgar, and Foole,"* which contradicts Kent's speech a few lines later "What art thou that dost grumble there i'th' straw? Come forth"), Edgar utters a line that Q lacks: "Fathom, and halfe, Fathom and halfe; poore *Tom*"; this offstage cry makes a chilling theatrical introduction to Edgar-as-Tom, and it is moreover the event that, coupled with his entrance, appears to propel Lear finally into madness. Later in the third act F omits material that Q includes. F lacks the trial of Goneril that Lear conducts with the support of Edgar and the Fool (3.6.17–56). While F provides the Fool with a new last line in the play "And Ile go to bed at noone" (3.6.88), it omits Kent's tender speech over Lear in Q, which begins "Oppressed nature sleepes" (3.6.100–104). However, very important alterations in this middle section of the play follow immediately; they are F's omission of the soliloquy with which Edgar closes 3.6 in Q and F's minor amplification of Edgar's first speech in the fourth act, two speeches that provide the transitions to and from the climactic scene of the blinding of Gloucester. These alterations need to be discussed in the larger context of the character and function of Edgar in the play.

In recent years serious challenges have been made to the traditional conception of Edgar as the good, devoted, abused but patient, loving son. Some of this examination has led to the formulation of extreme positions in which Edgar has appeared as almost as culpable and vicious as Edmund, dedication to an ideal of self-

---

1. See *Pelican Shakespeare*, p. 31.

less virtuous support being interpreted as an unconscious psychic violence, a dangerous self-righteousness that must exercise itself on others.[2] It is unnecessary, however, to censure Edgar so strongly to accommodate some of the distance that one frequently feels from him; one may allow him his virtue while still seeing its weakness. Speaking much in aside and soliloquy, Edgar is distanced theatrically from many of the events of the play. However, despite his involvement with Lear in the mad scenes, he also appears at times to be distanced emotionally from the events around him; his moral commentary reflects his response to the events, his assessment of his philosophical position in their light. The problem is that his response is frequently inadequate. As the play proceeds Edgar is obliged to confront the shallowness of his rationalizations, and yet much of the time he nevertheless appears impervious to the new knowledge that is being forced upon him. He possesses a naively pious and optimistic faith in the goodness of the world and the justice of the gods, and in his own youthful, romantic vision of his role in this world of conflict. In his mind his father's despair will be conquered by his endless encouragement; the triumphant climax will be the restoration to Gloucester of the knowledge of his son's existence and readiness to go off to recover his dukedom for him. The mode of Edgar's thought is Christian romantic-heroic, in which virtue usually triumphs spendidly. That it bears little relation to the realities of the universe in which the play takes place is evident; but it does save Gloucester from abject misery, and provides incidentally a happy, well-deceived death for him. We can appreciate Edgar's love and concern for his father, while doubting the maturity of many of his judgments.

It is in the context of this conception of Edgar, which is appropriate to either text, that I wish to demonstrate the major alterations in the role. When the soliloquy beginning "When we our betters see bearing our woes" is spoken at the close of 3.6. in Q (3.6.105–18), we are aware of Edgar's ability to comment upon the king's suffering, the power of fellowship, and his capacity to endure; in F, which lacks these meditations, Edgar has played a very

---

2. For sympathetic readings of Edgar, see (among others), R. B. Heilman, *This Great Stage* (Baton Rouge, La., 1948), and William R. Elton, *King Lear and the Gods* (San Marino, 1966). For more unsympathetic interpretations, see William Empson, "Fool in Lear," in *The Structure of Complex Words* (London, 1951); Nicholas Brooke, *Shakespeare: King Lear* (London, 1963); Stanley Cavell, "The Avoidance of Love," in *Must We Mean What We Say?* (New York, 1969); Marvin Rosenberg, *The Masks of King Lear* (Berkeley, Calif., 1972); S. L. Goldberg, *An Essay on King Lear* (Cambridge, 1974). However, there are signs of a restoration of honor and respect to Edgar; see, for instance, F. T. Flahiff, "Edgar: Once and Future King," in Rosalie L. Colie and F. T. Flahiff, eds., *Some Facets of King Lear: Essays in Prismatic Criticism* (Toronto, 1974), pp. 221–37, and Barbara A. Kathe, rsm, "The Development of the Myth of the Birth of the Hero in the Role of Edgar," a paper delivered at the International Shakespeare Association Congress in Washington, D.C., in April 1976.

small part in a rather brief scene, and the play rushes to the blinding of Gloucester. But F compensates for these cuts by expanding
the speech with which Edgar opens the fourth act in both texts by
adding an extra sentence. The speech reads:

> Yet better thus, and knowne to be contemn'd,
> Then still contemn'd and flatter'd, to be worst:
> The lowest, and most deiected thing of Fortune,
> Stands still in esperance, liues not in feare:
> The lamentable change is from the best,
> The worst returnes to laughter.
>
> (4.1.1–6)[3]

But F continues:

> Welcome then,
> Thou vnsubstantiall ayre that I embrace:
> The Wretch that thou hast blowne vnto the worst,
> Owes nothing to thy blasts.
>
> (4.1.6–9)

And then Gloucester enters. In both texts Edgar expresses the
philosophic confidence of the man who has reached the bottom,
but in F Edgar speaks still more facilely courageous lines of resolution against fortune just prior to having the inadequacy of his vision
exposed by the terrible entrance of his father. What the revision in
F achieves is this. The play is shortened and speeded by the loss
from 3.6 and the opening of 4.1 of about 54 lines (three minutes of
playing time at least). The absence of Edgar's moral meditation
from the end of 3.6 brings the speech at 4.1.1 into sharp focus, iso-
lating it more obviously between the blinding and the entrance of
Gloucester; in F the two servants do not remain onstage after
Cornwall's exit. The additional lines at this point emphasize the
hollowness of Edgar's assertions; while the quantity of sententious-
ness is reduced, its nature is made more emphatically evident.
Edgar gains in prominence, ironically enough, by the loss of a
speech, and the audience becomes more sharply aware of his character.

The last act reveals major alterations that surpass those briefly
described in the discussion of Albany. In both texts Edgar describes
the death of his father with rhetorical fullness and elaborate emotional dramatization (5.3.181–99). In Q, however, he is given an
additional speech of seventeen lines (5.3.204–21) only briefly in-
terrupted by Albany, in which he reports his meeting with Kent.
The removal of this speech not only speeds the last act by the elim-

---

3. At 4.1.4 Q reads "experience" for "esperance."

ination of material of no immediate importance to the plot, but also reduces the length of the delay between Edmund's "This speech of yours hath mou'd me, / And shall perchance do good" (5.3.199–200) and the sending of an officer to Lear. It also diminishes the sense of Edgar as the immature, indulgent man displaying his heroic tale of woe, for in F Albany's command "If there be more, more wofull, hold it in" (5.3.202) is obeyed; in Q by contrast Edgar nevertheless continues:

> This would haue seemd a periode to such
> As loue not sorow, but another to amplifie too much,
> Would make much more, and top extreamitie . . .
>
> (5.3.204–7)

and the speech reveals Edgar's regard for his own dramatic role in the recent history:

> Whil'st I was big in clamor, came there in a man,
> Who hauing seene me in my worst estate.
> Shund my abhord society, but then finding
> Who twas that so indur'd . . .
>
> (5.3.208–11)

F, then, maintains the fundamental nature of Edgar as philosophical agent through the play, but in the last act reduces somewhat his callowness, his easy indulgence of his sensibility in viewing the events through which he is living. In so doing F develops Edgar into a man worthy to stand with the dukes at the close of the play, capable of assuming power.

The elevation of Edgar at the close and relative reduction of Albany that distinguish F from Q can be documented from three other places. At 5.3.229[4] in Q Edgar says to Albany "Here comes Kent sir," but "Here comes Kent" in F. The transfer of the command "Hast thee for thy life" (5.3.251) from Albany in Q to Edgar in F gives Edgar a more active role in the urgent events; indeed, Q may indicate that it is Edgar who is to run. All Edgar's lines after "Hast thee for thy life" are shared by Q and F apart from the last four, which Q assigns to Albany. Though they are partial lines at most, they are susceptible of quite different interpretations according to whether Edgar speaks the last lines or not. If one considers Edgar's behavior in Q in the light of his lachrymose speech about Kent and his apparently subordinate role to Albany, he appears to be silenced by Lear's death: initially in Q he cries out "He faints my Lord, my Lord" (5.3.311), then appeals to Lear "Look vp my Lord" (312), only to say after Kent has assured him of the death "O he is gone indeed" (315), and to fall silent for the rest of the play. By

---

4. This is the Arden placing that follows F; Q places this line in the middle of Albany's next speech at 5.3.232.

contrast, F omits the "O" in this last statement, and then gives Edgar the last lines. In Q, then, Edgar concludes the play stunned to silence by the reality of Lear's death, a very young man who does not even answer Albany's appeal "Friends of my soule, you twaine, / Rule in this Realme" (5.3.319–20), so that Albany reluctantly but resolutely accepts the obligation to rule: "The waight of this sad time we must obey" (323). This characterization of Edgar is a far cry from the Edgar of F who comes forward as a future ruler when he enables Albany to achieve his objective of not ruling; F's Edgar is a young man of limited perceptions concerning the truth of the world's harsh realities, but one who has borne some of the burdens and appears capable of handling (better than anybody else) the responsibilities that face the survivors.[5]

In summary, Q and F embody two different artistic visions. In Q Edgar remains an immature young man and ends the play devastated by his experience, while Albany stands as the modest, diffident, but strong and morally upright man. In F Edgar grows into a potential ruler, a well-intentioned, resolute man in a harsh world, while Albany, a weaker man, abdicates his responsibilities. In neither text is the prospect for the country a matter of great optimism, but the vision seems bleaker and darker in F, where the young Edgar, inexperienced in rule, faces the future with little support.

V

In discussing these two texts I have focused on what seem to me to be the two major issues of the revision; I have not attended to the absence of 4.3 from F, nor to the relatively minor but nevertheless significant differences in the speeches of Lear, the Fool, and Kent. However, I submit that this examination of the texts and the implications of their differences for interpretation and for performance make it clear that they must be treated as separate versions of *King Lear*, and that eclecticism cannot be a valid principle in deciding readings. Conflated texts such as are commonly printed are invalid, and should not be used either for production or for interpretation. Though they may give their readers all of "what Shakespeare wrote," they do not give them Shakespeare's play of *King Lear*, but a play created by the craft and imagination of learned scholars, a work that has no justification for its existence. The principle that more is better, that all is good, has no foundation. What we as scholars, editors, interpreters, and servants of the theatrical craft have to accept and learn to live by is the knowledge

---

5. If this distinction between the presentations of Edgar in the two texts is made, the subtitle of Q makes more than merely conventional sense in its place: "*With the unfortunate life of* Edgar, *sonne and heire to the Earle of Gloster, and his sullen and assumed humor of* TOM *of Bedlam.*"

that we have two plays of *King Lear* sufficiently different to require
that all further work on the play be based on either Q or F, but not
the conflation of both.

LYNDA E. BOOSE

From The Father and the Bride in Shakespeare†

The aristocratic family of Shakespeare's England was, according to
social historian Lawrence Stone, "patrilinear, primogenitural, and
patriarchal." Parent-child relations were in general remote and formal, singularly lacking in affective bonds and governed solely by a
paternal authoritarianism through which the "husband and father
lorded it over his wife and children with the quasi-authority of a
despot" (*Crisis* 271). Stone characterizes the society of the sixteenth and early seventeenth centuries as one in which "a majority
of individuals . . . found it very difficult to establish close emotional
ties to any other person" (*Family* 99)[1] and views the nuclear family
as a burdensome social unit, valued only for its ability to provide
the means of patrilineal descent. Second and third sons counted
for little and daughters for even less. A younger son could, it is true,
be kept around as a "walking sperm bank in case the elder son died
childless," but daughters "were often unwanted and might be regarded as no more than a tiresome drain on the economic resources of the family" (Stone, *Family* 88, 112).[2]

Various Elizabethan documents, official and unofficial, that com-

---

† From *PMLA* 97 (1982). Reprinted by permission of the Modern Language Association.
Some notes have been renumbered.
1. Stone accounts for the drama and poetry of the sixteenth and early seventeenth centuries by modifying his "rather pessimistic view of a society with little love and generally
low affect" to allow for "romantic love and sexual intrigue . . . in one very restricted social group . . . that is the households of princes and great nobles" (*Family* 103–04). This
qualification does not extend to his view of parent-child relationships.
2. Stone also points out that the high infant-mortality rate, "which made it folly to invest
too much emotional capital in such ephemeral beings," was as much responsible for this
lack of affective family ties as were any economic motives (*Family* 105). For Stone, paternal authority—not affection—was the almost exclusive source of the family's coherence. Furthermore, the domestic patriarchy of the sixteenth century was not merely a
replica of family structures inherited from the past but a social pattern consciously exploited and reinforced by the state to emphasize the injunctions of obedience and authority; nor was it replaced until absolute monarchy was overthrown (see *Family*
151–218). Meanwhile, because of the prevalent child-rearing practices, the maternal
impact was relatively insignificant, hence not nearly so important to the psychological
process of maturation; in Stone's estimate, our familiar "maternal, child-oriented, affectionate and permissive mode" of child rearing did not emerge till about 1800 (*Family*
405). During the Elizabethan, era, the upper-class practice of transferring a newborn infant immediately to a village wet nurse, who nurtured the child for two years, substantially muted any maternal influence on child development and no doubt created an
inestimable psychological distance between mother and child. Stone cites the strained

ment on family relations support Stone's hypothesis of the absence of affect.[3] Yet were we to turn from Stone's conclusions to those we might draw from Shakespeare's plays, the disparity of implication—especially if we assume that the plays to some extent mirror the life around them—must strike us as significant. Shakespeare's dramas consistently explore affective family dynamics with an intensity that justifies the growing inference among Shakespearean scholars that the plays may be primarily "about" family relations and only secondarily about the macrocosm of the body politic.[4] Not the absence of affect but the possessive overabundance of it is the force that both defines and threatens the family in Shakespeare. When we measure Stone's assertions against the Shakespeare canon, the plays must seem startlingly ahistorical in focusing on what would seem to have been the least valued relationship of all: that between father and daughter.

---

and formal relationship between Juliet and Lady Capulet as vivid testimony of the absence of affective mother-child bonds that results from such an arrangement (106); in the Capulet household, it is even left up to the nurse, not the mother, to remember Juliet's birthday. Yet Stone does not measure the relationship between Juliet and her father against his hypothesis of the absence of affect. Old Capulet is indeed the authoritarian dictator of Stone's model, but he is also a "careful father" who deeply loves his child. Instead of being eager to have her off his hands, Capulet is notably reluctant to give up the daughter he calls "the hopeful lady of my earth" (1.2.15; all Shakespeare quotations are from the Evans ed.); his bull-headed determination to marry her to Paris following Tybalt's death is born, paradoxically enough, from the deeply rooted affection that Stone's hypothesis excludes.

3. As Christopher Hill suggests in his review of Stone's *Family*, much of the evidence used could well imply its opposite: "The vigour of the preachers' propaganda on behalf . . . of breaking children's wills, suggests that such attitudes were by no means so universally accepted as they would have wished" (461). Hill and others have criticized Stone for asserting that love and affection were negligible social phenomena before 1700 and for presuming throughout "that values percolate downwards from the upper to the lower classes" (Hill 462). Because of the scope and importance of Stone's subject, his book has been widely reviewed. As David Berkowitz comments, "the possibility of endless symposia on Stone's vision and performance looms as a fashionable activity for the next half-dozen years" (396). Hill's review and the reviews by Keith Thomas and John Demos seem particularly well balanced.

4. One could chart the new emphasis on the family by reviewing the Shakespeare topics at recent MLA conventions. The 1979 convention featured Marriage and the Family in Shakespeare, Shirley Nelson Garner chairing, as its Shakespeare Division topic and also included a related special session, The Love between Shakespeare's Fathers and Daughters, Paul A. Jorgensen chairing. Before becoming the division topic, the subject had been examined in special sessions for three consecutive years: 1976, Marianne Novy chairing; 1977, John Bean and Coppélia Kahn chairing; and 1978, Carol Thomas Neely chairing. Special sessions continued in 1980 and 1981, with Shirley Nelson Garner and Madelon S. Gohlke as chairs. A parallel phenomenon has meanwhile been taking place in sixteenth-, seventeenth-, and eighteenth-century historical scholarship, which Hill explains by saying that ". . . the family as an institution rather suddenly became fashionable, perhaps as a by-product of the women's liberation movement" (450).

Most of the work on fathers and daughters in Shakespeare has been done, as might be expected, on the romances. See the essays by Cyrus Hoy, D. W. Harding, and Charles Frey. Of particular interest is the Schwartz and Kahn collection, which was published after I had written this paper but which includes several essays that express views related to my own. See esp. David Sundelson's "So Rare a Wonder'd Father: Prospero's *Tempest*," C. L. Barber's "The Family in Shakespeare's Development: Tragedy and Sacredness," and Coppélia Kahn's "The Providential Tempest and the Shakespearean Family."

While father and son appear slightly more often in the canon, figuring in twenty-three plays, father and daughter appear in twenty-one dramas and in one narrative poem. As different as these father-daughter plays are, they have one thing in common: almost without exception the relationships they depict depend on significant underlying substructures of ritual. Shakespeare apparently created his dramatic mirrors not solely from the economic and social realities that historians infer as having dictated family behavior but from archetypal models, psychological in import and ritual in expression. And the particular ritual model on which Shakespeare most frequently drew for the father-daughter relationship was the marriage ceremony.[5]

In an influential study of the sequential order or "relative positions within ceremonial wholes," Arnold van Gennep isolated three phases in ritual enactment that always recur in the same underlying arrangement and that form, in concert, "the pattern of the rites of passage": separation, transition, and reincorporation.[6] The church marriage service—as familiar to a modern audience as it was to Shakespeare's—contains all three phases. When considered by itself, it is basically a separation rite preceding the transitional phase of consummation and culminating in the incorporation of a new family unit. In Hegelian terms, the ceremonial activities associated with marriage move from thesis through antithesis to synthesis; the anarchic release of fertility is positioned between two phases of relative stasis. The ritual enables society to allow for a limited transgression of its otherwise universal taboo against human eroticism. Its middle movement is the dangerous phase of

5. Margaret Loftus Ranald has done substantial work on the legal background of marriage in Shakespeare plays. I have found no marriages (or funerals) staged literally in the plays of Shakespeare or of his contemporaries. Although, for instance, the marriage of Kate and Petruchio would seem to offer a rich opportunity for an indecorously comic scene appropriate for *The Taming of the Shrew*, the action occurs offstage and we only hear of it secondhand. Nor do we witness the Olivia-Sebastian marriage in *Twelfth Night*. Even the fragment of the botched ceremony in *Much Ado* does not follow the liturgy with any precision but presents a dramatized version of it. This omission—apparently consistent in Elizabethan and Jacobean drama—may have resulted from the 1559 Act of Uniformity of Common Prayer and Divine Service in the Church, which stipulates sanctions against "any persone or persones whatsoever . . . [who] shall in anye Entreludes Playes Songes, Rymes or by other open Woordes, declare or speake anye thing in the derogation depraving or despising of the same Booke, or of any thing therein conteyned" (1 Elizabeth 1, c. 2, in *Statutes* 4:355–58). Given the rising tempo of the Puritan attack on the theaters at this time, we may reasonably infer that the omission of liturgy reflects the dramatists' conscientious wish to avoid conflict. Richmond Noble's study corroborates this assumption (82). Of the services to which Shakespeare does refer, Noble notes that the allusions to "distinctive features, words, and phrases of Holy Matrimony are extremely numerous" (83).

6. Van Gennep built his study on the work of Hartland, Frazer, Ciszewski, Hertz, Crowley, and others who had noted resemblances among the components of various disparate rites. His tripartite diachronic structure provides the basis for Victor W. Turner's discussions in the essay "Liminality and Communitas" (*Ritual Process* 94–203).

transition and transgression; its conclusion, the controlled reincorporation into the stability of family. But before the licensed transgression can take place—the transgression that generates the stability and continuity of society itself—the ritual must separate the sanctified celebrants from the sterile forces of social interdiction. The marriage ritual is thus a pattern of and for the community that surrounds it, as well as a rite of passage of and for the individuals who enact it. It serves as an especially effective substructure for the father-daughter relation because within its pattern lies the paradigm of all the conflicts that define this bond at its liminal moment of severance. The ceremony ritualizes two particularly significant events: a daughter and a son are being incorporated into a new family unit, an act that explicitly breaks down the boundaries of two previously existing families; yet, at the same time, the bonds being dissolved, particularly those between father and daughter, are being memorialized and thus, paradoxically, reasserted. In early comedies like *The Taming of the Shrew*, Shakespeare followed the Roman design of using the father of the young male lover as the *senex iratus*, a blocking figure to be circumvented. The mature comedies, tragedies, and romances reconstruct the problems of family bonds, filial obedience, and paternal possessiveness around the father and daughter, the relation put into focus by the marriage ceremony. When marriage activities are viewed from the perspective of their ritual implications, the bride and groom are not joined until the transitional phase of the wedding-night consummation; before that, a marriage may be annulled. What the church service is actually all about is the separation of the daughter from the interdicting father.

The wedding ceremony of Western tradition has always recognized the preeminence of the father-daughter bond. Until the thirteenth century, when the church at last managed to gain control of marriage law, marriage was considered primarily a private contract between two families concerning property exchange. The validity and legality of matrimony rested on the *consensus nuptialis* and the property contract, a situation that set up a potential for conflict by posing the mutual consent of the two children, who owed absolute obedience to their parents, against the desires of their families, who must agree beforehand to the contract governing property exchange. However true it was that the couple's willing consent was necessary for valid matrimony and however vociferously the official conduct books urged parents to consider the compatibility of the match, fathers like Cymbeline, Egeus, and Baptista feel perfectly free to disregard these requirements. Although lack of parental consent did not affect the validity of a marriage and, after 1604, affected the legality only when a minor was involved,[7] the family control over the dowry was a powerful psychological as well as economic weapon. Fathers like Capulet, Lear, and Brabantio depend on threats of disinheritance to coerce their children. When their daughters nonetheless wed without the paternal blessing, the marriages are adversely affected not because any legal statutes have been breached but because the ritual base of marriage has been circumvented and the psychological separation of daughter from father thus rendered incomplete. For in Shakespeare's time—as in our own—the ceremony acknowledged the special bond between father and daughter and the need for the power of ritual to release the daughter from its hold.

As specified in the 1559 *Book of Common Prayer*, the marriage ritual enjoins that the father (or, in his absence, the legal guardian)[8] deliver his daughter to the altar, stand by her in mute testimony that there are no impediments to her marriage, and then witness her pledge henceforth to forsake all others and "obey and serve, love honor and keep" the man who stands at her other side. To the priest's question, "Who giveth this woman to be married unto this man?"—a question that dates in English tradition back to the York manual (*Book of Common Prayer* 290–99; 408, n.)—the father must silently respond by physically relinquishing his daugh-

---

7. The church canons of 1604 seem to have confused the situation further by continuing to recognize the validity of the nuptial pledge but forbidding persons under twenty-one to marry without parental consent; this ruling would make the marriage of minors illegal but nonetheless binding for life and hence valid (Stone, *Family* 32). Until the passage of Lord Hardwicke's Marriage Act in 1753, confusion was rife over what constituted a legal marriage and what a valid one. In addition to bringing coherence to the marriage laws, this act was designed to protect increasingly threatened parental interests by denying the validity as well as the legality of a religious ceremony performed without certain conditions, including parental consent for parties under twenty-one (Stone, *Family* 35–36).

   The concern for parental approval has always focused on, and in fact ritualized, the consent of the bride's father. In 1858, the Reverend Charles Wheatly, a noted authority on church law, attributed the father's giving away his daughter as signifying the care that must be taken of the female sex, "who are always supposed to be under the tuition of a father or guardian, whose consent is necessary to make their acts valid" (496). For supportive authority Wheatly looks back to Richard Hooker, whose phrasing is substantially harsher. Hooker felt that the retention of the custom "hath still this vse that it putteth we men in mind of a dutie whereunto the verie imbecillitie of their [women's] nature and sex doth binde them, namely to be alwaies directed, guided and ordered by others . . ." (215).

   Even though the validity of a marriage was not vested in parental consent, "the Protestants, including the Anglicans, considered the consent of the parents to be as essential to the marriage as the consent of the bride and bridegroom" (Flandrin 131). Paradoxically, "both Church and State claimed to be supporting, at one and the same time, freedom of marriage and the authority of parents" (Flandrin 132). The ambiguity arose because the child was obliged, under pain of mortal sin, to obey the parent. Technically, the child was free to choose a marriage partner, but since the church never took steps against the prerogatives of the father, the notion of choice was problematic.

8. Given the high parent mortality rate, a number of brides necessarily went to the altar on the arms of their legal guardians. Peter Laslett notes that in Manchester between 1553–1657 over half of the girls marrying for the first time were fatherless (103), but some historians have criticized his reliance on parish registers as the principal demographic barometer.

ter, only to watch the priest place her right hand into the possession of another man. Following this expressly physical symbolic
transfer, the father's role in his daughter's life is ended; custom dictates that he now leave the stage, resign his active part in the rite,
and become a mere observer. After he has withdrawn, the couple
plight their troths, and the groom receives the ring, again from the
priest. Taking the bride's hand into his, the groom places the ring
on her finger with the words, "With this ring I thee wed, with my
body I thee worship, and with all my worldly goods I thee endow,"
thus solemnizing the transfer in its legal, physical, and material aspects.[9]

Before us we have a tableau paradigmatic of the problematic
father-daughter relation: decked in the symbols of virginity, the bride
stands at the altar between her father and husband, pulled as it
were between the two important male figures in her life. To resolve
the implied dilemma, the force of the priest and the community
presides over and compels the transfer of an untouched daughter
into the physical possession of a male whom the ceremony author-
izes both as the invested successor to the father's authority and as
the sanctified transgressor of prohibitions that the father has been
compelled to observe.[1] By making the father transfer his intact

9. The groom's pledge suggests the wedding ring's dual sexual and material symbolism.
   Historically, the ring symbolizes the dowry payment that the woman will receive from
   her husband by the entitlement of marriage; it apparently superseded the custom of
   placing tokens of espousal on the prayer book (see *Book of Common Prayer* 408). It also
   signifies the physical consummation, a point frequently exploited in Renaissance drama
   and also implied by the rubrics in the older Roman Catholic manuals, which direct the
   placing of the ring. The Martène manual specifies that the bride is to wear it on the left
   hand to signify "a difference between the estate and the episcopal order, by whom the
   ring is publicly worn on the right hand as a symbol of full and entire chastity" (Legg
   207). *The Rathen Manual*, which follows the Use of Sarum, contains a rather charming
   piece of folklore widely believed through the eighteenth century. It, too, allusively suggests the sexual significance of the ring: "For in the fourth finger there is a certain vein
   proceeding to the heart and by the chime of silver there is represented the internal affection which ought always to be fresh between them" (35–36; see also Wheatly 503). Even
   after the priest took over the ceremonial role of transferring the bride's hand from her
   father's to her husband's, he did not also become the intermediary in transferring the
   ring from the groom's keeping to the bride's finger. Such an incorporation of duties
   might seem logical were it not that this part of the ritual simultaneously imitates and licenses the sexual act.
      The English reformers retained both the symbol of the ring and the groom's accompa-
   nying pledge to "worship" his wife's body, a retention that generated considerable attack
   from the more radical reformers. The controversy over this wording occupies the major
   portion of Hooker's defense of the Anglican marriage rite (see also Stone, *Family* 522, on
   the attempts in 1641 and 1661 to alter the wording of the vow from "worship" to
   "honor"). Hooker justifies the husband's "worship" as a means of transferring to the wife
   the "dignitie" incipient in her husband's legitimizing of the children he now allows her to
   bear. She furthermore receives, by this annexation of his worship, a right to participate
   in his material possessions. The movement of the vow, from sexual to material pledge,
   thus sequences a formal rite of passage, a pattern alluded to in Hooker's phrase, "the
   former branch hauing granted the principall, the latter graunteth that which is annexed
   thereunto" (216).
1. The ceremonial transfer of the father's authority to the husband is acknowledged by the
   Reverend John Shepherd in his historical commentary accompanying the 1853 *Family*

daughter to the priest in testimony that he knows of no impediments to her lawful union, the service not only reaffirms the taboo
against incest but implicitly levels the full weight of that taboo on
the relationship between father and daughter. The groom's family
does not enter into the archetypal dynamics going on at this altar
except through the priest's reference to marriage as the cause why
a man "shall leave father and mother and shall be joined unto his
wife." The mother of the bride is a wholly excluded figure—as indeed she is throughout almost the entire Shakespeare canon. Only
the father must act out, must dramatize his loss before the audience of the community. Within the ritual circumscription, the father is compelled to give his daughter to a rival male; and as
Georges Bataille comments:

> The gift itself is a renunciation. . . . Marriage is a matter less
> for the partners than for the man who gives the woman away,
> the man whether father or brother who might have freely en-
> joyed the woman, daughter or sister, yet who bestows her on
> someone else. This gift is perhaps a substitute for the sexual
> act; for the exuberance of giving has a significance akin to that
> of the act itself; it is also a spending of resources.[2]

Prayer Book: ". . . the ceremony shows the father's consent; and that the authority, which
he before possessed, he now resigns to the husband" (Brownell 465). By implication,
however, the ceremony resolves the incestuous attraction between father and daughter
by ritualizing his "gift" of her hand, a signification unlikely to be discussed in the commentary of church historians. When first the congregation and next the couple are asked
to name any impediments to the marriage, there are, Wheatly says, three specific impediments the church is charging all knowledgeable parties to declare: a preceding marriage
or contract, consanguinity or affinity, and want of consent (483). The final act of Ben
Jonson's *Epicoene* enumerates all the possible legal impediments that might be sub-
sumed under these three.
   The bride's father, by virtue of his special prominence in the ritual, functions as a select witness whose presence attests to the validity of the contract. The Friar in *Much
Ado* asks Hero and Claudio whether they "know any inward impediment why you should
not be cojoin'd" (4.1.12–13). Leonato dares to respond for Claudio, "I dare make his answer, none," because, as father of the bride, he presumes to have full knowledge that no
impediment exists. When he learns of Hero's supposed taint, the rage he vents over the
loss of his own honor is the more comprehensible when we understand his special position in the ceremony as a sworn witness to the transfer of an intact daughter.
2. The sections on the celebration of "Festiuall daies" and times of fast that precede
   Hooker's defense of the English "Celebration of Matrimonie" are especially helpful in
   understanding Elizabethan ritual, for in these sections Hooker expands his defense of
   the Anglican rites into an explanation of, and rationale for, the whole notion of ritual.
   Having first isolated three sequential elements necessary for festival—praise, bounty,
   and rest—he goes on to justify "bountie" in terms remarkably compatible with the theories of both Bataille and Lévi-Strauss on the essential "spending-gift" nature of marriage.
   To Hooker, the "bountie" essential to celebration represents the expression of a "charita-
   ble largenesse of somewhat more then common bountie. . . . Plentifull and liberall expense is required in them that abounde, partly as a signe of their owne joy in the
   goodnesse of God towards them" (292, 293). Bounty is important to all festival rites, but
   within the marriage rite this "spending" quality incorporates the specific idea of sexual
   orgasm as the ultimate and precious expenditure given the bride by her husband, a notion alluded to in Bataille and one that functioned as a standard Elizabethan metaphor
   apparent in phrases like "Th' expense of spirit" (sonnet 129) or Othello's comment to
   Desdemona, "The purchase made, the fruits are to ensue; / That profit's yet to come

By playing out his role in the wedding ceremony, the father implicitly gives the blessing that licenses the daughter's deliverance from family bonds that might otherwise become a kind of bondage. Hence in *A Midsummer Night's Dream*, a play centered on marriage, the intransigent father Egeus, supported by the king-father figure Theseus, poses a threat that must be converted to a blessing to ensure the comic solution. In *Love's Labor's Lost*, the sudden death of the Princess' father, who is likewise the king-father figure for all the French ladies, prevents the necessary blessing, thus cutting sharply across the movement toward comic resolution and postponing the happy ending. In plots constructed around a daughter without a father, the absent father frequently assumes special dramatic prominence. This absence felt almost as a presence may well contribute to the general unease and unresolved tensions emanating from the three "problem plays," for Helena, Isabella, and Cressida are all daughters severed from their fathers.

Within the father-daughter plays, the daughter's association of father with husband is so strong that even when a woman as independent as Rosalind or Viola first thinks about the man she will eventually marry, her thoughts immediately call to mind her father. Her movement toward conjugal love unconsciously resuscitates a mental movement back to the father to whom she will remain emotionally as well as legally bound until the ritual of marriage transfers her loyalties from one domain to the other. The lack of narrative logic in the association emphasizes its subconscious quality. When Viola first hears the governor of Illyria named, she responds: "Orsino! I have heard my father name him. / He was a bachelor then" (*TN* 1.2.28–29). When Rosalind meets Orlando she instantly tells Celia, "The Duke my father lov'd his father dearly,"

'tween me and you" (2.3.9–10). The wedding ceremony ritualizes this notion of bounty as the gift of life by having the father give the groom the family treasure, which the father cannot "use" but can only bequeath or hoard. The groom, who ritually places coins or a gold ring on the prayer book as a token "bride price," then fully "purchases" the father's treasure through his own physical expenditure, an act that guarantees the father's "interest" through future generations. This money-sex image complex is pervasive and important in many of Shakespeare's plays. The pattern and its relation to festival are especially evident in Juliet's ecstatic and impatient speech urging night to come and bring her husband:

> O, I have bought the mansion of a love,
> But not possess'd it, and though I am sold,
> Not yet enjoy'd. So tedious is this day
> As is the night before some festival.
>   (3.2.26–29).

In another context, this pattern enables us fully to understand Shylock's miserly refusal to give or spend and the implications of his simultaneous loss of daughter and hoarded fortune. His confusion of daughter and ducats is foreshadowed when he recounts the story of Jacob and equates the increase of the flock through the "work of generation" to the increase of money through retentive "use." To Antonio's question, "Or is your gold and silver ewes and rams?" Shylock responds, "I cannot tell, I make it breed as fast" (*MV* 1.3.95–96).

making a connection that Celia pointedly questions in her response, "Doth it therefore ensue that you should love his son dearly?" (*AYL* 1.3.29–32). Once inside Arden Forest—ostensibly on a journey to find her father—Rosalind pays scant attention to her purpose, instead asking Celia, "But what talk we of fathers, when there is such a man as Orlando?" (3.4.38–39). But at the conclusion of the play, when Rosalind prepares to become Orlando's wife, she seeks out her father as the necessary figure who must ritually enable her to do so. Whereas she can freely don male clothing and shift her identity back and forth between Rosalind and Ganymede without the assistance of ritual, marriage is not merely the transposition of assumed roles but the actual transition from daughter to wife. And the movement must be ceremonialized through its distinct, sequential phases. Having spent the play testing various roles and disguises, Rosalind at the end chooses a fixed identity as wife; but that identity depends on her first having reentered the role of daughter. To be incorporated into a new stasis, she must have one from which to be separated; she must be reunited as child to her father before she can be joined to her "child's father" (1.3.11). Thus in ritual language she repeats the vow of incorporation first to her father and then to Orlando: "To you I give myself, for I am yours" (5.4.116, 117). The play itself becomes paradigmatic of the ritual movement that concludes it: Rosalind's search to be reunited with her father metamorphoses into a journey to be united with the husband who replaces and supersedes him. And instantly on completion of the ceremony, having first been rejoined with his daughter and having then fully performed the father's formulaic role, Duke Senior is miraculously reinstated in his dukedom, regaining the paternal authority over his domain that he had lost at the same time as he had lost that over his daughter. In *King Lear* and *The Tempest*, Shakespeare uses the same pattern, making the King's ability to govern his state depend on his ability to enact his ritual role as father. In *Lear*, however, the dual restitution of paternal roles that concludes the two comedies is reversed into an opening scene staging the dual divestiture of daughter and kingdom.

* * *

In *King Lear*, the father's grudging recognition of the need to confer his *daughter* on younger strengths while he unburdened crawls toward death should be understood as the basal structure underlying his divestiture of his kingdom. Lear has called his court together in the opening scene because he must at last face the postponed reckoning with Cordelia's two princely suitors, who "Long in our court have made their amorous sojourn, / And here are to be answer'd" (1.1.47–48). But instead of justly relinquishing his daughter, Lear tries to effect a substitution of paternal divesti-

tures: he portions out his kingdom as his "daughters' several dowers," attaching to Cordelia's share a stipulation designed to thwart
her separation. In substituting his public paternity for his private
one, the inherently indivisible entity for the one that biologically
must divide and recombine, Lear violates both his kingly role in the
hierarchical universe and his domestic one in the family. Nor is it
accident—as it was in *Hamlet* 5.1—that brings these two incompatible rituals into collision in *Lear* 1.1. It is the willful action of
the king and father, the lawgiver and protector of both domain and
family, that is fully responsible for this explosion of chaos.

Yet of course Lear's bequest of his realm is in no way an uncon-
ditional transfer of the kingdom from one rulership to another. Instead, Lear wants to retain the dominion he theoretically casts off
and to "manage those authorities / That he hath given away"
(1.3.17–18). Likewise, the bequest of his daughter is actually an attempt to keep her, a motive betrayed by the very words he uses.
When he *dis*claims "all my paternal care" and orders Cordelia "as a
stranger to my heart and me / Hold thee from this for ever" (113,
115–16), his verb holds to his heart rather than expels from it the
daughter he says is "adopted to our hate" (203), another verbal usage that betrays his retentive motives. His disastrous attempts to
keep the two dominions he sheds are structurally linked through
the parodic divestiture of his kingdom as dowry. In recognition of
the family's economic interest in marriage, the terms of sixteenth-
century dowries were required to be fully fixed before the wedding,
thus making the property settlement a precondition for the wedding.[3] But Lear the father will not freely give his daughter her endowment unless she purchases it with pledges that would nullify
those required by the wedding ceremony. If she will not love him
all, she will mar her fortunes, lose her dowry, and thus forfeit the
symbolic separation. And yet, as she asserts, she cannot marry if
she loves her father all. The circularity of Lear's proposition frus-
trates the ritual phase of separation: by disinheriting Cordelia, Lear
casts her away not to let her go but to prevent her from going. In
Lévi-Strauss' terms, Lear has to give up Cordelia because the father
must obey the basic social rule of reciprocity, which has a necessarily communal effect, functioning as a "distribution to undo excess."
Lear's refusal is likewise communal in its effect, and it helps create
the universe that he has "ta'en too little care of."

Insofar as Burgundy's suit is concerned, Lear's quantitatively
constructed presumption works. Playing the mime priest and inten-

---

3. *Measure for Measure* provides the most dramatic testimony to the importance of fixing
the dowry provisions before the wedding. Although Juliet is nearly nine months pregnant
and although she and Claudio believe themselves spiritually married, they have not le-
galized the wedding in church because of still unresolved dowry provisions.

tionally desecrating the sacramental ritual question he imitates,
Lear asks the first bridegroom-candidate:

> Will you, with those infirmities she owes,
> Unfriended, new adopted to our hate,
> Dow'r'd with our curse, and stranger'd with our oath,
> Take her, or leave her?   (1.1.202–05)

Burgundy's hedged response is what Lear anticipates—this suitor
will gladly "take Cordelia by the hand" only if Lear will give "but
that portion which yourself propos'd" (243, 242). Shrewdly intuit-
ing that France cannot be dissuaded by so quantitative a reason as
"her price is fallen," Lear then adopts a strategy based on qualitative assumptions in his attempt to discourage the rival he most
greatly fears. Insisting to France that

> For you, great King
> I would not from your love make such a stray
> To match you where I hate; therefore beseech you
> T'avert your liking a more worthier way   (208–11)

Lear tries to avoid even making the required ritual offer. By calling
his own daughter "a wretch whom Nature is asham'd / Almost t'acknowledge hers" (212–13), Lear implies by innuendo the existence
of some unnatural impediment in Cordelia that would make her
unfit to marry and would thus prevent her separation. Effectively,
the scene presents an altar tableau much like that in *Much Ado*,
with a bride being publicly pronounced unfit for marriage. In *Lear*,
however, it is the father rather than the groom who defames the
character of the bride, and his motives are to retain her rather than
to reject her. In this violated ceremony, the slandered daughter—instead of fainting—staunchly denies the alleged impediments by demanding that her accuser "make known / It is no vicious blot . . .
No unchaste action, or dishonored step, / That hath deprived me of
your grace and favor" (226–29). And here the groom himself takes
up the role implicit in his vows, defending Cordelia's suborned
virtue by his statement that to believe Lear's slanders would require
"a faith that reason without miracle / Should never plant in me"
(222–23). The physical separation of the daughter from the father
is finally achieved only by France's perception that "this unpriz'd
precious maid . . . is herself a dowry" (259, 241); France recognizes
the qualitative meaning of the dowry that Burgundy could only understand quantitatively.

In Cordelia's almost archetypal definition of a daughter's proper
loyalties (1.1.95–104), Shakespeare uses a pun to link the fundamental predicament of the daughter—held under the aegis of the
father—to its only possible resolution in the marriage troth: "That

lord whose hand must take my plight shall carry / Half my love with him" (101–02), says Cordelia. When France later addresses his bride as "Fairest Cordelia, that art most rich being poor, / Most choice forsaken, and most lov'd despis'd" (250–51), he echoes the husband's traditional pledge to love "for richer, for poorer" the daughter who has "forsaken all others." And France himself then endows Lear's "dow'rless daughter" with all his worldly goods by making her "queen of us, of ours, and our fair France" (256–57). His statement "Be it lawful I take up what's cast away" (253) even suggests a buried stage direction through its implied allusion to the traditional conclusion of the *consensus nuptialis* as explained in the Sarum and York manuals: the moment when the bride, in token of receiving a dowry of land from her husband, prostrates herself at her husband's feet and he responds by lifting her up again.

The visual and verbal texts of this important opening scene allude to the separation phase of the marriage ritual; the ritual features are emphasized because here, unlike the similar scene in *Othello*, the daughter's right to choose a husband she loves is not at issue. Because the ritual is sacred, Cordelia dispassionately refuses to follow her sisters in prostituting it. Lear, in contrast, passionately destroys his kingdom in order to thwart the fixed movement of the ritual pattern and to convert the pattern's linear progression away from the father into a circular return to him.[4] The discord his violation engenders continues to be projected through accumulating ritual substructures: in a parody of giving his daughter's hand, Lear instead gives her "father's heart from her" (126); in a parody of the ring rite, Lear takes the golden round uniting king and country and parts it, an act that both dramatizes the consequences of dividing his realm and demonstrates the anguish he feels at losing his daughter to a husband.

Once Lear has shattered the invoked sacred space by collapsing two incompatible rituals into it, he shatters also all claims to paternal authority. From this scene onward, the question of Lear's paternal relation to his daughters and his kingdom pervades the drama through the King's ceremonial invocations of sterility against the daughters he has generated and the land he has ruled. In the prototype of a harmonious wedding that concludes. *As You Like It*, Hy-

---

4. Alan Dundes points out the psychological dimensions of various folktale types underlying a number of Shakespeare's plays; significantly, the central figure in the folktale is usually the daughter-heroine. The theme of incest, which Freud himself recognized as a powerful undercurrent in *King Lear*, is manifest in the folk-tale father who demands that his daughter marry him; Shakespeare transforms the overt demand into a love test requiring that she love her father all (358). In Dundes' interpretation, the more obvious father-daughter incest wish is actually an Electral daughter-father desire that has been transformed through projection. Dundes also lists other discussions of the father-daughter incest theme in *King Lear* (359).

men—who "peoples every town"—defines Duke Senior's correct paternal role as that of the exogamous giver of the daughter created in heaven:

> Hymen from heaven brought her,
>   Yea, brought her hither,
> That thou mightst join her hand with his
> Whose heart within his bosom is.
>
> (5.4.112–15)[5]

Hymen characterizes the generating of children as a gift from heaven, an essential spending of the self designed to increase the world. By contrast, Lear's image of the father is the "barbarous Scythian, / Or he that makes his generation messes / To gorge his appetite" (1.1.116–18). The definition is opposite to the very character of ritual. It precludes the possibility of transformation, for the father devours the flesh he begets. Here, generation becomes primarily an autogamous act, a retention and recycling of the procreative energies, which become mere extensions of private appetite feeding on its own production. The unnatural appetite of the father devouring his paternity is implicit even in the motive Lear reveals behind his plan to set his rest on Cordelia's "kind nursery" (124), an image in which the father pictures himself as an infant nursing from his daughter. The implied relationship is unnatural because it allows the father to deflect his original incestuous passions into Oedipal ones, thus effecting a newly incestuous proximity to the daughter, from whom the marriage ritual is designed to detach him. And when this form of appetite is thwarted by France's intervention, Lear effects yet another substitution of state for daughter: having ordered Cornwall and Albany to "digest the third" part of his kingdom, he and his gluttonous knights proceed to feed off it and through their "Epicurism and lust / Make . . . it more like a tavern or a brothel / Than a grac'd palace" (1.4.244–46). Compelled by nature to give up his daughter, he unnaturally gives up his kingdom; when his appetites cannot feed on her, they instead devour the paternity of his land.

The father devouring his own flesh is the monstrous extension of the circular terms of Lear's dowry proposal. The image belongs not only to the play's pervasive cluster of monsters from the deep but

5. Hymen's verses emphasize the religious sense of the marriage ritual. In this context the genetic father is only a surrogate parent, appointed by the heavenly parent to act out the specific role of bequeathing the daughter to a new union; Hymen himself functions as the mythic priest, the agent authorized by heaven to oversee the transfer. Wheatly's notes reflect this same sense of the religious meaning of the roles played by father and priest: ". . . the woman is to be given not to the man, but to the Minister; for the rubric orders, that the minister shall receive her *at her father's or friend's hands*; which signifies, to be sure, that the father resigns her up to God, and that it is God, who, by His Priest, now gives her in marriage . . ." (497).

also to its dominant spatial pattern of circularity. Within both the narrative movement and the repeated spatial structure inside the drama, the father's retentive passions deny the child's rite of passage. When Cordelia departs from the father's realm for a new life in her husband's, ostensibly fulfilling the ritual separation, the journey is condemned to futility at its outset, for Cordelia departs dowered with Lear's curse: "Without our grace, our love, our benison" (1.1.265). Although the bride and groom have exchanged vows, the denial of the father's blessing renders the separation incomplete and the daughter's future blighted. Cordelia, like Rosalind, must therefore return to be reincorporated with her father before she can undergo the ritual severance that will enable her to progress. She thus chooses father over husband, returning to Lear to ask his blessing: "look upon me, sir, / And hold your hand in benediction o'er me" (4.7.56–57). In lines that indicate how futile the attempt at incorporation has been when the precedent rites of passage have been perverted, Cordelia asserts, "O dear father, / It is thy business that I go about" (4.4.23–24), and characterizes her life with France as having been one of constant mourning for the father to whom she is still bound.

Shakespeare rewrote the source play *Leir* to make Cordelia remain in England alone (rather than with France at her side) to fight, lose, and die with her father, a revision that vividly illustrates the tragic failure of the family unit to divide, recombine, and regenerate. The only respite from pain the tragedy offers is the beauty of Lear's reunion with Cordelia, but that reunion takes place at the cost of both the daughter's life and the future life of the family. And for all the poignancy of this reunion, the father's intransigence—which in this play both initiates and conditions the tragedy—remains unchanged: it is still writ large in his fantasy that he and his daughter will be forever imprisoned together like birds in a cage.[6] At the end of the play, excluding any thought of Cordelia's new life with France, Lear focuses solely on the father-daughter merger, which he joyfully envisions enclosed in a perpetuity where no interlopers—short of a divine messenger—can threaten it: "He that parts us shall bring a brand from heaven, / And fire us hence like foxes" (5.3.22–23). The rejoining is the precise opposite of that in *As You Like It*. To Rosalind's question, "if I bring in your Rosalind, / You will bestow her on Orlando here?" Duke Senior responds, "That would I, had I kingdoms to give with her" (*AYL* 5.4.6–7, 8). In the Duke's characterization of Orlando's newly received endowment as "a potent Dukedom"

6. See Barber's essay in Schwartz and Kahn, esp. pp. 198–221. Barber additionally provides a striking iconographic association, noting the image of Lear with Cordelia in his arms as being effectively "a *pietà* with the roles reversed, not Holy Mother with her Dead Son, but father with his dead daughter" (200).

(5.4.169), the implied fertility of both kingdom and family is ensured through the father's submission to the necessary movement of ritual. In *King Lear*, the father who imagined that he "gave his daughters all" extracts from his daughter at the end of the play the same price he demanded in the opening scene—that she love her father all. The play's tragic circles find their counterpart in its ritual movements. Cordelia returns to her father, and the final scene stages the most sterile of altar tableaux: a dead father with his three dead daughters, the wheel having come full circle back to the opening scene of the play. Initially barren of mothers, the play concludes with the death of all the fathers and all the daughters; the only figures who survive to emphasize the sterility of the final tableau are Albany, a widower, and Edgar, an unmarried son.

* * *

Works Cited

Barber, C. L. *Shakespeare's Festive Comedy*. Princeton: Princeton Univ. Press, 1959.
Bataille, Georges. *Death and Sensuality: A Study of Eroticism and the Taboo*. 1962; rpt. New York: Arno, 1977.
Berkowitz, David. *Renaissance Quarterly* 32(1979): 396–403.
The Book of Common Prayer, 1559. Ed. John E. Booty. Charlottesville: Univ. of Virginia Press, 1967.
Boose, Lynda E. "Othello's Handkerchief: 'The Recognizance and Pledge of Love.'" *English Literary Renaissance* 5(1975): 360–74.
Brownell, Thomas Church, ed. *The Family Prayer Book; or*, The Book of Common Prayer *according to the Use of the Protestant Episcopal Church*. New York: Stanford and Swords, 1853.
The Church and the Law of Nullity of Marriage. Report of a commission appointed by the archbishops of Canterbury and York in 1949. London: Society for Promoting Christian Knowledge, 1955.
Demos, John. *New York Times Book Review*, 25 Dec. 1977, 1.
Dundes, Alan. "'To Love My Father All': A Psychoanalytic Study of the Folktale Source of *King Lear*." *Southern Folklore Quarterly* 40(1976):353–66.
Eliade, Mircea. *The Sacred and the Profane*. Trans. Willard R. Trask. New York: Harcourt, 1959.
Evans, G. Blakemore, ed. *The Riverside Shakespeare*. Boston: Houghton, 1974.
Flandrin, Jean-Louis. *Families in Former Times: Kinship, Household and Sexuality*. Trans. Richard Southern. Cambridge: Cambridge Univ. Press, 1979.
Frey, Charles. "'O sacred, shadowy, cold, and constant queen': Shakespeare's Imperiled and Chastening Daughters of Romance." *South Atlantic Bulletin* 43(1978): 125–40.
The Geneva Bible. 1560; facsim. rpt. Madison: Univ. of Wisconsin Press, 1961.
Harding, D. W. "Father and Daughter in Shakespeare's Last Plays." *TLS*, 30 Nov. 1979, 59–61.
Hill, Christopher. "Sex, Marriage and the Family in England." *Economic History Review*, 2nd ser., 31(1978): 450–63.
Hooker, Richard. *Of the Lawes of Ecclesiasticall Politie*. 1594; facsim. rpt. Amsterdam: Theatrum Orbis Terrarum, 1971.
Howard, George Elliott. *A History of Matrimonial Institutions*. London: T. Fisher Unwin, 1904.
Hoy, Cyrus. "Fathers and Daughters in Shakespeare's Romances." In *Shakespeare's Romances Reconsidered*. Ed. Carol McGinnis Kay and Henry E. Jacobs. Lincoln: Univ. of Nebraska Press, 1978, 77–90.
Kelly, Henry Ansgar. *The Matrimonial Trials of Henry VIII*. Stanford, Calif.: Stanford Univ. Press, 1976.
Laslett, Peter. *The World We Have Lost*. 2nd ed. 1965; rpt. London: Methuen, 1971.
LeClercq, R. V. "Crashaw's Epithalamium: Pattern and Vision." *Literary Monographs* 6. Madison: Univ. of Wisconsin Press, 1975, 73–108.

Legg, J. Wickham. *Ecclesiological Essays*. London: De La More Press, 1905.
Lévi-Strauss, Claude. *The Elementary Structures of Kinship*. Trans. James Harle Bell. Ed. John Richard von Sturmer and Rodney Needham. Paris, 1949; rpt. Boston: Beacon, 1969.
McCown, Gary M. "'Runnawayes Eyes' and Juliet's Epithalamion." *Shakespeare Quarterly* 27(1976): 150–70.
Noble, Richmond. *Shakespeare's Use of the Bible and* The Book of Common Prayer. London: Society for the Promotion of Biblical Knowledge, 1935.
Partridge, Eric. *Shakespeare's Bawdy*. 1948; rpt. New York: Dutton, 1969.
Rabkin, Norman. *Shakespeare and the Problem of Meaning*. Chicago: Univ. of Chicago Press, 1981.
Ranald, Margaret Loftus. "'As Marriage Binds, and Blood Breaks': English Marriage and Shakespeare." *Shakespeare Quarterly* 30(1979): 68–81.
The Rathen Manual. Ed. Duncan MacGregor. Aberdeen: Aberdeen Ecclesiological Society, 1905.
Schoenbaum, S. *William Shakespeare: A Compact Documentary Life*. Oxford: Oxford Univ. Press, 1975.
Schwartz, Murray M., and Coppélia Kahn, eds. *Representing Shakespeare: New Psychoanalytic Essays*. Baltimore: Johns Hopkins Univ. Press, 1980.
The Statutes of the Realm. London: Record Commissions, 1820–28; facsim. ed. 1968.
Stone, Lawrence. *The Crisis of the Aristocracy: 1558–1660*. Abridged ed. London: Oxford Univ. Press, 1971.
———. *The Family, Sex and Marriage in England: 1500–1800*. New York: Harper, 1977.
Thomas, Keith. *TLS*, 21 Oct. 1977, 1226.
Tufte, Virginia. *The Poetry of Marriage*. Los Angeles: Tinnon-Brown, 1970.
Turner, Victor W. *The Ritual Process: Structure and Anti-Structure*. Chicago: Aldine, 1969.
Van Gennep, Arnold. *The Rites of Passage*. Trans. Monika B. Vizedom and Gabrielle L. Caffee. 1908; rpt. London: Routledge and Kegan Paul, 1960.
Wheatly, Charles. *A Rational Illustration of* The Book of Common Prayer *according to the Use of the Church of England*. Cambridge: Cambridge Univ. Press, 1858.

JANET ADELMAN

From Suffocating Mothers†

It may at first seem merely perverse to understand *King Lear* as in part the adumbration of fantasies about maternal power, particularly given the entire absence of literal mothers in the play; at first glance, *Lear* seems overwhelmingly about fathers and their paternity rather than about mothers. The motherlessness of Lear's world is striking particularly if one comes to it from the source play, *The True Chronicle Historie of King Leir*, in which the emotional starting point is the king's dismay at the death of his wife and the motherlessness of his daughters; in that play, the king's decision to abdicate and divide the kingdom is presented in part as his response to her loss.[1] But our King Lear has no wife, his daughters no mother; nor, apparently, have they ever had one: Queen Lear goes unmentioned, except for those characteristic moments when Lear

---

† From *Suffocating Mothers*, pp. 104–14. Copyright © 2006. Reproduced by permission of Routledge/Taylor & Francis Group, LLC. Notes have been renumbered and edited.
1. See *The True Chronicle Historie of King Leir*, 1.1.1–31, reproduced in Geoffrey Bullough, *Narrative and Dramatic Sources of Shakespeare*, vol. 7 (London: Routledge and Kegan Paul, 1973), pp. 337–38.

invokes her to cast doubt on his paternity. *Leir* starts with the fact of maternal loss; *Lear* excises this loss, giving us the uncanny sense of a world created by fathers alone.[2]

But Lear's confrontation with his daughters (I will argue) repeatedly leads him back to the mother ostensibly occluded by the play:[3] in recognizing his daughters as part of himself he will be led to recognize not only his terrifying dependence on female forces outside himself but also an equally terrifying femaleness within himself—a femaleness that he will come to call "mother" (2.4.56). For this text about fathers insistently returns to mothers: discovering what he is father to, confronting the implications of his own paternity, Lear is brought to acknowledge their absent presence; and even Gloucester, unproblematically father to sons, is made the victim of their awesome power. I take as a central text of the play the fool's bitter "thou mad'st thy daughters thy mothers; . . . thou gav'st them the rod and putt'st down thine own breeches" (1.4.179–81), with its painfully literal suggestions of both generational and gender reversal, of infantile exposure and maternal punishment. Much of the play's power comes, I think, from its confrontation with the landscape of maternal deprivation or worse, from the vulnerability and rage that is the consequence of this confrontation and the intensity and fragility of the hope for a saving maternal presence that can

2. This uncanniness of course serves ideological ends; see, for example, Jonathan Goldberg's account of the extent to which "the natural event of procreation becomes an extension of male prerogative and male power in Stuart portraiture of families" ("Fatherly Authority: the Politics of Stuart Family Images," in *Rewriting the Renaissance: the Discourses of Sexual Difference in Early Modern Europe*, ed. Margaret W. Ferguson, Maureen Quilligan, and Nancy J. Vickers [Chicago, Ill.: University of Chicago Press, 1986], esp. pp. 16–25). Many have noted the absence of mothers specifically in *Lear*; see, for example, Stephen Greenblatt's suggestive comparison of *Lear* with Francis Wayland's (successful) attempt to "displace the nurturing female body" ("The Cultivation of Anxiety: King Lear and His Heirs," *Raritan* 2 [1982]: 105). For psychoanalytic critics, this absence often functions as a "decoy" (Peter Erickson, *Patriarchal Structures in Shakespeare's Drama* [Berkeley: University of California Press, 1985], p. 110), serving "to highlight her psychological presence" (Coppélia Kahn, "Excavating 'Those Dim Minoan Regions': Maternal Subtexts in Patriarchal Literature," *Diacritics* 12 [1982]: 37; amplified in "The Absent Mother in *King Lear*," in *Rewriting the Renaissance*, pp. 33–49).

3. It is by now a familiar trope of psychoanalytically informed criticism to note that Lear makes his daughters into mothers; see, for example, Marianne L. Novy (*Love's Argument: Gender Relations in Shakespeare* [Chapel Hill: University of North Carolina Press, 1984], pp. 152–53), Marvin Rosenberg (*The Masks of King Lear* [Berkeley: University of California Press, 1972], p. 120), and Diane Elizabeth Dreher (*Domination and Defiance: Fathers and Daughters in Shakespeare* [Lexington: University Press of Kentucky, 1986], pp. 7, 64–65). Many see in this exchange Lear's specifically incestuous and oedipal desire for his daughters; for full accounts, see especially Norman N. Holland (*Psychoanalysis and Shakespeare* [New York: Octagon Books, 1979], p. 343) and William H. Chaplin ("Form and Psychology in *King Lear*," *Literature and Psychology* 19 [1969]: 32). Like other critics who ground their work in object-relations psychoanalysis, I read in Lear's relationship to his daughters-made-mothers a reiteration of dynamics that are primarily preoedipal rather than oedipal; my account is, as always, heavily indebted to the combined work of Richard Wheeler, C. L. Barber, Madelon (Gohlke) Sprengnether, Murray Schwartz, Peter Erickson, and Coppélia Kahn.

undo pain. In the characteristic way of the return of the repressed, that is, the excision of the mother that seems initially to allow for a fantasy of male parthenogenesis ends by releasing fantasies far more frightening than any merely literal mother could be, fantasies that give emotional coloration to the entire play in part because they are not localized in (and hence limited to) any single character.

We can see this process of repression and terrifying return played out in miniature in the Gloucester plot. In the opening lines of the play, Edmund's mother is invoked only to be absented, apparently for the rest of the play. The opening exchange between Kent and Gloucester is full of nervousness about the biological relation between fathers and sons, and about the place of mothers; Edmund's mother appears in the text only in response to a pun that emphasizes the differing reproductive roles of men and women:

> Kent   Is not this your son, my Lord?
>
> Glou.   His breeding, Sir, hath been at my charge: I have so often blush'd to acknowledge him, that now I am braz'd to't.
>
> Kent   I cannot conceive you.
>
> Glou.   Sir, this young fellow's mother could; whereupon she grew round-womb'd. . . . Do you smell a fault?
>
> Kent   I cannot wish the fault undone, the issue of it being so proper.
>
>   (1.1.8–18)

Kent could not conceive, but this fellow's mother could. The pun doubly turns on the tenuousness of this father's biological relation to his son: Gloucester's terms for his part in the making of Edmund ("his breeding . . . hath been at my charge") are so evasive[4] that Kent does not at first understand what Gloucester means; and their evasiveness is a function not only of Gloucester's shame but also of the tenuousness of the male role in reproduction *per se*. But there is nothing tenuous about that round womb: Edmund is unequivocally his mother's child, the "issue" from her "fault."[5] As though in response to that unequivocal round womb, Gloucester then turns from Edmund to the absent Edgar: "But I have a son, Sir, by order of law, some year elder than this" (1.1.19–20). His shift from one

---

4. "Breeding" can imply either biological reproduction or upbringing, "charge" either financial or moral responsibility: either "I have paid for his rearing" or "I have been blamed for his begetting," or some combination of the two. No wonder Kent is confused.

5. Astington argues for the use of "fault" as slang for the female genitals both generally and specifically here. But the term seems to me to carry the meaning of the pun of *foutre* as well: Edmund the Bastard is the proper (=fitting) issue not only of his mother's anatomical fault, but of any fault/*foutre*, since all faults turn out to be equally illegitimate.

son to the other—"but I have a son"—in effect distinguishes between Edmund as his mother's child and Edgar as his father's: if
Edmund is the product of a mother's womb, Edgar is the product of
patriarchal law, apparently motherless. In distinguishing between
his legitimate and illegitimate sons, Gloucester manages to do away
with the womb altogether, making Edgar all his.

The differences between these sons will be played out in the dy-
namic between them. But for the moment, let us ask what becomes
of Edmund's mother in this transaction. Present only as a site of illegitimacy, she—and the round womb of maternal reproduction—
are erased by Gloucester's reference to Edgar and by the rest of the
play. She may make a brief and covert reappearance under the
guise of "Nature" in Edmund's apostrophe to her when he next appears; at least his dedication of himself to Nature's "law" (1.2.1–2)
reminds us that there is more than one law and recalls the outlaw
status of Edmund's mother. For the most part, however, her erasure
seems total. But although exiled as a bodily presence or even as a
figure to whom others allude, she returns in full force in the last
moments of the play, when Edgar offers a moralized account of his
father's history:

> My name is Edgar, and thy father's son.
> The Gods are just, and of our pleasant vices
> Make instruments to plague us;
> The dark and vicious place where thee he got
> Cost him his eyes.
>
> (5.3.169–73)

In Edgar's account, the play comes full circle and we are returned
to its beginning. As legitimate Edgar identifies himself to his dying
brother. ("My name is Edgar, and thy father's son"), he stresses not
their fraternity but his claim to his father, reiterating the distinction
of the opening scene: once again, Edgar—the legitimate, the
would-be rescuer of his father—is his "father's son"; once again,
Edmund—the illegitimate, his father's scourge—is his mother's
derivative from her dark and vicious place. And now the vice lightly
acknowledged—and dismissed—by Gloucester is revealed as the
cause of all his suffering. But even as Edgar blames his father for
his own blinding, he constructs an alternate version of the story in
which the blinding is less the logical moral consequence of
Gloucester's vicious action than it is the analogical extension
of the place of vice; and in this version, the blinding is all the
mother's fault. Wholly excising Cornwall's role in Gloucester's
blinding, acknowledging even Edmund's only parenthetically
("where thee he got"), Edgar in effect names the female sexual

"place" as the blinding agent, metonymically making the darkness
of that place equivalent to the darkness into which Gloucester is
plunged. And at this moment, the presence occluded throughout
the play reinstates itself with a vengeance, and reinstates itself in
Gloucester's body: blinded by his commerce with her darkness, he
carries in himself the darkness of this "dark and vicious place" writ
large.[6]

In simultaneously marking the mother's child as illegitimate and
locating the place of female begetting as the father's scourge, the
Gloucester plot plays out a bizarre fantasy in which social anxieties
about illegitimacy and patriarchal inheritance are fused with psychological anxieties about sexuality and masculine identity. Patriarchal society depends on the principle of inheritance in which the
father's identity—his property, his name, his authority—is transmit-
ted from father to son; in the words of the Paphlagonian king who
is Gloucester's prototype in *Arcadia*, the father of a true son need
"envie no father for the chiefe comfort of moralitie, to leave an

6. Many readers are uncomfortable with both the tone and the substance of Edgar's judgment and would not permit him to speak for the play: for a representative sample, see,
for instance, A. C. Bradley, *Shakespearean Tragedy* (New York: Meridian Books, Inc.,
1955), p. 244; William Empson, *The Structure of Complex Words* (London: Chatto &
Windus, 1952), p. 150; S. L. Goldberg, *An Essay on King Lear* (Cambridge: Cambridge
University Press, 1974), pp. 80, 82; Stephen Booth, *King Lear, Macbeth, Indefinition
and Tragedy*, p. 47; and James R. Siemon, *Shakespearean Iconoclasm* (Berkeley: University of California Press, 1985), pp. 274–75. But others disagree; see, for instance, May-
nard Mack's strong defense of the play's homiletic character at this moment: "The
blindness is not what will follow from adultery, but what is implied in it. Darkness
speaks to darkness" (*King Lear in Our Time* [Berkeley: University of California Press,
1965], p. 70). Mack would dissociate these words from Edgar conceived as a naturalistic character with motives, partly to preserve the play's homiletic nature; although I find
Edgar's words of a piece with his anger at his father (see "Introduction," *Twentieth Century Interpretations of "King Lear,"* ed. Janet Adelman [Englewood Cliffs, N.J.: Prentice-
Hall, Inc., 1978[, pp. 8–20], my formulation here and elsewhere is very much indebted
to Mack's. For the logic Edgar expresses is not isolated in him: Edmund's status as second son would have sufficed to motivate his plot against his brother (as in *As You Like It,
Hamlet,* and *The Tempest*); Shakespeare's insistence on his bastardy traces both his outlaw viciousness and his father's blinding to the dark and vicious place where he was got.
Moreover, Edgar's judgment relies on cultural commonplaces linking blindness with sexuality. The "blind Cupid" that Lear sees in Gloucester (4.6.139) is the sign of the brothel
(see Muir's note, Arden *King Lear*, p. 178) partly because blindness was thought to be a
consequence of sexuality: according to the pseudo-Aristotelian *Aristotle's Masterpiece*,
excess sexuality "destroys the sight, dries the body, and impairs the brain" (cited by Vern
L. Bullough, *Sex, Society, and History* [New York: Science History Publications, 1976],
p. 94); according to Bacon, "It hath been observed by the ancients, that much use of
Venus doth dim the sight" (cited by Stephen Booth in his rich commentary on "expense
of spirit" in Sonnet 129, *Shakespeare's Sonnets* [New Haven, Conn.: Yale University
Press, 1977], p. 442). Loss of the eyes or blindness was moreover sometimes recognized
as a symptom of syphilis; see, for example, Charles Clayton Dennie (*A History of Syphilis*
[Springfield, Ill.: Charles C. Thomas, 1962], pp. 17, 36), and James Cleugh (*Secret Enemy: The Story of a Disease* [London: Thames and Hudson, 1954], pp. 47, 66). Whether
or not this symptomology was commonly known, the association between sexual excess
and blindness was familiar to Shakespeare; see Pompey's pitying description of Mistress
Overdone as "you that have worn your eyes almost out in the service" (*Measure for Measure*, 1.2.101–2).

other ones-selfe after me."[7] But this transmission from father to
son can take place only insofar as both father and son pass through
the body of a woman;[8] and this passage radically alters them both.
This is the weak spot in patriarchal inheritance: maternal origin
and illegitimacy are synonymous in the Gloucester plot—and
throughout *Lear*—because sexuality *per se* is illegitimate and illegit-
imizes its children; whether or not the son is biologically his
father's, the mother's dark place inevitably contaminates him, com-
promising his father's presence in him.[9] For the son who has tra-
versed the maternal body cannot be wholly "an other ones-selfe" for
his father; the mother's part in him threatens the fantasy of perfect
self-replication that would preserve the father in the son. As Fal-
staff tells us, "the son of the female"—any female—"is the shadow
of the male" (*2 Henry IV*, 3.2.126–28). And the father himself will
be deeply compromised by the sexual concourse that produces the
son. Edgar's bizarre metaphor for his father's blindness—"in this
habit / Met I my father with his bleeding rings, / Their precious
stones new lost" (5.3.188–90)—makes plain what his earlier equa-
rion of blindness with the place of female generation (5.3.172–73)
had implied: both the secondary meaning of "stones" as testicles

7. Cited in Bullough, *Narrative and Dramatic Sources in Shakespeare*, vol. 7, p. 404. Anxiety about the transmission of paternal identity and property is played out when Edmund
   the Bastard is made Earl of Gloucester (3.5.17–18) and the designation "Gloucester" is
   abruptly emptied of fixed meaning: after Cornwall renames Edmund (3.5.17–18),
   "Gloucester" refers both to father and son, most strikingly within two lines (see 3.7.13,
   15). This confusion raises primary questions about who—or what—is "Gloucester": not
   only what that identifier means, but who has the right to it, and who confers that right.
   (Naming in the speech-headings is conservative, locating the right to name only in the
   king: they designate as Gloucester the man Lear recognizes as Gloucester.) Anxiety
   about names and legitimacy is of course at the heart of the Gloucester plot; see, for example, William C. Carroll's meditation on legitimacy and the natural body in Edgar
   (" 'The Base Shall Top Th'Legitimate': The Bedlam Beggar and the Role of Edgar in *King
   Lear*," *Shakespeare Quarterly* 38 [1987]: 426–41). But by giving one of his fathers sons
   and one daughters, Shakespeare is able to play out anxieties inherent in each of the two
   different systems of property inheritance operating in the play. The father-son plot oper-
   ates under the rules of primogeniture, where the replication of patriarchal identity is at
   stake; illegitimacy is thus its central anxiety. But the love test of the father-daughter plot
   seems to operate under the system that became increasingly common in the sixteenth
   century as the entails maintaining strict primogeniture were broken and the father became increasingly capable of disposing of his property as he saw fit, rewarding or pun-
   ishing his children at will (see Lawrence Stone, *The Family, Sex and Marriage in
   England, 1500–1800* [New York: Harper and Row, 1979], pp. 112–13). It makes sense
   that the central anxieties of this system—anxieties about sincerity and insincerity, about
   bribery and misplaced trust—should be played out in relation to daughters, especially
   daughters whose impending marriage threatens the fantasy that they love their fathers
   all.
8. This is the dilemma played out in the travels of Bertram's father's ring in *All's Well*; see
   Chapter 4, pp. 81–82.
9. In *King John*, however, bastardy serves the function of a classic family romance, allowing the son to replace his "real" and decidedly unheroic father with Cordelion, the play's
   mythic Ur-father. It can serve this function partly because the fantasy is written decidedly from the perspective of the son, not the father, and partly because disruptive
   maternal presence is invoked only to be contained and almost comically dismissed
   (4.2.120–23).

and the frequent association of rings with the female genitals rewrite Edgar's reassuringly cold and hard metaphor for loss as an image of castration, in effect registering the transformation of his father into a woman with a bleeding ring.[1] In Edgar's image, that is, the father bears the corrosive signs of his concourse with the female; the occluded maternal presence is in effect etched on his face.

The pattern of repression and return visible in Edmund's illegitimacy and in the blinding of Gloucester is played out again in the Lear plot, where the presence of daughters *per se*—daughters instead of sons—has a function equivalent to the presence of illegitimacy in the Gloucester plot, that of returning the father to the occluded maternal place. Shakespeare in fact arranges matters so that we will feel the presence of Lear's daughters as a slight disturbance, a perplexing substitution for the sons we expect him to have: in the play's opening lines, both Gloucester's reference to his own two sons and the talk of dividing the kingdom between two men we know nothing about predispose us to think of these men as Lear's sons; and Lear himself refers to Albany and Cornwall as his sons (1.1.41–42) before he mentions that he has daughters (1.1.44). Our carefully induced surprise at the sudden substitution of daughters—three of them for the two sons we had apparently been promised—registers something like Lear's unspoken problem:[2] by definition, his daughters disrupt the patriarchal ideal, both insofar as they disrupt the transmission of property from father to son and insofar as they disrupt the paternal fantasy of perfect self-replication. Even more clearly than the mother's son, the daughter is but "the shadow of the male," carrying within her the disruptive sign of the mother's presence. (Why does this father have only daughters?)

In its representation of Lear's problematic relation to his daughters, the Lear plot simultaneously replicates and analyzes the logic

1. See Eric Partridge, *Shakespeare's Bawdy* (New York: E. P. Dutton, 1960) for sexualized instances of both "stones" (pp. 195–96) and "rings" (p. 179). (Partridge omits *Midsummer Night's Dream*, 5.1.188, a comic *locus classicus* for "stones.") Without commenting on these puns, David Willbern sees in Gloucester's bleeding eyes a traumatic mask of the "nothing" that is the female—or the castrated male—genitals ("Shakespeare's Nothing," in *Representing Shakespeare*, pp. 247, 253). The equivalence of blindness and castration is familiar to psychoanalysis and to psychoanalytic criticism, where it is usually read as punishment for oedipal crime: see, for example, Sigmund Freud ("The Uncanny," *The Standard Edition of the Complete Psychological Works of Sigmund Freud*, vol. 17, trans. James Strachey [London: Hogarth Press, 1955], p. 231); Alexander Grinstein ("King Lear's Impending Death," *American Imago* 30 [1973]: 135); Mark Kanzer ("Imagery in *King Lear*," in *The Design Within: Psychoanalytic Aproaches to Shakespeare*, ed. M. D. Faber [New York: Science House, 1970], p. 223); Holland (*Psychoanalysis and Shakespeare*, p. 344); and Chaplin ("Form and Psychology in *King Lear*," pp. 38, 39).
2. In *Leir*, the dilemma of the king's sonlessness is not unspoken (1.1.21, 44). I am indebted to Zan Marquis's wonderful undergraduate honors thesis on Lear's fear of female fertility (1978) for the perception that Lear's daughters arrive on stage in place of sons.

of illegitimacy in the Gloucester plot. If Gloucester's wicked son is literally illegitimate, Lear similarly imagines that his disobedient daughters are illegitimate, "degenerate bastard[s]" (1.4.262), the products of an adulterous womb (2.4.131–33). If the only mother of the Gloucester plot is Edmund's, the only mother of the Lear plot is the adulterous mother Lear thus imagines; and like Edgar,[3] Cordelia is motherless, purely her father's child. Once again, the female sexual place is necessarily the place of corruption, the "sulphurous pit" (4.6.130) that is Lear's equivalent to Edgar's "dark and vicious place";[4] present only as a site of illegitimacy, the mother once again transmits her faults to her issue, the children whose corrupt sexuality records their origin. And once again the plot sets the father's pure and a-sexual child[5] against the mother's, making his child the father's bulwark against her dark power as it is played out through her children.[6] But the logic of illegitimacy is played out with a difference in the Lear plot. For we know, as Lear comes to know, that Goneril and Regan are not in fact illegitimate; the whole of the play works to bring him to the recognition of his own complicity in their making. And this time the protective function of the fantasy of illegitimacy is made visible. Lear imagines his daughters illegitimate when he cannot tolerate their failure to meet his needs; he would rather imagine himself a cuckold than be forced to acknowledge that the female children who so imperfectly replicate him are part his. The fantasy of their illegitimacy is thus his pyrrhic solution to the larger problem of daughters: insofar as he can make their disruptive femaleness entirely derivative from their mother's sexual fault, he can dissociate himself wholly from it, in effect disowning them as he has earlier attempted to disown Cordelia.

3. Characteristically, Edgar's mother is mentioned only obliquely, and only when Gloucester believes Edgar false and hence attempts to disown him ("I never got him," 2.1.78).
4. The play makes a small move toward recuperating sexual origin in Kent's musing that "one self mate and make" have begotten both Goneril and Regan and Cordelia (4.3.35); this is the only place in which sexuality is imagined as an indifferent force, not one that necessarily breeds monsters, and the only place in which it is hinted that even Cordelia might have had a mother. (But see Robert H. West for a recuperative reading of sexuality in *Lear* ["Sex and Pessimism in *King Lear*," *Shakespeare Quarterly* 11 (1960): 55–60].)
5. The extent to which their exemption from sexuality is structurally important can be gauged by the extent to which we find Tate's inclusion of a sexual relation between them utterly alien to the play Shakespeare wrote.
6. Like Edmund, Goneril and Regan seem complicit with her dark and vicious place as they initiate Gloucester's blinding (3.7.4–5); Regan may in fact imagine that she is blinding her own father in blinding him (see Stanley Cavell, "The Avoidance of Love," *Disowning Knowledge in Six Plays of Shakespeare* [Cambridge: Cambridge University Press, 1987], p. 53). She and her sister are, in any case, the agents of a similar unmanning of their father: the Fool repeatedly interprets the "nothing" to which they bring him as castration; see especially the dense series of images at his first entrance in 1.4, where Lear is "an O without a figure" (ll. 200–201), "a sheal'd peascod" (208), a hedge-sparrow that "had it head bit off by it young" (225). (See Willbern's "Shakespeare's Nothing," especially pp. 245–46, on the fantasized equivalence of femaleness and castration here.)

But even while the logic of illegitimacy is thus stripped bare, the female site of generation nonetheless remains the site and sign of corruption in the Lear plot as in the Gloucester plot. For Lear's acknowledgment of complicity in the making of his daughters turns out to mean not so much his acknowledgment of his own sexual darkness as his acknowledgment that he too has been contaminated by the dark and vicious place. Far from recuperating the place of female sexuality by freeing it from blame, his recognition that his daughters are legitimate merely invests the horror of that place in him. Recognizing his part in Goneril and Regan entails recognizing their part in him; if they are his, then he is intolerably implicated in their femaleness.[7] Forced to acknowledge his own part in the making of Goneril, he identifies her as the disease in his own body:

> We'll no more meet, no more see one another;
> But yet thou art my flesh, my blood, my daughter;
> Or rather a disease that's in my flesh,
> Which I must needs call mine: thou art a boil,
> A plague-sore, or embossed carbuncle,
> In my corrupted blood.
>
> (2.4.222–27)

Even as he would disown her ("We'll no more meet"), he must acknowledge that she is inextricably his, and hence the sign of corruption in him. For if she is his, then he is complicit with the dark and vicious place that made her: both her name and the imagery of skin disease make her the sign of the specifically venereal disease that registers his own participation in the sexual fault.[8] And as he

---

7. My formulation here, and in the pages that follow, is heavily indebted to Madelon [Gohlke] Sprengnether's classic essay, " 'I wooed thee with my sword': Shakespeare's Tragic Paradigms," in which she argues that Shakespeare's tragic heroes struggle against the signs of "femininity" in themselves and see these signs especially in their powerlessness, "specifically in relation to a controlling or powerful woman" (*Representing Shakespeare*, p. 175); she notes, for example, that Lear reads his own tears—evoked by his daughters—as dangerously feminine. Many recent critics comment on Lear's fear of his own feminization: see, for example, Patrick Colm Hogan ("*King Lear*: Splitting and Its Epistemic Agon," *American Imago* 36 [1979]: 40); Carolyn Asp, for whom Lear himself becomes a type of the (French) feminine (" 'The Clamor of Eros': Freud, Aging, and *King Lear*," in *Memory and Desire*, ed. Kathleen Woodward and Murray M. Schwartz [Bloomington: Indiana University Press, 1986], pp. 196–97); and especially Coppélia Kahn, whose formulations are closest to my own, especially in her emphasis on Lear's identification with his daughters and his fear of the mother within ("Excavating 'Those Dim Minoan Regions,' " pp. 37–39; "The Absent Mother in *King Lear*," pp. 36, 43–44). Paul Jorgensen tends to replicate—rather than analyze—Lear's fear; for him, Lear's progress toward self-knowledge necessarily entails his sex-nausea and mysogyny because "only woman's body could suffice to illustrate the full depravity of man" (*Lear's Self-Discovery* [Berkeley: University of California Press, 1967], p. 126); his is nonetheless a good early account of these elements in the play.
8. By naming Goneril a disease in Lear's flesh, Shakespeare characteristically takes a name that he found lying inert in his sources and transforms it into a dense center of meaning. The term "gonorrhea" was current. Before 1767, it referred to one of the symptoms of syphilis rather than to a separate disease (see James Cleugh, *Secret Enemy: The Story of*

imagines her a swelling within him—"a boil, / A plague-sore, or embossed carbuncle" in his corrupted blood—he takes that dark place
into himself; his language figures his body as grotesquely female,
pregnant with the disease that is his daughter. Acknowledging
Goneril his flesh and blood entails making his own body the site of
her monstrous femaleness.[9]

Lear cannot ultimately sustain the protective fantasy that his
daughters are bastards, wholly separate from him, and the collapse
of this fantasy illustrates what it is designed to protect him from: if
Goneril is his, then her female corruption is within him; in attempting to disown her, he finds her inside himself. Like Edgar's account
of the blinding of Gloucester, this moment seems to me characteristic of the broader pattern of repression and return that governs the
play's treatment of mothers: for the play that apparently excludes
mothers simultaneously plays out a dark fantasy about the interior
of the female body, about the position of the male who traverses that
body, and about the traces the female body consequently leaves
within the male. This fantasy everywhere shapes Lear's encounters
with his daughters, the literally female flesh that he must needs call
his. But it is most terrifyingly expressed not through them but
through the storm that is their avatar; its traces in fact determine
the logic that governs Lear's meditative reworking of the storm in his
meeting with Gloucester in 4.6, the logic that links his greeting of
Gloucester ("Goneril, with a white beard" [l. 97]), his recollection
of the rain that came to wet him once (ll. 102–8), his bitter acknowledgment that his daughters were "got 'tween the lawful
sheets" (l. 119), his recoil from the "sulphurous pit" (l. 130), and
the smell of mortality on his own hands (l. 135). For he concludes
his meditation by arriving at the place of his birth, acknowledging
his mortality as he remembers his origins: "We came crying hither: /

---

a Disease, p. 136); William Clowes, for example, writes of a syphilitic patient who had "a
stinking Gonorrhea and running of the reines" (A Brief and Necessary Treatise Touching
the Cure of the Disease called Morbus Gallicus [London, 1585], p. 195). The skin erup-
tions Lear describes were characteristic of syphilis in the early stages: Cleugh describes
boils and other swellings very much like Lear's embossed carbuncles (pp. 46–49); the
Spanish in fact named the disease bubas from these swellings (Cleugh, p. 57). "Plague
sore" may be a general term, or it may reflect an association between syphilis and specifically Black Plague; see Frankie Rubenstein for the relation between (generalized)
plague and pox ("They Were Not Such Good Years," Shakespeare Quarterly 40 [1989]:
70–74). Rubenstein identifies the "good years" Lear wishes on Goneril and Regan
(5.3.24) as venereal disease; if she is right, then Lear is attempting to retaliate specifically for the disease he imagines in his flesh. Insofar as blindness was associated specifically with venereal disease (see n. 6, p. 361), it makes sense that it should be Goneril
who first suggests blinding Gloucester.
9. Recognition of his own flesh in his daughters may again lead to Lear's sense of himself
as feminized in 3.4.74–75, where Lear figures himself as a grotesque version of the maternal pelican; Muir cites several instances of the pelican who feeds or revives her children with her blood (Arden King Lear, pp. 118–19). Perhaps in response to Lear's
apparent gender confusion, Edgar/Poor Tom immediately transforms the pelicans into
decidedly male pillicocks (3.4.76).

Thou know'st the first time that we smell the air / We wawl and cry"
(ll. 180–82). Within the logic of these associations, the storm comes
to function as the sign of the female place of origin; in remembering
it, Lear records its traces in himself.

Initially, the storm seems to Lear to be the place of the male
thunderer classically associated with its powers. In his initial response to it, he invokes this thunderer, rewriting his impotence in
the face of the daughters who have thrust him into the storm—the
daughters who can "shake [his] manhood thus" (1.4.306)—by
imagining himself on the side of the "all-shaking thunder" (3.2.6)
that makes the caitiff shake (3.2.55). And he invokes this masculine authority specifically against the female site of origin, "round-
womb'd" as Edmund's mother (1.1.14): commanding the thunder
to "Strike flat the thick rotundity o' th' world! / Crack Nature's
moulds, all germens spill at once" (3.2.7–8), he cosmologizes his
earlier attack on Goneril's womb ("Into her womb convey sterility! /
Dry up in her the organs of increase" [1.4.287–88]). But Lear cannot reinstate his own masculine authority by joining with the thunderer in his destruction; he cannot command this or any other
power. Recourse to male authority—his own or that of the gods—
will not protect him; as the storm speaks his impotence, exposing
him as "a poor, infirm, weak, and despis'd old man" (3.2.20), it
reiterates not his lost power but his own helplessness in the face
of his daughters' rage, and the elements themselves come to seem
less the signs of male authority than the exfoliations of their
power, "servile ministers / That will with two pernicious daughters
join / . . . 'gainst a head / So old and white as this" (3.2.21–24).

For if the storm is classically the domain of the male thunderer,
it is simultaneously the domain of disruptive female power: associated both with the storms that witches were commonly suspected
of raising and with the storms that conventionally figure the turbu-
lence of Fortune (the "arrant whore" who—like Lear's daughters—
"ne'er turns the key to th' poor" [2.4.52–53]), this storm becomes
in effect the signature of maternal malevolence, the sign of her
power to withhold and destroy.[1] As Poor Tom reminds us, this storm

1. As *Macbeth*'s witches imply (1.3.10–25), witches were traditionally able to raise storms.
See, for example, *The Malleus Maleficarum of Heinrich Kramer and James Sprenger*,
trans. Montague Summers (New York: Dover Publications, 1971), pp. 147–49; Reginald
Scot, *The Discoverie of Witchcraft* (London, 1584; reprint, with an introduction by Hugh
Ross Williamson [Carbondale: Southern Illinois Press, 1964], p. 31); King James's *Dae-
monologie* (London, 1603), p. 46; and the failure of the witches to raise a storm in Jonson's *Masque of Queens*, ll. 134–37, 209–20. Johnson's learned note to 1.134 gives his
classical sources for the witches' association with storm and chaos; see *Ben Jonson: The
Complete Masques*, ed. Stephen Orgel (New Haven, Conn.: Yale University Press, 1969),
pp. 531–32. For the association of Fortune with storms, especially in the visual arts, see
Frederick Kiefer, who reproduces some spectacular instances in his *Fortune and Elizabethan Tragedy* (The Huntington Library, 1983), p. 287; he comments specifically on the
presence of this traditional association in Lear's storm.

is witch's turf, where "Swithold . . . met the night-mare, and her nine-fold; / . . . And aroint thee, witch, aroint thee!" (3.4.123–27). It is no accident, I think, that Poor Tom himself defines his place in this nightmare world by what he has been forced to eat: asked who he is, he answers with a catalogue that anticipates the "eye of newt, and toe of frog," the toad and dog and lizard, of *Macbeth* (4.1.6–17); he is

> Poor Tom; that eats the swimming frog, the toad, the todpole, the wall-newt, and the water; that . . . eats cow-dung for sallets; swallows the old rat and the ditch-dog; drinks the green mantle of the standing pool.
>
> (3.4.132–37)

This is the landscape of the witches' cauldron, the obverse of the landscape on Lear's map,[2] with its "plenteous rivers and wide-skirted meads" (1.1.65) reassuringly abundant and reassuringly under male control; here, the kind goddess nature whom Lear thought he could command (1.4.284) is revealed under the aspect of Hecate. No wonder that he should attempt to invoke the masculine authority of the gods against her, as though he could uproot her monstrous generativity.

Despite Lear's recurrent attempts to find a just Thunderer in the storm, that is, its violence ultimately epitomizes not the just masculine authority on which Lear would base his own but the dark female power that everywhere threatens to undermine that authority. No longer under the aegis of a male thunderer, the very wetness of the storm comes to seem a sexual wetness, a monstrous spilling of germens that threatens to undo civilization and manhood itself, spouting rain until it has "drench'd our steeples, drown'd the cocks" (3.2.3), its power an extension into the cosmos of Goneril's power to shake Lear's manhood. Fantasized site of Poor Tom's "act of darkness" (3.4.87–88), the storm takes on the aspect of the hellish "Lake of Darkness" in which Nero is an angler (3.6.7), becoming itself the dark and vicious place writ large.[3] Hence, I think, the logic according to which Lear's memory of the storm—"when the rain came to wet me once and the wind to make me chatter, when the thunder would not peace at my bidding" (4.6.102–4)—leads him to

2. Mack, *King Lear in Our Time*, p. 94; for him, the play is "the greatest anti-pastoral ever penned" (p. 65).
3. This lake is identified with the female sexual place by Shakespeare's other uses of fishing for sexual intercourse; see *Measure for Measure*, 1.2.83, and especially *The Winter's Tale*, 1.2.195. Many understand the storm as sexual: see, for example, Kanzer ("Imagery in *King Lear*," p. 223), Rosenberg (*The Masks of King Lear*, pp. 126, 191–92), and Lisa Miller ("A View of 'King Lear,'" *Journal of Child Psychotherapy* 4 [1975]: 102); for Chaplin, it is specifically female, "Nature's womb-like upheaval," which is "given a new location and iconology" in the sulphurous pit ("Form and Psychology in *King Lear*," pp. 40–41).

imagine that female place, and to imagine concentrated in it the dispersed elements of the storm:

> But to the girdle do the Gods inherit,
> Beneath is all the fiend's: there's hell, there's darkness,
> There is the sulphurous pit—burning, scalding,
> Stench, consumption; fie, fie, fie! pah, pah!
>
> (4.6.128–31)

For the "sulph'rous and thought-executing fires" (3.2.4) of that "hell-black night" (3.7.59) are replicated in the hell and darkness and burning and stench of this "sulphurous pit" (4.6.129–31); in arriving at this pit, Lear in effect traces the elements of the storm back to their origin.

The fantasy given darkest expression in the storm is of Lear's subjection to the realm of Hecate, in which masculine identity and the civilization that upheld it are dissolved in a terrifying female moisture. Hence, I think, the logic behind the awful simultaneity of Lear's exposure on the heath and Gloucester's blinding, instigated by Lear's daughters. The oscillation of scenes throughout Act III—indoors and outdoors equally brutal—serves to intensify the audience's pain, as each promises momentary relief from the other and then drives in a different mode toward the same dark place. For the one acts out the subjugation that has been implicit in the other: in the blinding of Gloucester, the punitive female power of the storm—the power of the dark and vicious place—is given a local habitation and a name. We begin the rush into the storm with the womanish tears Lear attempts to suppress, the tears that threaten to stain his "man's cheeks" (2.4.280); we end with a Gloucester vulnerable as a woman, a Gloucester whose man's cheeks are stained with the blood and jelly of his weeping eyes. We begin with the "eyeless" storm (3.1.8) and end with the blinded Gloucester. As Lear is driven toward the nightmare state of the naked baby, exposed to the rage of the punitive mother in the storm, Gloucester is transformed into a woman by the daughters who are her human agents: her dark and vicious place newly recorded in his own eyelessness, Gloucester is mistaken by Lear for that monster-woman herself, "Goneril, with a white beard" (4.6.97).

The storm as Lear recalls it is the testing place of masculine power, the site of the punitive sexualized mother; in greeting the feminized Gloucester as Goneril, Lear sees her signs in him. And as he traces the elements of the storm back to their origin in her, he comes to find the same elements in himself. This recoil onto the self is registered in part through smell, the most primitive of infant senses, the one that Lear later makes synonymous with breathing itself (4.6.181). Initially smelling out the flattery of others in the storm ("there I found 'em, there I smelt 'em out. Go to, they are not

men o' their words" [4.6.105–6]), he comes via the stench of the
sulphurous pit to the smell of mortality on his own hands:

> *Lear* There is the sulphurous pit—burning, scalding,
> Stench, consumption; fie, fie, fie! pah, pah!
> Give me an ounce of civet, good apothecary,
> To sweeten my imagination.
> There's money for thee.
>
> *Glou.*   O! let me kiss that hand.
>
> *Lear* Let me wipe it first; it smells of mortality.
>
>   (4.6.129–35)

In tracing his mortality to its source, he revises the bravado of his
triumphant "there I found 'em, there I smelt 'em out": the smell becomes specifically female and implicates him in its stench. Spitting
out his words ("pah, pah!") as though he would violently expel the
tormenting thought of that female stench within him, Lear finds it
in his own body. For the stench of the sulphurous pit and the smell
of mortality turn out to be one:[4] his own flesh—traditionally derivative from the woman's part in conception—carries that stench
within it, as the mark of her female corruption in him.[5] This—his
origin in and vulnerability to the sulphurous pit—is what Lear
smells out in the storm.

Attempting to disown Goneril, Lear finds her a disease within his
own body; attempting to separate himself from her corrupt femaleness, he finds himself pregnant with her. Attempting to escape his
own feminizing emotions by rushing out into the storm, he finds
himself caught in the female maelstrom; attempting to smell out
the faults of others, he finds the stench of the sulphurous pit on his
own hands. But despite his attempts to suppress its presence in
himself, he has always known that that pit was within him; his rush
out into the storm was in part one more attempt to avoid that
knowledge. Lear wants to think that his daughters drive him out
into the storm (3.4.17–19). But he is driven toward the storm less
by his daughters' actions than by the intensity of feeling with which
he responds to their actions; he invents his exposure to the storm
(2.4.210–13) well before they close their doors against him. When
the storm he imagines materializes, it announces itself as an exter-
nalization of his feelings, in effect a projection outward of everything he cannot tolerate within:

---

4. Rosenberg (*The Masks of King Lear*, p. 271), Novy (*Love's Argument*, p. 157), and Kay
   Stockholder (*Dream Works: Lovers and Families in Shakespeare's Plays* [Toronto: University of Toronto Press, 1987], pp. 135–36) note this connection.
5. This nexus of ideas informs Erickson's account of Lear's "mortification of the flesh" in
   the storm: "Lear punishes his body in order to purify it while at the same time destroying the universal power of procreation that corrupted him" (*Patriarchal Structures in
   Shakespeare's Drama*, p. 110).

> You think I'll weep;
> No, I'll not weep:
> I have full cause of weeping, [*Storm and Tempest.*][6]
>   but this heart
> Shall break into a hundred thousand flaws
> Or ere I'll weep.
>
> (2.4.284–88)

Attempting to mobilize masculine rage against his intolerable feelings—as he will later attempt to invoke the male Thunderer in the
storm—he identifies these feelings specifically as female: "touch
me with noble anger, / And let not women's weapons, water-drops, /
Stain my man's cheeks" (2.4.278–80). Rushing out into the storm
made of his own tears, Lear rushes out to confront what is inside
him: for if the storm is the embodiment of the female force that
shakes his manhood, that force is from the start the enemy within.[7]

Earlier, before the storm, Lear has given this female force her
proper name:

> O! how this mother swells up toward my heart;
> *Hysterica passio!* down, thou climbing sorrow!
> Thy element's below. Where is this daughter?
>
> (2.4.56–58)

The bizarreness of these lines has not always been appreciated; in
them, Lear quite literally acknowledges the presence of the sulphurous pit within him. Suffocated by the emotions that he thinks
of as female, Lear gives them the name of the woman's part, as
though he himself bore that diseased and wandering organ within:
for "mother" is a technical term for the uterus; "Hysterica passio"
or "the suffocation of the mother" is the disease caused by its wandering.[8] Like Richard III, Lear discovers his origin in the suffocat-

---

6. This is Folio's stage direction; Muir uses Capell's "Storm heard at a distance" (Arden *King Lear*, p. 99).
7. See Kahn's powerful insight that Shakespeare's portrayal of the storm as the "breaking open of something enclosed" makes it resemble "Lear's heart cracking, letting out the hungry, mother-identified part of him in a flood of tears" ("The Absent Mother in *King Lear*," p. 46).
8. See Edward Jorden, *A Briefe Discourse of a Disease called the Suffocation of the Mother* (London, 1603): "This disease is called by diverse names amongst our Authors. Passio Hysterica, Suffocatio, Prasocatio, and Strangulatus uteri, Caducus matricis, etc. In Eng-lish the Mother or the Suffocation of the Mother, because most commonly it takes them with choaking in the throat: and it is an affect of the Mother or wombe" (pp. 5–6); the suffocation is caused by "the rising of the Mother wherby it is sometimes drawn upwards or sidewards above his natural seate, compressing the neighbour parts" (p. 6). Not sur-prisingly, all Jorden's victims are women. According to The Right Honorable Lord Brain, this passage makes Shakespeare the first person to describe hysteria in a man ("The Concept of Hysteria in the Time of William Harvey," *Proceedings of the Royal Society of Medicine*, 56 [1963]: 321); but Samuel Harsnett notes that Richard Maynie "had a spice of the *Hysterica passio*, as seems from his youth, he himselfe terms it the Moother" (cited in Kenneth Muir, "Samuel Harsnett and *King Lear*," *Review of English Studies* N.S. 2 [1951]: 14). Maynie does not, however, think that he has a uterus; he says that a

ing maternal womb and traces his vulnerability to it: if he was once
inside it, it is now inside him, and his suffocating emotions are its
sign. Thus naming his pain, Lear localizes in himself the nightmare
that Poor Tom will later evoke in the storm:[9] finding her within and
calling her "mother," he traces his internal femaleness to her presence within him, the presence that now rises up to choke him. And
at this moment, Shakespeare shows us the place of the repressed
mother: her organ the epitome of the woman who refuses to stay in
her proper place,[1] she turns up at the very center of masculine au-

Scottish doctor in Paris told him that the disease "riseth . . . of a wind in the bottome of
the belly" (Muir, p. 14). By 1667, Thomas Willis had dissociated the disease from the
womb, partly on the basis of its occurrence in men (see Brain, "The Concept of Hysteria," pp. 321–22, and L. R. Rather, "Pathology at Mid-Century: A Reassessment of
Thomas Willis and Thomas Sydenham," in *Medicine in Seventeenth Century England*,
ed. Allen G. Debus [Berkeley: University of California Press, 1974], p. 107). But *hysterica passio* remained overwhelmingly associated with women: Harsnett notes that "a
thousand poore girles in England" had the disease worse than Maynie (Muir, p. 14),
Willis that "women of every age, and condition, are obnoxious to these kinds of Distem-
pers . . . yea, sometimes the same kind of Passions infest Men" (Brain, p. 322). Moreover, whether or not Shakespeare knew from Harsnett or elsewhere that the disease
could occur in men, Lear's words imply not only that he has the disease but also that he
has the female organ (the "mother") itself: even if one wants to make this passage less
bizarre by reading "this mother" (2.4.56) as the name of the disease rather than the organ, Lear's reference to the mother's swelling upward associates it unmistakably with the
rising womb itself. Despite Muir's note pointing out the connection with Jorden (Arden
King Lear, p. 85), most recent commentators have missed the precision of the anatomical reference; see, for example, Mark S. Shearer, for whom the term functions vaguely as
a birth metaphor ("The Cry of Birth: King Lear's Hysterica Passio," *Postscript* 1 [1983]:
60–66), and Margaret Hotine, who thinks that it refers to abdominal pain like that suffered by King James ("Lear's Fit of the Mother," *Notes and Queries* N.S. 28 [1981]:
138–41). The bizarreness of the anatomical reference is noted by Lisa Jardine (*Still
Harping on Daughters: Women and Drama in the Age of Shakespeare* [Sussex: Harvester
Press, 1983], p. 110) and especially by Kahn, whose account most fully anticipates my
own; but even in Kahn's account, the bizarreness of the reference tends to be displaced
by the speed with which the "mother" becomes metaphorical, serving simultaneously to
indicate Lear's sense of loss of maternal presence ("Those Dim Minoan Regions," p. 38;
"The Absent Mother in *King Lear*," p. 40), his repressed identification with the mother
("Minoan," p. 37; "Absent Mother," p. 36), and the female domain of feeling that refuses
to stay in its place ("Minoan," pp. 38–39; "Absent Mother," p. 36).

9. Suffocation was the primary sign of the nightmare's or incubus's presence as it was the
primary symptom of *hysterica passio*; inside (as the "mother") or outside (as the night-
mare), the female remains the cause of suffocation. See Robert Burton, who notes that
such sleepers "as are troubled with Incubus, or witch-ridden (as we call it); if they lie on
their backs, they suppose an old woman rides, & sits so hard upon them, that they are
almost stifled for want of breath" (*The Anatomy of Melancholy*, ed. Floyd Dell and Paul
Jordan-Smith [New York: Tudor Publishing Company, 1948], p. 220). Though etymolog-
ically "nightmare" is derived from Old English *mare* and "has no connection with the
word meaning a female horse" (Muir, Arden *King Lear*, p. 124), the linguistic accident
that combines woman and horse in "nightmare" may have helped to shape Lear's horrific
portrayal of woman as centaur (4.6.126).

1. Lear asks "Where is this daughter?" as though she too could suddenly turn up inside
him. The conjunction of "Thy element's below" and "Where is this daughter?" moreover
connects the medical discourse of hysteria with the social discourse of hierarchy, making
the rising female element the center of anxiety for both social and bodily instability; see
Kahn ("The Absent Mother," pp. 33–34, 36) and Lisa Jardine (*Still Harping on Daughters*, p. 110). Lear's discovery that he has a uterus seems to invert the Galenic model
that would make the female body merely an inverted version of the male (see Thomas
Laqueur's description of this model, "Orgasm, Generation, and the Politics of Reproductive Biology," *Representations* 14 [1986]: esp. 2–6); it thus serves to destabilize the reas-
suring primacy of the male. Moreover, the conception of the female body that would

thority, in the king's own body; excluded outside, she returns within, undermining the gender divide and so shaking the foundations of masculine identity. It is no wonder that the storm seems a near-psychotic experience for us as for Lear, for it plays out the terror of this discovery: in the storm made of his own irrepressible femaleness, the storm that is the maternal signature, all boundaries dissolve, and Lear is once more inside what is inside him.

Insofar as the Lear plot insists on Lear's complicity in the making of his daughters and on the presence of the female within him, it scrutinizes, and criticizes, the scapegoating logic of the Gloucester plot—the logic that would make only the female the agent of darkness. In fact the play at one point thematizes the logic of this scapegoating, as though to distance itself from it. Faced with the hard evidence of Edgar's mutilated body, Lear invents wicked daughters to account for his suffering, as though only they could be to blame:

> Lear Now all the plagues that in the pendulous air
>   Hang fated o'er men's faults light on thy daughters!
> Kent He hath no daughters, Sir.
> Lear Death, traitor! nothing could have subdu'd nature
>   To such a lowness but his unkind daughters.
>   Is it the fashion that discarded fathers
>   Should have thus little mercy on their flesh?
>   Judicious punishment! 'twas this flesh begot
>   Those pelican daughters.
>
>   (3.4.66–75)

Inventing these wicked daughters, Lear in effect rewrites a tale of fraternal and paternal abuse as a tale of abuse by daughters. And this invention serves a patently defensive function: having invented them, he can righteously call punishment down upon them, deflecting onto them the plague that "hangs fated o'er men's faults." But this is the punishment that hangs specifically over Lear's own fault/foutre. In diverting the plagues that hang fated over men's faults onto the daughters who can be made to suffer in their stead,

---

allow for the rising womb might in any case partly destabilize the hierarchical tidiness and stability implicit in the Galenic model; the body in which a womb can wander— what Edgar imagines as the "indistinguish'd space of woman's will" (4.6.273)—may figure not a comfortable homology with the male but rather a fearful interior and exterior chaos, as I think it does in Lear's storm. According to Foucault, mobility and permeability remain the keynotes of hysteria even when etiology has passed from the wandering womb to the wandering animal spirits; he asks, "If the body is firm and resistent, if internal space is dense, organized, and solidly heterogeneous in its different regions, the symptoms of hysteria are rare. . . . Is this not exactly what separates female hysteria from the male variety?" (Michel Foucault, *Madness and Civilization: A History of Insanity in the Age of Reason*, trans. Richard Howard [New York: Random House, 1965], p. 149).

Lear attempts to insulate himself from acknowledgment of the "plague-sore, or embossed carbuncle" (2.4.226) in his own corrupted blood; relocating plague outside the boundaries of his body, in the wicked daughters he invents, he ensures that the daughters—rather than their fathers—are to be punished for the faults/foutres that have made them.

The mechanism of scapegoating is laid bare here, in Lear's attempt to redirect the plague from his own fault; but the plague nonetheless lights on his daughters. Even while the play enables us to see Lear's need for wicked daughters, and hence undermines the scapegoating logic, it nonetheless replicates that logic,[2] construing Lear's fault itself as the legacy of the female, the contaminating maternal inheritance that cannot be disowned or suppressed. And it moreover represents Goneril and Regan in accordance with the demands of that logic; in their portrayal, the play's dramaturgy is entirely complicit with the fantasy of the dark and vicious place. For the play simultaneously illuminates their genesis in Lear's need and embraces Lear's vision of them, making them as monstrous as he himself could have wished: as it progresses, they are increasingly identified as the source of evil; finally removed wholly from the realm of human sympathy—as Edmund never is—they die as monsters, consumed by their own excess.[3]

2. The scapegoating mechanism has frequently been noted; see, for example, Herbert Coursen ("The Death of Cordelia: A Jungian Approach," *Hebrew University Studies in Literature* 8 [1980]:7), Novy (*Love's Argument*, p. 156), Leonard Tennenhouse (*Power on Display: The Politics of Shakespeare's Genres* [New York: Methuen, 1986], p. 138), and especially Kahn ("Those Dim Minoan Regions," p. 38; "The Absent Mother in *King Lear*," p. 44) and Erickson ("Displaced from the male body and projected exclusively onto the female, sexuality becomes female sexuality," *Patriarchal Structures*, p. 109). Coursen and Novy exempt Shakespeare from this mechanism, locating it only in his male characters; but for Tennenhouse and Erickson, Shakespeare is clearly complicit in it.

3. See Kathleen McLuskie's discussion of the ideological weight Goneril and Regan are made to bear ("The Patriarchal Bard: Feminist Criticism and Shakespeare: *King Lear* and *Measure for Measure*," in *Political Shakespeare*, ed. Jonathan Dollimore and Alan Sinfield [Ithaca, N.Y.: Cornell University Press, 1985], pp. 98–99). For Bradley, there is no question that they are more monstrous than Edmund, "for Edmund, not to mention other alleviations, is at any rate not a woman" (*Shakespearean Tragedy*, p. 239). Stephen Reid's attempt to make Goneril and Regan plausible and perhaps even sympathetic by constructing numerous childhood setbacks for them is not markedly successful ("In Defense of Goneril and Regan," *American Imago* 27 [1970]: 226–44); but see Harry Berger's more sophisticated attempt to derive their characteristic stance toward the world from the Lear family dynamics ("*King Lear*: The Lear Family Romance," *The Centennial Review* 23 [1979]: 357). Claudette Hoover wisely notes that the text "teases us with explanations that consistently prove inadequate to our questions and that each of these hints involves traditions and myths about the nature of women" ("Goneril and Regan: 'So Horrid as in Woman,'" *San Jose Studies* 10 [1984]: 62).

MARGOT HEINEMANN

"Demystifying the Mystery of State": *King Lear* and the World Upside Down†

King Lear is very much a political play—that is, a play concerned with power and government in the state, with public and civil life, and not solely with private relationships and passions. Of course it is not *only* political; but it seems necessary to restate the point because recent productions so often try to make it a *purely* personal, familial, and psychological drama (much in the manner of A. C. Bradley, though a Bradley who has read Freud, Laing, and Foucault). However, even if this is intended to render the play acceptable to modern audiences (who are assumed to be very simple-minded), it is still a distortion, and makes much of the action unintelligible. As Peter Brook put it, the fact that the play is called *King Lear* does not mean that it is primarily the story of one individual[1]—or, one may add, of one family. Shakespeare himself, by introducing the Gloucester parallel plot from quite another source, seems concerned to generalize the issues, to show that Lear's personal psychology or 'character' is not the only force at work.

There was a period, of course, when an exclusively timeless, ahistorical way of reading was more or less taken for granted. It was a great illumination for me, then, to read studies like John Danby's *Shakespeare's Doctrine of Nature* (1949), and the chapters by Kenneth Muir and Arnold Kettle in *Shakespeare in a Changing World* (1964), which attempted to read the play in the light of its contemporary historical and political significance, whatever reservations one may now have about some of their particular interpretations. Many years later, when my own highly intelligent and dominating mother reached the age of eighty-six, my sister and I discovered in ourselves marked Goneril and Regan tendencies. In one sense, as Goethe has it, 'an old man is always a King Lear'. The frustrations of old age ('I will do such things / What they are yet I know not, but they shall be / The terrors of the earth!'); the pain of confusion and weakness, are superbly given. The play needs inescapably to be seen *both* as an individual's loss of power and control *and* as the breakdown of a social and political system: that is indeed its point.

Why, for instance, some critics ask, does not Cordelia humour her old father, in the opening scene, by telling him what he wants

---

† From *Shakespeare Survey* 44, edited by Stanley Wells, pages 75–83. Reprinted by permission of the Cambridge University Press.
1. Peter Brook. *The Empty Space* (London, 1968), p. 91.

and expects to hear—that she loves him above everything? If he were *only* her father, that could perhaps be a reputable argument. But he is also the King, he wields absolute power in the state, and for Cordelia to join in the public competition of flattery and cadging would be to collude with the corruption of absolute power—a matter which preoccupied many of James I's most politically thoughtful subjects in 1604–7. This she cannot do, as Kent cannot do it, and we admire their courage, come what will. If we take it only as a personal story (which the legendary history of course does not), it becomes plausible to imagine Cordelia as culpably stubborn, opinionated, self-righteous and selfish, the inherited mirror-image of Lear's personal failings. But one cannot play it like this without destroying the force of the legendary narrative and the interaction in the theatre.

Demystifying the Mystery of State

The main political thrust is not, of course, to propound an ideal, simplified, harmonious solution for conflicts and contradictions that were genuinely insoluble in the society of the time. Shakespeare is not writing Agitprop. School pupils and students who ask: 'What is Shakespeare putting over?' can be given only a negative answer—some things he is clearly not putting over.

The political effect is, rather, sharply to represent the complex conflicts of interest and ideology in his own world; to dramatize them as human conflicts and actions, not ordained by fate; to present images of kings and queens, statesmen and counsellors as simultaneously holders of sacred office and fallible human beings who may be weak, stupid, greedy or cruel (in itself a central contradiction). Hence the drama empowers ordinary people in the audience to think and judge for themselves of matters usually considered 'mysteries of state' in which no one but the 'natural rulers'—the nobility and gentry and professional élites—should be allowed to meddle. Sir Henry Wotton commented after seeing *Henry VIII* at the Globe that it was 'sufficient in truth within a while to make greatness very familiar, if not ridiculous'. If this was what he thought about *Henry VIII*, the most spectacular and ceremonious of Shakespeare's history plays, what would he have said of *King Lear*, which produces this effect in its extremest form?

Reinforcing Dominant Ideology?

It has been argued that the dramatists necessarily reinforce the dominant ideology which holds the society together, within which institutions such as the theatre function and provide them with a living, so that on balance criticism is safely 'contained'. In the early seventeenth century, however, it becomes increasingly evident that no single dominant ideology or consensus is capable of holding the society together. The existence of different ideologies and of deep ideological and political conflicts over the nature and limits of monarchic power and prerogative, and the rights and liberties of subjects (however masked by the pervasive censorship), has been clearly demonstrated and documented for the years 1603–40 by younger historians, notably J.P. Sommerville, Richard Cust, and Peter Lake.[2] The Essex circle, where so many contesting ideological viewpoints were articulated and discussed in the 1590s, was a marvellous seedbed for Shakespeare's multivocal historical and political drama. But that complex clash of ideologies—bastard-feudal, politique, scientific-Machiavellian, republican, radical-Puritan crusading and anti-clerical—ended in the disaster of the Essex revolt. In the drama, optimistic confidence in political and military action to fulfil national destiny gave place to a sense of history as tragedy, and modern English history became for the time being a banned subject.

What the Politics of King Lear Cannot Be

The politics of the play cannot then be the assertion of absolute monarchal power, prerogative, and magnificence against mean-spirited Parliamentary attacks on royal expenditure and pleasures, symbolized allegorically in Goneril and Regan, though this has been seriously argued. The Parliament of 1604 was certainly no flatterer of the monarch. Neither does the play show that any interference with or diminution of the King's absolute power is unnatural and must lead to chaos: for it is Lear's refusal to listen to wise counsel, his insistence on his own will as paramount and absolute, that opens the way to chaos and disintegration. The patriarchalist view of monarchy, that equates kingly power with the power of the father within the family, is strongly present in the play, above all in the mind of Lear himself. Patriarchalism does not, however, necessarily entail an absolutist view of kingly power; the importance of paternal power was supported by many anti-absolutist and even some revolutionary and Leveller political thinkers.[3] Yet Cordelia, who challenges her father's use of absolute power, retains the audience's sympathy in so doing. To read the play as unequivocally patriarchalist is to read against the grain.

The assertion of the traditional and necessary rights and privi-

---

2. See in particular the chapters by these authors in *Conflict in Early Stuart England*, ed. R. Cust and A. Hughes (London, 1989); and J. P. Sommerville, *Politics and Ideology in England, 1603–1640* (London, 1989).
3. Sommerville, *Politics and Ideology*, pp. 28–32.

leges of Parliament against government by royal prerogative was not something invented in the 1620s and 1630s, just in time for the Civil War, but goes back to the moment of *King Lear* and beyond it. James I was confused and annoyed by the institution of Parliament as he found it in his new kingdom, and the loyal Commons tried to explain to him that their right to be consulted and to criticize Crown policies did not imply disloyalty. The 'Apology of the Commons' in 1604 expressed their fears, based on what was happening to elected assemblies elsewhere in Europe:

> What cause your poor Commons have to watch over our privileges is manifest in itself to all men. The prerogatives of princes may easily and do daily grow: the privileges of subjects are for the most part at an everlasting stand. They may be by providence and good care preserved, but being once lost are not recovered but with much disquiet.[4]

The Apology itself (never finally passed through parliament or officially presented) was drafted by Sir Edwin Sandys, MP, thereafter a close associate of Shakespeare's former patron the Earl of Southampton, with other surviving Essexians (such as Sir Thomas Ridgway) taking an important part. Sandys himself, one of the foremost exponents of anti-absolutist thinking in Jacobean times, claimed that the King's power had originally been introduced by popular consent; he declared in Parliament that now 'it is come to be almost a tyrannical government in England'.[5] The tension between King and Parliament was indeed to continue throughout James's reign.

We do not know very much about Shakespeare's later connections with Southampton and his circle, but there is no evidence that they were broken off. Shakespeare apparently celebrated his former patron's release from the Tower with a congratulatory sonnet (No. 107), and continuing links with his circle are demonstrated by G. P. Akrigg.[6] *The Tempest*, begun around the time when Southampton (with Sandys) helped to found the Virginia Company, shows continuing cross-fertilization, and revolves (though sceptically) the colonialists' dream of creating a juster empire in the New World.[7]

---

4. From 'A Form of Apology and Satisfaction', drawn up at the end of the 1604 session by a Committee of the House. Cited Conrad Russell, *The Crisis of Parliaments* (London, 1971), p. 270.

5. Cited Derek Hirst, *Authority and Conflict in England 1603–1648* (London, 1986), p. 117.

6. G. P. Akrigg, *Shakespeare and the Earl of Southampton* (London, 1968), pp. 264ff.

7. Other links with Parliamentarian circles can be traced through the Digges brothers, who are connected in various ways with Shakespeare and later with anti-absolutist opposition trends. Their stepfather, Thomas Russell, was overseer of Shakespeare's will. Leonard Digges published eulogies of Shakespeare in 1623 and 1640. (*Shakespeare, Complete Works* (Oxford, 1986), pp. xlvi and xlviii). Dudley Digges, who is believed to have shown Strachey's confidential report on the state of Virginia to Shakespeare (see *The Tempest*,

In the context, it seems that Goneril, Regan, and Edmund were likely to be identified by the audience not with the Parliamentary oppositionists, but with what they saw as contemporary flatterers, cadgers, and upstarts at the Jacobean court, who were being rewarded for their obsequiousness with land, monopolies, offices and gifts—people like James's unpopular Scottish favourites. The land and the peasants who live on it are given away by Lear as if they were his private property. The decay of the old social order, with an alternative not yet ready to be born, gives rise to such morbid growths—as Gramsci expresses it.

Nature of the Political Interest

The heart of the political interest is not in the division of the kingdom or the issue of unification with Scotland, though there may well be allusions to this. The *division* as such does not in fact cause the war and barbarity that we see. The sole rule of Goneril, the eldest, would scarcely make for peace and harmony, and the single rule of Cordelia could only be secured if primogeniture were ignored. The causes of disaster lie deeper than that. The central focus is on the horror of a society divided between extremes of rich and poor, greed and starvation, the powerful and the powerless, robes and rags, and the impossibility of real justice and security in such a world. Lear himself, like the faithful Gloucester, discovers this only when his own world is turned upside down, when he himself is destitute and mad, and at last sees authority with the eyes of the dispossessed. Central to the language as well as the stage images is the opposition between 'looped and window'd raggedness', utter poverty, and the 'robes and furred gowns' that hide nakedness and crimes. All the difference lies in clothes and ceremony: 'a dog's obeyed in office'.

This crazy world is directly the responsibility of the King and of the rich and powerful in general, and the verse continually underlines this: 'You houseless poverty', cries Lear on the heath,

> O, I have ta'en
> Too little care of this. Take physic, pomp,
> Expose thyself to feel what wretches feel,
> That thou mayst shake the superflux to them
> And show the heavens more just. (3.4.32–6)

And Gloucester, blind and helpless, echoes this conclusion:

---

ed. Frank Kermode (London, 1964), pp. xxvii–xxviii) was a prominent anti-absolutist MP, and in 1629 drafted the Petition of Right.

    Heavens deal so still!
Let the superfluous and lust-dieted man
That slaves your ordinance, that will not see
Because he does not feel, feel your power quickly.
So distribution should undo excess,
And each man have enough.   (4.1.60–5)

This is a note not struck in the earlier Histories, and certainly not in the other 'deposition play', *Richard II*.

The indictment is still, for us, very direct and near the bone. Audiences going to the South Bank to see in 1990 *King Lear* at the National Theatre passed by Cardboard City, the modern equivalent of Edgar's hovel, where the homeless shelter in cardboard boxes on the pavement. Mother Teresa of Calcutta, visiting London, said on television that she had seen such sights in the Third World, but in a rich country like Britain she could not understand it. Many of those sleeping rough are the mentally disturbed and the old, made homeless by the closing of mental hospitals and old people's homes, the cuts in home helps, the lack of funds for care in the community. Lear bitterly tells Goneril, 'Age is unnecessary'. It still is.[8]

This interest, and the rôle-reversal of riches and poverty, power and powerlessness, is stressed in Quarto and Folio alike, despite the many alterations. Nor is it just our modern prejudice that leads us to focus on this as a central concern. It is surely significant that so many of what are now widely believed to be Shakespeare's own revisions relate to this aspect of the play—the inverted world, the counterposing of king and clown, wisdom and madness, insight and fooling. Clearly he was particularly anxious to get this right. He has two goes at presenting the 'upside-down' view of monarchy and absolute power. Once this appears as a powerful stage image, the 'mock-trial' of the Quarto text, in which the very possibility of securing justice in such an unjust and unequal society is parodied and mocked. This scene can be much more effective on the stage than it looks on the page (*pace* Roger Warren),[9] since the parallel

---

8. During the year to October 1990 London local authorities had to place over 31,000 families in temporary accommodation (a new high), and 8,000 in bed and breakfast accommodation. (Chairman of Association of Local Authorities Housing Committee, the *Guardian*, 12 October 1990). Even in prosperous Cambridge, 307 homeless families had to be rehoused in the year 1990–1, an increase of 44 on the previous year and the highest number on record. For England as a whole official statistics show homeless households have increased by 131 per cent in 1979–89 to a total of 122,680: recent research (by Professor John Greve) shows that in 1990 some 170,000 households were accepted as homeless by Local Authorities, amounting to about half a million people. Estimates of single homeless (who are not entitled to be rehoused) in London vary between 65,000 and 125,000: according to the housing charity *Shelter*, about 3,000 are currently sleeping rough in London.

9. Roger Warren, 'The Folio Omission of the Mock Trial: Motives and Consequences', in Gary Taylor and Michael Warren, eds., *The Division of the Kingdoms* (Oxford, 1983), pp. 45ff.

with Lear dispensing 'justice' from his throne in the opening scene can be made visually much sharper and more shocking.

In the Folio text the upside-down view of justice is presented purely in language, in the extended speech of Lear to Gloucester, which, after the brilliant images (already in Quarto) of the dog obeyed in office and the beadle lashing the whore he lusts for, adds the explicit general moral:

> Plate sin with gold,
> And the strong lance of justice hurtless breaks;
> Arm it in rags, a pygmy's straw does pierce it.
> None does offend, none, I say none. I'll able 'em.
> Take that of me, my friend, who have the power
> To seal th'accuser's lips.   (4–5.161–6)

The 'upside-downness' is emphasized and made more explicit verbally in Folio—*extended* from Quarto but not *amended*. 'None does offend' suggests that no one has the right to accuse or judge since all are sinners, or that no one will dare to accuse if the king opposes it and has the power to silence the accusers and pardon the offenders. But there may also be an echo of antinomian discourse, implying that our categories of right and wrong, sin and righteousness, are meaningless and evil. The dreams of persecuted underground Familist groups at the time when *King Lear* was written surface again in the revolutionary years in the antinomian vision of Abiezer Coppe:

> Sin and transgression is finished and ended . . . Be no longer so horribly, hellishly, impudently, arrogantly wicked, as to judge what is sin, what not.[1]

Although I understand Roger Warren's point about the difficulty of staging the 'mock-trial', which *may* have prompted the revision, it has (as he concedes) been successfully done, for example in our time by Peter Brook, and it is difficult to accept that by cutting it Shakespeare made a better play. For the 'mock-trial' vividly makes the case not against a particular legal injustice or the corruption of individual judges (as Middleton does in, say, *The Phoenix*), but against the whole intrinsically ridiculous pretence of justice in an unjust society.

Warren criticizes the scene as ineffective on the grounds that the Fool and Edgar as Poor Tom, seated on the farmhouse bench alongside Lear, fail to keep to the legal-satirical point, though Lear himself does so.[2] But this is surely the essence. The entire set up is absurd—the rich and respectable are no more qualified to dispense

---

1. Abiezer Coppe, *A Fiery Flying Roll*, pt 1, ch. 8 (London, 1649).
2. R. Warren, p. 46.

justice than the whores and thieves, or the fools and madmen. To make this strike home and shake our complacency, the speech of madness and folly at this moment needs to sound truly mad, wild and disorganized, not the coherently composed discourse of a satirist in disguise. The image flashes on us as a moment of dreadful insight—enough, one might say, to drive the beholder mad.

Christopher Hill perceptively notes that many prophets of the upside-down world in the seventeenth century were thought by contemporaries to be mad, and some probably were—the vision was too much for their sanity.[3] But in some cases madness was a useful protection for the expression of opinions dangerous to the social order. There can be no doubt that the Ranter Thomas Webbe was being prudent when he called himself Mad Tom in a pamphlet foretelling the downfall of Charles II in 1660.[4]

This reversal of degree finds no easy resolution in the play. Edgar's final speech provides no strongly felt reassurance that the world is now once more firmly the right way up. It is deliberately quiet and bleak.

Resistance Upside Down

The resistance to evil too has an 'upside-down' dimension, coming first from the weak, the oppressed lower orders, the peasants and servants. This is highlighted in the first violent check to tyranny, when the Nazi-type brute Cornwall, about to put out the other eye of Gloucester, is defied and wounded by his own servant. In the few lines he speaks this unnamed man declares himself a lifelong servant of the Duke, not a casual hireling; but the bonds of feudal loyalty and rank cannot hold in face of such dishonourable cruelty:

> I have served you ever since I was a child,
> But better service have I never done you
> Than now to bid you hold.   (3.7.71–3)

This echoes Kent's justification of his insubordination to Lear. A 'villein' of Cornwall's draws on his lord as an equal, and Regan screams out the indignation of the 'natural rulers':

> A *peasant* stand up thus!   (3.7.77)

She kills him, running at him from behind. But the resistance has started, and Cornwall will not be there to help crush it.

For the audience, this action—quite unprepared—by one of the

---

3. Christopher Hill, *The World Turned Upside Down* (London, 1972), p. 224. The whole chapter 'The Island of Great Bedlam' is illuminating on the relation between lower-class prophecy and accusations of madness.
4. Hill, p. 227.

stage 'extras' is startling, and evidently meant to be so. It is followed, in Quarto, by the sympathy and indignation of the horrified servants, who despite their terror do their best to help Gloucester and bandage his wounds. This first tentative rallying of humane forces against the tyrants was cut in the Folio text, and also in a famous production by Peter Brook, who said he wished to prevent reassurance being given to the audience. One wonders why. The reassurance provided in these depths of agony hardly seems excessive. Was the suggestion of a justified *popular* rising against despotic power perhaps felt to be going too far? However that may be, Edgar when he kills Oswald is disguised as a peasant, wearing the 'best 'parel' provided by the honest old man, Gloucester's tenant, and talking stage country dialect. His peasant cudgel beats down the gentleman's sword and his fancy fencing:

> 'I's' try whether your costard or my baton be the harder . . . 'Chill pick your teeth, sir. Come, no matter vor your foins.
>
> (4.5.240–4)

Ordinary countrymen were of course forbidden to wear a sword, which was the exclusive privilege of gentlemen.[5] Hence this victory must register in the theatre as symbolic of the common people defeating the hangers-on of court and wealth, though since Edgar is really a nobleman in disguise, and the audience knows this, the effect is less subversive than it might be. However, if we compare this fight with the concluding duels between Hamlet and Laertes, Prince Hal and Hotspur, or Coriolanus and Aufidius, this image is strikingly a contest of social unequals, in which the plain but righteous man wins against the odds. It may also have suggested a further symbolic meaning for some in the audience. The Surrey group of Familists, whose pacifist principles forbade them to bear arms, found that this made them too conspicuous, and therefore compromised by carrying staves (cudgels).[6]

Lear's Fool is of course the most obvious source of upside-downness in both texts, speaking wisdom in the proverbial idiom of the people, often coarsely, in contrast to the hypocrisy and folly of formal and ceremonial utterance by the great. (The distinction that has been suggested between a 'natural' Fool in Quarto and an 'artificial', skilful courtier-Fool in Folio has to my mind been greatly overstated.) The Fool's jokes and aphorisms are consistently in the irreverent upside-down style, often literally so, and some as old as Aesop:

---

5. Oswald, as Kent points out earlier, while technically allowed to wear a sword, is too dishonourable to have a right to it.
6. See Janet E. Halley, 'The Case of the English Family of Love', in *Representing the English Renaissance*, ed. Stephen Greenblatt (London, 1988), pp. 319–20. See also John Rogers, *The displaying of an horrible sect of gross and wicked heretics* (London, 1578).

e'er since thou madest thy daughters thy mothers . . .
and puttest down thine own breeches . . .

(1.4.153–4)

May not an ass know when the cart draws the horse?

(1.4.206)

When thou clovest thy crown i'th' middle and gavest away both
parts, thou borest thine ass o'th' back o'er the dirt.

(1.4.142–4)

This echoes the images of the topsy-turvy world in scores of songs
and broadsides,[7] such as the popular ballad, 'Who's the fool now',
favoured by James's own provocative Fool Archy Armstrong (and
still in use at folksong festivals to this day). Textual revision has not
substantially changed this effect. The King himself reduced to a
fool is a key image in both texts. The main difference may be in the
greater emphasis given to it in the Quarto:

LEAR   Dost thou call me fool, boy?
FOOL   All thy other titles thou hast given away.
    That thou wast born with.   (Q.4.143–5)

And one may note also the obviousness of the topical application in
Quarto, which it is suggested the censor may have jibbed at.[8]
Among the lines excised is the Fool's jingle:

That lord that counselled thee
To give away thy land,
Come, place him here by me;
Do thou for him stand.
The sweet and bitter fool
Will presently appear,
The one in motley here,
The other found out there.   (Q.4.135–142)

So too is the Fool's complaint that he has failed to secure a monopoly of folly, because:

lords and great men will not let me. If I had a monopoly out, they
would have part on't, and ladies too, they will not let me have all
the fool to myself—they'll be snatching.

(Q.4.147–50)

---

7. See Peter Burke, *Popular Culture in Early Modern Europe* (London, 1978), especially
the illustrated broadsides of the mice burning the cat; the woman with the gun and the
man with the distaff; and the peasant riding on the nobleman's back (between pp. 98
and 99).
8. See Gary Taylor in *The Division of the Kingdoms*, pp. 104–9.

There is indeed a double topical reference here (1) to the land given away by the King to his favourites, and (2) to anti-monopoly pressure by the Commons, culminating in the Apology of 1604.

The Fool stands in a direct theatrical tradition from Tarlton, appearing as Simplicity in the 'medley' plays of the 1580s. Even his jokes are traditional.[9] The clown as prophet appears in *The Cobbler's Prophecy* (printed 1594) where the poor cobbler, endowed with prophetic gifts by the gods, denounces the rich and foresees the world turned upside down at the Day of Judgement, when widows and starving children will be avenged. The most direct analogy, however, is with Rowley's comic-historical presentation in 1605 of Henry VIII and his famous jester Will Summers, who in this rendering is an iconoclastic, egalitarian, anti-Popish clown and a champion of the poor. It would be better, he says, if Henry had their prayers rather than the Pope's, for the Pope is at best St Peter's deputy, 'but the poor present Christ, and so should be something better regarded'—an old anti-clerical aphovism traceable back to the Lollards.[1]

Not Only 'Carnivalesque'

The upside-down discourse here is not simply 'carnivalesque', if by that we mean providing a recognized safety-valve for the release of tensions in a repressive society—a temporary holiday from hierarchy which enables it to be reimposed more effectively afterwards, as we see in the Feast of Fools, the Lords of Misrule, or the iconoclastic Christmas entertainments customary to this day in the London teaching hospitals.

The deriding of accepted categories of sin, adultery, property and officially enforced law echoes Utopian ideas which survived in a serious and organized form, more or less underground, in late-Elizabethan and Jacobean times, among radical religious sects such as the Family of Love, and were to surface again forty to fifty years later in the revolutionary years, first with the Levellers, and after their defeat with Ranters and Seekers. A Presbyterian divine, denouncing the sect under Elizabeth, had emphasized the 'topsy-turvy' aspect of Henry Niclaes' teaching as especially subversive of order:

9. The Fool's joke about the cockney's brother who, 'in pure kindness to his horse, buttered his hay' (*Lear* 2.4) is anticipated by Tarlton's story about the inn where they greased the horses' teeth to prevent them eating, and so saved the cost of the fodder (*Three Ladies of London*, Dodsley's Old Plays (London, 1874), vol. 6, p. 255).
1. Samuel Rowley, *When You See Me You Know Me* (London, 1605) (Malone Society Reprint, 1952, line 1568).

> To be brief in this matter of doctrine, H.N. turneth religion upside down, and buildeth heaven here upon earth: maketh God, man; and man, God; heaven, hell; and hell, heaven.[2]

The existence of such ideas was topical knowledge about the time when *King Lear* was first produced. In *Basilikon Doron* King James had particularly attacked Familists as an example of *dangerous* Puritanism:

> their humours . . . agreeing with the general rule of all Anabaptists, in the contempt of the civil magistrate, and in leaning to their own dreams and revelations.[3]

The Familists, replying to this, petitioned King James for toleration, disavowing any intent to overthrow the magistrate and place themselves in his seat: an appeal almost certainly drafted by Robert Seale, one of a group of Familists in the royal Guard.[4] They did not obtain the toleration they sought. In 1606 a confutation of their *Supplication* was printed (together with the text) and thereafter little is known about the sect as such. The ideas, however, were in the air, and theatre people could have picked up their acquaintance with them around the court as well as in artisan circles (often no doubt in distorted form).

Not Mad from the Beginning

The 'world upside down' effect in the play is easily destroyed, though, if the King is played (as has happened in some recent productions) as deranged, undignified and in senile dementia from his first entrance. Dramatically, no fall or reversal is then possible, and 'Let me not be mad, not mad, sweet heaven!' loses all its agonizing force. No moral or political point can then be made, except perhaps that kings ought to be retired early, so that they can be replaced by sane people like Goneril and Regan.

It is not a question of the sacred untouchability of the text. As Brecht once said, 'I think we can alter Shakespeare if we can alter him'; but wrong alterations will 'mobilise all Shakespeare's excel-

---

2. John Knewstub, *A Confutation of Monstrous and Horrible Heresies* (London, 1579). Preface.
3. Cited by Halley.
4. Seale was briefly imprisoned on suspicion of Familism in 1580, but was still in a position of trust at court as clerk of the Cheque of the Guard in 1599, a position which he continued to hold in 1606. In the reply confuting the Familists' Supplication (which includes their text) the editor refers (p. 18) to leading Familists 'receiving yearly both countenance and maintenance from her princely coffers, being her household servants': and on p. 28 states that the Elizabethan Familists are 'yet living and in Court', with 'their children in right ancient place about his majesty'. The Familists included both an educated élite and an organized popular following, mainly of artisans, in such areas as Wisbech, Surrey, Suffolk, and Cambridge. See Alastair Hamilton, *The Family of Love* (1981), especially Chapter 6 on the Family in England.

lences against us'. This particular one seems to me the kind of alteration that distorts the original to the point where the chemistry
of the play no longer works. A successful production has to convince us that a King, however grand and mighty he has been, is a
fool anyway, and mortal anyway. Lear's fearful experience makes
him and the audience aware of this. Hence the need of any king for
wise and courageous advisers prepared to tell him the truth and set
limits to his power—the role played by Kent here, and in the contemporary political context, unevenly but increasingly, in their own
mind at least, by some opposition elements in Parliament.

Censorship and the Reception of the Play

Direct censorship (as distinct from cautious self-censorship) has
been argued as possibly accounting for some of the differences between the two texts—notably the omission of several of the Fool's
speeches in Scene 4. It was a tricky moment to write in this tone
about a *British* Court and Crown, even if legendary ones. But it may
just have been that the bitter jokes against royalty did not please,
and some were therefore cut by the dramatist and the players in a
revised acting version. That, however, may not have been enough.
No London revival of *Lear* after 1606, which might have used a revised text, is actually known, though there were many repeats, at
court and elsewhere, of *Othello, Hamlet, Richard II*, and the late romances. The chances are that this play, directly representing a King
as foolish, the rich as culpable, and the poor as victims, may have
been felt as altogether too disturbing and subversive.

There is indeed evidence that the company was in political trouble with the Court around this time. The King's Men had, it seems,
displeased James by a play performed 'in their theatre' reported to
him as containing many 'galls', 'dark sentences / Pleasing to fac-
tious brains,' with 'every otherwhere a jest / Whose high abuse shall
more torment than blows'. The company made their peace with a
Court performance of the old romantic—heroic popular favourite
Mucedorus, including a specially rewritten Epilogue, in which the
characters appealed on their knees to the 'glorious and wise Arch-
Caesar on this earth' to pardon 'our unwitting error'.[5] The references to the offending play in this Epilogue (attributed by several
scholars to Shakespeare) sound more appropriate to *King Lear* than

---

5. I am grateful to Richard Proudfoot for drawing my attention to the *Mucedorus* Epilogue
and its significance. The revised Epilogue, first printed in the 1610 edition, is included
in *The Shakespeare Apocrypha*, ed. C. Tucker Brooke (1908), from which all the above
phrases are quoted. The matter is discussed in *The Comedy of Mucedorus*, ed. K. Warnke
and Ludwig Proeschold (1878); and by R. Simpson in *Academy*, (29 April 1876). The
play is described in the Epilogue as a 'comedy' but this does not rule out a reference to
Lear: Hamlet, after all, referred to *The Murder of Gonzago* as a 'comedy'.

to anything else recently performed by the King's Men. However
that may be, the company had certainly been warned; and the
marked change of tone in Shakespeare's later plays—*Pericles* and
Winter's Tale, Cymbeline and *Tempest*—may in part reflect this.

R. A. FOAKES

From Hamlet *versus* Lear†

Let me begin with two lists, so as to provide an orientation for the
first part of this book. One is a short anthology of comments prais-
ing either *Hamlet* or *King Lear* as the best, the greatest, or the chief
masterpiece of Shakespeare. The claims for *Hamlet* pretty much
died out by the 1950s, while those for *King Lear* become common-
place only from the 1950s onwards, though notably anticipated by
Hazlitt and A. C. Bradley. The second list records some of the major international events in the period 1956–65, which is when the
great shift in the status of *King Lear* took place. I do not claim that
there is a direct connection, or that what was happening politically
in the world at that time explains the way Shakespeare's plays were
assessed, but only that critics consciously or unconsciously reflect
the mood of their time; and the mood of that period was dominated
by the expansion of nuclear arsenals and the fear of a war that
might destroy the world. This mood was indicated in two of the
films that made a huge impact, Stanley Kramer's *On the Beach*
(1959), a film about the end of civilization in a world devastated by
atomic waste, based on a 1957 novel by Nevil Shute; and Stanley
Kubrick's *Dr. Strangelove: or, How I Learned to Stop Worrying and
Love the Bomb* (1963), a satirical reflection of the nightmares of
the age. Here, then are the lists:

> 1 The anthology: (a) *Hamlet*
> '*Hamlet*—the noblest and greatest of all [Shakespeare's] trag-
>   edies' (John Keble, 1830).
> 'Other works of the human mind equal *Hamlet*; none sur-
>   passes it' (Victor Hugo, 1864).
> '*Hamlet* is the greatest creation in literature that I know of'
>   (Alfred Lord Tennyson, as reported by Hallam Tennyson,
>   1883).
> '*Hamlet* is the greatest of popular dramas' (J. Dover Wilson,
>   1935).
> 'The play [*Hamlet*] is almost universally considered to be the

---

† From *Hamlet* versus *Lear*. Reprinted by permission of the Cambridge University Press.

chief masterpiece of one of the greatest minds the world has known' (Ernest Jones, 1949).

'[*Hamlet* is] one of the few great masterpieces of the European spirit' (Salvador de Madariaga, 1948).

(b) *King Lear*

'[*King Lear*] is the best of all Shakespeare's plays' (William Hazlitt, 1817).

'*King Lear* seems to me Shakespeare's great achievement, but it seems to me *not* his best play' (A. C. Bradley, 1904).

'The greatest of plays [*King Lear*]' (D. G. James, 1951).

'In the twentieth century *Hamlet* has yielded to *King Lear* the distinction of being the play in which the age most finds itself' (L. C. Knights, 1960).

'For a number of critics it [*King Lear*] is self-evidently the greatest of Shakespeare's tragedies' (Emrys Jones, 1971).

'The play that has come to be regarded as the definitive achievement of Shakespearean tragedy' (Howard Felperin, 1977).

'The tragedy of Lear, deservedly celebrated among the dramas of all Shakespeare, is commonly regarded as his greatest achievement' (Stephen Booth, 1983).

2 Some major events 1954–65

1954, March   Americans explode hydrogen bomb on Bikini atoll; fallout affected Japanese fishing boats, and also islanders more than a hundred miles away.

1956, October   Uprisings in Hungary and Poland crushed by the Soviet Union.

1956, November   Outbreak of Suez war; Britain, France and Israel invade Egypt, are defeated and humiliated.

1957, October   Sputnik, first Soviet space rocket, placed in orbit.

1958, February   Launching of the Campaign for Nuclear Disarmament.

1959, January   Fidel Castro takes over in Cuba. First two Americans killed in Vietnam.

1960   France explodes its first atomic device.

1960, March   Sharpeville massacre in South Africa.

1960, May   U2 spy plane shot down over Russia; after repeated denials that they were spying, the United States was forced to admit it when Gary Powers was produced alive.

1961, January   Inauguration of President John F. Kennedy.

1961–3   Build-up of American arms; Kennedy announced in 1963, 'In less than three years we have increased by 50 per cent the number of Polaris submarines—increased by 70 per

cent the proportion of our strategic bombers on fifteen
minute alert—increased by 100 per cent the total number of
nuclear weapons in our strategic alert forces . . . increased
by 60 per cent the tactical nuclear forces displayed in Western Europe.'[1]

1961, April   Bay of Pigs; invasion of Cuba backed by the CIA
fails disastrously.

1961, August   East Berlin closed off from the West by completion of the Berlin Wall.

1962, October   Cuban missile crisis.

1963, November   Assassination of President Kennedy.

1964, August   Tonkin Bay incident; two American destroyers
said to be attacked by North Vietnamese gunboats.

1964, October   Kruschev ousted by Leonid Brezhnev.

1965, October   China explodes its first atomic bomb.

1965, February   First sustained bombing of North Vietnam
by Americans; first marine battalions land in Vietnam;
200,000 combat troops there by December.

1965, August   Watts riots in Los Angeles.

*** About 1960 *** an intriguing double shift took place. On
the one hand, *King Lear* regained its ascendancy in critical esteem,
and since that time most critics seem to have taken it for granted
(see the quotations above from Emrys Jones, Howard Felperin and
Stephen Booth) that they can refer to it as Shakespeare's greatest
play. On the other hand, *King Lear* changed its nature almost
overnight: the main tradition of criticism up to the 1950s had interpreted the play as concerned with Lear's pilgrimage to redemption,
as he finds himself and in 'saved' at the end, but in the 1960s the
play became Shakespeare's bleakest and most despairing vision of
suffering, all hints of consolation undermined or denied.*** There
is no simple explanation for this shift in the 1960s, but it strikingly
coincided with a period of political change, as indicated in the
chronology above, that affected the mood of people in Britain and
in the United States *** and which have a bearing on the way
Hamlet and *King Lear* were interpreted. Criticism, as most now realize, is never an innocent activity; it always has a hidden agenda,
even if the critic remains largely unconscious of it. For criticism always reflects the ideology of the critic and the conditions of the age
in which he writes, however much it may claim to be independent
and concerned only with the text.

*** Although Hamlet was, as a character, abstracted from the
play and privatized as a representative of everyman by Romantic

1. Seyom [Brown], *The Faces of Power* (New York: Columbia University Press, 1968),
p. 196.

and later critics, he also became in the nineteenth century an important symbolic political figure, usually typifying the liberal intellectual paralysed in will and incapable of action. By contrast, *King Lear* was depoliticized, even by the radical Hazlitt, perhaps at that time because of a possible association with the mad old monarch, George III; and until the 1950s the play was, in the main, seen as a tragedy of personal relations between father and daughter, or as a grand metaphysical play about Lear's pilgrimage to discover his soul. All this changed after 1960, since when *King Lear* has come to seem richly significant in political terms, in a world in which old men have held on to and abused power, often in corrupt or arbitrary ways; in the same period *Hamlet* has lost much of its political relevance, as liberal intellectuals have steadily been marginalized in Britain and the United States.

*** Each play has had its champions to assert vigorously that either *Hamlet* or *King Lear* is the 'greatest' of Shakespeare's plays. *** Yet in all the vast mass of critical writing on these plays, there is hardly any consideration of the grounds for such judgements. Aesthetic questions are generally ignored, or the artistic value of the plays taken for granted. Indeed, criticism has increasingly been equated with interpretation, so that the post-structuralist claim that criticism is a discursive practice no different from other discursive practices such as those we call literature, and the further claim that 'only the critic *executes* the work'[2] and constructs its meanings, appears from one point of view as the culmination of a long tradition in which interpretation has become the central activity of criticism, especially in the academy. The meanings critics find relate to their own political or social ideology, whether conservative, quietist, liberal or revolutionary.

STANLEY CAVELL

From The Avoidance of Love:
A Reading of *King Lear*†

This is the way I understand that opening scene with the three daughters. Lear knows it is a bribe he offers, and—part of him anyway—wants exactly what a bribe can buy: (1) false love; and (2) a public expression of love. That is: he wants something he does not

2. Roland Barthes, "From Work to Text," in *Textual Strategies: Perspectives in Post-Structuralist Criticism*, ed. Josue V. Harari (Ithaca: Cornell University Press, 1976).
† From *Must We Mean What We Say?* Second Edition, by Stanley Cavell, pages 289–301. Reprinted by permission of the Cambridge University Press.

have to return *in kind*, something which a division of his property
fully pays for. And he wants to *look* like a loved man—for the sake of
the subjects, as it were. He is perfectly happy with his little plan, until Cordelia speaks. Happy not because he is blind, but because he is
getting what he wants, his plan is working. Cordelia is alarming precisely because he *knows* she is offering the real thing, offering something a more opulent third of his kingdom cannot, must not, repay;
putting a claim upon him he cannot face. She threatens to expose
both his plan for returning false love with no love, and expose the
necessity for that plan—his terror of being loved, of needing love.

Reacting to over-sentimental or over-Christian interpretations of
her character, efforts have been made to implicate her in the
tragedy's source, convicting her of a willfulness and hardness kin to
that later shown by her sisters. But her complicity is both less and
more than such an interpretation envisages. That interpretation depends, first of all, upon taking her later speeches in the scene (after
the appearance of France and Burgundy) as simply uncovering
what was in her mind and heart from the beginning. But why? Her
first utterance is the aside:

> What shall Cordelia speak? Love, and be silent.

This, presumably, has been understood as indicating her decision to
refuse her father's demand. But it needn't be. She asks herself what
she can say; there is no necessity for taking the question to be
rhetorical. She wants to obey her father's wishes (anyway, there is
no reason to think otherwise at this stage, or at any other); but
how? She sees from Goneril's speech and Lear's acceptance of it
what it is he wants, and she would provide it if she could. But to
pretend publicly to love, where you do not love, is easy; to pretend
to love, where you really do love, is not obviously possible. She hits
on the first solution to her dilemma: Love, and be silent. That is,
love *by being* silent. That will do what he seems to want, it will
avoid the expression of love, keep it secret. She is his joy; she
knows it and he knows it. Surely that is enough? Then Regan
speaks, and following that Cordelia's second utterance, again aside:

> Then poor Cordelia!
> And yet not so; since I am sure my love's
> More ponderous than my tongue.
>
> (I, i, 76–78)

Presumably, in line with the idea of a defiant Cordelia, this is to be
interpreted as a re-affirmation of her decision not to speak. But
again, it needn't be. After Lear's acceptance of Regan's characteristic outstripping (she has no ideas of her own, her special vileness is

always to increase the measure of pain others are prepared to inflict; her mind is itself a lynch mob) Cordelia may realize that she will *have* to say something. "More ponderous than my tongue" suggests that she *is* going to move it, not that it is immovable—which would make it more ponderous than her love. And this produces her second groping for an exit from the dilemma: to speak, but making her love seem less than it is, out of love. Her tongue will move, and obediently, but against her condition—then poor Cordelia, making light of her love. And yet *she* knows the truth. Surely that is enough?

But when the moment comes, she is speechless: "Nothing my lord." I do not deny that this can be read defiantly, as can the following "You have begot me, bred me, lov'd me" speech. She is outraged, violated, confused, so young; Lear is torturing her, claiming her devotion, which she wants to give, but forcing her to help him betray (or not to betray) it, to falsify it publicly. (Lear's ambiguity here, wanting at once to open and to close her mouth, further shows the ordinariness of the scene, its verisimilitude to common parental love, swinging between absorption and rejection of its offspring, between encouragement to a rebellion they failed to make, and punishment for it.) It may be that with Lear's active violation, she snaps; her resentment provides her with words, and she levels her abdication of love at her traitorous, shameless father:

> Happily, when I shall wed,
> That lord whose hand must take my plight shall carry
> Half my love with him . . . .
>
> (I, i, 100–102)

The trouble is, the words are too calm, too cold for the kind of sharp rage and hatred real love can produce. She is never in possession of her situation, "her voice was ever soft, gentle and low" (V, iii, 272–273), she is young, and "least" (I, i, 83). (This notation of her stature and of the quality of her voice is unique in the play. The idea of a defiant *small* girl seems grotesque, as an idea of Cordelia.) All her words are words of love; to love is all she knows how to do. That is her problem, and at the cause of the tragedy of King Lear.

I imagine the scene this way: the older daughters' speeches are public, set; they should not be said to Lear, but to the court, sparing themselves his eyes and him theirs. They are not monsters first, but ladies. He is content. Then Cordelia says to him, away from the court, in confused appeal to their accustomed intimacy, "Nothing"—don't force me, I don't know what you want, there is nothing I can say, to speak what you want I must not speak. But he is alarmed at the appeal and tries to cover it up, keeping up the front, and says, speaking to her and to the court, as if the ceremony is still in full effect: "Nothing will come of nothing; speak again." (*Hysterica passio* is already stirring.) Again she says *to him*: "Unhappy that I am, I cannot heave my heart into my mouth"—not the heart which loves him, that always has been present in her voice; but the heart which is shuddering with confusion, with wanting to do the impossible, the heart which is now in her throat. But to no avail. Then the next line would be her first attempt to obey him by speaking publicly: "I love your Majesty according to my bond; no more no less"—not stinting, not telling *him* the truth (what is the true *amount* of love this loving young girl knows to measure with her bond?), not refusing him, but still trying to conceal her love, to lighten its full measure. Then her father's brutally public, and perhaps still publicly considerate, "How, how, Cordelia! Mend your speech a little, lest you may mar your fortunes." So she tries again to divide her kingdom (". . . that lord whose hand must take my plight shall carry half my love with him . . ."). Why should she wish to shame him publicly? He has shamed himself and everyone knows it. She is trying to conceal him; and to do that she cuts herself in two. (In the end, he faces what she has done here: "Upon such sacrifices, my Cordelia. . . ." Lear cannot, at that late moment, be thinking of prison as a sacrifice. I imagine him there partly remembering this first scene, and the first of Cordelia's sacrifices—of love to convention.)

After this speech, said in suppression, confusion, abandonment, she is shattered, by her failure and by Lear's viciousness to her. Her sisters speak again only when they are left alone, to plan. Cordelia revives and speaks after France enters and has begun to speak *for* her:

> Sure, her offence
> Must be of such unnatural degree
> That monsters it, or your fore-vouch'd affection
> Fall into taint; which to believe of her,
> Must be a faith that reason without miracle
> Should never plant in me.

> (*I, i*, 218–223)

France's love shows him the truth. Tainted love is the answer, love dyed—not decayed or corrupted exactly; Lear's love is still alive, but expressed as, colored over with, hate. Cordelia finds her voice again, protected in France's love, and she uses it to change the subject, still protecting Lear from discovery.

A reflection of what Cordelia now must feel is given by one's rush of gratitude toward France, one's almost wild relief as he speaks his beautiful trust. She does not ask her father to relent, but only to give France some explanation. Not the right explanation: What has "that glib and oily art" got to do with it? That is what her sisters needed, because their task was easy: to dissemble. Convention perfectly suits these ladies. But she lets it go at that—he hates me because I would not flatter him. The truth is, she *could* not flatter; not because she was too proud or too principled, though these might have been the reasons, for a different character; but because nothing she could have done would have *been* flattery—at best it would have been *dissembled flattery*. There is no convention for doing what Cordelia was asked to do. It is not that Goneril and Regan have taken the words out of her mouth, but that here she cannot say them, because for her they are true ("Dearer than eye-sight, space and liberty . . ."). She is not disgusted by her sister's flattery (it's nothing new); but heart-broken at hearing the words she wishes she were in a position to say. So she is sent, and taken, away. Or half of her leaves; the other half remains, in Lear's mind, in Kent's service, and in the Fool's love.

(I spoke just now of "one's" gratitude and relief toward France. I was remembering my feeling at a production given by students at Berkeley during 1946 in which France—a small part, singled out by Granville-Barker as particularly requiring an actor of authority and distinction—was given his full sensitivity and manliness, a combination notably otherwise absent from the play, as mature womanliness is. The validity of such feelings as touchstones of the accuracy of a reading of the play, and which feelings one is to trust and which not, ought to be discussed problems of criticism.)

It may be felt that I have forced this scene too far in order to fit it to my reading, that too many directions have to be provided to its acting in order to keep the motivation smooth. Certainly I have gone into more detail of this kind here than elsewhere, and I should perhaps say why. It is, first of all, the scene in which the problem of performance, or the performability, of this play comes to a head, or to its first head. Moreover, various interpretations offered of this scene are direct functions of attempts to *visualize* its progress; as though a critic's conviction about the greatness or weakness of the scene is a direct function of the success or unsuccess with which he has been able to imagine it concretely. Critics will invariably dwell on the motivations of Lear and Cordelia in this scene as a problem, even while taking their motivation later either as more or less obvious or for some other reason wanting no special description; and in particular, the motives or traits of character attributed to them here will typically be ones which have an immediate visual implication, ones in which, as it were, a psychological trait and its physical expression most nearly coalesce: at random, Lear is described as irascible (Schüking), arrogant, choleric, over-bearing (Schlegel), Cordelia as shy, reluctant (Schüking), sullen, prideful (Coleridge), obstinate (Muir). This impulse seems to me correct, and honest: it is one thing to say that Cordelia's behavior in the opening scene is not inconsistent with her behavior when she reappears, but another to *show* its consistency. This is what I have wanted to test in visualizing her behavior in that scene. But it is merely a test, it proves nothing about my reading, except its actabil-ity; or rather, a performance on these lines would, or would not, prove that. And that is a further problem of aesthetics—to chart the relations between a text (or score), an analysis or interpretation of it, and a performance in terms of that analysis or interpretation.

The problem is not, as it is often put, that no performance is ideal, because this suggests we have some clear idea of what an ideal performance would be, perhaps an idea of it as embodying all true interpretations, every resonance of the text struck under analy-sis. But this is no more possible, or comprehensible, than an exper-iment which is to verify every implication of a theory. (Then what makes a theory convincing?) Performances are actions, and the im-itations of actions. As with any action, a performance cannot con-tain the totality of a human life—though one action can have a particularly summary or revelatory quality, and another will occur at a crossroads, and another will spin tangentially to the life and circumstances which call it out, or rub irrelevantly or mechanically against another. Some have no meaning for us at all, others have more resonance than they can express—as a resultant force an-swers to forces not visible in the one direction it selects. (Then what makes action bearable, or comprehensible?) I cannot at will give my past expression, though every gesture expresses it, and each elation and headache; my character is its epitome, as if the present were a pantomime of ghostly selections. What is necessary to a per-formance is what is necessary to action in the present, that it have its autonomy, and that it be in character, or out, and that it have a specific context and motive. Even if everything I have said about Cordelia is true, it needn't be registered explicitly in the way that first scene is played—there may, for example, be merit in stylizing it drastically. Only there will be no effort to present us with a sullen or prideful or defiant girl who reappears, with nothing intervening to change her, as the purest arch of love.

Nor, of course, has my rendering of the first scene been meant to bring out all the motivations or forces which cross there. For exam-ple, it might be argued that part of Lear's strategy is exactly to put Cordelia into the position of being denied her dowry, so that he will not lose her in marriage; if so, it half worked, and required the magnanimity of France to turn it aside. Again, nothing has been said of the theme of politics which begins here and pervades the action. Not just the familiar Shakespearean theme which opens the interplay between the public and private lives of the public creature, but the particularity of the theme in this play, which is about the interpenetration and confusion of politics with love; something which, in modern societies, is equally the fate of private creatures—whether in the form of divided loyalties, or of one's relation to the State, or, more pervasively, in the new forms love and patriotism themselves take: love wielding itself in gestures of power, power extending itself with claims of love. *Phèdre* is perhaps the greatest play concentrated to this theme of the body politic, and of the body, torn by the privacy of love; as it is closest to *King Lear* in its knowledge of shame as the experience of unacceptable love. And Machiavelli's knowledge of the world is present; not just in his attitudes of realism and cynicism, but in his experience of the condition to which these attitudes are appropriate—in which the inner and outer worlds have become totally disconnected, and man's life is all public, among strangers, seen only from outside. Luther saw the same thing at the same time, but from inside. For some, like Edmund, this is liberating knowledge, lending capacity for action. It is what Lear wants to abdicate from. For what Lear is doing in that first scene is trading power for love (pure power for mixed love); this is what his opening speech explicitly says. He imagines that this will prevent future strife now; but he is being counselled by his impotence, which is not the result of his bad decision, but produces it: he feels powerless to *appoint* his successor, recognized as the ultimate test of authority. The consequence is that politics becomes private, and so vanishes, with power left to serve hatred.

The final scene opens with Lear and Cordelia repeating or completing their actions in their opening scene; again Lear abdicates, and again Cordelia loves and is silent. Its readers have for centuries wanted to find consolation in this end: heavy opinion sanctioned Tate's Hollywood ending throughout the eighteenth century, which resurrects Cordelia; and in our time, scorning such vulgarity, the same impulse fastidiously digs itself deeper and produces redemption for Lear in Cordelia's figuring of transcendent love. But Dr. Johnson is surely right, more honest and more responsive: Cordelia's death is so shocking that we would avoid it if we could— *if* we have responded to it. And so the question, since her death is restored to us, is forced upon us: Why does she die? And this is not answered by asking, What does her death mean? (cp: Christ died to save sinners); but by answering, What killed her? (cp: Christ was killed by us, because his news was unendurable).

Lear's opening speech of this final scene is not the correction but the repetition of his strategy in the first scene, or a new tactic designed to win the old game; and it is equally disastrous.

CORD. Shall we not see these daughters and these sisters?
LEAR. No, no, no, no! . . .

(V, iii, 7–8)

He cannot finally face the thing he has done; and this means what it always does, that he cannot bear being seen. He is anxious to go off to prison, with Cordelia; his love now is in the open—that much circumstance has done for him; but it remains imperative that it be confined, out of sight. (Neither Lear nor Cordelia, presumably, knows that the soldier in command is Gloucester's son; they feel unknown.) He is still ashamed, and the fantasy expressed in this speech ("We two alone will sing like birds i' the cage") is the same fantasy he brings on the stage with him in the first scene, the thwarting of which causes his maddened destructiveness. There Cordelia had offered him the marriage pledge ("Obey you, love you, and most honor you"), and she has shared his fantasy fully enough to wish to heal political strife with a kiss (or perhaps it is just the commonest fantasy of women):

CORD.   Restoration hang
Thy medicine on my lips. . . .

(IV, vii, 26–27)

(But after such abdication, what restoration? The next time we hear the words "hang" and "medicine," they announce death.) This gesture is as fabulous as anything in the opening scene. Now, at the end, Lear returns her pledge with his lover's song, his invitation to voyage (". . . so we'll live, and pray, and sing, and tell old tales, and laugh . . ."). The fantasy of this speech is as full of detail as a day dream, and it is clearly a happy dream for Lear. He has found at the end a way to have what he has wanted from the beginning. His tone is not: we will love *even though* we are in prison; but: because we are hidden together we can love. He has come to accept his love, not by making room in the world for it, but by denying its relevance to the world. He does not renounce the world in going to prison, but flees from it, to earthly pleasure. The astonishing image of "God's spies" (V, iii, 17) stays beyond me, but in part it contains the final emphasis upon looking without being seen; and it cites an intimacy which requires no reciprocity with real men. Like Gloucester toward Dover, Lear anticipates God's call. He is not experiencing reconciliation with a daughter, but partnership in a mystic marriage.

If so, it cannot be, as is often suggested, that when he says

Upon such sacrifices, my Cordelia,
The Gods themselves throw incense.

(V, iii, 20–21)

he is thinking simply of going to prison with Cordelia as a sacrifice. It seems rather that, the lines coming immediately after his love song, it is their love itself which has the meaning of sacrifice. As though the ideas of love and of death are interlocked in his mind— and in particular of death as a payment or placation for the granting of love. His own death, because acknowledging love still presents itself to him as an annihilation of himself. And her death, because now that he admits her love, he must admit, what he knew from the beginning, that he is impotent to sustain it. This is the other of Cordelia's sacrifices—of love to secrecy.

Edmund's death reinforces the juncture of these ideas, for it is death which releases his capacity for love. It is this release which permits his final act:

. . . some good I mean to do
Despite of mine own nature. Quickly send . . .

(V, iii, 243–244)

What has released him? Partly, of course, the presence of his own death; but that in itself need not have worked this way. Primarily it is the fact that all who have loved him, or claimed love for him, are dead. He has eagerly prompted Edgar to tell the tale of their father's death; his reaction upon hearing of Goneril's and Regan's deaths is as to a solution to impossible, or illegitimate, love: "All three now marry in an instant"; and his immediate reaction upon seeing their dead bodies is: "Yet Edmund was belov'd." *That* is what he wanted to know, and he can acknowledge it now, when it cannot be returned, now that its claim is dead. In his following speech he means well for the first time.

It can be said that what Lear is ashamed of is not his need for love and his inability to return it, but of the *nature* of his love for Cordelia. It is too far from plain love of father for daughter. Even if we resist seeing in it the love of lovers, it is at least incompatible with the idea of her having any (other) lover. There is a moment, beyond the words, when this comes to the surface of the action. It is the moment Lear is waking from his madness, no longer incapable of seeing the world, but still not strong enough to protect his thoughts: "Methinks I should know you and know this man . . ." (*IV, vii*, 64). I take it "this man" is generally felt to refer to Kent (disguised as Caius), for there is clearly no reason to suppose Lear

knows the Doctor, the only other man present. Certainly this is
plausible; but in fact Lear never does acknowledge Kent, as he does
his child Cordelia.[1] And after this recognition he goes on to ask,
"Am I in France?" This question irresistibly (to me) suggests that
the man he thinks he should know is the man he expects to be with
his daughter, her husband. This would be unmistakable if he di-
rects his "this man" to the Doctor, taking him for, but not able to
make him out as, France. He finds out it is not, and the next time
we see him he is pressing off to prison with his child, and there is
no further thought of her husband. It is a standing complaint that
Shakespeare's explanation of France's absence is perfunctory. It is
more puzzling that Lear himself never refers to him, not even when
he is depriving him of her forever. Either France has ceased to exist
for Lear, or it is importantly from him that he wishes to reach the
shelter of prison.

I do not wish to suggest that "avoidance of love" and "avoidance
of a particular kind of love" are alternative hypotheses about this
play. On the contrary, they seem to me to interpret one another.
Avoidance of love is always, or always begins as, an avoidance of a
particular kind of love: men do not just naturally not love, they
learn not to. And our lives begin by having to accept under the
name of love whatever closeness is offered, and by then having to
forgo its object. And the avoidance of a particular love, or the acceptance of it, will spread to every other; every love, in acceptance

---

1. Professor Jonas Barish—to whom I am indebted for other suggestions about this essay
as well as the present one—has pointed out to me that in my eagerness to solve all the
King Lear problems I have neglected trying an account of Kent's plan in delaying making
himself known ("Yet to be known shortens my made intent" (*IV, vii*, 9)). This omission is
particularly important because Kent's is the one delay that causes no harm to others,
hence it provides an internal measure of those harms. I do not understand his "dear
cause" (*IV, iii*, 52), but I think the specialness of Kent's delay has to do with these facts:
(1) It never prevents his perfect faithfulness to his duties of service; these do not require—Kent does not permit them to require—personal recognition in order to be performed. This sense of the finitude of the demands placed upon Kent, hence of the harm
and of the good he can perform, is a function of his complete absorption into his social
office, in turn a function of his being the only principal character in the play (apart from
the Fool) who does not appear as the member of a *family*. (2) He does not delay reveal-
ing himself to Cordelia, only (presumably) to Lear. A reason for that would be that since
the King has banished him it is up to the King to reinstate him; he will not presume on
his old rank. (3) If his plan goes beyond finding some way, or just waiting, for Lear to
recognize him first (not out of pride but out of right) then perhaps it is made irrelevant
by finding Lear again only in his terminal state, or perhaps it always consisted only in
doing what he tries to do there, find an opportunity to tell Lear about Caius and ask for
pardon. It may be wondered that we do not feel Lear's fragmentary recognitions of Kent
to leave something undone, nor Kent's hopeless attempts to hold Lear's attention to be
crude intrusions, but rather to amplify a sadness already amplified past sensing. This
may be accounted for partly by Kent's pure expression of the special poignance of the
servant's office, requiring a life centered in another life, exhausted in loyalty and in
silent witnessing (a silence Kent broke and Lear must mend); partly by the fact that
Cordelia has fully recognized him: "To be acknowledg'd, Madam, is o'er-paid" (*IV, vii*, 4);
partly by the fact that when his master Lear is dead, it is his master who calls him, and
his last words are those of obedience.

or rejection, is mirrored in every other. It is part of the miracle of the vision in *King Lear* to bring this before us, so that we do not care whether the *kind* of love felt between these two is forbidden according to man's lights. We care whether love is or is not altogether forbidden to man, whether we may not altogether be incapable of it, of admitting it into our world. We wonder whether we may always go mad between the equal efforts and terrors at once of rejecting and of accepting love. The soul torn between them, the body feels torn (producing a set of images accepted since Caroline Spurgeon's *Shakespeare's Imagery* as central to *King Lear*), and the solution to this insoluble condition is to wish for the tearing apart of the world.

Lear wishes to escape into prison for another old reason—because he is unwilling to be seen to weep.

> The good years shall devour them, flesh and fell,
> Ere they shall make us weep: we'll see 'em starved first.
>
> (V, iii, 24–25)

See them shalt thou never. And in the end he still avoids Cordelia. He sees that she is weeping after his love song ("Wipe thine eyes"). But why is she in tears? Why does Lear think she is? Lear imagines that she is crying for the reasons that he is on the verge of tears—the old reasons, the sense of impotence, shame, loss. But *her* reasons for tears do not occur to him, that she sees him as he is, as he was, that he is unable to take his last chance; that he, at the farthest edge of life, must again sacrifice her, again abdicate his responsibilities; and that he cannot know what he asks. And yet, seeing that, it is for him that she is cast down. Upon such knowledge the Gods themselves throw incense.

It is as though her response here is her knowledge of the end of the play; she alone has the capacity of compassion Lear will need when we next see him, with Cordelia dead in his arms: "Howl, howl, howl! O! you are men of stones." (Cp. the line and a half Dante gives to Ugolino, facing his doomed sons, a fragment shored by Arnold: "I did not weep, I so turned to stone within. They wept. . . .") Again he begins to speak by turning on those at hand: "A plague upon you, murderers, traitors all!" But then the tremendous knowledge is released: "I might have saved her. . . ." From the beginning, and through each moment until they are led to prison, he might have saved her, had he done what every love requires, put himself aside long enough to see through to her, and be seen through. I do not mean that it is clear that he could, at the end, have done what Edmund feared (". . . pluck the common bosom on his side, And turn our impress'd lances in our eyes . . ."); but it is not clear that he could not. And even if he had not succeeded, her death would not be on his hands. In his last speech, "No, no, no, no" becomes "No, no, no life!" His need, or his interpretation of his need, becomes her sentence. This is what is unbearable. Or bearable only out of the capacity of Cordelia. If we are to weep her fortunes we must take her eyes.

ADAPTATIONS AND
RESPONSES

NAHUM TATE

From The History of King Lear†

[5.2] *Scene, A Prison.* LEAR *asleep, with his Head on* CORDELIA'S *Lap.*

CORDELIA   What Toils, thou wretched King, hast Thou endur'd
    To make thee draw, in Chains, a Sleep so sound?
    Thy better Angel charm thy ravisht Mind
    With fancy'd Freedom; Peace is us'd to lodge
    On Cottage Straw, Thou hast the Begger's Bed,   5
    Therefore shou'dst have the Begger's careless Thought.
    And now, my Edgar, I remember Thee,
    What Fate has seiz'd Thee in this general Wreck
    I know not, but I know thou must be wretched
    Because Cordelia holds Thee Dear.   10
    O Gods! a suddain Gloom o'er-whelms me, and the Image
    Of Death o'er-spreads the Place.—ha! who are These?

    Enter CAPTAIN *and* OFFICERS *with Cords.*

CAPTAIN   Now, Sirs, dispatch, already you are paid
    In part, the best of your Reward's to come.
LEAR   Charge, charge upon their Flank, their last Wing haults;   15
    Push, push the Battel, and the Day's our own.
    Their Ranks are broke, down, down with Albany.
    Who holds my Hands?—O thou deceiving Sleep,
    I was this very Minute on the Chace;
    And now a Prisoner here—What mean the Slaves?   20
    You will not Murder me?
CORDELIA   Help Earth and Heaven!
    For your Souls sake's, dear Sirs, and for the Gods.
OFFICER   No Tears, good Lady, no pleading against Gold and
        Preferment;   25
    Come, Sirs, make ready your Cords.

† From *The History of King Lear, Acted at the Duke's Theatre. Reviv'd with Alterations* (London: Printed for E. Flesher, 1681), signatures A2r–v, A3r. In his revision of the play, which replaced Shakespeare's play from 1681 to 1834, when William Macready returned Shakespeare's version to the London stage, Tate kept most of Shakespeare's original plot, other than the ending; however, Tate changed the play's structure, added or cut characters (including the Fool, who is eliminated), and modernized the language to suit Restoration taste. He retained 3.7, and its blinding of Gloucester by Regan and Cornwall. In his revised ending, Tate has Goneril and Regan poison each other and Albany return the kingdom to Lear, who makes Cordelia queen and betrothes her to Edgar, who has rescued her three times in the play. In the epilogue, Cordelia tells the audience: "Still so many Master-Touches shine / Of that vast Hand that first laid this Design."

CORDELIA   You, Sir, I'll seize,
  You have a humane Form, and if no Pray'rs
  Can touch your Soul to spare a poor King's Life,
  If there be any Thing that you hold dear,   30
  By That I beg you to dispatch me First.
CAPTAIN   Comply with her Request, dispatch her First.
LEAR   Off Hell-hounds, by the Gods I charge you spare her;
  'Tis my Cordelia, my true pious Daughter:
  No Pity?—Nay then take an old Man's Vengeance.
    Snatches a Partizan, and strikes down two of them; the
    rest quit CORDELIA, *and turn upon him.*

        Enter EDGAR *and* ALBANY.

EDGAR   Death! Hell! Ye Vultures hold your impious Hands,   35
  Or take a speedier Death than you wou'd give.
CAPTAIN   By whose Command?
EDGAR   Behold the Duke your Lord.
ALBANY   Guards, seize those Instruments of Cruelty.
CORDELIA   My Edgar, Oh!   40
EDGAR   My dear Cordelia, Lucky was the Minute
  Of our Approach, the Gods have weigh'd our Suffrings;
  W'are past the Fire, and now must shine to Ages.
GENT   Look here, my Lord, see where the generous King
  Has slain Two of 'em.   45
LEAR   Did I not, Fellow?
  I've seen the Day, with my good biting Faulchion
  I cou'd have made 'em skip; I am Old now,
  And these vile Crosses spoil me; Out of Breath!
  Fie, Oh! quite out of Breath and spent.   50
ALBANY   Bring in old Kent, and, Edgar, guide you hither
  Your Father, whom you said was near,   *Exit* EDGAR
  He may be an Ear-witness at the least
  Of our Proceedings.

        KENT *brought in here.*

LEAR   Who are you?   55
  My Eyes are none o'th' best, I'll tell you streight;
  Oh Albany! Well, Sir, we are your Captives,
  And you are come to see Death pass upon us.
  Why this Delay?—or is't your Highness pleasure
  To give us first the Torture? Say ye so?   60
  Why here's old Kent and I, as tough a Pair
  As e'er bore Tyrant's Stroke:—but my Cordelia,
  My poor Cordelia here, O pitty!—
ALBANY   Take off their Chains—Thou injur'd Majesty,

The Wheel of Fortune now has made her Circle,   65
And Blessings yet stand 'twixt thy Grave and Thee.
LEAR   Com'st Thou, inhumane Lord, to sooth us back
To a Fool's Paradise of Hope, to make
Our Doom more wretched? go too, we are too well
Acquainted with Misfortune to be gull'd   70
With Lying Hope; No, we will hope no more.
ALBANY   I have a Tale t'unfold so full of Wonder
As cannot meet an easy Faith;
But by that Royal injur'd Head 'tis True.
KENT   What wou'd your Highness?   75
ALBANY   Know the noble Edgar
Impeacht Lord Edmund since the Fight, of Treason,
And dar'd him for the Proof to single Combat,
In which the Gods confirm'd his Charge by Conquest;
I left ev'n now the Traytor wounded Mortally.   80
LEAR   And whither tends this Story?
ALBANY   E'er they fought
A blacker Scrowl of Treason, and of Lust
Than can be found in the Records of Hell;
There, Sacred Sir, behold the Character   85
Of Gonerill the worst of Daughters, but
More Vicious Wife.
CORDELIA   Cou'd there be yet Addition to their Guilt?
What will not They that wrong a Father doe?
ALBANY   Since then my Injuries, Lear, fall in with Thine: 90
I have resolv'd the same Redress for Both.
KENT   What says my Lord?
CORDELIA   Speak, for me thought I heard
The charming Voice of a descending God.
ALBANY   The Troops by Edmund rais'd, I have disbanded;   95
Those that remain are under my Command.
What Comfort may be brought to cheer your Age
And heal your savage Wrongs, shall be apply'd;
For to your Majesty we do Resign
Your Kingdom, save what Part your Self conferr'd   100
On Us in Marriage.
KENT   Hear you that, my Liege?
CORDELIA   Then there are Gods, and Vertue is their Care.
LEAR   Is't Possible?
Let the Spheres stop their Course, the Sun make Hault,   105
The Winds be husht, the Seas and Fountains Rest;
All Nature pause, and listen to the Change.
Where is my Kent, my Caius?
KENT   Here, my Liege.

LEAR   Why I have News that will recall thy Youth;   110
   Ha! Didst Thou hear't, or did th'inspiring Gods
   Whisper to me Alone? Old Lear shall be
   A King again.
KENT   The Prince, that like a God has Pow'r, has said it.
LEAR   Cordelia then shall be a Queen, mark that: 115
   Cordelia shall be Queen; Winds catch the Sound
   And bear it on your rosie Wings to Heav'n.
   Cordelia is a Queen.

      Re-enter EDGAR *with* GLOSTER.

ALBANY   Look, Sir, where pious Edgar comes   120
   Leading his Eye-less Father: O my Liege!
   His wondrous Story will deserve your Leisure:
   What He has done and suffer'd for your Sake,
   What for the Fair Cordelia's.
GLOUCESTER   Where is my Liege? Conduct me to his Knees to hail   125
   His second Birth of Empire; my dear Edgar
   Has, with himself, reveal'd the King's blest Restauration.
LEAR   My poor dark Gloster;
GLOUCESTER   O let me kiss that once more sceptred Hand!
LEAR   Hold, Thou mistak'st the Majesty, kneel here;   130
   Cordelia has our Pow'r, Cordelia's Queen.
   Speak, is not that the noble Suffring Edgar?
GLOUCESTER   My pious Son, more dear than my lost Eyes.
LEAR   I wrong'd Him too, but here's the fair Amends.
EDGAR   Your leave, my Liege, for an unwelcome Message.   135
   Edmund (but that's a Triffle) is expir'd;
   What more will touch you, your imperious Daughters
   Gonerill and haughty Regan, both are Dead,
   Each by the other poison'd at a Banquet;
   This, Dying, they confest.   140
CORDELIA   O fatal Period of ill-govern'd Life!
LEAR   Ingratefull as they were, my Heart feels yet
   A Pang of Nature for their wretched Fall;—
   But, Edgar, I defer thy Joys too long:
   Thou serv'dst distrest Cordelia; take her Crown'd: 145
   Th'imperial Grace fresh Blooming on her Brow;
   Nay, Gloster, Thou hast here a Father's Right;
   Thy helping Hand t' heap Blessings on their Head.
KENT   Old Kent throws in his hearty Wishes too.
EDGAR   The Gods and You too largely recompence   150
   What I have done; the Gift strikes Merit Dumb.
CORDELIA   Nor do I blush to own my Self o'er-paid
   For all my Suffrings past.

GLOUCESTER   Now, gentle Gods, give Gloster his Discharge.
LEAR   No, Gloster, Thou hast Business yet for Life;   155
    Thou, Kent and I, retir'd to some cool Cell
    Will gently pass our short reserves of Time
    In calm Reflections on our Fortunes past,
    Cheer'd with relation of the prosperous Reign
    Of this celestial Pair; Thus our Remains   160
    Shall in an even Course of Thought be past,
    Enjoy the present Hour, nor fear the Last.
EDGAR   Our drooping Country now erects her Head,
    Peace spreads her balmy Wings, and Plenty Blooms.
    Divine Cordelia, all the Gods can witness   165
    How much thy Love to Empire I prefer!
    Thy bright Example shall convince the World
    (Whatever Storms of Fortune are decreed)
    That Truth and Vertue shall at last succeed.   *Exeunt Omnes.*

FINIS.

JOHN KEATS

On Sitting Down to Read
King Lear Once Again†

O golden-tongued Romance, with serene lute!
Fair plumed Siren, Queen of far-away!
Leave melodizing on this wintry day,
Shut up thine olden pages, and be mute:
Adieu! for, once again, the fierce dispute
Betwixt damnation and impassioned clay
Must I burn through; once more humbly assay
The bittersweet of this Shakespearian fruit:
Chief poet! and ye clouds of Albion,
Begetters of our deep eternal theme!
When through the old oak forest I am gone,
Let me not wander in a barren dream,
But, when I am consumed in the fire
Give me new phoenix wings to fly at my desire.

† From *The Complete Poetical Works of John Keats,* ed. H. B. Forman (London: Henry Frowde, 1907), pp. 302–03.

EDWARD BOND

From Lear†

[1.1] *Near the wall.*

> *A stack of building materials—shovels, picks, posts and a tar-paulin. Silence. Then (offstage) a sudden indistinct shout, a crash, shouts.* A FOREMAN *and* TWO WORKERS *carry on a* DEAD WORKER *and put him down. They are followed by a* SOLDIER.

FIRST WORKER.   Get some water! He needs water.

FOREMAN.   He's dead.

SOLDIER.   Move 'im then!

FOREMAN.   Get his legs.

SOLDIERS   (*to* FOREMAN). Can yer see 'em? Look an' see! They're comin' up the ditch on the other side.

> FOREMAN *goes upstage to look off.* THIRD *and* FOURTH WORK-ERS *come on.*

THIRD WORKER   (*coming on*). I shouted to him to run.

FOREMAN   (*coming downstage*). Go back, go back! Work!

> FOURTH WORKER *goes off again.*

THIRD WORKER.   You heard me shout!

FIRST WORKER.   He says he's dead.

FOREMAN.   Work!

SOLDIER   (*to* FIRST WORKER). You!—make yerself responsible for 'andin' in 'is pick t' stores. (*Suddenly he sees something off stage and runs down to the others.*). Cover 'im! Quick!

FOREMAN   (*points to tarpaulin*). Take that!

> *They cover the body with the tarpaulin.* LEAR, LORD WARRING-TON, *an* OLD COUNCILLOR, *an* OFFICER, *an* ENGINEER *and* LEAR'S DAUGHTERS—BODICE *and* FONTANELLE—*come on. The* SOLDIER, FOREMAN *and* WORKERS *stand stiffly.* WARRINGTON *signs to them and they work by the tarpaulin.*

BODICE   (*to* FONTANELLE). We needn't go on. We can see the end.

ENGINEER.   The chalk ends here. We'll move faster now.

COUNCILLOR   (*looking at his map*). Isn't it a swamp on this map?

---

† Scene One from *Lear* by Edward Bond. Copyright © 1972, 1978 by Edward Bond. Reprinted by permission of Methuen Drama and Casarotto Ramsay & Associates Ltd. All rights whatsoever in this play are strictly reserved, and application for performance, etc., must be made before rehearsal to Casarotto Ramsay & Associates Ltd., 7-12 Noel Street, London W1F 8GQ. No performance may be given unless a license has been ob-tained.

FONTANELLE   (*to* BODICE). My feet are wet.

LEAR   (*points to tarpaulin*). What's that?

ENGINEER.   Materials for the—

WARRINGTON (*to* FOREMAN).   Who is it?

FOREMAN.   Workman.

WARRINGTON.   What?

FOREMAN.   Accident, sir.

LEAR.   Who left that wood in the mud?

ENGINEER.   That's just delivered. We're moving that to—

LEAR.   It's been rotting there for weeks.   (*To* WARRINGTON.) They'll never finish! Get more men on it. The officers must make the men work!

BODICE   (*shakes* ENGINEER's *hand*). Our visit has been so enjoyable and informative.

FONTANELLE.   Such an interesting day.

WARRINGTON.   We can't take more men. The countryside would be left derelict and there'd be starvation in the towns.

LEAR.   Show me this body.

> WARRINGTON *and the* SOLDIER *lift the tarpaulin.*

Blow on the head.

FOREMAN.   Axe.

LEAR.   What?

FOREMAN.   An axe, sir. Fell on him.

LEAR.   It's a flogging crime to delay work.   (*To* WARRINGTON.) You must deal with this fever. They treat their men like cattle. When they finish work they must be kept in dry huts. All these huts are wet. You waste men.

COUNCILLOR   (*making a note*). I'll appoint a hut inspector.

LEAR   They dug the wall up again last night.

OFFICER.   Local farmers. We can't catch them, they scuttle back home so fast.

LEAR.   Use spring traps.   (*To* FOREMAN.) Who dropped the axe?

WARRINGTON   (*to* FOREMAN). Be quick!

> FOREMAN *and* SOLDIER *push* THIRD WORKER *forward.*

LEAR.   Court martial him. Fetch a firing squad. A drumhead trial for sabotage.

> *Quiet murmur of surprise. The* OFFICER *goes to fetch the* FIRING SQUAD.

FONTANELLE.   My feet are wet.

BODICE.   She'll catch cold, father.

LEAR.   Who was a witness?

WARRINGTON   (*points to* FOREMAN). You!

FOREMAN.   He dropped a pickaxe on his head. I've had my eye on him, sir. Always idle and—

LEAR   (*to* THIRD WORKER). Prisoner of war?

FOREMAN.   No. One of our men. A farmer.

LEAR.   I understand! He has a grudge. I took him off his land.

     The FIRING SQUAD *is marched in by the* OFFICER.

OFFICER.   Squad as a squad—halt!

LEAR.   I shall give evidence. He killed a workman on the wall. That alone makes him a traitor. But there's something else suspicious about him. Did you dig up the wall last night?

BODICE   (*sighing*). It can easily be checked if he missed their roll calls.

LEAR.   I started this wall when I was young. I stopped my enemies in the field, but there were always more of them. How could we ever be free? So I built this wall to keep our enemies out. My people will live behind this wall when I'm dead. You may be governed by fools but you'll always live in peace. My wall will make you free. That's why the enemies on our borders—the Duke of Cornwall and the Duke of North—try to stop us building it. I won't ask him which he works for—they're both hand in glove. Have him shot.

THIRD WORKER.   Sir.

FONTANELLE   (*aside to* BODICE). Thank god we've thought of ourselves.

OFFICER.   Squad as a squad to firing positions—move!

LEAR   (*indicating the* FIRING SQUAD). They must work on the wall, they're slow enough. (*Turns to* WARRINGTON.) See this is done. I'm going down to the swamp.

BODICE.   Father, if you kill this man it will be an injustice.

LEAR.   My dear, you want to help me, but you must let me deal with the things I understand. Listen and learn.

BODICE.   What is there to learn? It's silly to make so much out of nothing. There was an accident. That's all.

LEAR.   (*half aside to her*). Of course there was an accident. But the work's slow. I must do something to make the officers move. That's what I came for, otherwise my visit's wasted. And there *are* saboteurs and there *is* something suspicious about this man—

BODICE.   But think of the people! They already say you act like a schoolboy or an old spinster—

LEAR.   Why are they waiting? It's cruel to make him wait.

OFFICER.   } Sir—you're—
WARRINGTON   } Move, sir.

     LEAR *moves out of the* FIRING SQUAD's *way.*

BODICE   (*loudly*). Listen to me. All of you notice I disassociate myself from this act.

LEAR.   Be quiet, Bodice. You mustn't talk like that in front of me.

FONTANELLE.   And I agree with what my sister says.

LEAR.   O my poor children, you're too good for this world.   (*To
the others.*) You see how well they'll govern when I'm dead.
Bodice, you're right to be kind and merciful, and when I'm dead
you *can* be—because you will have my wall. You'll live inside a
fortress. Only I'm not free to be kind or merciful. I must build
the fortress.

BODICE.   How petty it is to be obstinate over nothing.

LEAR.   I have explained and now you must understand!

BODICE.   It is small and petty to make—

LEAR.   I have explained.

BODICE.   Small and petty! All these things are in your head. The
Duke of Cornwall is not a monster. The Duke of North has not
sworn to destroy you. I have proof of what I say.

LEAR.   They're my sworn enemies. I killed the fathers therefore the
sons must hate me. And when I killed the fathers I stood on the
field among our dead and swore to kill the sons! I'm too old now,
they've fooled me. But they won't take my country and dig my
bones up when I'm dead. Never.

FONTANELLE   (to BODICE). This is the moment to tell him.

BODICE.   I'm going to marry the Duke of North and my sister's going to marry the Duke of Cornwall.

FONTANELLE.   He's good and reliable and honest, and I trust him
as if we'd been brought up together.

BODICE.   Good lord!—how can they be your friends if you treat
them like enemies? That's why they threatened you: it was political necessity. Well, now that's all in the past! We've brought them
into your family and you can pull this absurd wall down. There!
(*Slight laugh.*) You don't have to make your people slaves to protect you from your sons-in-law.

LEAR.   My sons-in-law?

FONTANELLE.   Congratulate us, father, give us your blessing.

BODICE.   I'm marrying North.

FONTANELLE.   And I'm marrying Cornwall.

LEAR   (*points to* THIRD WORKER). Tie him straight! He's falling!

BODICE.   So now you don't have to shoot him. Our husbands could
never allow you to, anyway.

FONTANELLE.   I know you'll get on with my husband. He's very understanding, he knows how to deal with old people.

LEAR.   Straighter!

BODICE.   You'll soon learn to respect them like your sons.

LEAR.   I have no sons!—I have no daughters!   (*Tries to be calmer.*)

Tell me—(*Stops, bewildered.*)—you are marrying North and you are marrying—. No, no! They've deceived you. You haven't met them. When did you meet them? Behind my back?

FONTANELLE.   We sent each other photographs and letters. I can tell a man from his expression.

LEAR.   O now I understand! You haven't met them. You're like blind children. Can't you see they only want to get over the wall? They'll be like wolves in a fold.

BODICE.   Wall, wall, wall! This wall must be pulled down!

FONTANELLE.   Certainly. My husband insists on that as part of the marriage contract.

BODICE   (*to* OFFICER). I order you not to shoot this man. Our husbands will shoot anyone who shoots him. They offer us peace, we can't shoot innocent men because we think they're their spies!

LEAR.   Shoot him!

BODICE.   No!

LEAR.   This is not possible! I must be obeyed!

WARRINGTON.   Sir, this is out of hand. Nothing's gained by being firm in little matters. Keep him under arrest. The Privy Council will meet. There are more important matters to discuss.

LEAR.   My orders are not little matters! What duke are you marrying? Who have you sold me to?

BODICE.   If the king will not act reasonably it's your legal duty to disobey him.

WARRINGTON.   Ma'am, you make this worse. Let me—

LEAR   (*takes pistol from the* OFFICER *and threatens the* FIRING SQUAD). Shoot him!

BODICE.   There, it's happened. Well the doctors warned us, of course.   (*Loudly.*) My father isn't well. Warrington, take the king back to his camp.

FONTANELLE.   He shouldn't have come out today. This mud's too much for him. My feet are wringing.

LEAR.   My enemies will not destroy my work! I gave my life to these people. I've seen armies on their hands and knees in blood, insane women feeding dead children at their empty breasts, dying men spitting blood at me with their last breath, our brave young men in tears—. But I could bear all this! When I'm dead my people will live in freedom and peace and remember my name, no—venerate it! . . . They are my sheep and if one of them is lost I'd take fire to hell to bring him out. I loved and cared for all my children, and now you've sold them to their enemies! (*He shoots* THIRD WORKER, *and his body slumps forwards on the post in a low bow.*) There's no more time, it's too late to learn anything.

BODICE.   Yes, you'll ruin yourself. Our husbands can't let you terrorize these people—they'll be *their* people soon. They must protect them from your madness.

LEAR.   Work! Get your men to work! Get them on the wall!

> WORKERS, SOLDIERS *and* FOREMAN *go out. They take the two bodies with them.*

I knew it would come to this! I knew you were malicious! I built my wall against *you* as well as my other enemies! You talk of marriage? You have murdered your family. There will be no more children. Your husbands are impotent. That's not an empty insult. You wrote? My spies know more than that! You will get nothing from this crime. You have perverted lusts. They won't be satisfied. It *is* perverted to want your pleasure where it makes others suffer. I pity the men who share our beds. I've watched you scheme and plan—they'll lie by you when you dream! Where will your ambition end? You will throw old men from their coffins, break children's legs, pull the hair from old women's heads, make young men walk the streets in beggary and cold while their wives grow empty and despair—I am ashamed of my tears! You have done this to me. The people will judge between you and me.

> LEAR *goes out. The* ENGINEER *and the* OLD COUNCILLOR *follow him.*

WARRINGTON.   I'm sorry, ma'am. If you'd spoken another time—

FONTANELLE.   You should have taken him away when you were told—

BODICE.   You were caught out. Well, learn your lesson. As it happens, no harm's done. Go and keep in with him. We'll let you know what must happen next.

> WARRINGTON *and the others go out.* BODICE *and* FONTANELLE *are left alone.*

We must go to our husbands tonight.

FONTANELLE.   Happiness at last! I was always terrified of him.

BODICE.   We must attack before the wall's finished. I'll talk to my husband and you talk to yours. The four of us will sit in the Council of War. We must help each other. Goodbye.

FONTANELLE.   Goodbye.

> *The daughters go out.*

Selected Bibliography

A basic search in an online bibliography database reveals over 1850 items of criticism on *King Lear*; a more complex search would offer hundreds more. Criticism of the play shifted sharply in the 1960s from the main two approaches, through its characters and tragic genre, to performance and gender study. The renewed interest from the 1970s in Shakespeare's practice of authorial revision, with *King Lear* as the test-case, also resulted in substantial re-investigations and re-interpretations of early twentieth-century "new bibliographic" theories about the textual transmission of Shakespeare's plays from author to stage to print.

In addition to searching online databases, readers can examine a full range of criticism of the play since the eighteenth century by consulting the following printed resources: New Variorum edition of *King Lear*, edited by Horace Howard Furness (Lippincott, 1908); Samuel A. Tannenbaum, *Shakespeare's King Lear: A Concise Bibliography* (New York, 1940); G. R. Hibbard, "*King Lear*: A Retrospect 1939–1979," *Shakespeare Survey* 33 (1980): 1–12; Kenneth Muir's entry on the play in Stanley Wells's *Shakespeare: A Bibliographical Guide* (Oxford: Clarendon, 1990), pp. 241–58; and Rebecca W. Bushnell, *King Lear and Macbeth: An Annotated Bibliography of Shakespeare Studies, 1674–1995* (Asheville, NC: Pegasus, 1996). Biographies of Shakespeare, such as the standard work, Samuel Shoenbaum's *Shakespeare's Lives* (Oxford University Press, 1979), can shed light on his life during the time in which he was composing *King Lear*. These may also prove useful: Park Honan, *Shakespeare: A Life* (Oxford: Clarendon Press, 1998); Katherine Duncan-Jones, *Ungentle Shakespeare* (London: Arden Shakespeare, 2001); Stephen Greenblatt, *Will in the World: How Shakespeare Became Shakespeare* (New York: Norton, 2004); and Peter Ackroyd, *Shakespeare: The Biography* (London: Chatto and Windus, 2005).

Below is a selected bibliography, offering some seminal books and articles that can lead readers to a much wider range of general or specific criticism of *King Lear*. Texts excerpted in the "Criticism" section of this Norton Critical Edition are not listed below.

Abbreviations:

Aligarh	*The Aligarh Journal of English Studies*
HLQ	*Huntington Library Quarterly*
Library	*The Library*
LFQ	*Literature Film Quarterly*
N&Q	*Notes and Queries*
NYRB	*The New York Review of Books*
PMLA	*Publications of the Modern Language Association*
RD	*Renaissance Drama*
RES	*Review of English Studies*
SEL	*Studies in English Literature 1500–1900*
SS	*Shakespeare Survey*
SQ	*Shakespeare Quarterly*

CRITICAL ANTHOLOGIES, CASEBOOKS, AND STUDY GUIDES

Specific collections on *King Lear* include Janet Adelman, *Twentieth-Century Interpretations of "King Lear"* (London: Prentice Hall, 1978); Grace Ioppolo, *A Routledge Literary Sourcebook on William Shakespeare's "King Lear"* (London: Routledge, 2003); Frank Kermode, "*King Lear*": *A Casebook* (London: Macmillan; rev. ed. 1992); Alexander Leggatt, *Harvester New Critical Introductions to Shakespeare: "King Lear"* (New York: Harvester Wheatsheaf, 1988); *Aspects of "King Lear,"* ed. Kenneth Muir and Stanley Wells (Cambridge: Cambridge University Press, 1982); Jay Halio, *Critical Essays on "King Lear"* (New York: Hall, 1996); *Lear from Study to Stage: Essays in Criticism,* ed. James Ogden and Arthur H. Scouten

(Newark, DE: Associated University Presses, 1997); and *King Lear and Its Afterlife*, ed. Peter Holland, *SS* 55 (2002).

CONTEMPORARY THEATRE AND CULTURE

On general theatre history, see E. K. Chambers, *The Elizabethan Stage*, 4 vols. (Oxford: Clarendon Press, 1923–1934), and G. E. Bentley, *The Jacobean and Caroline Stage*, 6 vols. (Oxford: Clarendon Press, 1941). Also see Leeds Barroll, *Politics, Plague and Shakespeare's Theater: the Stuart Years* (Ithaca: Cornell University Press, 1991), and Andrew Gurr, *The Shakespearean Stage, 1574–1642*, 3rd ed. (Cambridge: Cambridge University Press, 1992); on specific issues, see H. F. Lippincott, "*King Lear* and the Fools of Robert Armin," *Shakespeare Quarterly* 26 (1975): 243–53.

Two excellent reference guides to the history and culture of Shakespeare's age are David Cressy, *Birth, Marriage and Death, Ritual, Religion and the Life Cycle in Tudor and Stuart England* (Oxford: Oxford University Press, 1997) and Antonia Fraser, *The Weaker Vessel: Woman's Lot in Seventeenth Century England* (London: Weidenfeld and Nicholson, 1984). On the court of King James I, see Robert Ashton, *James I by His Contemporaries: An Account of His Career and Character as Seen by Some of His Contemporaries* (London: Hutchinson, 1969). On general literary issues, see Jonathan Goldberg, *James I and the Politics of Literature* (Stanford: Stanford University Press, 1989) and Annabel Patterson, *Censorship and Interpretation* (Madison: University of Wisconsin Press, 1984). On specific historical issues in *King Lear*, see Richard Dutton, "*King Lear*, The Triumphs of Reunited Britannia, and 'The Matter of Britain'," *Literature and History* 12 (1986): 139–51; O. B. Hardison, Jr., "Myth and History in *King Lear*," *SQ* 26 (1975): 227–42; Margaret Hotine, "Two Plays for St. Stephen's Day," *N&Q* 29. 227 (1982): 119–21; Alvin B. Kernan, "*King Lear* and the Shakespearean Pageant of History," in *On King Lear*, ed. Lawrence Danson (Princeton: Princeton University Press; 1981), pp. 7–24; Arthur Kinney, "Speculating Shakespeare, 1605–1606," in *Elizabethan Theater: Essays in Honor of S. Schoenbaum*, ed. R. B. Parker, S. P. Zitner (Newark: University of Delaware Press, 1996), pp. 252–70; Kaara L. Peterson, "*Historica Passio*: Early Modern Medicine, *King Lear*, and Editorial Practice," *SQ* 57 (2006): 1–22; and Christopher Wortham, "James I and the Matter of Britain," *English: The Journal of the English Association* 45 (1996): 97–122.

KING LEAR: SOURCES

A collection of Shakespeare's possible sources is printed in Volume 7 of Geoffrey Bullough's *The Narrative and Dramatic Sources of Shakespeare's Plays* (London: Routledge and Kegan Paul, 1973). Additional studies of sources are Irving Ribner, "Shakespeare and Legendary History: *Lear* and *Cymbeline*," *SQ* 7 (1956): 47–52; Gary Taylor, "A New Source and an Old Date for *King Lear*," *RES* 33 (1982): 396–413; Diane Speed, "*King Lear* and the Brut," in *Imperfect Apprehensions: Essays in English Literature in Honour of G. A. Wilkes*, ed. Geoffrey Little (Sydney, Aus.: Challis; 1996), pp. 56–73; Marie-Françoise Alamichel, "Layamon et Shakespeare: De Leir à Lear," *Etudes Anglaises* 45 (1992): 62–76; Peter Pauls, "The True Chronicle History of King Leir and Shakespeare's *King Lear*: A Reconsideration," *The Upstart Crow* 5 (1984): 93–107; Martin Coyle, "*King Lear* and *The Faerie Queene*," *N&Q* 31 (1984): 205–207; Michael Cameron Andrews, "*Arcadia* and *King Lear*," *N&Q* 31 (1984): 205; Kenneth Muir, "Samuel Harsnett and *King Lear*," *RES* 2 (1951): 11–21; Robert Stevenson, "Shakespeare's Interest in Harsnett's *Declaration*," *PMLA* 67 (1952): 898–902; Leo Salingar, "*King Lear*, Montaigne and Harsnett," *Aligarh* 8 (1983): 124–66; Stephen Greenblatt, "*King Lear* and Harsnett's 'Devil Fiction',," *Genre* 15 (1982): 239–42; F. W. Brownlow, *Shakespeare, Harsnett, and the Devils of Denham*, Newark: University of Delaware Press 1993; and Amy Wolf, "Shakespeare and Harsnett: 'Pregnant to Good Pity'?," *SEL* 38 (1998): 251–64.

TEXTUAL STUDIES

Most recent bibliographic studies of the play focus on authorial revision and its effect on textual transmission. Earlier and standard studies include Madeline Doran, *The Text of 'King Lear'* (Stanford: Stanford University Press, 1931); W. W. Greg, *The Shakespeare First Folio: Its Bibliographical and Textual History* (Oxford: Clarendon Press, 1955); E. A. J. Honigmann, *The Stability of Shakespeare's Text* (London: Edward Arnold, 1965); T. H. Howard-Hill, "New Light on Compositor E of the Shakespeare First Folio," *Library*, ser. 6, 2

(1980): 156–78, and "The Problem of Manuscript Copy for Folio *King Lear*," *Library*, ser. 6, 4 (1982): 1–24. However, the groundbreaking work is Peter W. M. Blayney's *The Texts of 'King Lear' and Their Origins* (Cambridge: Cambridge University Press, 1982), which established that Quarto 1 was not printed surreptitiously (and was thus not a "bad" quarto as previously argued) but most likely from authorial foul papers. On theories of the "new revisionists" see Steven Urkowitz, *Shakespeare's Revision of "King Lear"* (Princeton: Princeton University Press, 1980); Gary Taylor, "The War in *King Lear*," *Shakespeare Survey* 33 (1980): 27–34; *The Division of the Kingdoms: Shakespeare's Two Versions of "King Lear*," ed. Taylor and Michael Warren (Oxford: Clarendon Press, 1983); Grace Ioppolo, *Revising Shakespeare* (Cambridge: Harvard University Press, 1991). William Shakespeare, *The Complete King Lear 1608–1623*, prepared by Michael Warren (Berkeley: University of California Press, 1989), offers a complete set of facing-page facsimiles of the Quarto 1 and Folio texts.

THEATRICAL PERFORMANCE AND FILM STUDIES

The performance history of the play has been most fully documented in Christie Carson and Jacky Bratton's edition of *The Cambridge "King Lear" CD-Rom: Text and Performance Archive* (Cambridge: Cambridge University Press, 2000); other full-length studies include Marvin Rosenberg, *The Masks of "King Lear"* (London: Associated University Presses, 1972); Bratton, *Plays in Performance: King Lear, William Shakespeare* (Bristol: Bristol Classical Press, 1987), and Alexander Leggatt, *Shakespeare in Performance: "King Lear"* (Manchester: Manchester University Press, 1991). More specialized studies of modern stage performance include: Tetsuo Anzai, "Directing King Lear in Japanese Translation," in *Shakespeare and the Japanese Stage*, ed. Takashi Sasayama, J. R. Mulryne, and Margaret Shewring (Cambridge: Cambridge University, Press), 1998, pp. 124–37; Brian Cox, *The Lear Diaries: The Story of the Royal National Theatre's Productions of Shakespeare's "Richard III" and "King Lear"* (London: Methuen, 1992); William W. French, "A Kind of Courage: *King Lear* at the Old Vic, London, 1940," *Theatre Topics* 3 (1993): 45–55; Jay L. Halio, "Five Days, Three *King Lears*," *Shakespeare Bulletin* 9 (1991): 19–21; Dympna Callaghan, "Buzz Goodbody: Directing for Change," in Jean I. Marsden, *The Appropriation of Shakespeare: Post-Renaissance Reconstructions of the Works and the Myth* (New York: St. Martin's; 1991), pp. 163–81; Michael Hattaway, "Possessing Edgar: Aspects of *King Lear* in Performance," in *Shakespeare Performed: Essays in Honor of R. A. Foakes*, ed. Grace Ioppolo (University of Delaware Press, 2000), pp. 198–215; Grace Ioppolo, "The Performance of Text in the Royal National Theatre's 1997 Production of *King Lear*," in Ioppolo, *Shakespeare Performed*, pp. 180–97; Philippa Kelly, "'See What Breeds about Her Heart': King Lear, Feminism, and Performance," *RD* 33 (2004): 137–57; Charles Marowitz, "Lear Log," *The Drama Review*, 8 (1963): 103–21; David Richman, "The *King Lear* Quarto in Rehearsal and Performance," *SQ* 37 (1986): 374–82; Daniel Seltzer, "*King Lear* in the Theater," in *On King Lear*, ed. Lawrence Danson (Princeton: Princeton University Press, 1981), pp. 163–85; Antony Sher, *Beside Myself: An Autobiography* (London: Hutchinson, 2001); Zdenek Stríbrný, *Shakespeare in Eastern Europe* (Oxford: Oxford University Press, 2000); and J. L. Styan, "A Theatrical Approach: *King Lear* as Performance and Experience," in *Approaches to Teaching Shakespeare's "King Lear*," ed. Robert H. Ray (New York: Modern Language Association, 1986), pp. 111–18.

On stage adaptations of the play, from the seventeenth to the nineteenth centuries, see Arthur John Harris, "Garrick, Colman, and *King Lear*: A Reconsideration," *SQ* 22 (1971): 57–66; Nancy Klein Maguire, "Nahum Tate's *King Lear*: 'the King's blest restoration'," in *The Appropriation of Shakespeare: Post Renaissance Reconstructions of the Works and the Myth*, ed. Jean Marsden (New York: Harvester Wheatsheaf, 1991), pp. 29–43; Harry William Perricord, "Shakespeare, Tate, and Garrick: New Light on Alterations of *King Lear*," *Theatre Notebook* 36 (1982): 14–21; and Adele Seeff, "Charles Kean's *King Lear* and the Pageant of History," in *Shakespeare, Man of the Theater*, ed. Kenneth Muir, Jay L. Halio, and D. J. Palmer (Newark: University of Delaware Press, 1983), pp. 231–42.

On *King Lear* on film, see Todd S. Gilman, "The Textual Fabric of Peter Brook's King Lear: 'Holes' in Cinema, Screenplay, and Playtext," *LFQ* 20 (1992): 294–300; J. Lawrence Guntner, "*Hamlet, Macbeth* and *King Lear* on Film," in *Shakespeare on Film*, ed. Russell Jackson (Cambridge: Cambridge University Press, 2000), pp. 117–34; Tony Howard, "When Peter Met Orson: The 1953 CBS *King Lear*," in *Shakespeare, the Movie: Popularizing the Plays on Film, TV, and Video*, ed. Lynda E. Boose and Richard Burt (London: Routledge, 1997), pp. 121–34; Michael Mullin, "Peter Brook's *King Lear*: Stage and Screen," *LFQ* 11 (1983): 190–96, and "Peter Brook's *King Lear*: A Reassessment," in *Screen Shakespeare*, ed. Michael Skovmand and Tim Caudery (Cambridge, UK: Aarhus University Press, 1994), pp. 54–63; Kenneth S. Rothwell, "Representing *King Lear* on Screen: From

Metatheatre to 'Meta-Cinema'," *SS* 39 (1987): 75–90; and Mark Sokolyansky, "Grigori Koz-intsev's *Hamlet* and *King Lear*," in *Shakespeare on Film*, ed. Jackson, pp. 199–211.

On film adaptations of *King Lear*, see Samuel Crowl, "'The Bow Is Bent and Drawn': Kurosawa's *Ran* and the Shakespearean Arrow of Desire," *LFQ* 22 (1994): 109–16; Ib Jo-hansen, "Visible Darkness: Shakespeare's *King Lear* and Kurosawa's *Ran*," in *Screen Shake-speare*, ed. Skovmand and Caudery (Cambridge, Eng.: Aarhus University Press, 1994), pp. 64–86; Ann Thompson, "Kurosawa's *Ran*: Reception and Interpretation," *East-West Film Journal* 3 (1989): 1–13; and Iska Alter, " '*King Lear*' and '*A Thousand Acres*': Gender, Genre, and the Revisionary Impulse," in *Transforming Shakespeare: Contemporary Women's Re-Visions in Literature and Performance*, ed. Marianne Novy (New York: St. Martin's, 1999), pp. 145–58.

CRITICISM

Genre
For many years, G. Wilson Knight's *The Wheel of Fire* (Cleveland: World Publishing, 1962), first printed in 1930, was the standard reference work on Shakespearean tragedy; it is still influential. Also see Stephen Booth, *"King Lear," "Macbeth": Indefinition and Tragedy* (New Haven: Yale University Press, 1983); Jonathan Dollimore, *Radical Tragedy*, 2nd ed. (Brighton: Harvester Press, 1989); William Elton, *King Lear and the Gods* (Lexington: University Press of Kentucky, 1988); Tom McAlindon, "Tragedy, *King Lear*, and the Politics of the Heart," *SS* 44 (1992): 85–90; and Susan Snyder, *The Comic Matrix of Shakespeare's Tragedies: Romeo and Juliet, Hamlet, Othello, and King Lear* (Princeton: Princeton University Press, 1979).

Structure, Style, and Themes
Modern criticism is wide-ranging; a small sample of topics includes Jonathan Bate, "Ovid and the Mature Tragedies: Metamorphosis in *Othello* and *King Lear*," *SS* 41 (1989): 133–44, and "Shakespeare's Foolosophy," *Shakespeare Performed*, ed. Ioppolo (Newark: University of Delaware Press, 2000), pp. 17–32; Fredson Bowers, "The Structure of *King Lear*," *SQ* 31 (1980): 7–20; James L. Calderwood, "Creative Uncreation in *King Lear*," *SQ* 37 (1986): 5–19; Steven Doloff, " 'Let Me Talk with This Philosopher': The Alexander/Diogenes Paradigm in *King Lear*," *HLQ* 54 (1991): 253–55; John X. Evans, "Erasmian Folly and Shakespeare's *King Lear*: A Study in Humanist Intertextuality," *Moreana: Bulletin Thomas More* 27 (1990): 3–23; Dorothy C. Hockey, "The Trial Pattern in *King Lear*," *SQ* 10 (1959): 389–95; Arthur Kirsch, "The Emotional Landscape of *King Lear*," *SQ* 39 (1988): 154–70; Emily W. Leider, "Plainness of Style in *King Lear*," *SQ* 21 (1970): 45–53; and Susan Snyder, "*King Lear* and the Prodigal Son," *SQ* 17 (1966): 361–69. Caroline Spurgeon's *Shakespeare's Imagery and What It Tells Us* (Cambridge: Cambridge University Press, 1935) is still a standard reference work for all of Shakespeare's plays, including *King Lear*.

Characters
A. C. Bradley's *Shakespearean Tragedy*, excerpted above, is the standard reference work on Shakespeare's characters; for some more recent, and specific, studies, see Jay Halio, "Gloucester's Blinding," *SQ* 43 (1992): 221–23; Arnold Isenberg, "Cordelia Absent," *SQ* 2 (1951): 185–94; Ivor Morris, "Cordelia and Lear," *SQ* 8 (1957): 141–58; Carol Rutter, "Eel Pie and Ugly Sisters in *King Lear*, I & II," *Essays in Theatre/Etudes Theatrales* 13 (1995): 135–58, 14 (1995), 49–63; Harry Rusche, "Edmund's Conception and Nativity in *King Lear*," *SQ* 20 (1969): 161–64; Antony Sher, "The Fool in *King Lear*," in *Players of Shake-speare, II*, ed. Russell Jackson and Robert Smallwood (Cambridge: Cambridge University Press, 1988), pp. 151–65; and Allan R. Shickman, "The Fool's Mirror in *King Lear*," *ELR* 21 (1991): 75–86. Also see the individual essays in *The Division of the Kingdoms*, ed. Taylor and Warren, for the effects of revision on characters' representations.

Theoretical Approaches
The most recent theoretical approaches focus on gender and new historicism; a classic essay using this methodolgy is Kathleen McLuskie's "The Patriarchal Bard: Feminist Criticism and Shakespeare: *King Lear* and *Measure for Measure*," in *Political Shakespeare: Essays in Cultural Materialism*, ed. Jonathan Dollimore and Alan Sinfield (Manchester: Manchester University Press, 1994), pp. 88–108. A very brief selection of other theory-based discussions of the play includes Barbara J. Bono, " 'The Chief Knot of All the Discourse': The Maternal Subtext Tying Sidney's *Arcadia* to Shakespeare's *King Lear*," in *Gloriana's Face: Women, Public and Private, in the English Renaissance*, ed. S. P. Cerasano and Marion Wynne-Davies (Detroit: Wayne State University Press, 1992), pp. 105–27; Stephen Green-blatt, "Shakespeare and the Exorcists," in *Shakespeare and the Question of Theory*, ed. Patri-

cia Parker and Geoffrey Hartman (New York: Methuen, 1985), pp. 163–87; Lisa Jardine, *Still Harping on Daughters: Women and Drama in the Age of Shakespeare* (Harvester Press, 1983); Ania Loomba, *Gender, Race, Renaissance Drama* (Manchester: Manchester University Press, 1989); Coppélia Kahn, "The Absent Mother in *King Lear*," in *Rewriting the Renaissance: The Discourses of Sexual Difference in Early Modern Europe*, ed. Margaret W. Ferguson, Maureen Quilligan, and Nancy J. Vickers (Chicago: University of Chicago Press, 1986), pp. 33–49; Carol Thomas Neely, *Distracted Subjects: Madness and Gender in Shakespeare and Early Modern Culture* (Ithaca, NY: Cornell University Press, 2004); and Martin Orkin, "Cruelty, *King Lear* and the South African Land Act 1913," in *Shakespeare and Race*, ed. Catherine M. S. Alexander and Stanley Wells (Cambridge: Cambridge University Press, 2000), pp. 151–64. For an invaluable analysis of modern theory, see Brian Vickers, *Appropriating Shakespeare* (New Haven: Yale University Press, 1993).